A Vast Simplicity

"Jesus Christ the same, yesterday, today, and forever." HEBREWS 13:8

REV. DOUGLAS DETERT

A Vast Simplicity

Copyright © 2013 by Douglas Detert.

All rights reserved. No Part of this book may be reproduced in any form except for brief quotations, without written permission from the author.

ISBN/EAN 978-0-9854421-7-0
eBook ISBN/EAN 978-0-9854421-8-7

Unless otherwise noted, Scripture quotations are from the Holy Bible, King James Version (Public Domain).

Scripture quotations marked (AMP) are from the Amplified® Bible. Copyright © 1954, 1958, 1962, 1964, 1965, 1987 by The Lockman Foundation. Used by permission. (www.Lockman.org)

Scripture quotations marked (NIV) are from the Holy Bible, New International Version®, NIV®. Copyright © 1973, 1978, 1984, 2011 by Biblica, Inc.™ Used by permission of Zondervan. All rights reserved worldwide. www.zondervan.com The "NIV" and "New International Version" are trademarks registered in the United States Patent and Trademark Office by Biblica, Inc.™

Scripture quotations marked (NKJV) are from the New King James Version®. Copyright © 1982 by Thomas Nelson, Inc. Used by permission. All rights reserved.

Scripture quotations marked (RHM) are from the Emphasized Bible by Joseph Bryant Rotherham. Kregel Publications, Grand Rapids, MI, reprinted 1994.

Contents

Foreword 7
Preface 9
Prologue 11

1. Vignettes 19
2. Converging Streams 25
3. Jesus as All–In–All 33
4. The Original Work, 1907–1914 Part One............................49
5. The Original Work, 1907–1914 Part Two............................61
6. The Rising and Falling Work, 1914–1921...........................73
7. The Secondary Work, 1921–1936..83
8. The Slowly Disintegrating Work, 1936–1947......................93
9. The Resurrected Work, 1947–1949 Part One....................101
10. The Resurrected Work, 1947–1949 Part Two....................111

INTERLUDE ONE:
   Living on Charity, by Dorrel Healey...............................125

11. The Resurgent Work, 1949–1996.......................................133
12. A Color Sketch of Ruth M. Brooks....................................171
13. A Black & White Sketch of Rex B. Andrews
   Part One...187
14. A Black & White Sketch of Rex B. Andrews
   Part Two...207
15. Particular Expressions of God's Wisdom...........................233
16. What is Mercy?...247

INTERLUDE TWO:
   Taking Mercy for Free..269

17. Poverty of Spirit and Lowliness 275
18. Kingdom Praying 293
19. What Are You Here For? 305

INTERLUDE THREE:
  Jesus Is Coming in the Glory of His Father 351

20. To What End is God Working? 357
21. The Inside World vs. The Outside World 371
22. The Opening of the Sixth Seal 385

Epilogue 397

Afterword 399

Appendices
  Appendix A: Studies in Psalms 136, The Great Halal 401
  Appendix B: The Definition of Mercy: Is It Biblical? 407
  Appendix C: Two Possible Great Calls 411
  Appendix D: Lake's Letter and Brooks' Reply 413
  Appendix E: To One Asking For Forgiveness 423
  Appendix F: Thoughts on Being "Possessed" 433

Notes 439

Foreword

My experience of the Zion Faith Homes began in 1946 when, as a teenager, I attended a Monday Night Service with my sister and brother-in-law.

In 1949 I entered the Faith Homes as a trainee and lived there under the leadership of those precious saints for one and a half years.

There seemed to be no help for my sinful condition and for freedom from the power of sin in my life. The teaching I heard about Lowliness, Poverty of Spirit, and Mercy seemed out of reach to me; an impossibility for me to experience in my life. Yet I somehow knew it was the truth of God's Word. The love, support, and acceptance from the saints of the Zion Faith Homes raised faith and hope in my heart and brought me face to face with Jesus.

Today I leave it with Jesus as to how well I possess these truths in my life, but I can say with gratitude that I am enjoying the wonder of fellowship with Jesus in the knowledge of those things I was taught.

I am glad that the Lord has led Rev. Doug Detert to write this book. No one else had both the background as a resident for nearly thirty years in the Faith Homes, and the dedication required to search out the history of God's work and will in that unique ministry, and to put it in writing. The grace of God in Doug's life qualifies him to present this important record. It is a history worth recording, not only because the facts of that history need to be preserved, but also because the spiritual implications are vital for the present generation of believers to grasp.

May this book birth in you the hunger for union with Jesus in His Spirit of Lowliness, Poverty, and Mercy.

God bless you,

Rev. Fred Sindorf, Sr.
Retired Pastor

Preface

The story of God's work in this world is a never-ending one.

The Apostle John ends his account of Jesus' life with a disclaimer. Referring to all the things that Jesus said and did, John supposed "that even the world itself could not contain the books that should be written" (John 21:25).

This book begins with a similar disclaimer.

For a relatively small ministry like the Zion Faith Homes, but which has a history spanning nearly one hundred years and affecting uncounted thousands of lives, there is simply no way to write a definitive history of that ministry and limit it to one volume. Though the author lived and worked there for nearly thirty years, he can only include a small fraction of what could, or should be written.

A Vast Simplicity captures a portion of that history, but more importantly, presents the spiritual nature of that history. As such, it is not merely a record of that which has come and gone, but of that which belongs to the present working of God in and among His people. The Word of God is continually rising.

There was a time when the Law, and all its attendant duties and ceremonies, seemed the epitome of God's revelation to man, but it turned out to be our schoolmaster to bring us to Christ. "The law came by Moses, but grace and truth came by Jesus Christ" (John 1:17). By all accounts we have been living for two thousand years in the outworking of that Grace.

If this has been "the Day of Grace," then the Rising Word will usher in what the Psalmist calls "the Day of God's Power" (Psalm 110:3). The story of the Faith Home Work gives us a glimpse – a preview – of that coming Day. It also illuminates the pathway into that Day of Power. Law – Grace – Power. It is a Divine Progression leading to the overthrow of "the kingdoms of this world" which must give way to "the kingdoms of our Lord and of His Christ" (Revelation 11:15). It is also the Triumph of Love, for God is Love. Jesus was Love Embodied. His Life must now be unveiled in His Body on Earth, filled with Incorruptible Love. Then,

Jesus who died shall be satisfied, and earth and Heav'n be one![1]

I want to say at the outset that this book is not merely a history of the Zion Faith Homes. It is a record of what Jesus Christ accomplished through a specific group of people in a specific place throughout most of the Twentieth Century. It is the story of what He Himself has done, for His Glory alone.

By His grace I will never disavow this story, for it is true. It is not about any one person or place, nor even about the wonderful life in the Faith Homes, though it truly was wonderful. This story is about your Savior, your Jesus, who loves you and gave Himself for you in a way that most of us only dimly comprehend. Paul, however, who did comprehend such love, prayed that we might "know the love of Christ, which passes knowledge, that we might be filled with all the fullness of God" (Ephesians 3:19). Jesus wants to give Himself to us – now. Apparently it is His time for His people – now. Being more than a matter of historical interest, then, this record presents a fullness of God now being offered to His children, as this present age comes to a close.

Although I am well aware of the value of scholarship and the need for verifiable research, what follows should be thought of as "devotional" rather than "scholarly." Therefore, not every source will be cited, not every account substantiated by "two or three witnesses." I am in my 70th year, still actively involved in ministry, still teaching and preaching the truth of Christ as we heard and saw it in the Faith Homes for nearly 30 years. My heart is in this record, not merely my mind and memory. Some may question the wisdom of "putting it on paper"; others may question my motive in doing so. My intent, however, is BLESSING, not controversy, and I know of no one else still living who could provide such a record. May God's people be edified!

Admittedly, the full story can never be told, for it covers a period of ninety years, involving uncounted thousands of individuals, all of whom have their own testimonies of God's blessing on their lives in and through the Faith Homes. I do have several large notebooks packed with transcribed talks, letters, teachings, notes, *etc.*, but I have not attempted to track down additional letters and notes from others that pertain to this history. It is an acknowledged limitation. This record is limited as well by the shortcomings of the writer. Despite these things, my hope is that Jesus Christ will be glorified by the effort to preserve this history.

Prologue

God's Interaction With Man

Examples from the Old Testament

We first pose a question: What does the Scripture tell us about God interacting directly with individuals?

We begin in Genesis, the book of beginnings. God created Adam and Eve in his own image, thus making it possible for them to commune with Him in the cool of the day. Enoch walked with God for three hundred years. Noah found grace in the eyes of the Lord and became the builder of an ark designed by God Himself, who gave the plan to Noah in explicit detail. There were no atheists in those days because everyone knew who had created the human race. For more than 900 years, anyone could ask Adam to recount the story of his origin.

The narrative in Genesis, however, lengthens out the story of God's interaction with Abraham, whom God called, "My friend" (Isaiah 41:8). Their encounters are personal, intimate, and sometimes painful. They converse often. God leads Abraham out of his tent to show him the stars and to speak of his future. Abraham reasons with God over the impending destruction of Sodom. God allows Himself to be known by this "man who is a child," shall we say, preserving the sacred record in thirteen chapters of Genesis. If you were to talk to Abraham and hear him tell about his encounters with God, you would find it impossible to be an atheist.

In Exodus we meet another man with whom God speaks "as a man does with his friend, face to face" (Exodus 33:11). His name is Moses, and the story of his interaction with God (and the obvious results) occupies most of Exodus' forty chapters. For the last third of his life, Moses converses with God daily, in actual words. Moses has no problem hearing God's voice – no, not at all. Moses spends eighty days in the fiery luminescence with which God clothes Himself and finds he needs neither food nor water for the duration. His face radiates the effects of their sacred *tête-à-tête*. When Moses is an infant, God saves his life; when it is time for Moses to die, God gives this meek man a private burial.

Anyone who knew Moses could be a rebel (and there were some!), but no one could be an atheist. It was simply impossible.

The Books of Joshua, Judges, Ruth and Samuel contain many beautiful stories of men and women who interacted with God, but none is so poignant, so vivid, as David's story. The Shepherd-God of Psalm 23 sings many songs through the future Shepherd-King. Together they defeat a bear, then a lion, then a giant, then the entire Philistine nation. God and David know each other well, having become intimate in the wilderness for thirteen years. David even knows the voice of God as his confronter, when God rebukes his sin through the prophet Nathan. David also knows how to answer God's charges, and live. God entrusts into David's hands the plans for the future Temple that Solomon would construct, overlaying His hand on David's hand as he wrote (I Chronicles 28:19). No one who knew David could deny David's God.

In First Kings we meet Elijah, the man who *stood before the Lord.* This is the man who brings down fire from Heaven with a prayer of sixty-four words; who runs (in God's power) faster than Ahab's horse-drawn chariot; who hears what Ahab says in his bedchamber miles away, but who also hears the *still small voice of God* while hiding in a cave. This is the man who eats food cooked by God's angel, that so energizes his earthly body, he doesn't need to eat again for nearly six weeks. Interaction with God? Yes, repeatedly; even to the end, when God orders a chariot for Elijah's home-going instead of a grave. For the toughest skeptic who might have known Elijah, it was enough to convince him that "God is."

Did anyone visit God in His Throne-Room, while still living on earth? Yes, Isaiah did. He *saw the Lord on His throne, high and lifted up,* and he conversed with the Holy One in the presence of seraphim. He survived the touch of the glory-hot coal on his lips, a touch that affected his speech for the rest of his life. The Poetic Prophet wrote page after page of exquisitely worded verse, inspired by the Poetic God who had commissioned him. Isaiah the see-er "saw" the Crucifixion centuries before it happened and preserved what he saw in perfect prose. So close was he to God that he plumbed the mystery of His lowliness: *The Most High is also the Most Low* (Isaiah 57:15). If you talked to Isaiah, you knew there was a God, and you knew what God was like.

Jeremiah, Ezekiel, Daniel – true prophets who "saw" God and often engaged in dialogue with Him. God sent the Archangel Gabriel to "show"

Daniel the answer to his prayers for his people, an answer that stretches into our days. "The people that do know their God shall be strong, and do exploits," said Daniel (Daniel 11:32). His body was distasteful to lions, and the bodies of his three friends were impervious to fire. He "saw" mysteries that no one will unravel until God unveils their meaning. Daniel, a "greatly beloved" man of God, made believers out of heathen kings.

Examples from the New Testament

Peter, James, John, and the other nine disciples interacted with God-in-the-flesh for three and a half years. They walked with God, literally. They fell asleep in His presence, and when they awoke each morning, He was there. Their meals were provided by Him whose faith met all their needs. He spoke, they answered. They spoke, and He answered. What was it like to hear Him say, "Good morning, James"; "Good morning, Peter"? To sing psalms with Him? To witness His authority over disease, and devils, even over the weather? "What manner of man is this, that even the winds and the sea obey Him?" (Matthew 8:27). Out of Peter's mouth tumbled the great confession of faith: "You are the Christ, the Son of the Living God!" (Matthew 16:16).

What did the Apostle Paul say about his interaction with God? What kind of an experience with God did he have? Though he thought he knew God, his understanding of God changed forever when he encountered God's Anointed One for the first time. The heavens were opened to him on the Damascus Road and he heard Jesus Christ speaking to him directly, in words, "Saul, Saul, Why are you persecuting Me?" (Acts 9:4). He was blinded by the glory of that Heavenly Light and humbled by the loving authority of the One who addressed him by name. He wrote of his experience in these words: "When it pleased God, who separated me from my mother's womb, and called me by his grace, *to reveal His Son in me*..." (Galatians 1:15-16a).

What did he mean by that expression, *to reveal His Son in me*? He explains it partially in the next chapter: "I am crucified with Christ: nevertheless I live; yet not I, but Christ liveth in me: and the life which I now live in the flesh I live by the faith of the Son of God, who loved me, and gave himself for me" (Galatians 2:20). His entire life was built around such truth. "For me to live is Christ," he wrote to the Philippians (Philippians 1:21).

This is difficult for us to understand. Consider the following comment in *Ellicott's Commentary on the Whole Bible*, in regard to Galatians 2:20:

> One main way of conceiving of the specially Christian life is through the idea of union with Christ. This idea, when ultimately pressed to precise logical definition, must necessarily contain a certain element of metaphor. Consciousness, rigorously examined, tells us that even in the most exalted souls there is no such thing as an *actual* union of the human and divine.[1]

Yet Paul testified to such an "actual union" in many ways. *Since ye seek a proof of Christ speaking in me*, he wrote to the Corinthians (II Corinthians 13:3). *Before whose eyes Jesus Christ hath been evidently set forth, crucified among you* [*before whose eyes Jesus Christ was publicly portrayed as crucified* (RSV)], he protested to the Galatians (3:1). His life and writings were more, much more, than the product of a brilliant Jew, highly trained, a man possessed of an unusually forceful personality. No, that wasn't it. His body had become *the temple of the living God*, as he wrote to the Corinthians (II Corinthians 6:16). *He that is joined unto the Lord is one spirit*, he told them (I Corinthians 6:17). If you met the Apostle Paul, you had met the One who dwelt in him.

For those of us who are acquainted with the history of the Zion Faith Homes and the testimony of eyewitnesses of the glory of God manifested in its founders, we can only conclude that *God does interact with individuals here on earth now* as described in many places in the Scripture, with amazing results in the world of men. If it were not so, there never would have been such a place as the Zion Faith Homes.

Martha Wing Robinson's Testimony

There exists a written record of the testimony of the founder of the Zion Faith Homes, Mrs. Martha Wing Robinson, which describes God's interaction with her. It is the truth of what Jesus did in the life of this woman who loved Jesus more than her own life and who lived in *a vast simplicity* of union with Jesus. The story of her life, *Radiant Glory*, by Gordon P. Gardiner (1915-1986), who knew her from childhood until her death in 1936, furnishes the interested reader with many details of God's interaction with her. It is not a history of the Zion Faith Homes as such;

nonetheless, because she spent half of her life in the Homes, her biography cannot be understood apart from the setting in which she lived.²

From her written testimony of what she called "Passing Over" (from her own life into Jesus' life), we find the following descriptive statements:

> ...We passed over into a change, which was not like anything which we had ever heard of. It included everything from head to foot. We found out it was A TASTE OF SOMETHING GOD IS GOING TO DO IN THE LAST DAYS. At that time we did not understand that we had come into it by the crucifixion, or death to self. In a moment we were gone and a Greater One was there. Entire spirit and soul and body were in a new and divine control. We walked out of the natural into the spiritual, in BODY as well as in soul...
>
> God got the light to me that it would be blessed to be utterly gone. And that was a Real Light. We PASSED OVER. It was simply a manifestation of The King's Life...
>
> In such tremendous mystery the very Presence of God comes upon us and we just feel bowed before God in that wonderful experience. It was the mystery of THE INDWELLING CHRIST.*

From the time of her "Passing Over" (1907) until her death (1936), Mrs. Robinson lived out the Jesus-life together with those whom God ordained to live in His glory. The Zion Faith Homes became a place of encouragement for thousands of the Lord's followers, who, like Paul, were praying "that I may know Him, and the power of His resurrection, and the fellowship of His sufferings, being made conformable unto His death" (Philippians 3:10), and who were walking the pathway of "the loss of all things for the excellency of the knowledge of Christ Jesus my Lord" (Philippians 3:8).

Mrs. Robinson passed away six years before this writer was born, but when he came to live in the Homes in 1967, he met many people who had known her firsthand. Not a single one he talked to doubted the reality of Jesus' possession of her. All were profoundly affected by her life.

Thus the visible, audible reality of the revelation of Jesus Christ within his people took on a deeper, fuller meaning than what ordinarily

---

* This testimony will be quoted in full in Chapter 3, Jesus As All-in-All.

is grasped by Jesus' followers. The Holy Spirit repeatedly pressed home the point: Jesus wants to possess His people to make them fully His, not only in theory, but in actual experience. John 14:21 was used frequently by the Lord to draw attention to the enormity of what He had promised:

He that hath my commandments, and keepeth them, he it is that loveth Me: and he that loveth Me shall be loved of my Father, and I will love him, and will manifest Myself to him.

And again in John 14:23:

If a man love Me, he will keep My words: and My Father will love him, and we will come unto him, and make our abode with him.

Since Jesus addressed those words to His disciples, in the atmosphere of loving intimacy that characterized The Last Supper, we, too, as His disciples/followers, are entitled to believe His promises are meant for us today. We may expect Him to appear within our very lives to the same degree as He appeared within John, James, Peter, and Paul, and within all who have given their lives to know Him so intimately.

The power of such Scriptures, as well as the fire of God in the leaders of the Zion Faith Homes, burned deeply into our lives when my wife and I first came there to live in January 1967, and the Holy Spirit has fanned that fire in a special way in recent years. The late evangelist Leonard Ravenhill gave us our first copy of Madame Guyon's *Autobiography* when we were still working at Brooklyn Teen Challenge. I read it through twice, with many tears, and cried out involuntarily to Jesus as I read: "Jesus, if I could know You like this woman did, I would pay any price." Having been led to leave New York and enter the Faith Homes as trainees, we were surprised and humbled that Jesus had brought us to a place where that prayer could begin to be answered, a place where the union with Jesus which Madame Guyon experienced was as real and as fresh as today's Quiet Time with Jesus.

Many *dangers, toils, and snares* have beset us since then, but the grace of God has led us on in a persistent hunger to know Jesus in the fullest possible way. I believe God's intention is to reveal Jesus within His people in these days in a manner which exceeds our customary but partial grasp of His promises.

A Cautionary Word

Before concluding this introduction, it is necessary to insert a word of caution about the natural tendency to exalt an individual rather than Jesus. In Revelation 19, and again in Revelation 22, the Apostle John, who certainly was a devout and exemplary disciple, made two mistakes. That is, he made the same mistake twice — and did so in Heaven. He to whom God entrusted the most complete fore-view of the Last Days, nonetheless was rebuked twice for inappropriate behavior. What did he do wrong?

He worshiped an angel-messenger, instead of Jesus.

Rex Andrews, a co-worker of Martha Robinson and an eyewitness of the things I intend to describe, had this to say about "the man-worshiping spirit":

> How powerful is the tendency to worship creatures! The man-worshiping spirit so easily arises in people for those whom they greatly admire. It becomes a form of idolatry. Beware, woe to the one who touches the man-idol for whom one may fight. God help us! It is written in our files, by Martha Robinson, "You see a great woman instead of a great God." That was a word to one of the intimate workers among whom she labored. We are hardly capable of enduring to see the angelic beauty and glory [such as John saw]. It will require a pure heart. It will mean to be sealed in the forehead. And that means: "The utter annihilation of your will."[3]

> "God help His poor children, in these days to walk in Divine Love, and not be trapped in the man-worshiping spirit!"[4]

This word of caution is directly intended to remove any hindrance to *seeing no man, save Jesus only* (Matthew 17:8). This is the story of HIS WORK, not the story of anyone's greatness. The purpose is to keep in view the reality of God's interaction with mankind NOW, so as to prepare loving hearts for The Second Coming of Our Savior, the Lord Jesus Christ, "who shall change our vile body [natural, but vile in comparison to His body], that it may be fashioned like unto His Glorious Body, according to the working whereby He is able even to SUBDUE all things unto Himself" (Philippians 3:21). If you are praying "to know the love of Christ, that passes knowledge…that you may be filled with all the fullness of God" (Ephesians 3:19-20), then you will likely benefit from the account that follows. If you are merely curious, you won't find much interest in reading it. If you want to be subdued under Jesus, I believe this account will fan that flame of desire.

Prayer

Father, thank You in Jesus' name that the truth of God never dies; never will die; cannot die. Thank You for the Gospel. Thank You for the revelation of Jesus Christ, not yet seen, but as certain as anything can be. Truly it is easier for heaven and earth to pass away than for one word of Yours to remain unfulfilled. We open ourselves to Jesus. To each one who may read this, grant a prepared heart. In Jesus' Name. Amen.

CHAPTER ONE

VIGNETTES

The young missionary from Brazil couldn't wait for the meeting to begin that night in the Faith Homes. Fresh from his first four-year term on the field, and eager to be seen and known, Rev. George Rowe strode from the Guest House at 2736 Eschol Avenue in Zion, Illinois to the Meeting House situated one block south on the corner of Eschol Avenue and 29th Street. He bounded up the steps and burst into the front room "chapel" of the large three-story home, where he sized up the situation and seated himself in the first row of chairs, directly in front of the Faith Home ministers, who were themselves seated in two rows along the east and south corner walls of the room, facing the gathering of worshipers.

"I was exalted in my own eyes," he stated, in telling the story to me many years later.

But the Presence of Jesus in the service that night, and the power of the Holy Spirit, together with obvious deep humility on the part of the ministers, weakened his self-confidence. The next night, he decided to sit in the *second row*, and by the end of the week (services were held nightly except Saturday) he was sitting in the *last row* with his back to the wall.

"The fire was too hot up front," he said, "and besides that, I now wished to be as inconspicuous as possible."

One minister in particular commanded George Rowe's attention and respect, a man who went by the title of "Elder Brooks." Someone once described The Elder as "bearing the closest resemblance to an Old Testament prophet one could imagine." His preaching was powerful and direct. It alarmed the sinners in Zion and scorched the flesh of carnal saints.

To add to the fear of God that descended on Rev. Rowe, all the ministers in the front of the room – and there were several of them – actively participated in the meetings, being used of God to speak His word, not only to the congregation, but also to specific individuals, often revealing their deepest needs and sometimes the secrets of their hearts. Repentance was the order of the day. Miraculous deliverances and healings took place. The joy of the Lord descended and the meeting room reverberated with the praises of God's people, loudly and at length. It was quite a lot for the young missionary to absorb!

One memorable night, after "seeing and hearing" the work of God for a week or more, Rev. Rowe sat quietly in his usual seat against the back wall as the service unfolded. Suddenly Elder Brooks rose from his chair at the opposite end of the room and walked straight down the aisle, not stopping until he stood directly in front of the awe-struck missionary.

"In a loud voice," related Rev. Rowe, "and with great authority, Elder Brooks gave a message in tongues as he stood in front me. When he finished, he looked directly into my eyes and thundered, 'Interpret that!' To my utter surprise, I opened my mouth and the Lord filled it with the interpretation of the message Elder Brooks had spoken. That night God imparted to me the gift of the interpretation of tongues, and I have been used that way to bless others for more than 40 years."

The above incident happened in the 1930s, approximately twenty-five years after the first Faith Home meeting was held on February 17, 1909, conducted by some of the same ministers who led the meetings referred to in George Rowe's testimony. From that modest beginning a Work of God sprang up that has affected thousands of lives. It is a long and fascinating history that takes the reader from Zion, Illinois to Toronto, Canada, and back again to Zion, and from there to South America, Africa, Israel, India, China, and the islands of the sea. More than that, however, it sheds light on the ways of God for our time and gives encouragement to those who long for the fulfillment of God's "exceeding great and precious promises" (II Peter 1:4) – all of them, – fulfillment that will "surely come and will not tarry" (Habakkuk 2:3).

It is the story of Jesus' Presence among His people, yes, and IN His people.

The veil of flesh that obscures Jesus' face and eyes and voice was rendered exceedingly thin or even transparent in the Zion Faith Homes. That is the testimony of a multitude of Christian believers who made their way to an unadvertised ministry in a small town in northeast Illinois, a town which was once the laughingstock of metropolitan Milwaukee and Chicago and, in recent years, became the target of atheists who successfully forced the city of Zion to remove the phrase "God Reigns" from its water tower, its street signs, and its stationery.

It is impossible now to conduct person-to-person interviews with more than a handful of "old-timers" whose lives were transformed by Jesus through contact with the Zion Faith Homes. Most of them have left us for their "long home" inside the Eastern Gate. Perhaps it could be said, "The *principals* are dead, but the *principles* remain." God gave this author the privilege of knowing scores of such eye-witnesses of God's power and glory, and the still greater privilege of living and working in the Faith Homes for nearly thirty years. The story needs to be told, not only to preserve its history in writing, but also to stir prepared hearts in these last hours before the final clashing of spirits takes place – in the heavenlies – and Jesus appears "without sin unto salvation" (Hebrews 9:28).

Not that no record exists, for Rev. Gordon P. Gardiner's fine biographies of two founding ministers of the Faith Homes tell part of the story.[1] Various articles in publications of limited circulation contain brief references to the Homes. (More about these sources will appear later in this history.) But the existing records do not cover the lengthy history of the Homes, nor do they involve the testimony of one who resided in the Homes and learned its story from ministers who gave their lives to maintain the simplicity and purity of that ministry.

Of course the Kingdom of God grows quietly throughout the earth, and a man "knoweth not how," as Jesus said in Mark 4:27. The Faith Homes are only a small part of the increase of the Word of God that takes place in the world every single day. Jesus is "the Head of the Body, the church" (Colossians 1:18), and in His wisdom He is forming that Body into a "perfect man, unto the measure of the stature of the fullness of Christ" (Ephesians 4:13). Without apology, however, it is stated that Jesus Himself founded the Faith Homes, and in those Homes He succeeded in blazing a trail that many will follow in the last days. The author of this history hopes the following account makes the trail markers visible for anyone longing to walk the path thus blazed but not yet well-worn.

Each year in November, the Faith Homes holds a homecoming of sorts, similar, for example, to Moody Bible Institute's annual *Founders' Week Convention*. Old friends gather to share God's goodness through lifetimes of ministry; new friends get a chance to taste the flavor of the early days; often the Lord Himself sets the tone of the meetings and prepares the congregants for the year ahead. The messages look to the future as well as backward to the past.

To such a celebration in Zion came a gentleman from New Jersey whose life had been touched by Jesus in the Faith Homes. This visitor was well known to Ruth Brooks, the daughter of Elder and Mrs. Brooks, who recounted the incident to the author. As the meeting progressed, one of the ministers, no doubt a lady, came quietly to this "wise man from the East" and "gave him a message," (as the phrase came to be used for a message of prophecy).

"The Lord desires you to write down every day for a year something you are thankful for," he was told. That was all. He did as he was instructed to do, faithfully recording his gratitude to God for various favors showed to him daily.

The following year he decided to return to Zion for another visit at the time of the homecoming services. With no thought that anyone – not even the Lord – would remember the previous year's message, he gladly entered into the services with a humble and eager spirit.

Presently the same minister who had been used by God to speak to him the previous year stood beside him to deliver another message from God: "Because you have been obedient to My Word, and have recorded with gratitude My favors day by day, I am giving you a thankful spirit for the rest of your life."

And thus it was! Ruth Brooks testified to the truth of that prediction, saying, "That brother was the most gracious and thankful person you would ever want to meet."

In 1985 (or thereabouts), Rev. George Rowe, now a saintly old man in his eighties, also came with his wife to the yearly celebration in November. Once again he was seated in the front row, but this time not because of his own presumption, but rather by invitation of the ministers. Jesus manifested His Presence almost palpably, one could say, so that no admonitions were needed or given calling for reverence before Deity. A great chorus of praise began to ascend from the entire congregation, accompanied by unusual, Spirit-generated music from the organ, where Ruth Brooks played heaven's hymns "in the Spirit." Everyone stood to their feet, praising God audibly from the heart in acceptable worship of our Savior.

"Suddenly I was aware of *a presence* in front of me, in the small space between the front row and the ministers facing the congregation," said Rev. Rowe. "I saw the feet and legs of a very tall being standing before us, and I knew it was a mighty angel from God. He was fearful to look upon. He uttered nothing, but his demeanor was that of a judge, impassive and impartial and of righteous character.

"In my soul I heard these words, although they were not spoken audibly: *'Judgment has begun in the house of God.'*"

A year later he shared the memory of that occasion with the author. "I could not bring myself to speak of it before now," he said. "The angel's presence so sobered me, and the unspoken words I heard so overwhelmed me that I could not speak of what I saw until now."

The appearance of angels, and the operation of the gifts of the Spirit, characterized the early days of Pentecostal experience, to be sure. The Zion Faith Homes appeared within the wide stream of Spirit-breathed encounters with the supernatural, and it pleased God to keep the Homes within that stream for many decades. The *context* of His Work in the Faith Homes is the fitting subject of the next chapter.

Nothing takes place "in a vacuum," and that is especially true of spiritual things. God builds on all that has preceded His present work. "A text without a context is a pretext," said an experienced saint, referring to the need to observe context when preaching. The same is true of history, especially spiritual history. In order to appreciate fully the place and lasting influence of the Faith Homes, one needs to know the historical setting in which God birthed them. Thankfully, there exists a wealth of material concerning that historical setting, to which we now turn for a brief review of that context.

CHAPTER TWO

CONVERGING STREAMS

Many historians of trends within the Church, especially as it developed from the Reformation onward, have outlined the progression of "this Gospel of the Kingdom [which must] be preached in all the world for a witness unto all nations" (Matthew 24:14). Five of them with whom I am familiar, all "Pentecostal" in background, are:

> Dr. J. Edwin Orr, whose widely recognized work on the history of revivals sheds much light on the expansion of God's Kingdom in the past 400 years. I was present (1964) when he visited the *Assemblies of God Seminary* in Springfield, Missouri and taught on the progressive restoration of historic Christianity;[1]
>
> Arthur Wallis, mostly known for his book, *God's Chosen Fast,* but often quoted for his outstanding introduction to Frank Bartleman's record of the outpouring of the Spirit at Azusa Street in 1906, entitled *Another Wave Rolls In*;[2]
>
> Dr. William Menzies, respected Bible teacher and historian for the Assemblies of God, whose book *Anointed to Serve* is still in print. I was privileged to take his course, "History of Revival," in 1964-65;[3]
>
> Dr. Vinson Synans, currently Dean Emeritus of the College of Divinity at Regent University in Virginia Beach, Virginia, whose research into the background of the Pentecostal Movement can be found in his treatise, *The Origins of the Pentecostal Movement*;[4]
>
> Dr. Edith Blumhofer, who through her father, Rev. Edwin Waldvogel, and her uncle, Rev. Hans Waldvogel, learned much about the Zion Faith Homes. She authored a history of the Assemblies of God entitled *Restoring the Faith: The Assemblies of God, Pentecostalism, and American Culture.*[5]

It serves no purpose for me to summarize what these and other church historians have written about the religious and spiritual environment in the late 19th Century, especially the environment in America and England at the time. As indicated in the endnotes cited above, interested readers can pursue the subject at length if they wish. My limited approach to the subject is to point out three streams of God's working that converged into a single stream in the Zion Faith Homes. Please note the particle "a" in that statement. "There is a river," chanted the singer of Psalm 46, "the streams whereof shall make glad the city of God" (Psalm 46:4). Only God knows where all of the *streams* are! What God did in the Faith Homes is one of those streams.

Those three converging streams seem to me to be:

1. The Holiness Movement, as typified by the Keswick Conventions;
2. The Divine Healing Movement, as typified by Dowie's restorationist movement;
3. The Pentecostal Movement, as typified by the Azusa Street outpouring.

A brief sketch of each of these streams provides a context for the rest of the story about the Zion Faith Homes.

The Holiness Movement, as typified by the Keswick Conventions

The Holiness Movement appeared (divinely inspired, I believe), as the *Third Great Awakening* began to decline. The beginning of the *Third Great Awakening* in 1857 (common designation) coincided roughly with the publication in 1859 of Charles Darwin's *Origin of the Species*, proposing the Theory of Evolution. Both of those events, one profoundly religious, and the other profoundly secular, had lasting effects on society at the time, and continue to influence the course of history to the present.[6]

The first *Keswick Convention* in 1875 became part of the resurgence of Evangelicalism when the *Awakening* seemed to taper off. It has had, and continues to have, a strong "holiness" emphasis with regard to Christian character and deportment.[7] Many teachers of what was often called "the deeper life" were connected with Keswick, including Hudson Taylor, Amy Carmichael, F. B. Meyer, T. Austin-Sparks, Andrew Murray, Watchman Nee, and Stephen Olford, to name but a few.[8] The convention practically launched what is called "The Holiness Movement," with an emphasis on the deeper life in Christ and the necessity of having a pure heart.

The Divine Healing Movement, as typified by Dowie's restorationist movement

At the same time, Dr. John Alexander Dowie (independent of *Keswick*, however) received a large gift of healing in Australia, and in 1888 he brought his message of "salvation, healing, and holy living" to America, first in California, then to various cities in the States and Canada. In 1894 he established his headquarters in Chicago, after his successful public ministry at the World's Fair in Chicago, 1893-94. By July of 1901 the City of Zion was under construction, and somewhere in the neighborhood of 6,000 people took up residence. In some ways Dowie was the talk of the nation, with his fearless denunciation of social evils, the liquor industry, and the medical establishment, not to mention dead churches, dead denominations and watered-down doctrines. The report of numerous healings, many of them spectacular, did much to enhance his stature and reputation in the eyes of the public.

Not many Pentecostal or Charismatic adherents today would recognize the name of John Alexander Dowie, but he was widely recognized from 1894 until his death in 1907. His story is told in three biographies that I know of.[9]

Dowie became a nationally known figure because of his bold, flamboyant sermons attacking his detractors; his building of a "city for God" (Zion, Illinois) from farmland purchased in northern Illinois; and because of the thousands of documented healings attributed to his prayers and ministry.[10] The (mostly hostile) press followed his endeavors with delight. His around-the-world trip in 1906 also gave him international exposure.[11]

The following remarks attest to his popularity and influence:

Among the many who were greatly blessed and influenced by the ministry of Dr. Dowie were: F.F. Bosworth (1877-1958); Eli N. Richey and family, including his famous evangelist son, Raymond T. Richey (1893-1968); Gordon Lindsay (1906-1973); William H. Piper, Zion's Overseer At Large (1868-1911), who later became founder and pastor of the old Stone Church in Chicago; and the popular song writer/evangelist F. A. Graves, whose daughter married a prominent Assemblies of God college professor. The list also includes such men of God as Fred Vogler and J. Roswell Flower (1888-1970), who was instrumental in the founding of the Assemblies of God in 1914.[12]

The Pentecostal Movement, as typified by the Azusa Street outpouring

In 1901 (January 1st), in Charles Parham's Bible school in Topeka, Kansas, one of the students received the Baptism of the Holy Spirit accompanied by speaking in other tongues. That event is generally accepted as the beginning of the Great Outpouring of the Holy Spirit that came to be known as "The Pentecostal Outpouring." The power of the Spirit was no more evident than at the Azusa Street Mission in Los Angeles, California where the Lord poured out his Spirit mightily upon the seekers in that simple barn in April 1906. It was the American locus of *the Holy Ghost and fire* ignited by God and reaching to the ends of the earth – in connection, of course, with the revivals in Wales, India, China, and other places.

So we have at least three streams of spiritual stirrings that define the context in which the Faith Homes arose, and each of those stirrings contributed directly to the Work of God as it unfolded in the Homes.

The connection of these three streams with the founders of the Faith Homes stands out clearly:

Connection with the Holiness Movement

We know that Martha Robinson read *The Christian's Secret of a Happy Life*, by Hannah Whitehall Smith. We know that she also read Mrs. Smiley's book on Joshua, likening the Spirit-led life to the conquering of Canaan by Joshua and the Israelites.[13] She loved and used the deep-life hymns that came out of the Keswick movement. In Edith Blumhofer's writings, she traces the influence that the Keswick movement had on all the early Pentecostal pioneers, including, of course, those who became leaders in the Zion Faith Homes.[14] The first hymnal used in the Faith

Homes was replete with hymns sung at Keswick Conventions, with their special emphasis on Holiness. It was God's resuscitation for a barely breathing church, battered by Darwinism and Liberalism in the last half of the 19th Century.

Connection with the Divine Healing Movement

Nine of the pioneers of the Zion Faith Homes either came out of Dowie's work, or were connected with it in some way. Young Martha Wing worked as a secretary and mission worker in Zion before she married Harry Robinson, who had distinguished himself as one of Zion's better preachers. The Mitchells owned a farm just outside the city when the Lord showed them they were to sell all and move into the first Faith Home in Zion in 1910. Mrs. Judd's husband, H. Worthington Judd, held a high position in Dr. Dowie's "business cabinet,"[15] and they were living in Zion when Faith Home ministers began holding meetings in that city. Stella Leggett was ordained under Dr. Dowie. Eva Leggett (nee MacPhail) and Mrs. Brooks were sisters. The exceptions were: Mr. Campbell; Hilda Nilsson (a student at Wheaton); Ursie Naylor; and Rex Andrews, although the latter worked with John G. Lake and Cyrus Fockler, both of whom were associates of Dr. Dowie.

The biography of Martha Wing Robinson contains a full account of her association with Dr. Dowie, following her remarkable healing of diseases that had reduced her to invalidism.[16] She was present at the "all night service with God" on December 31, 1899, when Dr. Dowie unveiled his plans for a city for God at the stroke of midnight. Back at her home in Davenport, Iowa, her success in establishing "Zion" in that city attracted the attention of Dr. Dowie (who kept close track of all his workers), and at his request she returned to Zion and was ordained into the ministry by him on May 24, 1901. In November, again at Dr. Dowie's request, she left Davenport permanently and took up residence in Zion to help with the grand effort of "building a city for God" under Dr. Dowie's theocratic rule. She and her husband Harry, whom she married on August 10, 1905, maintained their allegiance to Zion until January, 1907, when it became obvious that the Zionites would not change their stance of being "against" the Pentecostal Movement.

Though the name of Dr. John Alexander Dowie has faded into the "dustbin of history," in actual fact his life and ministry, controversial as they were, attracted much press throughout the United States and Canada. He also had many friends and contacts in high places, including the Presidents of the United States at that time, William McKinley and Theodore Roosevelt. In 1903 Dr. Dowie and 3,000 of the faithful in Zion, called "The Restoration Host," traveled to New York City in eight chartered trains. Dr. Dowie preached nightly in Madison Square Garden – the same venue where Billy Graham's Crusade took place fifty years later, and which Graham also filled nightly for six weeks.

Connection with the Pentecostal Movement

As noted earlier, many of the men whom God used so greatly in the late 1940s and early 1950s traced their spiritual anointing back to Zion City and the ministry of Dr. Dowie. In certain respects Dr. Dowie became a model for such men as T. L. Osborne, Raymond Richey, O. L. Jaggers, Oral Roberts, Hobart Freeman, Gordon Lindsay, and many others. As one of his biographers noted, Dr. Dowie's "teaching on healing helped usher in the modern Pentecostal movement."[17] However, there was this difference, *viz.*, the later divine healing evangelists were all "Pentecostal" in belief and practice, whereas the leaders of Zion City, especially Dr. Dowie's immediate successor, Wilbur Glenn Voliva, all rejected the Pentecostal testimony when it came to Zion City in 1906.*

Be that as it may, there were several leaders, ministers, and associates of the Zion Work who embraced what God had begun in 1901. The carrier of the testimony to Zion was Charles F. Parham himself, who had received the Baptism in the Spirit at his Bible School in Topeka. One of his students was William J. Seymour, whose name became associated with Azusa Street where the "fire fell" in the spring of 1906. Seymour was the "pastor" of the Azusa Street Mission in its halcyon days; he is also the author of the beloved hymn, *Jesus the Son of God*. The link to Zion was through a Mrs. Waldron, who had received the baptism with speaking in tongues in Lawrenceville, Kansas, under Parham's

---

* Ruth Brooks told this author that her father Elder Brooks had met on at least one occasion with Overseer Voliva to share with him the Pentecostal testimony, but Voliva would not accept the work of the Spirit as Elder had experienced it.

ministry in that city. Subsequently Mrs. Waldron moved to Zion City in 1904, where she shared her testimony with others. Prayer meetings began in her home, and the Lord duplicated Mrs. Waldron's experience in another lady. Despite opposition from the authorities, the desire to experience more of God's working fed the hunger and thirst of many in the city. This occurred at the time that Zion City's utopian dream had been shattered by financial and spiritual troubles and by Dr. Dowie's death early in 1906. Many people earnestly sought God for answers. At the same time, tidings came to Zion of the outpouring of God's Spirit in Wales, increasing their hunger for God to breathe upon them.[18]

In any event, it was probably Mrs. Waldron who sent word to Parham to pay a visit to the hurting saints in Zion and to proclaim the testimony of being baptized in the Holy Spirit. Some four months earlier Parham had seen a vision of the troubled city of Zion, and heard a voice saying to him, "Arise and go to Zion and take up the burden of an oppressed people." Thus he was eager to come when the invitation was issued.[19] Pentecostal services began on September 20, 1906, in the large frame building on Elijah Avenue (now Sheridan Road) known as the Elijah Hospice. Overseer Voliva forced the pray-ers out of the building, but thankfully he could not force the prayers out of the pray-ers. They re-gathered in the home of Mrs. Ames, and shortly afterward in five other homes besides, with the result that the group of Pentecostal seekers now numbered about 200. Truly a great move of God was at hand! Events occurring in Zion City, Illinois in September and October of 1906, affected "not only thousands in that place but also would literally change the life and history of the church the world over during the twentieth century," observes Gordon Gardiner.[20]

Mrs. Martha Robinson, who is rightly called the founder of the Zion Faith Homes, was visiting relatives and friends in Zion at the time of these special meetings, and it was there she first heard Pentecostal teaching. Although she did not receive the Baptism in the Spirit at that time, she searched the Scriptures and saw that such an experience was truly Biblical. In December, just three months later, she received the sought-for and longed-for baptism, as the Holy Spirit spoke one word over her lips: "Baptized." Two months later, on February 11, 1907, she spoke in an unknown tongue for the first time.[21]

Naturally, as mentioned above, this fact, together with Harry's acceptance of a doctrine that Zion opposed, led to their resignation from the organization. As painful as the separation was, in God's view it was a necessary step for His plan to be fulfilled in their lives. The time had come for God to birth something He desired. Though by His direct will the Faith Homes would remain largely hidden (unlike Dowie's Zion),† nevertheless it would be important to Him as a place where He could manifest Himself as He is; a place and a people who would constitute another link in the great chain of people and places who wanted Jesus alone, for Himself alone, that Christ might be magnified in them by life and by death.

The influence and legacy of the Holiness Movement contributed much to the emergence of the Pentecostal Movement, and in its own way, so did the Divine Healing ministry of Dr. John Alexander Dowie, his later delusion and decline notwithstanding. And those streams converged and swelled in the founders of the Zion Faith Homes. They became conduits of His power for the glory of God alone.

---

† See Appendix C, *Two Possible Great Calls.*

CHAPTER THREE

JESUS AS ALL-IN-ALL

The foregoing thumbnail sketch of the three streams contributes to an understanding of the larger picture of God's intentions for His people, both then and now. It is not in the province of this book to follow out each of those streams as they flowed into the 20th Century – where they went, the instances of when and where they converged, the amazing results thus produced, and the story of how they continue to replenish the Sea of God's Mercy, even into the 21st Century. Others have done so already. This account focuses in detail on the result of their convergence in the Faith Homes that flowered in Toronto in 1907 and came to full bloom in Zion, Illinois over a span of more than eighty years.

As may be gathered from the previous chapter, Mrs. Martha Wing Robinson became a key figure in the Faith Homes, and it is necessary to share further biographical details of her life.*

In 1961 one of her associates in the ministry gave an oral history of the Faith Homes which has never been put into print. It consists of three talks that were recorded and transcribed, primarily for the edification of friends of the Faith Homes. The subject of the first talk was Martha Wing's early life from her birth (1874) to the climax of her prayer to know Jesus (1907). It is worth inserting much of this account at this point, especially because it highlights her spiritual hunger for Jesus, and the pathway by which He led her to the fulfillment in Him that she sought. The original transcription was edited slightly, and this writer has taken the liberty to edit it again, only for the sake of grammar, clarity, *etc.* Please remember that this was spoken to an audience, not written for publication. The speaker was Rex B. Andrews.

---

* Only one biography is known to this writer, and the interested reader is urged to obtain a copy for himself. It is entitled *Radiant Glory: The Life of Martha Wing Robinson*, by Gordon P. Gardiner, and it is available in full on the internet.

The story of the Faith Home Work is the story primarily of one life. There are other lives that were gathered together around that life at a certain period, but the story of the Faith Home Work, beginning and ending, is the story of one life – what God DID in that life. It was such a simple thing that He did, and it is all over the pages of the New Testament described in one way or another, but it is not a thing which is commonly understood or known. There are now in the world quite a good many persons and groups who have taken the position for such things as incorruptibility, eternal life now in the flesh, various kinds of movements where one and another claims to be that one. I have read little extracts from them, but there is one thing missing: Christ Himself. It is a peculiar thing how easy it is to leave Christ out of the very position where, when you leave Him out, there is not anything left but you. People do not KNOW that. In This Work God fought it out and has been fighting it out for fifty years...

But as I said, the story of the Work is really the story of one person. It begins way back in the 1870s when Martha Wing was born in Sand Spring, Iowa. As a young girl in the Methodist church, she grew up (like many young people do) in a church where the Christian life and faith is comparatively nominal. When she was about 14 years old she had a desire to do something for the Lord. She does not claim that she was yet saved, but she had that desire like young people sometimes get in the church to work for Him. She got the young people together in that Methodist church in Sand Spring, Iowa, and got them to covenant that they would give up dancing, card playing and such things, for in those days Methodist evangelists lashed out pretty strongly against dancing, card playing, smoking, and drinking.

So Martha Wing as a 14-year-old girl was inspired in that church to get the young people together. In a year or two she went to visit an uncle in Canada. At that time God began to deal with her to give Him her life, to consecrate, to give up to Him, surrender ALL to Him. [Her uncle had said to her, "Mattie, something tells me the Lord wants you to live and work just for Himself."[1]] Then she came up against something opposite to God's dealing with her: She had an ambition to write and she felt that she had a real gift for writing and a gift for poetry – and she DID. The Lord said by His wisdom word in later years that that was true, but now she came up against that point and it faced her squarely: Would she give up her love and ambition for writing and give her life and will to the Lord? Would she GIVE UP this darling thing of hers, her ambition to be a writer?

The adversary, who had already been building up this point in her to resist God, caused her to come up against it in a stubbornness; she felt she could *not* give up that writing, not even for the Lord, not even for God, not even for His will. And she fought it back and forth until she CAME to the decision, a positive, out-and-out decision, "I WILL NOT give up my writing for the will of God." Maybe she did not say, or dare to say, actually the last words, "the will of God," but her position was clear. "I WILL NOT give up my writing ambition for the Lord."

Well, you know what it does to people when they WILL NOT GIVE UP the thing which the Lord is seeking to take OUT of their lives, that He may have that place. She got into darkness, and it got darker and darker, and it was leading her right on into infidelity. She had become a school teacher by the time she was 18 years old, and she taught school for several years. Gradually she became afflicted physically. Difficult diseases or afflictions fastened on her one after another. In those days you did not have as many ways of trying to cure yourself as you have nowadays.

By the time she was 23 years old she was a hopeless and helpless invalid. She had a complication of, I believe it was said, thirteen diseases, incurable things of one kind of another. One of them, I think, was dropsical, and also her nerves were simply shattered. She had gotten to the place where she was bedridden most of the time. To get out of bed and walk across the room, or to do just a little something more than ordinary exercise, so shattered her nerves that it would be two or three days before she could hardly move her arm or move her head or anything at all. She was given up by doctors.

There was a physician and his wife who were very interested in her personally. The physician admitted he could not help her, but he and his wife asked her to come and live in their home for a while. She stayed nearly two months. They were very kind to her, but he was an infidel. He was definitely an infidel, and when you are definitely a thing, you like to have other people be definitely what you are yourself. He was giving her infidelistic literature and talking to her along atheistic lines.

By some means the Lord began to work on her heart – and here is a little point I do not remember perfectly – but the Lord DID get her started praying to find out if there was a God. Oh, I think it happened as she was looking through a telescope into the skies, when the thought came across her heart and soul: "Well, there must be a God if all those stars are there; there MUST be a God. He must have made those stars."

I believe it was that night, when she was being wheeled back into her room, that she began to pray. Her testimony was that for six weeks she prayed eighteen hours a day to KNOW if there was a God, and to know if there was a Savior. [Her illnesses kept her in bed most of that time each day.] At the end of that time, she felt the discouragement which tests us all in the pathway of faith and in the pathway of earnest prayer. She felt it was useless to continue praying; the Lord had not answered her.

She did not give up at that point, however; she did make one more step – and that is one of the characteristics of the life I am talking about: she NEVER gave up. She always went on just one more step. She said, "Well, I will pray tonight, and if God does not answer me tonight, if something does not happen tonight, then I will never pray again. I will know there is no God. I will believe infidelity is correct and never pray anymore. I'm through."

That night, while she was praying, the Lord, (as she described it), seemed to open the gates of heaven, and for a few minutes the Lord revealed Himself to her heart – just made her to know there is a God. There IS a Jesus. There IS a Savior. So her whole heart knew it. Then the gates, so to speak, closed up again just like it was before. Now she KNEW there was a God and she had prayed through for her salvation. She dates her born-again experience from that time. She had given her heart to the Lord.

That was the first of four stages of prayer in her life.

The first stage of prayer was for her salvation. The next stage of prayer was for her healing. The third stage of prayer in her life was to know Jesus and to lose her own life, which was after she received the Baptism of the Holy Spirit. The fourth stage in her life was the twenty-eight years from 1907 to 1936 when she was involved in what we now call the Faith Home Work. So this life, that life that I am speaking of, Martha Wing, can be understood or described as four stages of prayer....

Taking a break from the narrative for a moment, it should be noted that God did answer her persistent prayer for healing by arranging for her to learn of Dr. Dowie's healing ministry in Chicago, as mentioned in Chapter 3. Her story is told in her own words in Dr. Dowie's weekly periodical *Leaves of Healing*,[2] and it was reprinted in its entirety in the quarterly publication of the Zion Faith Homes, *Feed My Lambs*.[3]

We resume the talk by Rex Andrews, leaving out a few paragraphs for the sake of brevity.

> It came home to her heart that it was not so important for her to keep struggling on to get the healing, but if she would get to the Healer, if she would get to Jesus Himself, she would be healed. That also is another one of the characteristics of her life which carried right through to the end of her life. You are enjoying the results of those characteristics today by the working of God in the offering up by His fire of the sacrifice provided by Him for it. So that made a change in her praying. She decided she would not pray any longer just for her healing, but she would pray to know the HEALER.
>
> That is almost the central pillar of fact in her life from then on. She started to pray to find Jesus, to know Jesus, to know the Healer, and there came a time when He answered the prayer. She sought the Lord for Himself, and she found Him as her healer. That is the second stage in that life which is altogether a prayer life. The story of This Work is composed primarily of one person's life with four stages of prayer in it.
>
> She was moved by Dr. Dowie to Zion. He made a match for her to marry a Canadian evangelist by the name of Harry Robinson. They were married in Detroit in 1905. As it turned out in later

years, it was not God's best will for her to marry Harry Robinson. Detroit, however, was the place that God wanted to start This Work. There came in several confusions which entered into the thing, and they never quite got straightened out in later years. We cannot take time to explain them. They are very simple to me after forty-nine years have passed since I first came into the anointing of This Work, but sometimes they are hard to explain.

Finally they moved to Toronto and there they got into Pentecostal meetings and began to seek the baptism. She received her baptism in cleansing, an experience she called cleansing, followed by her baptism in the Holy Spirit, I believe, in December 1906. In February 1907 she spoke with tongues. The anointing of the Holy Ghost on her issued finally THEN as a great desire for Jesus. She began to pray, "Oh, to know Jesus; oh, to know Jesus." He had baptized her with the Spirit and she loved Him more than she ever had before. Her new birth was a birth of His love, and her healing was an increasing of the love. The birth and the healing comprised two stages of praying in which she prayed and prayed and prayed until the answer came.

Now the third stage of praying began without her realizing it. She just wanted Jesus and to pray in the power of the Holy Spirit on her. The anointing of God urged her along little by little. She spent time in prayer and gradually the simple prayer formed and became established. "Let me know Jesus. I want Jesus. Oh, let me have Jesus." It was the love of God propelling her, as you have it in the song, *O Love that Wilt Not Let Me Go,* and others like it. It was intercession and it kept increasing. She sought for Him and took more and more time to pray and seek the Lord.

Before finishing the account of her intense longing to know Jesus, let us take a moment to compare her experience with that of the 17th Century French quietist, Madame Jeanne de La Mothe Guyon. Many readers know the name because of her *Autobiography*.[4] No one knows how many millions of copies have been made of that book. Other readers may have read the modern English version published by Gene Edwards. Her testimony continues to bring encouragement and blessing to those who want to know Jesus in a fuller way.

Jesus As All-In-All

In the first chapter, Madame Guyon writes,

> But let me assure you, this [sanctification] is not attained, save through pain, weariness and labor; and it will be reached by a path that will wonderfully disappoint your expectations. Nevertheless, if you are fully convinced that it is on the NOTHING in man that God establishes his greatest works — you will in part be guarded against disappointment or surprise. He destroys that He might build; for when He is about to rear His sacred temple in us, He first totally razes that vain and pompous edifice which human art and power had erected, and from its horrible ruins a new structure is formed, by His power only.[5]

At a tender age, the Lord arranged for a devoted man of God to visit the home of her father, and to him she poured out her heart's frustration. His reply changed her life: *"It is, madame, because you seek without what you have within. Accustom yourself to seek God in your heart, and you will there find Him."*[6]

> Nothing was now more easy to me than prayer [she says of the change effected in her]. Hours passed away like moments, while I could hardly do anything else but pray. The fervency of my love allowed me no intermission. It was a prayer of rejoicing and possessing, devoid of all busy imaginations of the head, wherein the taste of God was so great, so pure, unblended and uninterrupted, that it drew and absorbed the power of my soul into a profound recollection without act or discourse. For I had now no sight but of Jesus Christ alone. All else was excluded, in order to love with the greater extent, without any selfish motives or reasons for loving.[7]

Her *Autobiography* contains many such passages, particularly when she leaves off her narrative to speak to God directly. Consider this example:

> I believe there is hardly a torment equal to that of being ardently drawn to retirement [being alone with God, she means], and not having it in one's power to be retired [her husband and mother-in-law endeavored to prevent her from praying thus]. But O my God, the war they raised, to hinder me from loving Thee, did but augment my love; and while they were striving to prevent my

addresses to Thee, Thou drewest me into an inexpressible silence; and the more they labored to separate me from Thee, the more closely didst Thou unite me to Thyself. The flame of Thy love was kindled, and kept up by everything that was done to extinguish it.[8]

Eventually she was imprisoned by the King of France at the request of the religious authorities, because of their vehement opposition to her published views about "inwardness," as we would call it today.

The point is, there are remarkable parallels between Madame Guyon's experience and that of Martha Wing Robinson. In 1907, however, Mrs. Robinson had not yet encountered the writings of Madame Guyon.

We resume quoting now from Rex Andrews' oral history of Mrs. Robinson's seeking.

As the love of God increased, she wanted more of it and more of Him, until it became so intense and consuming in her life and in her prayer, that without her realizing it, she was crossing over the line beyond which you do not go back. You get there and then you keep on going and going. You are drawn farther and farther into God. That, dear ones, is what God has wanted for This Work for more than 50 years – for us to get far enough along in our praying and in our tarrying, in the anointing of the Holy Ghost, so that the love of God can constrain us, as Paul says. The love of God constrains, and it is very much around that boundary line in the pathway of seeking that most of us float back and forth somehow. But I believe we are making definite progress... It is appearing to me in my heart that the love of God is winning the day, seeping through... More individuals are being wooed and weaned away from the love of the world and the love of the self into that area where we will not be able to get out of it, because we will be so consumed in that drawing love of God, that He will carry us on. That is what He did with her.

She and her husband were taking care of a little church in Toronto, Canada. It really was Elder and Mrs. Brooks' church. Elder Brooks was one of the real good old-fashioned elders in every sense of the word. He pastored a small church which met in a rented hall, but he had not yet been baptized in the Holy

Spirit. In those days they believed you should not minister from the platform to preach until you had the baptism. So sometimes the ministers had to go and sit down in the audience while some little person who had had the Baptism of the Holy Spirit came up on the platform to preach and to lead the assembly.

Well, they had a good one there, really, as far as the spiritual life is concerned, in Mrs. Robinson, because what she wanted was the kind of meeting where you sit and love Jesus, or you sing songs about love. She called it "inward." The word "inward" got to be quite a bug-a-boo to some of us in after years because we were outward. Outward means you are kind of looking out away from the Lord; inward means you are coming right into Jesus and want to be there. She loved that and wanted inward meetings. She had the Baptism of the Holy Spirit, but she was only in the process of a prayer which brought her to a great wonderful answer in her life. Elder Brooks asked her to lead the meetings while he continued to tarry for his baptism in the Spirit. Her husband Harry was in the same position as Elder, leaving her in the awkward position of being the main preacher.

Harry could not get through to the baptism very easily, and he wanted her to go on and take care of the platform, but she wanted him to be with her. That is another characteristic of her life: she always wanted somebody else to be with her and be the one that really did the ministering. She would be there rooting for them in prayer and holding them up and wanting them to get ahead and be something. She, of course, wanted her husband to be a good Pentecostal preacher, but he did not have the baptism yet.

But a curious thing happened. She was seeking the Lord and the intensity of it increased and increased. In the diary which she kept for some of those months she described it as, "Oh, Jesus, let us have a feast of love. Oh, I want you. Oh, draw me into Yourself. I must have You. I must have more of You. I cannot live unless I have You. I want You, Jesus. I do not want anything but You, Jesus." She was praying this prayer for nine long months and it increased all the time, but a curious thing happened. Though her heart was being drawn out in an overwhelming and all-consuming love for just Jesus, the meetings dropped down and people did not come. It seemed to get dryer and deader, and she decided in her own heart the Lord was trying to show her she did not amount to anything and was no good and could not be a preacher.

Along in August 1907, they closed that hall. By this time they were living in Elder and Mrs. Brooks' apartment in Toronto, upstairs in Mrs. Mallaby's house, if I remember correctly. The Brooks had invited the Robinsons to live in their apartment while they visited relatives in Virginia. The prayer that Mrs. Robinson was in was increasing and increasing all the time.

As the weeks went by, her praying grew more intense. She got to such a place in her praying that she could not bear to think of there being such a person as Mrs. Robinson anymore at all. "Oh, that I were gone and that Jesus possessed my body and my life completely! Oh, that there was not anymore of me and that it was all Christ, all Jesus." She meant it LITERALLY. She prayed and prayed, and the prayer began to take the form that SHE might die, that SHE might be gone. She was praying then to be crucified, to be dead, to be gone and Christ alive and Christ living in her.

I have not touched on some important points about her praying, for she had prayed through on the Beatitudes, and she prayed through on such passages of scripture as you find in Philippians, the Third Chapter, – "that I may know HIM and the power of His resurrection, and the fellowship of His sufferings, being made conformable unto His death." I do not advise anybody to pray to "die" unless God puts it on you in such a way you cannot do anything else. I have tried it, but I found I could not do it. The Lord was not putting it on me, and I found that the adversary was plenty ready to take advantage of that. If you get that Holy Ghost holiness fixation in you, and it is the love of God controlling your heart and your spirit and the eyes of your heart, – well, perhaps you could pray some such a prayer as "Let me die."

She prayed on and on until it just became practically three words: "Let me die." It came to the point, along at the end of October it was, that she would get out of bed when Harry was asleep and kneel down beside the bed to pray all night, until she heard him stir. Then she got back in bed, and he never knew the difference, because she was there when he woke up. She wanted to spend all her time seeking the Lord.

One night it came up, would they go to the Pentecostal meeting downtown? She said, "I want to stay home. I do not think I want to go tonight." Harry said he was going. He left and took the key so he would not have to disturb her when he came home. He was not anymore out of the door than she was on her knees by a chair in the kitchen, praying her prayer. She did not know that was the night the prayer was going to be answered.

Dear ones, none of us ever know when it is going to be. We never know, though sometimes we can tell a little bit that we are getting there if God is drawing on us so much that we are loving Him more and more. We cannot bear anything possibly of any kind to get in between in any way, shape, or form. She had been praying, "Oh, let me die," if I remember right, for three days and nights. Suddenly, (as she told the story), it was as though the ticking of a great clock had stopped. Everything around her was perfectly still. And we have had some of those stillnesses. I could testify about it, but if I did it would seem like boasting.

So it was a great silence as though everything had stopped. (We read in the Book of Revelation of such a great silence.) Jesus was standing in front of her. It was Jesus. IT WAS JESUS. The Lord talked to her for a couple of hours or more, and she has not told us much of what He said to her. Some things, of course, came out in the course of conferences and teachings and arrangements of the Lord in later years. Finally she heard the Lord speaking to her, but she did not realize that the Lord was speaking through her own mouth. The Lord was speaking through her mouth to herself. I have heard her say at one time, "I have not spoken a word of my own for seventeen years." That continued right on to the end of her life, for twenty-eight years and more. That was because the Lord had done what Paul describes in various ways: He had made her body to be the body of the Lord. "The Lord is for the body, and the body is for the Lord," but you see, we do not preach much upon those subjects because most people have not got under the Blood yet far enough to even dare to contemplate much along these lines. They would easily run into some style of fanaticism. He had done that in her. "What? Know ye not that your body is the temple of God, and you are not your own; you are bought with a price?" The Lord had taken possession of her body. It was so real and so simple that her husband did not know it.

He came in from the meeting and the Lord talked to him through her mouth. He could not tell the difference at all. I do not doubt but he may have thought, "Well, she is a little sweeter than ordinary," but I think she was pretty near sweet enough for him. He did not know anything about it until she later told him. Not only did the Lord speak through her mouth, but the Lord also moved her body. Her feet were moved. Her hands were moved. Her whole body was moved. Her head was moved. Her whole body was moved by the Lord. She was in the power of God and it was a very simple thing.

The most amazing wonders of God are probably the greatest simplicities. The greatest power that ever was manifested in This Work was the power of God in such a simplicity that unless somebody knew it, they would not know that it was God at all.

And I want to say in great big blazing capital letters, no matter what anybody else may have ever been like, this one person was not *the person*; she never claimed, "Well, I am the great one, I have it," and all those things. She never did it.

That is the point to which the third stage of her prayer life came, and that is where This Work began. It began in that experience.

Once again we interrupt this narrative by Rex Andrews to insert Mrs. Robinson's own words about her experience at that time. This testimony has appeared in several places in longer or shorter versions.[9] My source is a paper made available to everyone attending a public meeting in the Faith Homes on Sunday morning, September 17, 1972. I have broken it into paragraphs to make it more readable. Otherwise it is copied *verbatim*.

Away back in the beginning of This Work, when we prayed through to our death, we passed over into a change, which was not like anything we had ever heard of. It included everything from head to foot. We found out it was A TASTE OF SOMETHING GOD IS GOING TO DO IN THE LAST DAYS. At that time we did not understand that we had come into it by the crucifixion, or death to self. In a moment we were gone and a Greater One was there. Entire spirit and soul and body were in a new and divine control. We walked out of the natural into the spiritual, in BODY as well as in Soul. That was the experience God opened This Work with.

And we dwelt in God, for a period, in a Great Mystery. We felt we had died, and Christ had come to dwell where we had been. And at that time there were mysteries that we had gone through. We passed up into God's Presence; saw and heard things that God has never let us tell – a number of weeks of the mysteries of God that we don't dare utter. We had it in our nature to maintain an absolute reserve of private experience.

We know that we had spent many, many long months in one great cry to God: "Let me die." We agonized before God, and wept and called upon God: "Let me die." God got the light to me that it would be blessed to be utterly gone. And that was a Real Light. We PASSED OVER.

It was simply a manifestation of The King's Life. We knew only God, and were hidden away in God. In such tremendous mystery the very Presence of God comes upon us and we just feel bowed before God in that wonderful experience.

It was the mystery of the INDWELLING CHRIST. He didn't explain it, till I found Him there and knew it was: "Nevertheless I live, yet not I, but Christ liveth in me." And the mystery was so enormous and so wonderful; and I felt my God moved – as it were eliminated me – Christ was living in me; and yet I didn't seem to live at all. My mind didn't work at all – my spirit off in heaven. It seemed that Christ was just borrowing, as it were, my body. <u>CRUCIFIXION IS THE UTTER ANNIHILATION OF YOUR WILL, AND THE YIELDING OF YOUR LIFE.</u> Martha Wing Robinson.

"IT IS NOT MEANT FOR ONE, BUT FOR MANY." M.W.R.

"THE WORLD IS WAITING FOR THE MANIFESTATION OF THE SONS OF GOD." M.W.R.[10]

Rex Andrews, whose life appears a bit later in this history, ran away from the Lord and the truth of that testimony, having "got tired of this kind of thing." He says,

> One of the reasons I am telling this is because, after my own rebellious and stubborn and wicked life, I knew some of these things. I will not be able to say very much in this series of talks where I was situated in it, or what I knew about it, or what was recovered for me in 1944, but [in 1936] I threw these things away. I rebelled. I got tired of this kind of thing and went out of the Work after I had been in it as a minister for four years.... Finally I got caught and trapped in a position that I could not get out of, and I was then gone to the devil for seven years.
>
> I have sometimes wondered if it could have been the result of just an unwillingness to be an out-and-out witness and say, "I KNOW THAT WAS JESUS" and stick to it. I did say those words, and I fought for it, and thought I was in it and believed it. But gradually I got away from it. I backed away from the person in whom the Lord Jesus never departed and never changed the fact of His possession and His residence there.
>
> I knew it was the Lord, because He gave me certain positions of light in my own soul when we first came here in 1913 and 1914. When the Lord restored me in 1944, He showed me the point where I had switched away from This Work: I had started to pray for poverty of spirit, but had never completed the prayer. In 1944 I resumed the prayer. I want to testify that during these now seventeen years, the Lord has increased and increased quietly the reality in my own heart and the certainty of these things. Certain things have gone on quietly unfolding that make me realize and believe that He has NEVER ceased to carry on and go on with what He was doing.
>
> I want to say point blank: THAT WAS JESUS CHRIST. It was the Lord Jesus Christ. If it was not, you would not be here

and I would not be here, and This Work would not be here, because there is a singular characteristic to This Work which is almost the opposite of most places, even "deep life" places. I will bring it out more as we go on, but the characteristic of This Work has been a giving Work, a faith life Work, where you give, you give, you give all the time. It is a crucifixion Work, to go ON to crucifixion of your will. It is a giving Work. To some favorable degree we have kept that principle alive here, to just go on by faith. The characteristic of the Work has been, from the beginning, to pour out, to give out. You can be reasonably safe that you are not in some kind of a radical fanaticism, when the life is GIVING, when that is the characteristic of it.[11]

Without an understanding of this manifestation of Christ to Mrs. Robinson, and the fruit that resulted from that transformation of her life by Jesus, it is impossible to understand the purpose, place, and calling of the Zion Faith Homes.

We will have occasion to return to the balance of the oral history given in 1961, but not before presenting a brief account of the three years in Toronto and the opening of the first Faith Home there in 1909.

CHAPTER FOUR

THE ORIGINAL WORK
1907 – 1914

PART 1

Introduction

What I am about to write seems impossible to put into words. That the subject matter exceeds my grasp I readily acknowledge. The thousands of precious saints who lived in or visited the Faith Homes for the past 90 years have their own stories to tell, though most of them have passed from this life into the next. My understanding of the Homes derives from my years of training in the Homes, from 1967 to mid-1973, followed by my years of service there as a minister, August 1973 to June 1996. God gave me a divine hunger to learn the history of the Work. Rex Andrews, who was one of the *Vessels* (a term explained later in this chapter), spoke frequently about the Homes in the course of his public and private ministry, and some things he shared with me personally.

In the 1980s, Miss Ruth Brooks, daughter of Elder and Sara Brooks, who were also among the Vessels, agreed to talk to me about the Work every Thursday afternoon for about a year, giving me access to her wonderful memory of things she had seen and heard from the time of her earliest childhood (she was born in 1903) through all the periods named in this record. We also read together a large number of written histories, letters, and other incidental papers pertaining to the Work. She encouraged me to ask questions as we were reading, giving me answers as she was able. For her willingness to take the time to share with me her knowledge of the Homes, I am forever deeply grateful.

I realize also that some reading this account may reject it as being fanciful, exaggerated, or colored by my own mind-set, or by my personality. Some may recoil when reading this story as though it is only a clumsy effort to turn ordinary people into heroes – "the usual process" (they say), "whereby history becomes myth or legend." And already some attribute Mrs. Robinson's experience, quoted in the previous chapter, to mental delusion or worse, as though such things could be dismissed by a few hints (or winks) to the undiscerning reader that what he is about to read is distorted and even laughable.

All I can do is tell the truth and leave the results to God. No one is compelled to believe this record. God is God, and all things will appear someday in the Light for what they are. Yet I can do one more thing: I can PRAY for everyone that reads these pages,

> *...that the God of our Lord Jesus Christ, the Father of glory, may give unto you the spirit of wisdom and revelation in the knowledge of Him...* (Ephesians 1:17)
>
> *...that you might be filled with the knowledge of His will in all wisdom and spiritual understanding; that ye might walk worthy of the Lord unto all pleasing, being fruitful in every good work, and increasing in the knowledge of God...* (Colossians 1:9-10)
>
> *...that your love may abound yet more and more, in knowledge and in all judgment [spiritual perception]; that you may approve things that are excellent; that ye may be sincere and without offense till the day of Christ...* (Philippians 1:9-10)
>
> *...and that Christ may dwell in your hearts by faith; that you, being rooted and grounded in love, may be able to comprehend with all saints what is the breadth, and length, and depth, and height; and to know the love of Christ, which passes knowledge, THAT YE MIGHT BE FILLED WITH ALL THE FULNESS OF GOD.* (Ephesians 3:17-19, emphasis added)

This history that follows needs to be prefaced by a quotation from a letter sent to Miss Ruth Lade, (later Mrs. David Schleicher), who entered the Faith Homes as a trainee shortly after receiving this letter, and who went on to become one of the ministers in the Faith Homes. She resided in the Homes for 33 years and passed on to her reward in 2002. The writer of this letter to her is Rex Andrews.

Almost no one realizes what KIND of a Work the Faith Home Work is. It is a "nothing" Work. That means: A come-to-NOTHING WORK. Consequently, when anyone tries to move forward into a Be-Something position, they sooner or later find they are stepping out on thin air — no foundation under them — no way at all to "BE" something... If anyone DOES start out to "be" something — in the sense of leadership — then they automatically enter the pathway of the discipline which the Faith Home leaders are all in, and have long been in...

Since 1948, the consecration of ALL the Faith Home ministers has been that: they see nothing before them but to lose their life, and come to nothing, in the service required in the Homes for others; IN ORDER TO LET THE LORD be the fountain-center — each one merely a hole in the ground for Him to flow through.

So, whoever sets out to "BE" something in the Faith Home ministry — or before the public so — finds himself automatically in a pathway which comes directly to "nothing" — a hole-in-the-ground.

This is a Work in which the working of the LORD is to bring us to self-nothingness IN the allness of Jesus.[1]

With that bit of introduction, we plunge ahead.

Description

What came to be called *The Zion Faith Homes* truly began in November 1907, as the outworking of the experience described by Mrs. Martha Robinson in her testimony in the previous chapter. *The Original Work* (a term the Lord used) lasted seven years. All that I know personally of the Faith Homes, and all that most of the 'old timers' knew of the Faith Homes, dates from *The Secondary Work* and not *The Original Work*. My personal knowledge of the Homes is limited, of course, to the period called *The Resurgent Work,* but what I learned about the other periods comes, as mentioned earlier, from eyewitness testimony.

The Original Work comprised a seven year period from 1907–1914. It was the Work in its purity. The best words I can use to describe it is a phrase God spoke into my heart many years ago. The words were, "The Faith Homes is *a vast simplicity*."

Those seven years could be termed the expression, the aura, or the after-effects of Jesus possessing Martha Robinson the way He did.

Jesus drew people into meetings where He Himself did everything, yes, everything, in a way that I cannot describe to you adequately in words. What happened in those years surpasses our present-day conceptions of Spirit-led meetings and anointed preaching.

I beg you to suspend for now the desire to overlay your experience in God on what I am saying. I know that sounds terribly arrogant, as though I am presenting something esoteric, understandable only by a few, "Gnostic heresy." I don't mean it that way. It needs to be said, however, because it is a shock to some people to find someone who knows God better than they do. When I have shared these simple things publicly, or semi-publicly, often the response is, "Oh yes, I know exactly what you're talking about. I've experienced that." And I think, "No, you haven't, but I realize you think you do." What a battle it is to stay out of the pride of spiritual knowledge!*

But the truth remains: The Work was formed into *a vast simplicity*. The meetings lasted hours and hours, yet it seemed but minutes had passed. Jesus ministered personally to one after another, using different individuals in a true First Corinthians 14 meeting. Jesus spoke and acted through the *Vessels* (His choice of wording, based on I Timothy 2:21) that were completely yielded to Him, without strife, competition, jealousy, or disputing among themselves. It was the innocence of Pentecost in a way that I still find difficult to comprehend.

My limited grasp of it was shaped by the simple Thursday night services in the Faith Homes, "trainee night" (more on that later), when afterward Rex Andrews would say, "Friends, that was the kind of meeting Mrs. Robinson wanted." Yet we hardly realized how great was Jesus' control over the actions and words in that service. It was so simple. The following description gives the atmosphere of those meetings:

> The greatest power ever manifested in the Faith Homes...was the power of God in such a simplicity that, unless somebody knew it, they would not know that it was God at all! And I want to say in great big blazing capital letters, no matter what anybody else may have been like, this one person [Mrs. Robinson] was not the person and never was the person who would go around claiming, "Well, I am the great one. I have it," and all those things. She never did it.[2]

---

* As was said to me one time, upon hearing from an eyewitness of these things, "If you ever get puffed up over what I am telling you, I will knock you down so fast you won't know what happened to you!"

Did you notice the expression, "The greatest power"?

Those meetings began in Toronto, Canada, in February 1909, and continued in Zion, Illinois from 1910 onward. You can read the story of those days when God began to put together the beginnings of the Faith Homes, and Faith Home meetings, in the biography of Martha Wing Robinson. How I love to be in meetings where Jesus is the whole thing!

Eventually, the small group of five people who later became *Vessels* in the Faith Homes when it moved to Zion City were directed by the Lord to rent a large home on Surrey Avenue in Toronto, where they would live and work together under the Lord's direction.

It was a remarkable start to a ministry that would continue for many decades and affect thousands of people. The leaders of the meetings were taught by the Lord to let Him have His way in the services – so different from the modern type of meetings – without the need for a song-leader, or worship team, or pre-planned programs. In the course of those meetings amazing things happened. To quote from *Radiant Glory*,

> All who attended the gatherings of the first year of the work in Toronto were unanimous in their testimony that they never witnessed before or after meetings upon which the presence of God rested so greatly and in which God worked so supernaturally. On the "platform" were Mr. and Mrs. Robinson, Elder and Mrs. Brooks, and Miss MacPhail. These five ministered as a unity, one or another being used of God as the Holy Spirit led or directed, supplementing or complementing the ministry of each other, all working in harmony and to one end. A marvelous example of the teaching set forth in First Corinthians twelve – "many members...one body," "diversities of gifts," of ministries, and of operations, but the same Spirit.
>
> "We always sat in silence until the Lord began to do something – give some prophecy...or some teaching by wisdom through Mrs. Robinson. Sometimes all of us just sat in silence, worshiping God for quite awhile, and then we would sometimes have wonderful praises." Such was the description of the meetings by Miss MacPhail.[3]

The Lord was free to do as He pleased, largely because nobody wanted to be "The One." Jesus was The One. He spoke His word through the

Vessels and reached out to those in the congregation to deliver and heal and release people from lifelong troubles of soul and body. "The power of God was present to heal," as Luke says in his account of the paralyzed man let down through the roof (Luke 5:17).

The ministers covenanted not to do anything in the meetings – not to speak, not to lay hands on anyone, nor to do anything – unless the power of God moved them to do it. They sat still and waited for God to raise them up on their feet, to walk them to the front of the room, and to open their mouths to speak His words without getting their minds into it at all.

Such things, of course, are in the Bible, especially in the lives of the Prophets, who experienced the power of God on their bodies, sometimes to restrain them and sometimes to enable them. I'm sure you can call to mind, for example, the testimonies of Ezekiel, or Elijah, or even Samson, in regard to the Lord's power on them physically. It was different from *leadings* with which Pentecostal people are familiar, and even different from what we commonly call *the anointing*.

In the Faith Home meetings all things were done with the utmost simplicity, so visitors not privy to the cause would never notice how directly the Lord Himself was carrying out His work.

One of the passages that (much later) meant so much to us living in the Faith Homes was Second Corinthians 6:16 (with the context).

> *And what agreement hath the temple of God with idols? For ye are the temple of the living God; as God hath said, I will dwell in them, and walk in them; and I will be their God, and they shall be my people.*

"Why don't you receive that promise literally?" we were asked. "It is meant that way." The Vessels knew what it was to have the Lord *walk in them*. (I do not know by experience such power on my physical body, but I know it is real.)

From Rev. George Rundblom, who was on the "platform" (the front end of the room where the appointed leaders sat) when my wife and I came to the Homes, we learned more about the Lord's power on the body. He told us the following story:

> As a young man in Chicago I found the Lord Jesus as my Savior and wanted to share His testimony with others. However, I was very shy and found it difficult to hand a tract to someone, for example, or to testify to strangers about Jesus. One day I determined to

board a city bus and hand out tracts to the people in the bus. Try as I would, I could not muster the courage to approach anyone. I finally gave up, feeling like a miserable failure, weak and fearful.

That night, however, as was my custom, I went to church to attend the prayer service. It was held in a Pentecostal church where the gifts of the Spirit operated frequently. As everyone was kneeling in fervent prayer, suddenly a tremendous message of prophecy came forth: "There's a Jonah among us! The Lord says you must go back to Nineveh where God sent you in the first place. You must repent of your unwillingness to go!"

The thought going through my mind was, "My, I wonder who gave that prophecy, and I wonder for whom it is intended?"

No one moved or responded or said anything. Suddenly the Lord spoke again: "Jonah! Go to your calling!"

A pastor among the praying saints finally cried out, "It's me, Lord; it's me! I'll go!" At the same time it dawned on me that the Lord had spoken over my own lips! I was the one who gave the prophecy, but I didn't know it the first time! This was God's answer to my fear of speaking to people about the Lord: "I will speak through you by the power of My Spirit!"

You ask, perhaps, "How can that be?" Well, I don't know. Like you, I need a greater appreciation for the God of the Bible. God is quite capable of doing anything He pleases, whenever He wants, using whomever He wants, and He doesn't need my prior permission or approval.

The power of God was on the Vessels in such a way that they walked as He moved their legs; they spoke as He gave them the opening of their mouths; He used their hands to bless others as He took control of their hands. It truly was "a taste of something God is going to do in the last days."

I am recalling right now an account of God's power told to me by Leonard Ravenhill. During evangelistic services held by General William Booth, founder of *The Salvation Army*, conviction fell so heavily on the crowds when Booth gave the invitation for salvation, that sometimes people were lifted bodily by the Spirit's power from the back of the crowd and deposited at the altar of repentance in front. Why do we limit God?

I mentioned the Thursday night meetings, how simple they sometimes were, but how greatly God's power rested upon them. The students were required to give a "talk" (a short sermon) on Thursday nights on a rotating basis. It worked out that each of us shared about once every six weeks. On one such evening, as one of the young men (who is still living) was giving his "trainee talk," he was baptized in the Holy Spirit while he was speaking! He simply slipped over the line from speaking naturally to speaking by the Spirit, "prophesying" without even realizing it. Rex Andrews heard the difference and later told the young man what had happened. "Do you realize that in the middle of your talk you went from speaking naturally to prophesying? And everything you said after a certain point was the Lord speaking through you?"

Again you might say, "That's impossible; I don't believe it." But did not even Caiaphas the High Priest prophesy unwittingly that Jesus would die for the nation (John 11:51)? Why do we limit God?

That *Original Work* came into being because (in February 1907) a great hunger rose in Martha Robinson to be baptized in the Holy Ghost, along Pentecostal lines. The testimony of what God had done on the West Coast, especially at Azusa Street in Los Angeles, had come eastward, and when Mrs. Robinson "searched the Scriptures to see if these things be so" (Acts 17:11), she concluded it was truly God's will to baptize His people with the Holy Ghost and fire.

Thus she began to pray to be filled. It was a very simple thing. The Lord cleansed her, gave her an experience of *sanctification* and filled her as an emptied and cleansed vessel. She knew God had baptized her before she spoke in tongues. She always held that the evidence of the Baptism of the Spirit was speaking in tongues, or prophesying, or both.

In any event, as a further result of her baptism, there came into her heart a tremendous hunger to know Jesus, a desire that only grew with each passing month. God enabled her to seek Jesus with unremitting passion, the likes of which is not commonly known. She kept a diary[4] of her seeking, and some of the entries in the diary are quoted at the end of Rex Andrews' *Meditations in the Revelation*.[5] She and her husband Harry were overseeing a small church in Toronto at the time, having been put into the Gospel ministry by Dr. John Alexander Dowie, healing evangelist and founder of the city of Zion, in the State of Illinois. From February to October, God fanned the spark of desire for

Jesus into a very bright flame. In early November, she "passed over into God," as told in the previous chapter.

Again you might say, "How can these things be? Surely you are exaggerating; or deluded." But these things are so, and I testify to their validity. You can read Gordon Gardiner's account of these things in Chapter 22 of *Radiant Glory,* entitled "The Manifestation of Christ." Paul said to Titus, "Unto the pure all things are pure" (Titus 1:15).

God had gotten the light through to her that "it would be blessed to be utterly gone. That was a real light," she said. Do you know what that "real light" was? (I will put it in my own words, as though she were saying it, however.)

> "O dear Lord, it would be better for everyone if I were gone and Jesus were here in place of me. O Jesus, please don't ever let me have my own way again. Please come to me. I'm so helpless. I'm so useless. Can't You just fill me? Why does it have to be Mrs. Robinson who does things? Why can't You just come and take over? O Jesus, I long for You, I long for You."

For nine months that prayer grew and grew and grew in her until Jesus answered the prayer He had given her.

And yet: She always knew that it was not because she was such a great pray-er, or such a wonderful woman, but rather because Jesus desires to give us Himself. He will give Himself to us FREELY if we will receive Him "as a little child" (Matthew 18:1). "Behold what it is the Lord has sought for you," she said in 1934. "It is to have Jesus."

The meetings developed naturally out of that experience about which I have been speaking.

The Hidden Pathway

It wasn't very long before the Lord offered Mrs. Robinson a choice that was to affect the pathway the Faith Homes would take in years to come. Her biographer tells it this way:

> Evidently it was about this same time (December 1907) that the Lord showed her two paths for her life and told her she might choose either one, just as she desired, for either one would be His will and that in either choice she made she would enjoy His

blessing. She could choose to be a successful evangelist, used to bless the multitudes, with the fame and acclaim which generally attends such a ministry, or she could choose to be a vessel hidden and comparatively unknown, with misunderstanding and great suffering as her main portion.

To the natural person, the first path, of course, would be the appealing one. On the basis of her experience as a young minister in the past nine years, she had reason to believe that she could indeed be successful. But Mrs. Robinson had passed out of the natural into the spiritual so that her own will "had, as it were, disappeared, or, rather, passed into another will." Therefore, Mrs. Robinson said to the Lord, "Jesus, I wouldn't know which to choose. You choose for me."

And He chose the hidden path, the path of suffering.[6]

And truly that became the pathway she trod until her death in 1936.

As one might imagine, such a choice would not lack its testings. One early example arose when the Lord told Mrs. Robinson He would remove the miraculous gifts and powers from her ministry for a time, to authenticate her love for Jesus Himself as the Giver of her gifts, and not merely because of the gifts He gave her.[†] Not only were her gifts and powers withdrawn, but she was unable to recall the Lord's word to her regarding the temporary loss.

This change in her created a stir in the church world of Toronto, causing many to believe her experience was not of God. Wild and exaggerated stories circulated that suggested her intense praying had affected her mind and she was now in delusion. Also the devil at this time sought to destroy what Jesus was doing through the avenue of her husband Harry's moody nature. He would go through periods of great openness to the Lord, and then he would back away from it. Apparently Harry asked a well-known minister in Toronto to come to their home to interrogate his wife. Though she answered humbly and well, the minister concluded her experience did not have its origins in God, confirming Harry's determination to order his wife to sever all connections with anything Pentecostal, even to the point of telling her not to speak in tongues any longer.

---

† Readers of Madame Guyon's *Autobiography* may recall a similar period of testing in her life.

The Original Work, 1907-1914 Part One

Mrs. Robinson was an intelligent young woman just 33 years of age in 1907, very talented in writing, diligent in business, capable in many ways. The humiliation and misunderstanding during this period accomplished the Lord's purposes, however, and in time Harry changed his mind, her gifts and powers were restored, and God began to construct the basic outlines of what became The Faith Home Work.‡

For seven years, from 1907-1914, the Lord continued His work in her and through her as I am describing and He added eight other workers to the five mentioned earlier, so that the original circle of ministers numbered thirteen in all, including Mrs. Robinson. They became known as *Vessels* by those who attended the meetings, because that is what God called them.

At various times, each of the Vessels experienced the power of God on their bodies, in much the same way that Mrs. Robinson did. God touched them physically, in ways reminiscent of His physical touch on Moses, for example, whose face shone with the glory of God, or Elijah who outran Ahab's chariot, or Ezekiel who was transported to Jerusalem in some manner and given a tour of the Temple, *etc.* All of these things had parallels in the Faith Homes. A diary kept by one of the Vessels during these years records many such examples, incidents perhaps too numerous and too sacred to share lest they serve to shift the emphasis onto the outward expressions of God's activity in the Faith Homes. The true essence of His work in the Homes was always inward, not the outward show of His power, but the simplicity of His inward possession (which necessarily preceded the miraculous manifestations).

For the record, here is a complete list of those thirteen men and women, part of the company of "those of whom the world is not worthy," as it says in Hebrews 11:37.

Harry Robinson	Loretta M. Judd
Martha W. Robinson	Alexander Campbell
Elder Eugene Brooks	Stella Leggett
Sara Brooks	Eva (MacPhail) Leggett
George Mitchell	Hilda Nilsson
Lydia Mitchell	Rex B. Andrews
	Ursie Naylor

---

‡ Gardiner's *Radiant Glory* contains a fuller account of this period.

I despair of telling properly the story of those first seven years. Like John's Gospel, I leave much unsaid. Though the Lord's perfect will had been to establish the Faith Homes in the American city of Detroit, Michigan, He gave grace for the first Faith Home to be located in Toronto, Canada. Within a year, however, for various reasons, the Work essentially shifted to Zion, Illinois where tent meetings began in 1910, followed by the rental of a meeting place at 2820 Eschol Avenue and the eventual purchase of other homes nearby.

As mentioned, those seven years were *a vast simplicity*, succinctly described later by Rex Andrews in the following words:

> That was the Great Coming of Jesus, [not His return when every eye shall see Him, but] the Passing Over into God, the Revelation of Jesus within, the complete possession of the body by The Holy Spirit, the issuing of THE WORD, and the projecting of what was called "The Power Work."[7]

As the nightmare of world war descended upon Europe in 1914, there came also furious opposition of the devil against the work Jesus was doing in the Faith Homes. I'm told by veterans of the Vietnam War that no one can really appreciate what it is like to be caught in a literal firestorm of destruction from the enemy unless he has experienced it. The same was true about the spiritual warfare in which the Vessels were involved.

It is that warfare we will examine next.

CHAPTER FIVE

THE ORIGINAL WORK
1907 – 1914

PART 2

As one might expect, the Lord's possession of Mrs. Robinson's life – "body, soul, and spirit" – precipitated fierce opposition from the enemy against her. If it was truly Jesus Christ who now controlled her thoughts and actions – and it was – then it constituted a very serious threat to the plans of the devil for these last days. Clearly his intention is to control and to possess a devil-filled human being who will rule the world: the Man of Sin, the Antichrist. God's possession of His people along the lines of Mrs. Robinson's experience spells failure for the Man of Sin.

God, by His power and wisdom alone, had CREATED something in Mrs. Robinson that He desires for all His own ones: "It is NOT meant for one," said Mrs. Robinson, "but for MANY."[1] In later years, the Lord taught that the devil will be overcome by those in whom Jesus dwells in all His fullness. Mrs. Robinson, and those whom God placed within her sphere of ministry, blazed a trail that many will follow in these last days. "The devil is doing terrible things these days," remarked Miss Nilsson to Mrs. Robinson. "Yes," was the reply, "but God will never be behind."[2] God always moves first; the devil can only seek to *prevent* the creative work of God, or to *destroy* it after it is produced. The devil tries to copy what God does, but the imitation always has in it the seeds of its own destruction; any attempted "clone" of God's true work cannot survive. The devil is NOT a creator, and indeed never can be; his title in Hebrew is *Abaddon* and in Greek it is *Apollyon*; both words mean "DESTROYER." The names describe his nature: he can NOT create; he seeks to destroy what God, the Creator, creates.

Many and fierce were the assaults on the Vessel in whom Jesus came to dwell.* With no one to teach her, she depended entirely on the Holy Spirit to lead her through a minefield of the enemy's devices – such things as fanaticism, false lights, the misuse and abuse of the Gifts of the Spirit, discouragements, criticism, etc., etc., – while experiencing the power of the Lord on her body, especially on her speech. To quote again from a short article by Rex Andrews:

> There would not have been any great opposition if there were nothing to oppose. But there was: The Greatest manifestation of the Word of God – well, let us just say, in our times.
>
> The details of many phases of this harrying opposition could be given...[the Lord] kept The Work in great power and glory even when the LIGHT was countered in inconceivable ways... It is one of the most amazing stories ever told...
>
> This is a partial record of the Truth of a spiritual conflict – a war – such as no one can imagine if they were not actually involved in it. They [the ministers] were the determined targets of the Adversary as he sought to obliterate, utterly, all trace of what The Word of God was doing in Mrs. Robinson and in them.
>
> What is being described? The position and power of the Great Delusion, "I" AM THE ONE! The whole world is wallowing in that spirit now.[3]

The origin of the Faith Homes dates from November 1907, when Jesus came to Mrs. Robinson, as described previously. For over a year the enemy assailed her, and some of the worst opposition came from those closest to her, including her husband, as mentioned earlier.[4] Gradually, however, it became apparent that her experience was the work of God, for it produced much blessing and edification in all who were exposed to it. In February 1909, meetings began in the parlor of Mr. and Mrs. Marlatt's home, where the Robinsons were staying. Without any advertisements or announcements, the Lord sent people of His choosing to the simple services. Soon the group of a dozen or more was meeting each Sunday at the Marlatt's, and Saturday nights in Mrs. Mallaby's home, with great effect on those attending. The group

---

* To repeat: "Vessel" was a word chosen by the Lord to describe those whom He thus filled. By capitalizing it, we do not mean to exalt them in any way, but to remain within the teaching of II Corinthians 4:7, which says, "But we have this treasure in earthen *vessels*, that the excellency of the power may be of God, and not of us."

included Mr. and Mrs. Robinson, of course, and Eva MacPhail (later, "Aunt Eva Leggett"), Elder and Mrs. Brooks, Professor and Mrs. Toews, and Mrs. Dunlop – names which were familiar to the early residents of the Faith Homes.

The words chosen as a title for this book arose as an apt description of God's grace to those who came to services that were distinctly different from church life as it was known and experienced at that time. Every aspect of the meetings was truly *a vast simplicity*. Without anyone using the term, the services were "inward" – which means "turned toward the Lord inside," as opposed to "outward," where one's attention is more on what is happening in the service, than on the Lord Himself.† If one has had the privilege of being in such services, one thinks instinctively of First Corinthians 14, where Holy Spirit-led meetings were normal. God speaks, to be sure, and all the gifts of the Spirit are in operation, but everything is done "decently, and in order"; the Spirit produces child*like*ness, but not child*ish*ness. Literally four or five hours might go by without weariness or boredom on the one hand, or excitement and "hype" on the other hand. It was "just Jesus"[5] as He is, present among those who are living in their "First Love."‡

In one of these small but wonderful meetings that had continued on through the spring, summer, and fall of 1909, the Lord's Word came to two of the ministers – Mrs. Robinson and Mrs. Brooks – that the Lord desired the leaders to secure a home in Toronto with suitable living quarters for the ministers, as well as a large enough room for public meetings. The announcement was made on Sunday night, December 12, 1909, on a cold and snowy evening, and it included the direction that it should be secured by the following Wednesday, December 15th! Providentially a man was present who had been directed by the Lord to bring an extra $75.00 to the meeting, and thus he was prepared to donate the money that night toward the cost of renting the home not yet found.[6]

As Mrs. Brooks and Miss MacPhail walked the streets the next morning, waiting for God's direction, the Lord spoke to them clearly when they passed the large home on 23 Surrey Place: "This is the house." Though

---

† Compare to the story in Luke 17:12-19, noting the response of the Samaritan to his healing.
‡ The Lord's Word which He gave concerning the meaning of "the first love" (Revelation 2:4) defined it as follows: "The First Love is not a great desire to go to work [for the Lord]; the First Love is the awakening of the heart to the wonder of just Jesus Christ Himself."

it turned out to be for sale, the owner agreed to rent it to the group for twenty-five dollars a month. With the money given by Mr. Campbell the night before, they paid the first three months' rent, and only then did they examine the house inside! If the Lord had chosen it, they believed it would be perfectly suited for their purposes. Indeed it was suitable, and thus December 15, 1909, marked the beginning of many decades of fruitful and influential ministry for the Kingdom of God.

Those in charge of the new "Faith Home" were six in all: Mr. and Mrs. Robinson; Elder and Mrs. Brooks; Eva MacPhail; and within a year, Alexander Campbell.

The arrangement in Toronto, however, did not become permanent. Due to circumstances which are beyond the purpose of this narrative to relate, the Faith Homes essentially moved to Zion, Illinois within a year. The Brookses moved first, in the spring of 1910, into a home secured by the Lord's direction by Mrs. Brooks' sister and her husband (Lydia and George A. Mitchell). The Mitchells had joined Dr. Dowie's venture several years earlier, but now knew that the venture had failed. In the nick of time, so to speak, practically the day before the Mitchells were to mail a signed contract to manage a ranch in the West, the Lord confirmed their call to join Elder and Mrs. Brooks in Zion City. Elder Brooks had been led to set up a tent on an empty lot near the downtown area, where Zion's poor and needy could be refreshed by the Holy Spirit.

It should be remembered that Zion City had gone through agonizing upheaval caused by the decline of Dr. Dowie, the bankruptcy into which the city had fallen, and the discouragement of the residents, many of whom had lost everything in the aftermath. The Lord, however, had sent a Pentecostal revival some six years previous, and many people were eager for the blessings to multiply. The power of the Lord was present in those tent services, both to heal the sick, and also to baptize with the Holy Spirit. Some who later became part of the Zion Faith Homes testified to the transformation in their lives through the ministry of Elder and Mrs. Brooks, and also through Mrs. Robinson, who came from Toronto to help lead the meetings.

One of Dr. Dowie's leading assistants, H. Worthington Judd, and his wife Loretta Mae Judd, were attracted to the tent meetings. Within a short time both were thoroughly convinced of the genuineness of the Spirit's work and joined the little band of Spirit-filled leaders, Mr.

Judd as the Faith Homes' organist for many years, and Mrs. Judd as one of the Vessels of His choosing. Also to the meetings came an African-American woman, Mrs. Ursie Naylor, whom the Lord chose to be a Vessel in the Faith Home Work.

When the tent meetings ended that fall of 1910, Mrs. Robinson returned to Toronto, but the Brookses and the Mitchells continued the services in the Faith Home which had been secured earlier that year. By the spring of 1911, new and larger quarters became a necessity, and the group moved to Emmaus Avenue and conducted the meetings in a large rented home on the corner of 29th Street and Eschol Avenue, which came to be known as the *Meeting House.* Mr. and Mrs. Robinson came from Toronto and moved into that home in June. The work continued to grow, attracting visitors from Pentecostal circles, necessitating further living quarters, and a third home was rented one block north of the Meeting House, at 2736 Eschol Avenue. From that point on, there were always three homes which constituted the Zion Faith Homes, with residents and visitors occupying some thirty-plus bedrooms and sharing meals together in each home's dining room. The Toronto Home closed and essentially the Faith Homes moved to Zion City in that year of 1911.

Miss Eva MacPhail married Sarah and Lydia Leggett's older brother William on August 30, 1911, and they too joined the group living in the Faith Homes. "Aunt Eva," as she was known, became an essential part of the leadership of the Homes. Although it is difficult to describe accurately how the Homes were run, and what kind of an atmosphere prevailed in them, the following description provides the reader with some helpful details:

> The three homes, each one of which maintained its own family life under the supervision of a ministerial couple, were under one administration which came to be known as the Faith Homes. <u>The fact is, the work never had an official name.</u> Nor did it have any formal organization as that term is generally used, for there were no officers such as president, secretary, *etc.* The affairs of the Homes were conducted by the entire group of ministers waiting upon the Lord for His direction and decision regarding *every thing* which pertained to them. <u>It was a "spiritual arrangement" made by the Lord Himself, whereby He, and no man or woman,</u>

was in reality the Head. This method proved a stronger bond for fellowship and basis of operation than any human organization with its constitution, by-laws, and elected or appointed officers. In this respect, the government of the Faith Homes was indeed unique.⁷

Much of this narration so far records the development of the Faith Homes in the natural realm, but simultaneously there was a deep inward, hidden work going on in the lives of those who were called to "blaze a trail" for others into the fullness of Christ. The first seven years dating from November 1907, when Jesus took control of Mrs. Robinson, until mid-summer of 1914, can properly be called *The Original Work*, and that term stands for the unusual purity, power, and simplicity that characterized the somewhat hidden nature of Jesus' pre-eminence among the leaders, thus precluding the acclaim and notoriety that often accompany giftings of the Spirit.

The term "hidden" has its roots in something that happened about a month after the experience of November 1907. As related earlier, the Lord had offered Martha Robinson a choice of two pathways: one, to become an evangelist who would bring the knowledge of salvation to multitudes; and two, to become hidden, unknown, and a vessel of suffering and misunderstanding. The Lord chose for her – not the first pathway, but the second. That choice then destined the work and ministry of the Homes to be largely hidden, as far as publicity and renown were concerned. It almost implied that the leaders would spend long hours of intercession on behalf of others, which equals, in Biblical understanding, the simple word "suffering." It also meant that the leaders would be pared down in their estimation of themselves, stripped of human ability and acumen, to have it all replaced by the life of Jesus, the Crucified One.

Looking at it from another angle, however, it meant that God would use the Faith Homes as a kind of "Bureau of Standards" against which error and fanaticism could be judged – something which developed into a source of immeasurable blessing in the lives of those whom God chose to walk the first pathway of large, evangelistic ministries.⁸

It is impossible to appreciate the value of the Faith Home Work without an understanding of this background "call" for Mrs. Robinson and for those whom God ordained to work with her.

To those who came to the meetings during that wonderful period of The Original Work, the Lord performed many visible miracles, but perhaps more importantly, He also performed mighty miracles in the invisible realm, "the inside world" of the soul. It seems quite clear that "psychology" as we know it has become a human substitute for God's divine method for changing people at the root of their personalities, or natures. God dealt with the flesh in those days, not gingerly, but with loving firmness and powerful wisdom, so that permanent changes were made in the "psyche" or "soul" of the willing recipients. "This is a life-changing Work," said Rex Andrews in later years.

For that to take place, strong work was necessary in the natures of the leaders. Consider the following remarks regarding this point:

Because we are in The Period NOW of that great crossing over – into God – it will be of great value, to anyone who is willing, to know the plain and simple facts which will unfold here. Why? Because that passing over was, and must needs be, THE DEATH OF OWN WILL. Mrs. Robinson called it "the annihilation of the will." She said, "A Will was given to us that death might be accomplished." It was also called "crucifixion." But these terms, "death" and "crucifixion," became bogged down in UNREALITY, partly by teaching what they did not comprehend, and partly by a joking use which came to be made of the words: "You have to die you know." "You must be crucified." The careless use of such terribly-meaningful terms – like many other "deep" truths – helped greatly to make them nearly void of power.

There are three degrees, or angles, to this Death of the will. And in some form or another each of these three factors has to be met. 1) What is your IDOL? 2) What you think you KNOW. 3) What you BELIEVE about yourself. In the ANNIHILATION of the WILL, God searches to the hidden and invisible root where "self," the "I," is located. There are very few people, even among Faith Home adherents, who have gone completely beyond the first named: What is your IDOL? To say nothing of death to what you think you KNOW, and what you believe about yourself.[9]

Those words describe somewhat the nature of the dealing of God with the Vessels – the actual leaders of the Faith Homes – who, although tremendously gifted and anointed, and spoken of as "a really brilliant constellation of ministers,"[10] nonetheless in private received "the clear, frank type of instruction" by the Lord's incisive word, so that they were "cut down to caterpillars unable to crawl – yet at the same time upheld mightily by God in power, and in gifts, and in glory."[11] One is reminded of the scene so vividly described by the Apostle Paul in Galatians 2:11-16, as the Lord by Paul reproved Peter publicly (not even in private!) "because he was to be blamed."

It bears repeating, that no one can properly understand the purpose of the Faith Homes, as far as God defined it, without feeling the sharpness of the sword of the Word of God clearly wielded without respect of persons – or even of a person's feelings, it might be added. In 1951 the following words of Rex Andrews summarized the calling of the Faith Homes in a letter to the congregation, (preserving his use of capital letters and hyphenation):

> There NEVER was any call, basically, over The Faith Homes, nor any one in them, but TO UTTERLY LOSE THEIR OWN LIFE in FINDING AND KNOWING JESUS, AND to give their life utterly, unto death, for Others, His Children, - A N Y others. You can't LOSE your life by SAVING it. And if you lose it you cannot keep it. Neither can you love your own way, and progress very far in "Knowing Jesus." God called The Faith Home Work, and its ministers and its people, to Just-One-Thing, *viz*: TO UTTERLY LOSE OWN-LIFE IN FINDING AND KNOWING JESUS. And I was among those ministers, and in the conferences, when The Lord SAID WHAT IT WAS that defeated Him and His Word.[12]

Notice the inclusive phrase, "its ministers and its people." In actual fact, the standard was much higher for the ministers than it was for the people, resulting in the "clear frank type of instruction" referred to previously.

In the passage where Paul the Apostle reveals his struggle with his "thorn in the flesh," he underscores the need for anointed persons to stay within sight of their smallness. The Lord arranged a circumstance tailor-made for Paul: There was given a thorn in the flesh, the messenger of Satan to buffet him, lest he be exalted above measure through the abundance of the revelation given to him (II Corinthians 12:7). A few verses later he correctly states his true position in God's eyes: "For in nothing am I behind the very chiefest apostles, *though I be nothing*" (II Corinthians 12:11, emphasis added).

Madame Guyon puts the same thought this way, "If you are fully convinced that it is on the NOTHING in man that God establishes his greatest works, – you will be in part guarded against disappointment or surprise."[13]

I have previously quoted from a letter Rex Andrews wrote to a young woman who at the time was considering the possibility of coming to the Faith Homes for training, on the nature of the Faith Home Work. I will put it in again here, because the truth of the words needs repeating. In a way, this quotation summarizes quite adequately an answer to those who pose the question, "What is the Faith Homes all about?"

> Almost no one realizes what KIND of a Work the Faith Home Work is. It is a "nothing" Work. That means: A come-to-NOTHING WORK. Consequently, when anyone tries to move forward into a Be-Something position, they sooner or later find they are stepping out on thin air – no foundation under them – no way at all to "BE" something... If anyone DOES start out to "be" something – in the sense of leadership – then they automatically enter the pathway of the discipline which the Faith Home leaders are all in, and have long been in...
>
> Since 1948, the consecration of ALL the Faith Home ministers has been that: they see nothing before them but to lose their life, and come to nothing, in the service required in the Homes for others; IN ORDER TO LET THE LORD be the fountain-center – each one merely a hole in the ground for Him to flow through.
>
> So, whoever sets out to "BE" something in the Faith Home ministry – or before the public so – finds himself automatically in a pathway which comes directly to "nothing" – a hole-in-the-ground.
>
> This is a Work in which the working of the LORD is to bring us to self-nothingness IN the allness of Jesus.§

---

§ Private letter from Rex Andrews to Ruth Lade [Schleicher]. It is interesting to note that "Ruthel" later became one of the platform ministers of the Faith Homes. There were several "Ruths" in the Homes, so this one became known as "Ruth L.," but in Hebrew the spoken sound meant "Ruth of God," or simply, "Ruthel," as we all affectionately called her.

The above quotations and references convey somewhat the quality of The Original Work, 1907 – 1914, a period of seven years which can be understood as the *expression*, the *aura*, or the *after-effects* of Jesus possessing Martha Robinson the way He did. Jesus drew people into meetings where He Himself did everything – yes, everything – in a way that is difficult to describe adequately. That is why the words, *a vast simplicity*, were chosen as the title of this book.

Though in later years the Lord altered the outward form of the meetings somewhat, He never changed the principles governing the services. Those principles included:

1) His Presence in the midst as the Center of every meeting.

2) The freedom of the Holy Spirit to minister through anyone present.

3) Plural leadership in the meetings.

4) Unity of the "platform" ministers.

5) Absolute commitment to "hear the Lord" in whomever might be speaking.

6) The Bible itself as the ultimate Rule and Authority in all things said and done.

7) All things done for the purpose of edifying.

The only way a group of leaders could conduct meetings according to those seven principles was their stated intention to live in the "nothingness" that characterized the Work itself, not a dismal "poor me" kind of nothingness, but a recognition of the All-ness of Jesus. In actual practice, people tended to think of the Vessels as being "great men and women of God," because of the powerful way God used them to bless others. The same balance had to be maintained that the Apostle Paul lived in, as quoted earlier in this chapter, namely, "For in nothing am I behind the very chiefest apostles, though I be nothing" (II Corinthians 12:11). It was a fight not easily comprehended by those who want to be something.

Such tremendous spiritual advances as were made in The Original Work, though opposed by the Adversary, were never completely overthrown by him. In the things of God, His Arising Word always triumphs! "Now thanks be unto God," wrote Paul in Second Corinthians 2:14, "which always causeth us to triumph in Christ." It would be advisable to keep that triumph clearly in view as this narrative moves to the next period in the history of the Faith Homes, a period characterized by advance and retreat, success and failure, starts and stops – but by the end of it God had established a position for the Work to hold until He recovered "at least One Position of the Original Work"[14]

CHAPTER SIX

THE RISING AND FALLING WORK
1914 – 1921

Introduction

If you have read this far, you might be saying to yourself, "But what difference does it make to me what happened in this obscure ministry one hundred years ago?"

The answer is, "It makes quite a difference to you, if you are seeking to know Jesus as He is in His fullness, His all-ness." The details of your conflict with the world, the flesh, and the devil may be a bit different, but the principles are the same. More to the point, we are one hundred years closer to *The Revelation of Jesus Christ*, and the stakes are very high, so to speak. Many are the Scriptures waiting to be fulfilled in the lives of God's people. We are at the very *threshold of His unveiling*, at the *intersection of "this present age"* with *"the world to come,"* as the writer of Hebrews puts it (Hebrews 2:5).

Nothing you do can stop God's Word from continually rising, but your relationship to the Rising Word is super-important.

This history of the Rising Word in the Faith Homes, and the spiritual opposition against it, can become an integral part of your preparation for the "the Day of the Lord."

With these things in mind, we continue the narrative of this titanic conflict between the Rising Word and The Accuser of the Brethren.

Opposition

The second phase of the Faith Home history lasted another seven years, from 1914-1921. By now the location of the Work had fully shifted from Toronto, Canada to Zion, Illinois. God upheld the workers through a series of difficulties while His work among them rose and fell like the waves of the sea. Some days everyone worked together beautifully and God's plan moved forward; other days progress stopped, or worse.

It would be hard to overstate the enormity of the spiritual opposition that came against the work God was bringing forth. It was the most terrible opposition you can possibly imagine, and then some. The Devil sought by every possible means to nullify and deride and destroy the reality of God's Word being spoken by vessels of clay, not to mention his strivings to keep it from being obeyed.

If you wish to grasp something of this conflict, study carefully the scene in the Garden of Gethsemane, where Jesus and the disciples faced the unbridled power of the enemy. Jesus broke into a blood-sweat; the disciples could not stay awake, though Jesus strongly urged them to pray for Him and for themselves. The ultimate go-through prayer of "Not my will, but Thine" had to be prayed three times, in the face of such pressure to "save one's life" that only the Son of God Himself could do it; even then Luke records the amazing fact that an angel came to the Garden to "strengthen Him."

In the Faith Homes at that time, God sought to give to all of the working ministers, the Vessels, the same experience into which He had brought Mrs. Robinson. All of them tasted it for shorter or longer periods, but none of them was able to hold it. They all spoke the Lord's Word at times, and they all experienced the power of God on their bodies. They all earnestly desired to be united with Jesus as their very life. Yet there were avenues in these individuals that had been opened to the enemy at different times in their past and present, and the devil rushed in through those avenues at every possible opportunity.

I have stayed in a cabin in the desert near Death Valley where the wind whips up the sand and throws it against that old house with amazing strength. I know what it is to enter the home and see an inch or two of sand covering anything near the doors and windows, even though it seemed the house had been sealed tightly!

The Devil threw sand (spiritually speaking) against the wills and natures of those precious saints of God with unbelievable force and deposited his darkness inside their inner worlds.* As a result, the Work would go up and down, up and down. Things would go well for a while, then a mistake would be made and opposition would arise. Anyone

---

* Chapter 21 will be devoted to the subject of *The Inside World vs. The Outside World*.

who has truly sought God with His whole heart has no difficulty understanding what I am describing.

For example, as you will read in a later chapter, the devil exploited a weakness in Rex Andrews to the *nth* degree. The same for Mrs. Loretta M. Judd. And the same for Mr. Harry Robinson, who became one of the enemy's greatest targets, for it was *God's stated plan that Mr. and Mrs. Robinson would take their place together as leaders of the Homes*; however, Harry's nature, briefly mentioned above, would often get the best of him. On top of that, though the Lord worked tirelessly to get the Vessels to uphold each other in prayer, the devil magnified the faults and failings of various ones and succeeded to a degree to make them dislike each other ever so slightly. The result was, they failed to intercede for each other as God pressed them to do. (Please understand they spent HOURS praying for each other, lest you think you would have done better.) But when it came to Harry Robinson, they lacked a sufficiently large "mercy-ing heart" toward him, to pray him through when he was ill and dying.

Mr. Robinson became like a soccer ball, almost, with the Lord on one side and the devil on the other. The Lord had said it was not His best will for Mrs. Robinson to be alone in her experience, and He offered to Mr. Robinson the very same experience of Jesus' possession that He had given to Mrs. Robinson, *provided Harry would take it for FREE*.†

As mentioned, it was God's best will for Harry and Martha Robinson to be together, to be equal in their union with Jesus, which Mrs. Robinson had already come into. Sometimes Harry would rise in faith to take what God was offering, and things would go well. (God's intention was to bring ALL the ministers into that same experience.) Then suddenly Harry would get an idea that he should go to Ohio, or some other place, and hold evangelistic meetings. "But Harry, this is not God's will," the Lord would say to him through his wife. "O yes it is," he would say, and off he would go.

Mrs. Robinson would convene the other ministers for prayer. "Would you intercede for Harry?" she would ask. "Can we pray and believe that God will win in Him?"‡

---

† The whole issue of "taking things from God for free" belongs to the subject of Poverty of Spirit and Lowliness, which Chapter 17 addresses.
‡ The studies on *What the Bible Teaches About Mercy* (more commonly known as the *Mercy Studies*) and the accompanying *Prayer of Mercy* had not been written yet in those days, of course; that all came later.

They didn't particularly like Harry, however. That was one of the areas where "the sand blew in." They liked Martha Robinson, but they didn't like her husband. "Can't you give up four hours today to intercede for Harry?" she asked.

Please don't laugh at this. If your eyes were opened to spiritual realities, you would truly be horrified at the lack of love among God's people — myself included. We have so little idea how self centered we are, selfish and self-absorbed to the core. But I go on.

Eventually Harry would return home. And the Lord would say to him, in words something like these, "Harry, it's true that you haven't prayed through like your wife did. No, you're not nearly as consecrated as she is. But I will give you everything I have given to your wife if you will just take it for free. If you will just humble yourself and say, 'Alright, I'll take it. And I won't resent my wife giving me the instruction I need. I will hear You speaking to me through her words, as well as through the words of the other Vessels. I will believe, Jesus, that You are not trying to shut me out of something, but rather that You are bringing me into something, and that You will give it to me for FREE.'" And the Lord would plead with him, as He did repeatedly with all the Vessels, "Won't you just believe?"

Now I have to introduce something I wish I didn't have to introduce. It was one of the most terrible things that ever happened in the Faith Homes. I speak of "spiritual ambition."

Among the Vessels whom God called to His work in the Faith Homes was a fairly new believer named Loretta Mae Judd. She was swept into "the Power Work" (as it came to be known) with ease and took to it like a duck takes to water. But hidden way down underneath, where hardly anyone could see it, was *spiritual ambition*. The words were never spoken openly, but the motive was there: "I will be the one to obey. I will be the one to consecrate. I want what I see [in Mrs. Robinson], and I'm going to have it."

Whether she realized it at the time or not, she became one whom the enemy used to interfere with God's plan in Harry Robinson's life. She also interfered with what God was doing to set Rex Andrews into his place in The Work. She rose up and blocked those two men from what God was trying to do in them because of her spiritual ambition — the opposite of lowliness and mercy. And it has a name. It's a snake called, "I Am The One." *Mercy* says,

The Rising And Falling Work, 1914-1921

"No, you are the one"; meaning, "I want God's fulfilling mercies in your life, regardless of what happens to me." And the *snake* clothes itself with light, in — subtle the cloak of, "O, I just want to be humble and broken." But underneath the snake is saying, "But I am the one, not you!" That thing came up and blocked Mr. Robinson, and blocked Rex Andrews in certain ways as well.

In lovingkindness I leave out much.

Nevertheless, that spirit continued to oppose God's plan, seeking whatever entrance could be found in any of the Vessels. Things came to a crisis in 1916. Harry Robinson lay ill unto death in one of the Faith Homes. Martha Robinson called all the ministers together to pray for his healing. Previously they had spent much time in prayer for Harry, but at this crisis moment they spent the entire day interceding for him.

At the end of that day, Harry Robinson died.

The dear Lord Jesus, who is the CENTER of everything we're talking about, who is lowly enough to reveal Himself in this world through redeemed sinners like you and me, walked Mrs. Robinson into the room where those precious people were praying and said through her mouth, "Harry has just passed away. Who will come into the room with me and take the answer to our prayers?" – with the unspoken expectation (which she knew to be true) that if one of the others, just one, would AGREE with her in prayer, God would raise Harry from the dead.

There is no question in my mind it would have happened. I have Miss Brooks' testimony to the truth of that statement. However, not one of them responded. Not one said to Mrs. Robinson, "I'll come in the room and AGREE with you in prayer for the answer to our prayers for Harry."

Why? Because they didn't love him enough!

This whole story has a point, of course, and the point lands right in the book of studies called, *What the Bible Teaches About Mercy*. The devil was there fighting to magnify their feelings of dislike toward Harry and to quench any faith they might have mustered. They couldn't bring themselves to go in and say, "All right, I want Harry to make it. I want Harry to fulfill. Dear Jesus, there lies his corpse. In Your great name, please raise him up and fulfill your will in him no matter what happens to me."

(I tremble to retell these things because of my own unmerciful condition of heart. But God is still looking for "Stephens" who will give their lives away for "Saul of Tarsus": "Lord, lay not this sin to their charge," Stephen prayed with his last breath.)

The day Harry died something changed, because the Lord had said, "If Harry Robinson dies, the Work as we know it will not fulfill." All the Vessels knew how much hung on Mr. Robinson's spiritual victory, which is one reason their failure was so serious. But the Work as they knew it did fail. It may be difficult for some to accept, but it is true.

A Glory Heart

Mrs. Robinson was deeply crushed. She loved her husband. She knew what the Lord had said: "The Work will fail if Harry dies." What now?

Mind you, Jesus occupied His place fully within Mrs. Robinson; He still spoke through her, and His Word and Work were still nascent in the Vessels; but now everything hoped for had seemingly fallen to pieces.

After Harry died, Elder Brooks, whom many considered a prophet in the mold of Jeremiah or Ezekiel, asked Mrs. Robinson, almost pitifully, "What do we do now, Mrs. Robinson?" It was a terrible crisis for everyone concerned.

Perhaps some of you reading this account have come to your own crisis and death of hope in certain ways. You have been there where all hope is extinguished. You have failed, and you knew what you were doing, and you did it wrong. You threw everything that you knew was right in the trash heap, just threw it away and now your future is going, going, gone...

Except for one thing, and one thing alone: JESUS.

Over Mrs. Robinson's lips came the answer to Elder's question that allowed the Work to go ahead, albeit in a slightly different fashion than it did at the beginning. Jesus said, "Well, I guess we have to have a 'glory heart' now, don't we?"

In so saying she turned defeat into victory. Perhaps you think you're pretty good at praising the Lord when you are disappointed, but when the disappointment strikes at the very center of your heart, at the very center of God's plans for you and for those you love, can you have a 'glory heart' then?

It is what God Himself faced when Eve took the fruit and shared it with Adam, and Satan said, "Now what are You going to do?"

It is what God faced when Israel slowly but surely pulled away from Him, their Husband, their One True Lover, and threw His prophet-messengers into their graves.

It is what God went through when Jesus Himself was killed and the devil smirked in God's face as he said, "Now what will You do?"

But a "glory heart" is the Holy of Holies where the Mercy Seat rests.

> *O for a heart to praise my God, A heart from sin set free*
> *A heart that always feels Thy blood, So freely shed for me.*
>
> *A heart resigned, submissive, meek, My great Redeemer's throne,*
> *Where only Christ is heard to speak, Where Jesus reigns alone.*[1]

Does not the Glory of God hover over the Mercy Seat?

None of us has anything by which to commend ourselves to Him. Paul understood that all his righteousness under the Law was as filthy rags before God; even his righteous works were wicked when God shone His light into Paul's innermost conscience. We could never earn God's favor, though we lived a hundred lifetimes trying to please Him. We would still need The Blood of Jesus. God is never stuck, because He can do by Mercy what Justice could never permit. All He asks is for us to BELIEVE in that Mercy, which Jesus' Blood established forever.

And on that basis – a "glory heart" – the Work went on.

Not long after Harry Robinson's death, Rex Andrews (about whom I will give more detail later on) began to back away from the Faith Homes, ever so slowly, but nonetheless definitely. By 1918 or thereabouts, he became the pastor of a "Branch Work" in nearby Waukegan, Illinois. Eventually he moved away with his family and traveled about the country without much further contact with Mrs. Robinson or the Faith Homes until shortly before her death.

Meanwhile Mrs. Judd, though outwardly very devoted to the Work and to Mrs. Robinson, fell into a series of spiritual delusions that kept her from finding her proper place in God's order of things. For, amazing as it may seem, the Lord had clearly indicated there were to be *three "wisdom teachers"* in The Work: Martha Robinson, Rex Andrews, and Mrs. Judd. That meant that the Work would increase as God had planned, provided each of the three embraced God's call, learned the lessons He would teach in order to establish them in The Gift of Wisdom, and progress along the pathway of NOTHINGNESS at the same time. By 1921, however, one was gone; one was compromised; only Martha Robinson remained.

Among those who later rejected the things Rex Andrews taught about Mercy, the view prevailed that his sinful backsliding disqualified him from being a teacher of spiritual things, much less from resuming his place as a Faith Home minister. Such a view failed to take into account the immense battle that ALL the Vessels were fighting, not just Rex Andrews, against their carnal natures. It was a *terrible, terrible conflict*, partly because of the weakness of their flesh, and partly because of what was referred to as the "New Body call" – *i.e.*, letting Jesus fully possess you in body, as well as in spirit and soul. The enemy, beloved, came against them with cannons, (spiritually speaking), and machine-guns, and every weapon that you could name, to destroy what God was doing. And the Work, for various reasons, went through an up and down phase until 1917, after Mr. Robinson passed away and the Work in its simplicity failed. Mrs. Robinson always referred to the Work after 1921 as the "secondary work." And anyone who came into the Work after that only knows the *secondary work*. They do not know or understand the simplicity of the Original Work. The Original Work ran from 1907 until 1914. After that, it was a rising and falling work – ebbing and flowing, ebbing and flowing. And finally, after 1921, it became a secondary work.

That is stated now because it provides a background for the colossal moral failure into which Rex Andrews fell.

I must explain somewhat my use of the terms "fail," "fallen to pieces," "blocked," *etc.*, lest those terms seem to cast the Vessels in a bad light. Personally, I am not qualified even to assess the relative strengths and weaknesses of a single one of them. Each one was a spiritual giant in his or her own right. Each one was an overcomer and has his or her reward. They "waxed valiant in fight," and a book of triumph could be written about each one.

The "failure" was explained to me this way: What the Lord wanted was *someone*, or *some ones*, to stand with Mrs. Robinson in the utterly childlike faith of Jesus, that God would give Jesus to them, **in the same quality and degree as He had given Jesus to Mrs. Robinson**, as though they had prayed through like she had, even though they had not! It was an offer of Mercy, PURE MERCY!

And not one of them could do it for more than a few days, or a few weeks at the most. That was *the failure.*

And the failure never could have been reversed, if 1) Jesus had not been IN Mrs. Robinson in the way He was, as she testified; and 2) if Jesus had not UNFOLDED the knowledge of God's Will of Mercy IN and THROUGH Mr. Andrews. And it is to their (the Vessels') eternal credit that all the Vessels who were still living when Mr. Andrews returned to the Homes in 1947 ACKNOWLEDGED that his message was of GOD. That is so even of Mrs. Judd, though she opposed the changes the Lord wanted to make.§

And yet!

How I love those words!

For God found a way to keep the Homes open, even though some possibilities had been forfeited. He did what could be done by mercy and still be true to His Word.

Thus began the third phase of the First Forty Years — what God called *The Secondary Work*, beginning in 1921 and continuing until 1936, the year of Mrs. Robinson's death.

---

§ These remarks only touch on the subject of, "How to Take Things from the Lord for Free." We make a simple thing to be very complicated by our natural-reasoning minds. Some further explanation is forthcoming in Chapter 17, *Poverty of Spirit and Lowliness.*

CHAPTER SEVEN

THE SECONDARY WORK
1921 – 1936

Suffering for Others

By 1921, Mr. Robinson had been dead for five years and Rex Andrews virtually absent for three years. The remaining Vessels found it very difficult to move forward spiritually. Mrs. Robinson remained as a Wisdom Teacher, of course, and the other Vessels continued to work in Power and in their own particular (and numerous) Gifts of the Holy Spirit. Mrs. Robinson upheld them by her faith and prayer. She literally laid her life down for the others in a pathway of suffering that is nearly impossible to describe; *i.e.,* through intercession which surpassed all natural strength and affection. The goal or purpose of God for the Work never changed, although the form of the Work did change necessarily, because of the losses described above. Here I quote again one of the clearest statements of God's goal for the Work, as written by Rex Andrews in July 1950:

> There NEVER was any call, basically, over The Faith Homes, nor any one in them, but TO UTTERLY LOSE THEIR OWN LIFE in FINDING AND KNOWING JESUS, AND to give their life utterly, unto death, for Others, His Children, – A N Y others. You can't LOSE your life by SAVING it. And if you lose it you cannot keep it. Neither can you love your own way, and progress very far in "Knowing Jesus." God called The Faith Home Work, and its ministers and its people, to Just-One-Thing, *viz*: TO UTTERLY LOSE OWN-LIFE IN FINDING AND KNOWING JESUS. And I was among those ministers, and in the conferences, when The Lord SAID WHAT IT WAS that defeated Him and His Word.[1]

There are several passages in Madame Guyon's *Autobiography* that shed light on this matter of suffering for others that they might find and know Jesus. For example, speaking of the maid who served her for many years, she wrote,

I freely resolved to suffer for her, as I did for Father La Combe. As she resisted God much more than he, and was much more under the power of self-love, she had more to be purified from... In proportion as this maid became inwardly purified, my pain abated, till the Lord let me know her state was going to be changed, which soon happily ensued. In comparison of inward pain for souls, outward persecutions, though ever so violent, scarce gave me any.[2]

The Lord through His Wisdom told Mrs. Robinson how to proceed, and she carried out His Will, even though things had slipped down from the *vast simplicity* of The Original Work. She poured herself into battling the natures, the flesh, and the failures of those around her. For example, in a personal interview, Rex Andrews told me he felt responsible for her death, mainly because of his unwillingness to surrender to God's will. Mrs. Robinson literally prayed him through into victory, although that victory did not come until eight years after her death.

The Apostle Paul hints at such an intercessory life in his writings.

> *I am afraid of you* ["I am afraid about you" – Vines], *lest I have bestowed upon you labor in vain... My little children, of whom I travail* [intolerable agony] *in birth again until Christ be formed in you...* (Galatians 4:11, 19)

> *But now when Timothy came from you unto us, and brought us good tidings of your faith and charity, and that ye have a good remembrance of us always, desiring greatly to see you: therefore brethren, we were comforted over you in all our affliction and distress by your faith: for now we live, if you stand fast in the Lord.* (I Thessalonians 3:6-8)

> *For God is my record, how greatly I long after you all in the bowels* [deep, inward tenderness of love] *of Jesus Christ.* (Philippians 1:8)

After the triumphant conclusion of Romans 8, that "we are more than conquerors through Him that loved us," the opening words of Romans 9 portray a Gethsemane-like agony of soul:

> *I say the truth in Christ, I lie not, my conscience also bearing me witness in the Holy Ghost, that I have great heaviness and continual sorrow in my heart. For I could wish that myself were accursed from Christ for my brethren, my kinsmen according to the flesh...*

There is something about "the Crucified Life" that cannot be understood unless we know Jesus as "the man of sorrows and acquainted with grief," and at the same time, know Him as "the happiest man that ever lived."* "*Love bears all things* [can take the strain of bearing others], *believes all things* [is full of faith], *hopes all things* [is filled with hope], *endures all things* [suffers long, and is kind]." UNION WITH JESUS makes it possible!

I have often remarked that, from the time of her "Passing Over" until her death, Mrs. Robinson's life was lived in LOVE, Christ's love, for others. One can see it in the numerous letters preserved by many who received them, where her concern is always *their* blessing and *their* spiritual growth.³ She simply poured out her life for others, regardless of the cost to herself.

Once, after a particularly difficult time of confrontation with Mrs. Judd, Miss Nilsson remarked to Mrs. Robinson, "Why do you keep trying to deal with her? You will eventually kill yourself if you keep it up."

"But I feel so sorry for her," was the reply.

We might do well to remember that the last week of Jesus' life is called "His passion" (Acts 1:3).

The Lord through wisdom taught Mrs. Robinson how to have a "glory heart," how to praise the Lord in spite of the most terrible failures. She did whatever He said regardless of personal cost. From that time on, the Work took the shape that most of the old-timers remember, with its daily schedule and established routines.

A Pattern for Daily Life in the Homes

Each day began with "Morning Prayers," where everyone (including visitors) in the three Homes remained at the table after breakfast for prayer and the Word, led by a resident minister of each home. People were taught to spend time alone with God, of course, but as far as the routine of the Faith Homes was concerned, all residents of each Home sat at the table with Bibles open, as a minister led them in prayer and worship and Bible reading. Lives were transformed during those sessions, partly because the ministers worked in large giftings of the Holy Spirit.

For many years the ministers conducted three meetings daily in "The Meeting House" at 2820 Eschol Avenue in Zion. Later it was reduced

---

* This will be touched on again in Chapter 14, *A Black & White Sketch of Rex B. Andrews, Part Two.*

to two meetings a day. Not all the ministers attended every service, of course, because their ministry to visitors and residents demanded much time, not to mention the hours spent in Vessels' prayer meetings and conferences. Truly their consecration was remarkable, and God is not unrighteous to remember their work of love, which they showed toward His name (Hebrews 6:10).

From time to time they were invited to speak in other churches from one end of the country to the other. God alone knows how many lives were transformed by their ministry outside of Zion, how many young people were thrust into the work of the ministry, how many believers were added to the Church, and healed, and delivered from the power of darkness.

Gradually the Faith Homes, under the Lord's direction, developed into a small but very effective Bible School. The students came to be known as "the young people," and later, "trainees." The three Homes, being large, contained rooms enough for 15 or 20 students at a time, spread among the three homes. This necessitated oversight and an authority structure. The Faith Home Council (as it came to be called) took responsibility for all the decisions affecting the life of the Homes. It consisted of the Vessels at first; others were added who were not in the original group of thirteen. Through them the Lord appointed "House Parents" for each home, almost always members of the Council, married couples if possible. Under them were "housekeepers" who oversaw meal preparation, cleaning, and maintenance in each home. In the "old days" (1920s) that meant chopping and splitting enough wood, and canning enough fresh vegetables and fruits, to supply heat and food though the long winters. Most years, between 50 and 60 persons took three meals daily, and slept in warm beds furnished with clean linens. It was a daunting task, all of it done "by faith," under what truly was "GREAT GRACE UPON ALL" (Acts 4:33). For many years the Homes raised their own produce, renting land in other parts of the city to do so. That enormous effort continued until Elder Brooks got the light they should have faith for enough money to purchase food directly, and not to be spending so much time on the gardens. God was faithful to supply all that was needed.

When one stops to think of the "logistics" of such a communal Work, it is truly amazing how smoothly things went.

The first trained missionary from the Faith Homes (whose name I've forgotten) was sent to South America in 1919, followed by Miss

Mabel Rigg, who went to South Africa in 1925, and Miss Kathryn Roth, who went to Kenya, East Africa in 1926. (This writer personally knew both Mrs. Mabel (Rigg) Richards and Miss Roth.) Miss Roth worked in Kenya for 39 years, taking only three furloughs; she gave most of her life there in a beautiful demonstration of what God taught her in the Faith Homes.†

It is a fact that at least 500 missionaries, pastors, and helpers went into the work of the Lord through the Faith Homes, either directly or indirectly. The influence of the Homes far exceeded its size. The writer of this story and his wife are two such workers. We thank God with all our hearts for the inexpressible privilege God gave us to live there for nearly thirty years.

Visitors

As you might expect, a large ministry to visitors developed rather quickly. In a ten-year period in the 1920s and '30s, over 30,000 visitors stopped in either for a meeting or two, or to stay in the Homes to seek the Lord for days or weeks. As mentioned before, because of the unusual manifestations of the Spirit in the meetings, the Homes' reputation spread far and wide in the Pentecostal world. Countless individuals benefited from personal encouragement that came directly from the Lord. The Gifts of the Spirit, as they were intended to do, edified the Body of Christ. The emphasis on "death to self" and "the crucified life" – an outgrowth of God's work in the Faith Home workers – kept their ministry largely free from error. It is hard to convey to the reader what I am describing, because so much ministry today that claims to be "in the Spirit" is mixed with and tainted by the flesh.

I have in my possession, for example, an envelope of notes that were sent to me by Rex Andrews over a period of nine years. They reflect the Gift of Wisdom that God gave to him at his Baptism in the Spirit, and restored to him when Jesus brought him back to Himself in 1944. Such Wisdom is life-changing; it is truly pure; it is from Jesus' own mind. And I am only one of the many, the very many, whose

---

† A brief recounting of her life is in my library, entitled *N'yangori Mother*. Many of us came to know her when she retired to Zion in 1967, and she was an example to all of us. When she passed away in a nursing home, the staff fought for the privilege of being on duty in order to witness her home-going. The thought of her life brings tears to my eyes even as I write.

lives were shaped by the Word of Wisdom (and other gifts) that came through the Vessels. To God be the glory.‡

Miss Ruth Brooks once shared with me a truly amazing illustration of God's power in the meetings, especially as He used the voices of the Vessels. She relates:

> On more than one occasion, when someone in the congregation needed to see himself as others saw him, the Lord inspired two of the Vessels to have a public dialogue. One Vessel was given the voice and manner of the person needing to see himself, and the other Vessel would provide the needed instruction. In reality the conversation between the two Vessels became a dramatic "skit" that left no doubt as to who was the focus of the instruction! Lovingly the Lord thus revealed the nature of the one being helped, so that even he could react with a good laugh about his own behavior! And it was all done supernaturally, with no forethought, and without a hint of malice.

Such things drew thousands of people to the Faith Homes at a time when transportation was not what it is today. But the Lord was there, and the Spirit moved, and people were helped. Everything happened spontaneously. There was no entertainment, no plan, no program in the meetings. Yes, there were various musical numbers, both instrumental and vocal, but the focus was on the worship of Jesus, not on the musicians. At the special "homecoming" meetings in 1934, two or three stenographers kept a record of all that took place that day, and it stands as a helpful glimpse into the kinds of meetings held in the Homes during those first forty years.[4]

This account should include mention of two ministers who came under the influence of the Faith Homes and whose lives affected so many others. They are Rev. Hans R. Waldvogel (1893–1969), and Rev. Joseph Wannenmacher (1903–1989). Their stories are included in *Radiant Glory*, but a brief mention of them here is appropriate for readers who may not have heard of them.

The Lord used Rev. Waldvogel to raise up the *Ridgewood Pentecostal Fellowship* in Brooklyn, New York, with influence that reached to many places in that area (including the development of *Pilgrim Camp* in upstate

---

‡ Please see Chapter 15, *Particular Expressions of God's Wisdom*

New York), and even to Germany, where the results of his ministry are still felt. He passed away in 1969. Through his ministry, several branch churches of *Ridgewood* were opened in and around New York City. Rev. Eddie Waldvogel, Hans' nephew, now pastors the main church and oversees the branch churches that remain to this day.

Rev. Wannenmacher, who trained in the Faith Homes for several years, opened seven churches in the city of Milwaukee, all affiliated with the Assemblies of God. Because of Rev. Wannenmacher's Faith Home background, many leaders of the Wisconsin District of the Assemblies of God kept a close relationship with the Faith Homes and benefited much from that association. Most of them have now passed away, as did Rev. Wannenmacher in 1989.

Joseph and Helen Wannenmacher's three children all entered full-time ministry. Their oldest son Philip became the Senior Pastor of *Central Assembly of God* in Springfield, Missouri, which is the flagship church where the Assemblies of God maintains its headquarters. Their son John pastored *Calvary Assembly of God* in Milwaukee, Wisconsin for forty years, after his father retired from that position. Their daughter Lois married Rev. Robert Graber, and together they ministered for years at *Bethel Assembly of God* in Canton, Ohio until retirement.

What a legacy is passed on to others from one laid-down life!

Mrs. Robinson's Passing

Visitors came from far and wide, and Mrs. Robinson's faith kept the Work relatively pure. Eventually some of the old-timers passed away, things changed, and the Work started to disintegrate after Mrs. Robinson passed away in 1936.

It must be stated clearly, however, that the Lord completed His work and ministry through her, especially in regard to her strong intercessory prayers concerning The Last Days.

Near the time of her death, as Miss Nilsson was attending to her dear friend's needs, Mrs. Robinson "had me lean over with my ear close to her, and said that 'Everything is done for the New Body – everything prayed through – victory over all enemies that could come against new bodies.'" In a similar vein, though earlier than the above word to Miss Nilsson, Mrs. Robinson said,

There is going to be a Great Work arise. It means that you must come to Jesus, and from the minute that you come to Jesus, you reckon yourselves dead. You reckon that you have no right to any desires and wishes, and no right to any decision. See God. You absolutely give your will to God, and you can do it by a heart that is perfect toward God, and every day of your life, you yield your flesh and give up to God.

There are some people who would enter the crucified life if they would say, "God, You take me to an utter crucifixion where my will is utterly subjected to Thine." And that is what God wants you to see for the crucified life; and the mystery is a perfectly yielded will and heart, and absolutely giving up of yourself to God, where between yourself and God, you know that if you know the mind of the Lord you are going to do it. Where you find the mind of the Lord you don't have feelings or fuss – that settles it.

THE ABIDING LIFE IS THE DEATH OF THE FLESH. ALSO YOU HAVE SEEN THE KING, SON OF GOD, AND DESIRE TO WORSHIP HIM. THERE ARE THOSE WHO WILL GET OUT BEYOND THE TEMPTATIONS OF THE FLESH. [emphasis in the original][5]

Such statements continue to uphold us as we intercede for God's answer to the needs of His people today. In our travels we meet sons and daughters of God who know these things and live for Jesus' glory alone. To quote again these encouraging words: "The devil is doing terrible things these days," Miss Nilsson remarked to Martha Robinson one day. "Yes," was the reply, "but God will never be behind."

On June 26, 1936, the Lord removed Mrs. Robinson from the sufferings she had gladly endured for the sake of others and took her home.

"What will happen to the Work now?" the other Vessels wondered. Several had already passed away; the remaining ones were older and hardly anyone knew what to do. Elder Brooks, though 80 years of age at the time of her death, shouldered the largest part of the burden for keeping the Faith Homes going. It was enough to test the mettle of the most seasoned veteran. The Work "was falling to pieces," wrote Rex Andrews, "because nearly all of The Older Workers were inactive, some having broken down under the long, long strain of oversight, and the drain of multiplied personal problems of a stream of needy souls, never ceasing... some of the most important and vital spiritual Truths which had constituted the Very Heart of The Work, were being lost to view."[6]

Would, nay, *could* the Work survive? God had an answer no one anticipated.

Before we enter into that wonderful part of this history, however, it seems wise to summarize some of the good things that transpired during those early years from 1907 onward, as well as to discuss briefly the subject of "natures," as the term came to be used in the Faith Homes.

CHAPTER EIGHT

THE SLOWLY DISINTEGRATING WORK
1936 – 1947

Good Things

The external view of the Faith Homes greatly impressed the many visitors who made their way to Zion, Illinois to see firsthand what they had heard from others. And they did see miracles, God's power, and all of the Gifts of the Spirit in operation in purity – in the words of Rex Andrews, they saw "the great meetings, the great blessings, the great gifts, the things that appeared in sight and sound; great vessels and great workers and this was a power work in those days and it was unique."[1] Even within Pentecostal circles it was unique.

There were missionaries, and missions represented. There were unusual personalities. And there were prayers, the likes of which are rarely seen. "This Work was founded in long prayers, and many," is the record of those early days. Such prayers were continued not for months or years, but for decades. The perseverance needed would test the patience of the most disciplined souls.

As seen from the outside, the Faith Homes also maintained a unique stand concerning finances. It truly was a "faith work." No one ever received a salary nor mentioned the lack of one. The ministers trusted God to supply all that was needed, not only for themselves as individuals, but also for the considerable expense of keeping the three Homes "warmed and filled." If there was food on the table, it was because God supplied it. Visitors always had a bed to sleep on, clean sheets and a warm room, and food at each meal, but few recognized the enormous miracle that made it possible. Miss Brooks told me, "Douglas, more than once I have seen platters passed around a table full of guests that contained nowhere near enough food for everyone to have a portion, but there was still food on the platter after everyone was fed."[2] None of the many students was ever charged tuition or room and board.

The Word had wisdom; it had impact; it had (what was called in those days) "impartation," which meant that something of God remained in the person to whom God's Word had been spoken. Everyone testified to that fact. God spoke life-changing words to receptive hearts. The "Guest Register" (no official record exists) included the names of many ministers known in their time as mighty men and women of God. Some had been associated with Dr. Dowie in his prime, such as John G. Lake and F. F. Bosworth. Catherine Booth-Clibborn, daughter of Gen. William Booth, founder of The Salvation Army, and her husband, Theodore Booth-Clibborn, visited the Homes with their children. Christine Gibson, the precious saint from Providence, Rhode Island who founded and oversaw the *Zion Bible Institute* in that city, was a great friend of Elder and Mrs. Brooks and the Faith Homes. The controversial but powerful evangelist Amy Semple MacPherson spent time in the Faith Homes after her "kidnapping," to counsel with its leaders, not long before Mrs. Robinson passed away.

Marie Burgess Brown, pastor for many years of *Glad Tidings Tabernacle,* the well-known Assemblies of God church in New York City, received the Baptism in the Holy Spirit during the tent meetings held by the Faith Home Vessels in 1910, and she remained a friend of the Homes throughout her life.

Declining Years

As the years went by, however, the Work began to change, and not for the better. "I have never seen a work that went so low, that ever recovered," remarked the late R. Edward Miller, missionary to Argentina and another long-time friend of the Faith Homes.

That statement sums up the years following Mrs. Robinson's death. It seemed no one knew what to do. The meetings continued, but occasionally things not prompted by the Holy Spirit would slip into the services. The united prayer of the remaining Vessels slacked off. Life in each of the three Homes became somewhat less life-changing. Cliques began to form. Much-needed discipline waned. It was a troubling time for all concerned. Mrs. Robinson was gone. Rex Andrews had backslidden terribly.* Mrs. Judd's ministry, while good in some ways, betrayed an area of her life that was uncrucified. Elder Brooks, the nominal "head," was aging, and would celebrate his 90th birthday in June of 1946.

---

* Chapters 13 and 14 will tell his life story in detail.

The Slowly Disintegrating Work, 1936-1947

From the outside, things didn't look too bad, perhaps. "Man looks on the outward appearance," God told Samuel, "but the LORD looks on the heart" (I Samuel 16:7). The outside view of the Faith Homes was wonderful, but what of the inside view?

Natures

What did God see, then, in the lives of those who were "like shining stars, almost"? In a phrase or two, God saw <u>uncrucified wills</u>, <u>positions of soul against the Word of God</u>, and <u>natures that did not conform to the image of Christ</u>.

"Natures." Oh, how people hate that word! "Natures!" The "works of the flesh" acting through "fallen natures."

We find such things in Scripture, but we seldom mention them. Paul wrote to Titus, to help him deal with the "natures" of his church members in Crete,

> *One of themselves, even a prophet of their own, said, The Cretians are always liars, evil beasts, slow bellies. This witness is true. Wherefore rebuke them sharply, that they may be sound in the faith.* (Titus 1:12-13)

Today such words would be condemned as "politically incorrect." Can you imagine any minister categorizing Italians, or the Irish, or Hungarians, or Indians... (or Americans!)... with such words?!

The point is, behind the scenes, in private conferences, the Lord, primarily through Mrs. Robinson, dealt very strongly with the "natures" of the Vessels, not in a mean-spirited way, of course, but directly and forcefully nonetheless. Here is a small excerpt that illustrates what I am saying...

> He [Rex Andrews, speaking of himself as a very young "vessel," green and unbroken] had to face, immediately, the clear frank type of instruction which was given to the vessels. They were everyone shining before his eyes like stars in the heavens almost. And almost suddenly he was involved in the drastic sight of vessels cut down to caterpillars unable to crawl – yet at the same time upheld mightily by God in power, and in gifts, and in glory. But there was always behind-the-scenes truth even about that.
>
> By this time Mrs. Robinson was the recognized Wisdom Teacher, but the Elder [Elder Brooks] had not yet ceased crossing

her, and he had a most exasperating way of picking up something she said and either greatly expanding on it until all resemblance was lost, or, expatiating in such a way as to amount to direct contradiction. The new young vessel had to be able to love, and reverence, and accept The Elder.

Each one of the vessels had oddities – some very pronounced ones. Mr. Mitchell balked – even got up out of conference and left the room when Mrs. Robinson said something which cut too deep...[3]

More proof could be adduced to show how important it is that the theology of Romans 6 be applied in a very personal way to every believer.

Let me interrupt this section to quote the famous hymn of Charles Wesley, *Love Divine, All Loves Excelling*. It will help us not to get bogged down with the narrative at this point.

> *Love Divine, all loves excelling, Joy of heaven, to earth come down!*
> *Fix in us Thy humble dwelling, All Thy faithful mercies crown.*
> *Jesus! Thou art all compassion, Pure, unbounded love Thou art;*
> *Visit us with Thy salvation, Enter ev'ry trembling heart.*
>
> *Come, Almighty, to deliver! Let us all Thy grace receive;*
> *Suddenly return, and never, Nevermore Thy temples leave:*
> *Thee we would be always blessing, Serve Thee as Thy hosts above,*
> *Pray and praise Thee without ceasing, Glory in Thy perfect love.*
>
> *Finish, then, Thy new creation! Pure and spotless let us be:*
> *Let us see Thy great salvation, Perfectly restored in Thee!*
> *Changed from glory into glory, Till in heaven we take our place,*
> *Till we cast our crowns before Thee, Lost in wonder, love, and praise.*

I also wish to insert here, by permission, a vision given to Annie Schisler, an Argentinian girl whom Jesus took into the Heavens following her conversion. This vision corresponds so beautifully and accurately with Charles Wesley's hymn just quoted, and with the teaching on "natures" in the Faith Homes.

A Place of Straightening

When He took me into the Spirit, He showed me some of His own ones whose eyes were twisted out of direction and focus; I realized that this was because of their carnal, unsanctified nature.

Then the Lord began to work on their spiritual eyes, to straighten their vision and redirect their eyes to see Him, and Him only. This work of straightening was a process, and not a single act or experience, and each operation of the straightening process was a process in itself. Not only was it a healing of their spiritual eyesight; but it was a straightening and an aligning of their whole spiritual being. It seemed as though not only their spiritual eyes, but their whole spiritual being also, was warped and twisted. As He straightened their vision so that their eyes focused solely upon Him, He was, at the same time, also straightening their whole spiritual being so that it would be perfectly aligned with Him.[4]

Anyone who has endeavored to implement "group leadership" in a church knows how easily little frictions turn into major disagreements. Each of the Faith Home ministers had his own "nature" to deal with, and the Lord asked for harmony despite their differing natures. Jesus expected them to "hear the Lord in each other," and to fervently pray for the other one "to fulfill," as the expression was.

Elder Brooks, for example, so mightily used in prophecy, had the most annoying habit of twirling his glasses in his hand, even when the Power of God was being manifested in the meeting in such a great way. Aunt Eva, another of the "power vessels" [Eva Leggett, sister to Sara Brooks], habitually came late to the meetings. Harry Robinson, as well as some of the others, simply didn't like Rex Andrews, almost resenting the presence of such a young vessel (24 years old) among the older ones. Mrs. Judd, as indicated earlier, let spiritual ambition blind her to the need of others to find their place in God's plan.

Dear reader, I wonder if you realize how many little judgments you make about others because of their "nature faults," or merely because you don't like their personalities? It's just the way the person is, and you don't like it. You cut them off in your heart, brand and label them, and you say, "Well, we get along well enough," but you don't really love that one enough to defend him in prayer and believe that God will come to him and speak through the one that irritates you so.

The point is simply this: The "weeds" in our natures that do not get plucked up when they are small become very difficult to uproot later on, and they spoil the work God wants to do through us as unhindered channels. The un-dug weeds in the ministers' natures grew into ugly, large blockages to God's efforts to "Finish, then, Thy new creation, Pure and spotless let us be."

Thus it was that behind the exterior of a very blessed Faith Home Work lay oppositions to the Lord's best will, and failures to let God uproot "weeds" in the natures of the leaders, all of which led to *The Slowly Disintegrating Work* after Mrs. Robinson's death.

Consider the following excerpt from a talk given to the trainees in the Faith Homes in 1968, one of seven such talks on the subject of "What Are You Here For?" The Scripture being used was Luke 14:25-33, where Jesus speaks of "hating your own life also."

> Here we are using this expression, "AND YOUR OWN LIFE ALSO," to give a grasp of what Jesus means when He says, "hate." Because the Love of God is something that is the exact opposite of the corrupting and corroding and destructive Love of the world. God's Love is healing. It is Divine Union. God's Love makes everything to come into union with everything else, in God's own Presence, and in His own unfolding increase in His creation, and in His purpose for it all. The word "hate" in God's mouth – and Jesus was God's mouth – was describing what it means to live forever; what the Kingdom of God is on the earth; what it means to be full of God now; what is it going to be on the earth in the Kingdom of God; this is it – HE MUST BE THE CENTER, AND THE FIRST, because that is WHAT HE IS.
>
> All through the Old Testament, as well as all through the New Testament, is expressed that FIRSTNESS of the Lord. So Jesus is saying, "If you want me, I will have to be first in your life. I will have to be first before father. I will have to be first before mother. I will have to be first before wife or husband. I will have to be first before children. I will have to be first before brothers or sisters. AND, I will have to be first before YOUR OWN life – Hate your own life also." And He goes on, "He cannot be my disciple otherwise." In the life of God it is THE WAY to really bless and help your own: love them in God – God first. Jesus must be in the place which, in all creation, is occupied, and must be occupied, by GOD, in whatever form or way He has ordained that it be in the creature. Jesus uses the term, or illustration, of a branch to a vine. You are a branch in

a vine. A branch in a vine needs the life which the vine itself has. It grows and develops by it. You are joined to Him. You do it by OFFERING IT ALL TO GOD. <u>Cross-bearing becomes TRANSFORMATION IN LOVE!</u>

"Unless you hate your own life also, you CANNOT be my disciple." Now this word "cannot" simply means, in its fundamental power, NOT ABLE; you are not able to be His disciple. And it should become apparent to every one of you, that you are NOT ABLE to be a learner of Jesus, to learn His Life, to be a disciple, to be a learner, unless you hate and forsake your own life also, because it says you "cannot." You are NOT ABLE to know, or learn to know Jesus, to be His disciple, IN THE NEW TESTAMENT SENSE, UNLESS YOU <u>HATE YOUR OWN LIFE AS YOUR PERSONAL POSSESSION, AND FORSAKE IT</u>. So, "Unless he hate his own life also, he is NOT ABLE to be my disciple," is the meaning there. You "learn" to be transformed in Love.[5]

Such teaching exemplifies the way God applied the Scriptures to the daily lives of the Faith Homes residents. If each one took the teaching to heart, then the "beauty of holiness" would descend on the three Homes and each day seemed "heaven on earth." On the other hand, if resistance to the Word of God arose in the hearts of one and another, scheduled duties soon became dreary, and uncrucified natures sparked strife and discord among the residents.

I am leaving out much that could be said, for I wish to move on to the gloriously terrible years in which God resurrected the Work –

...no, NOT TO RE-ESTABLISH MRS. ROBINSON'S WORK. No. But to raise up a section which belonged to it. A small section broken, crushed out of existence, yet vital. Whether this record seems to be self-presenting or not, is of no importance to me. I know whereof I speak. And The Lord Himself re-established in the Faith Home Work a central, vital though simple, area in which HE could maintain a forward progression of spiritual life – and light – which connects with what went before...[6]

The events that brought about such change reflect the infinite wisdom – and mercy – of our Blessed Savior Jesus Christ. To Him be all the glory forever. He alone is worthy of unending worship.

CHAPTER NINE

THE RESURRECTED WORK
1947 – 1949
PART 1

Background

Eugene Brooks, born in 1856, joined Dr. John Alexander Dowie's healing movement in the late 1800s after both he and his wife Sara experienced Divine Healing through Dr. Dowie's prayers.[1] Dr. Dowie had appointed 150 "Elders" to administer the utopian city he built in Zion, Illinois. Nearly 10,000 residents were under the care and spiritual oversight of these Elders, all of whom, of course, were supervised by Dr. Dowie himself, who called himself "The General Overseer."[2]

Eugene Brooks accepted his first pastorate in 1885 as Minister of The Carthage Christian Church in Cincinnati, Ohio. From that starting point, he earned a reputation for being a zealous, hard-hitting, successful pastor of congregations in the Midwest, in Colorado, and in Canada. He was afflicted with severe hemorrhoids for many years. With stern resolve he would minister in the pulpit despite the blood flowing down his legs into his socks as he preached. In 1898 the message of Dr. Dowie's Divine Healing Movement reached him. God wonderfully and miraculously healed him and led him to join Dr. Dowie's growing organization.

Dr. Dowie, having soon recognized Rev. Brooks' gifts and calling, gave him the title "Elder Brooks" and placed him among Zion's overseers. That designation stayed with him for the rest of his long and fruitful life of 98 years. The title was well-deserved, for he was a godly man by any measure and endowed with a large and powerful gift of prophecy, among other gifts. I have heard comments to the effect that "The Elder" (as he was affectionately called) best typified an Old Testament prophet such as Elijah or Jeremiah. It was said that his preaching flayed the flesh and laid it bare, after which his wife Sara would pour in the oil and wine for comfort and healing.

After Elder Brooks severed his relationship with Dr. Dowie, he sought and received the Baptism of the Holy Spirit, and in a short time joined with Martha Robinson and the other Vessels, as described earlier. The Faith Homes was to be his "parish" for nearly 50 years, and the Lord advanced him in leadership to such an extent that the Homes became known as the Brooks' Faith Homes, even when Mrs. Robinson was still living.

Elder Brooks' Prophecies

Well into the year 1944, Elder Brooks was now 88 years old. Rex Andrews was still terribly backslidden. It was a trying time, not only in the Faith Homes, but also in the world, for World War II was at its height. The German armies had driven the Allies out of Europe, and the Holocaust against the Jews was bringing death to upwards of 20,000 Jews per day in Hitler's death camps.

Without advance notice the Lord gave a most remarkable prophecy through Elder Brooks on Sunday, April 23, 1944. It was taken down in its entirety in shorthand and copies were made. The Lord made it clear that change was coming to the Homes, and that it would cause division among the people. Also the Lord pinpointed the shallowness in the Church – in 1944 – and called on the people to make complete consecrations. The following is a portion (about one-third) of this long prophecy, unedited.

> KNOW ALL MEN BY THESE PRESENTS:* that I, God Almighty, have spoken, and will speak again. Let your scribes take out their scrolls. I want these words taken.
>
> I want my people to understand a mystery. I want them to know that this work is set for the rise and fall again of many in America, and for a sign which shall be spoken against. There are many that are now your friends and your praisers, who will be otherwise before they finish their course. There are many movements in the world today that appear to be virtuous and wonderful and appear to be very spiritual, and the people are looking up to them and

---

* These are typical, time-honored words that introduce a legal instrument, especially deeds of conveyance and wills. The phrase comes from English Common Law, and means, "Know all people by the words in this document that…"

praising them and thinking they are the great power of God. These will turn and go against you and despise you and set you at naught.

There are those who are now your friends but who will become your enemies. You must understand that the breach is getting wider and wider between the true and the false, and men who love the truth will have to suffer for it. Those who profess the truth, but do not live in it will be your enemies...

Do not suppose because men make a fair show in the world that therefore they are favorites with God. Days are becoming darker and darker, and the powers of evil are becoming more apparent and more pronounced everywhere, until the children of God who love the truth will be tested beyond measure and many will fall away...

And to some of you who are sitting in this place, today, I will announce that unless you get into the Word of God and on your knees more definitely and constantly than you have done, you will become a persecutor and an opposer of this work, for as the breach grows wider, it will be because there is a neglecting of The Book and of prayer, and you will be among them, and those of you who think you are going to stand, take heed, lest you fall. For unless you get into The Book and on your knees in a very much more constant way than you are now doing, you too will become separated, you too will lose your light, and take darkness for light, and light for darkness.[3]

No one but God knew what amazing events lay ahead of that prophecy, less than two months hence, things "too wonderful for words." Jesus was about to end the backsliding of Rex Andrews, one of the three *Wisdom Vessels* and bring, not only him, but also the Faith Homes, back from the dead.

A year later (April 22, 1945), The Elder arose, stood behind his chair and gave another prophecy. By this time word had reached Zion that Mr. Andrews had gotten right with the Lord, though few possessed any details of his restoration. Rumors flew, and judgments were made. This prophecy is long (not as long as the previous one in its entirety), but the wording is so remarkable I will include all of it. Though it was given 68 years ago, its message still warns and convicts.

The paragraphing divides artificially, as the message was delivered verbally without breaks.

I want My messenger to stand up and tell My people what I have in store for them.

Are you not My people? Have I not called you? Have I not set you in this place as a sign? Have I not put My Spirit upon you and told you to go forward? And how long has it been since I started you, and how long is it unto this day and hour?

Have you anything to compliment yourselves about? Have you anything that I should give you laurels and a crown, that I should compliment you much? Examine your hearts and see if you have been faithful. Examine yourselves before Me and see if there is any reason why I should say wonderful and nice things about you — and yet have I not said that ye are My people and that I put My Spirit upon you? Have I not said that I would bring you through? It was all because of My faith over you — not because you have been wonderful.

Now I want to report to this people that judgment has begun at their house. It has already begun, and judgment will continue at this house until there is nothing to judge, and those of My people who do not like My way of doing things, and who resist whatever I say or do to them, they will be set aside.

And I say to those now who want to go on with Me: "You must prepare yourselves to take strong things. You must be ready to be dishonored and disgraced for the action required. You must be ready not to be flattered and praised, but you must be ready to receive criticism, not only privately, but publicly. I will deal with you in the wisdom of Myself, and if you reject and refuse the words and the message that I send you and give you, I will not argue and not plead — I will just let you know that you are set aside."

I have already spoken My word and started some little things, and you understand how much of a rumpus it raised. You understand what it has resulted in. I am not going to stop because there are those who do not understand and who are not willing to wait to see the result. They want to know — they want to have their way – therefore I say I have My people here – I have My own here. They are here, and they will go through with Me, they will take correction, they will take criticism, they will take teaching, they will take what I send in love.

There are some that will not. They are not as pious and not as wise as they think they are, and are not as willing to be told and taught as some others, and the day will reveal it. The time to come will reveal who they are, and if you are set aside, don't blame anybody but yourself, because My plan and My desire is that all men might come to the knowledge of the truth and be blessed by the Holy Spirit as I alone can bless.

I am saying these words carefully and not excitedly. I am speaking to you in the will of Myself. I have loved you much, and I have loved you long. You are the plant of My plantings. My Vessel started you in this wonderful path of light and righteousness, and for her sake and for My own glory I want to bring you into the blessing and to the light and the power of My glory.

I am waiting, have long waited, for the time to come when I might say this much to you, and I want you to understand that everything that will be done by Me in the future will be done by the deepest, and will be done by the profoundest, love of My heart that I have for you. Nothing could induce Me to lay one straw in the way of your spiritual and physical progress. No, children; no, children – every thought of My heart for you, and every desire that there is in Me is for your perfection and glory and beauty. I would never cease and never stop until the likeness of My Son is bestowed upon you, until you come into His image and His beauty.

Believe Me when I say I regard you every one as My own dear son and daughter, and I love you with all the power of the Spirit, and I would that there would be not one that would turn away. And so I very earnestly plead with you, "Pray much, pray much, pray much that you do not let the tempter get into your soul and say and do things against My work and against My messengers, whoever they may be, because there is where you are going to be in trouble."

You think you are alright because of the blessing I have given you, but you do not know the depths of Satan, you do not know the wiles of the enemy, and when you think that you can stand, take heed lest you fall. You have already had a little test, you've already said and done things that never ought to have been said and done, for you have not honored Me, but you have resisted Me in your spirit, and it is only a suggestion of what will be done in the future, because this purging and this cleansing must go on, and it will never succeed if there are going to be criticisms and fault-findings and judgments expressed.

So I say unto My children, it is not you – your spirits are good, – but your flesh is weak, and your flesh has things in it that you ought to resist and deny, and overcome, because it is going to lead you into the quagmire. You have let that flesh exercise itself, and it is going to lead you into rebellion and disobedience to My will.

And now I say, having said this, I want you to have no sorrow, no heaviness, nor anything else that is contrary to the Will of God. Rejoice, be happy, declare yourselves My messengers and My people. Declare yourselves My appointed of the Lord, and rejoice for I am with you.[4]

It would be hard to find a truer prediction of events as they transpired in the next several years in the Faith Homes. And no one dreamed that God's "messengers, whoever they may be" would turn out to be Rex Andrews.

Please remember the following words quoted in Chapter 1, because it could seem to you that this account over-emphasizes the person and ministry of Rex Andrews.

How powerful is the tendency to WORSHIP CREATURES! The Man-worshiping spirit so easily arises in people FOR THOSE WHOM THEY GREATLY ADMIRE. It becomes a form of idolatry.[5]

Everything you are about to read was the direct result of the Mercy offered freely by Jesus Christ to one who was totally and hopelessly LOST, paired with the Lowliness of Elder Brooks, who, unlike the "elder brother" of the parable, welcomed Rex Andrews back to the work and stood with him to the end. No self-credit was ever allowed by either man. All credit belongs to Jesus, as anyone who truly understands the Faith Homes gladly acknowledges.

How the Change Took Place

After walking with Jesus for two years in California, Rex Andrews knew it was time to return to Zion in repentance, to seek forgiveness for his sins from the leaders of the Faith Homes, and from all who had been under his ministry in those early years. As will be explained later, his letter to Elder Brooks requesting permission to do so never reached Elder. Still, the desire to return to Zion was so great, Rex wrote to his former colleague Loretta M. Judd, who responded and invited him to stay at her home (she owned her own home as a kind of fourth Faith Home), and, upon learning from Elder Brooks that Rex's letter had never been received, she told Rex that his public repentance would be permitted.

In late 1946 he traveled to Zion, met with Elder Brooks, and arranged to repent publicly at a meeting in the Faith Homes.

I can only imagine the intense emotions everyone experienced that day, as Rex Andrews kneeled before the aging Elder, confessed his sins, and repented utterly to the ministers and to the congregation. "I know there's talk about how wicked I've been," he said to the people. "It's all true, and I must tell you that no matter what you hear about my backslidings these past seven years, I was ten times more wicked than anything you've heard." He humbled himself to the bone, making no excuses, softening nothing. "This is God's doing," Elder Brooks affirmed, as he welcomed the Prodigal Son home.

As you might have already anticipated, his return precipitated the division the Lord predicted would come.

Soon God unexpectedly arranged for Mr. Andrews to address the older saints who had been in leadership positions in the Homes for many years. In the words of the record of those times,

> In July, 1947, Elder Brooks had Brother Eaton, who was at that time in the ministry of The Homes, to ask me [Rex Andrews] to talk to a selected group of "The Old Timers." Elder had had

a dream, on a Wednesday night, in which The Lord showed him that a "terrible contagious disease was going to sweep the Faith Home Work away, – BUT there was a chance of averting it." He told me that he trembled as he had never trembled in his life, and lay awake all the rest of the night PRAYING for God to do something. Thursday night after the meeting, Brother Eaton spoke to me saying that the Elder wished me to talk to them on REPENTANCE! I said that I did not see how I could possibly do that, but I would pray about it. That night The Lord showed me that I was to talk to them on Repentance, and what kind of Repentance, and WHY. On Friday the meeting was called. It was composed of nearly all of those who had been in the Work in the earlier years, and who had been under Mrs. Robinson's own ministry.

It is not necessary to give all the details, here, of what was done in that and subsequent meetings of that group. BUT, One Thing stood out starkly clear, *viz:*, it was absolutely necessary to FORM immediately some way by which The Faith Homes could proceed at all. Everyone in that group, which afterward became "The Council," agreed that the Work was falling to pieces, because nearly all of The Older Workers were inactive, some having broken down under the long, long strain of oversight, and the drain of multiplied personal problems of a stream of needy souls, never ceasing. The "contagious disease" was a spiritual condition which was slowly moving in on The Work, for lack of Strong Spiritual Oversight – and the fact that some of the most important and vital spiritual Truths, which had constituted the Very Heart of the Work, were being lost to view. There was some Very Strong Work done in those first few meetings, which only God would know how to do. It resulted in a clearing vision as to how to proceed.

Elder Brooks had called the meeting, and he never wavered from carrying out the things that became visibly necessary to do IF ANYTHING WAS TO BE CONSERVED of The Faith Home Work as it had been.[6]

Miss Brooks was present in those meetings. She told me, "Douglas, they were the most intense meetings I've ever been in." She said further,

"Nothing was spared." The Lord had instructed Rex Andrews, "When you speak to them about repentance, you will not start with the cooks, the helpers, and the young people; you will start at the top. You will start with Elder Brooks and show him his need for repentance."

"What I had to do was impossible, Brother Douglas," Rex Andrews told me privately. "How could I, the 'black sheep,' the 'Prodigal Son,' speak to the others about THEIR need for repentance?"

Truly it was unthinkable, UNLESS God Himself directed the proceedings of the next two and a half years. But Elder Brooks never wavered from God's purpose, as quoted above. In fact, as the Lord moved from one to the other to point out their faults and failings, Elder Brooks was no longer mentioned in some of the sessions. At such times The Elder would seek out Mr. Andrews afterward and say, "Brother Rex, you corrected the others today, but have you no correction for me?" Can you imagine that? Ninety-one years old, listening to the former Prodigal Son, and saying to him, "Have you no correction for me today?"

Perhaps we cherish the idea that we're pretty humble, but I wonder...?

That combination of lowliness on Elder Brooks' part, and mercy and obedience and the love of the truth on Rex Andrews' part, brought the Work back to life. It was a manifestation of Jesus Himself, "who calleth those things which be not, as though they were" (Romans 4:17).

Slowly the Work began to rise out of the disintegrating condition it had been in since Mrs. Robinson's death in 1936. The tide had turned and Jesus took His rightful place in the Homes once again.

CHAPTER TEN

THE RESURRECTED WORK
1947 – 1949

PART 2

Prayer

I confess, Lord, I don't know You very well. I know You, yes, but I don't know You very well. I'm just a branch, one of many. I am not The Vine. I'm only a little chick under Your wings. I'm one of the sheep in Your flock. I'm a passenger on a boat crossing life's stormy sea. I know You are in the boat, which means it cannot sink.

What we want, Lord, is for all us passengers in the boat to say, "What manner of man is this, that even the wind and the seas obey Him?"

Lord, if You would impress on us the enormity of that statement, "What manner of man is this?", if You will make that real to us, then we will be satisfied.

I ask that everyone reading this will receive his or her portion. Lord, not all readers have been walking with You for forty years. Some hardly have begun. But I pray that all will be encouraged by Your Spirit to follow You wholeheartedly.

I pray that you will not let us exalt ourselves over one another, or put others down, or act unkindly toward each other. All of us are in the deficiency of not knowing You very well. I ask You to help us see ourselves as we really are in Your sight, and then to see You as You really are.

I desire to present in some meaningful fashion what it will mean to be like You. Please, Lord, communicate to us the characteristics of this pathway, so nothing in the future will ever shake us from the pursuit of this Jesus who has pursued us. We want to apprehend that for which we are apprehended by Christ.

You shall certainly bring forth the likeness of Jesus in your people, for You have "seen the travail of His soul and shall be satisfied." By Your knowledge *shall many be justified. "We shall be satisfied when we awake in Your likeness." We declare that our "citizenship is in heaven from whence also we look for the Savior, the Lord Jesus Christ, who shall change our vile body that it might be fashioned like His glorious body, according to the working whereby He is able even to subdue all things [including us] unto Yourself."*

"Now unto Him who is able to keep you from falling and to present you faultless before the presence of His glory with exceeding joy, be glory and majesty, dominion, and power both now and forevermore." In Jesus' Name. Amen.

How God Reversed the Disintegration of the Faith Homes

We continue with the subject, "The Resurrected Work." The period is from 1947 to 1949, and I am focusing primarily on the restoration of Rex Andrews from his fall, and the subsequent restructuring of The Faith Home Work.

God spoke to Elder Brooks and asked him to invite Mr. Andrews to have meetings and talk to the old-timers about repentance, starting with Elder Brooks. It is one of the most amazing things that ever happened, that "the prodigal son" was used to bless "the elder brother." It is truly too long a story to recount, but it is most wonderful. In those two and one-half years God resurrected a dying work.

This leads to an introduction of *What the Bible Teaches about Mercy*, which will be the focus in Chapter 16 of this book. By filling in the background first, the reader will appreciate the value of the *Mercy Studies* a great deal more.

Many of the old-timers had become self-satisfied and self-righteous. After all, they had known Martha Robinson, had worked with her, and had listened to her teachings. What more could there be? In their conception of things, they had seen the pinnacle of Christian experience. They were confident in their knowledge of God.

Therefore, when Rex Andrews returned to Zion and, following his public repentance, began to share his testimony in the meetings, there was a slight resistance. "We are thankful that God has restored Rex Andrews," they said, "but let's get back to where we were," not realizing that the Work had almost disintegrated spiritually. After about six weeks, Mr. Andrews decided to depart. His planned destination was South Africa, where he would visit the Faith Home missionaries in that country, and then make his way northward to Kenya to be reunited with his wife Beulah, who was living with their daughter and son-in-law on a mission station near the equator. He ceased talking about mercy in the meetings, which was fine with many in the congregation. They did not want to hear about mercy any longer.

At this juncture two people came to him with a request. One was Ruth Brooks, the daughter of Elder Brooks, and the other was Matthew Eaton, one of the ministers at that time. They came to Mr. Andrews privately and said to him, "Please don't stop talking about mercy. We've noticed that you've tapered off. Please don't do that. We need this." Ruth Brooks was especially eager, for she had grown up in the Work, and she, being the way she was, could hardly bear the self-righteousness of some of the old-timers − "They acted so spiritual, but in their hearts they were hypocritical," she told me later. Miss Brooks was a real down-to-earth person, and she knew that what had happened to Mr. Andrews was genuine and recognized it as the work of God.

Mr. Andrews heeded the urgings of Miss Brooks and Matthew Eaton, and that became a turning point in the history of the Faith Homes.

Had that not happened, the Work would have completed its disintegration and disappeared entirely. The Lord confirmed to Rex Andrews during his *Night Watch** that he should stay, but he had no idea it would take over two years of intense ministry before The Work gradually became healthy again. One problem was that he did not look, act, nor sound like Martha Robinson. People had unconsciously elevated her to such a stature that all speakers had to be measured against her. It became necessary for a time to forbid mentioning Martha Robinson's name to prove one's point, and to forbid the quotation of anything she had said. The old-timers were horrified.

"But that was Jesus speaking through her," they said.

"Yes," Mr. Andrews replied, "but you don't understand at all what she meant by some of the things she said, and you have taken her words out of context, and you are spoiling the very essence of what she was teaching."

Is it any different in our Bible Colleges and seminaries today? The Word of God is studied, but men of unsanctified intellects pervert it until its truths are contradicted and abandoned.

---

* Beginning about June of 1944 until his death in 1976, God gave him the desire − and the strength − to seek the Lord in His Word and in prayer every night from 11 p.m. or midnight until sunrise. He never took any self-credit for doing so.

They were doing that with Mrs. Robinson's teaching. Yes, Mr. Andrew's style of ministry was different. But what really galled some listeners and made it difficult for them was the fact that he had been one of the Vessels. He had been in many private meetings with Mrs. Robinson and the other Vessels. He knew what had happened, and he knew what the Lord had said to Elder and Mrs. Brooks, and to the Mitchells and the Leggetts and Mrs. Judd. He knew how the Lord had cut through the exterior to the interior of their hearts and exposed their fleshly ways. Yes, they had great gifts and great powers and great ministries. People were practically falling down at their feet because of the amazing things that were done in the public meetings, but behind the scenes, the Lord was saying, "Get thee behind Me, Satan."

One example might be helpful here. The Lord was dealing with Aunt Eva Leggett through Mrs. Robinson. As the Lord Jesus pointed out something about Aunt Eva that "cut to the quick," she blurted out to Mrs. Robinson, "That's not true, and I don't have to take that." She rose and headed for the door. (Please remember you have no higher court of appeal when Jesus says to you, "This is what you are like." You can't go somewhere else and say, "I don't like that opinion. I'd like a better one.")

"If you leave this room, you will take an enemy," said the Lord. (When anyone resists the pure word of God, the enemy has access to that one.) She went out anyway and shut the door. The minute she did so, she experienced the truth of the warning just given; a frightful darkness descended on her. She felt it and knew it was an enemy. Thankfully she immediately knocked on the door she had just closed, and requested entrance. "Come in," said Mrs. Robinson. Aunt Eva threw herself down in repentance and begged for deliverance. The Lord in His mercy dispelled the darkness that had been allowed to come upon her because of her rebellion.

That is one small glimpse of the purity and power of the Lord's immanent Presence and Word with which the Vessels were instructed or corrected.†

Aunt Eva had gifts, amazing gifts, but God was not satisfied with the condition of her heart. He wanted her to be like His Son, of whom it is written, "The prince of this world cometh and hath nothing in Me." In

---

† For comparison, consider the immediate consequence of King Uzziah's brash entry into the Holy Place to offer incense, despite the priests' warning not to do so. He was instantly smitten with leprosy in the forehead and thrust out of the sacred precincts by the priests. See II Chronicles 26:16-21.

other words, every avenue by which the devil sought to enter Jesus and corrupt His work and destroy His power and effectiveness and purity — all those avenues were closed, so that he could not find one place to enter our Savior's outer or inner life and say, "This part of Jesus is mine." The devil never found one such avenue; no, not one.

Jesus never spoke a single word that He didn't hear His Father speak. Can you put your foot into such a shoe? Yet, so greatly did Jesus possess Mrs. Robinson that she spoke no words of her own for years on end. Some may think that was fanaticism, but it wasn't. It was the truth. She wouldn't speak unless Jesus actually spoke.

THAT'S WHERE WE ARE HEADED. But for that to happen God has to get at our hearts, because "out of the abundance of the heart the mouth speaketh" (Matthew 12:34).

God is relentless. (I want to say this accurately.) He is relentless in getting rid of everything in us that would interfere with the flow of His mercy through us. I like to put it that way because in holiness churches and deep-life circles, the emphasis is often on "sinless perfection" in a way that becomes a perversion of the truth. In developing a pure heart in His people, God eliminates everything that interferes with pouring out the mercy of God to other people. You only get that by sitting at the feet of Jesus. It doesn't come by studying the doctrine of it.

The Cross-Life of Travail

We may rightfully inquire, "What happened to Mrs. Robinson after her tremendous experience in 1907? What showed in her life that it was truly Jesus who came to her?"

The answer is that she never lived another minute for herself. She never did one thing out of self-will for the rest of her life. Was it wonderful? Indeed it was, but it was also a life of the most intense suffering you can imagine, unless you understand it from the record of God's intercessors in the Bible.

What kind of suffering was it? Was she suffering for her own troubles and sorrows, her flesh and her sins?

No, she bore the sins and troubles of those whom God brought to her.

You can see that quality of pure-hearted-ness — a life lived solely for others — in the Apostle Paul. Take, for example, what he says to the Galatians in Chapter 3. "O, foolish Galatians, who hath bewitched you that you should not obey the truth before whose eyes Jesus Christ hath been evidently set forth crucified among you?" What did he mean? *They saw the crucified Christ in the life of Paul. They saw "Christ crucified" before their very eyes.*

He had brought them to the birth of faith in Christ, but they were moving away from it. "I'm afraid for you," he writes in 4:9, "lest I have bestowed upon you labor in vain..." [and further on, vv. 19-20] "My little children, of whom I travail in birth again until Christ be formed in you, I desire to be present with you now, and to change my voice; for I stand in doubt of you."

What does Paul mean here? Certainly the first travail is for the conversion of souls – Paul travailed till they were brought to the birth. Now he travails again. For what purpose? That Christ may be formed in them. Travail involves pain and suffering, but it is for a purpose.

Martha Robinson's work with people followed those general lines for 28 years. It was the epitome of unselfishness. It was a life of suffering (birth-pangs) for others, that Christ might be formed in them.

The same could be said of Rex Andrews' life, after his restoration in 1944. "For fifteen years, 1944–1959," he wrote in the *Record of Truth*, "there has been but slight surcease [cessation], day or night, from the conflict – a raging conflict." Conflict for what? For Jesus' life to take root and grow in the lives of others. Even God's people shy away from that kind of a consecration. They don't want to suffer with Him.

One day while meditating on the story of the man with a legion of demons (Luke 8), I said in my heart, "Jesus, why did you not put those demons into the abyss? Why did you permit them to go into the swine instead?"

I felt an impression of an answer, "I allowed it so they would be present to attack me while I was on the Cross." Oh, Jesus! I am still trying to accommodate my thinking to that answer.

Then it seemed like another comment followed. "Even if I had cast out all the demons that were loose in Israel and in the rest of the world, yet mankind would still need redemption. You would have all gone back to what you are. I had to DIE. There is no redemption without death."

That has become a principle for me.

I'm describing how Jesus' possession of us means we will be plunged into conflict for the sake of others. I found out that there is no lasting work done in the Kingdom without it. "Except a grain of wheat fall into the ground and DIE, it abides alone," Jesus said just prior to His death (John 12:24, emphasis added). We are called to follow in His steps. We have to go to our own Gethsemane, our own crucifixion with Him, of course, before we can truly be the blessing that God wants us to be – emptied, broken, no confidence in the flesh – then filled with His power to lay our lives down for others. By such people, the work of God gets done in the world, His permanent work.

Occasionally visitors to the Faith Homes would say, "Why are there not more people visiting the Homes now? Why have you a congregation of only one hundred?" Rex Andrews explained, "The reason people don't flock to the Faith Homes is because they hear the sound of nails being driven into wood."

Rex Andrews stayed in the Faith Homes from 1947 until mid-1949. The Work was completely turned around, and he was as amazed as anyone else at what had happened. God did it.

Resistance and Division

One of the things that had to be dealt with was the issue of God's power on the body, as it related to "working in power," as it was called. Martha Robinson had given instructions to three different Vessels on how they should proceed with the Work if The Power of God were taken from the workers. Rex Andrews was one of those who heard those instructions, but it was only after returning to the Homes in 1944 that God brought it back to his memory.

"If anything happens to me," Mrs. Robinson had told him, "the remaining workers must lay down The Power Work and conduct the meetings along Pentecostal lines by leadings, as any other Pentecostal work is obliged to do." She added, "You will get into serious trouble if you don't remember this word and obey it."

Everyone was willing to do that except Mrs. Judd, who had built her ministry on her supposed excellence. Gradually the enemy had corrupted her work in the meetings, though she retained an unusual aura connected with The Power of God on her body. In addition to that fact, her teaching in the Gift of Wisdom had been tainted somewhat because she had disobeyed certain injunctions of the Lord pertaining to that teaching. She really did need to lay it all down, but when faced with the choice, she said, "I won't lay it down."

Eventually it came to a head, a momentous head. She was confronted with this directive from Mrs. Robinson, who had told it not only to Rex Andrews, but also to Elder Brooks and to Mrs. Naylor. "If anything happens to Mrs. Robinson, you must lay down the Power Work." What was Mrs. Judd's defense? "But Mrs. Robinson never said that to me."

A deadline was set for everyone to affirm their obedience, "Will you obey what God said to do, or will you not?" When the day came, Mrs. Judd knelt in front of Elder Brooks and said, "Elder, you know I can't do that. Besides, an angel appeared to me last night and said, 'Don't lay down the Power Work.'"‡ Elder Brooks stood firmly for the truth, however.

There came a division that never changed.

Perhaps a short digression on the subject of "Why Do Divisions Come?" would be worthwhile, for a number of critics have launched attacks against *What the Bible Teaches about Mercy*.

Jesus spoke of division in Luke 12:51-53.

Suppose ye that I am come to give peace on earth? I tell you, Nay; but rather division: For from henceforth there shall be five in one house divided, three against two, and two against three. The father shall be divided against the son, and the son against the father; the mother against the daughter, and the daughter against the mother; the mother in law against her daughter in law, and the daughter in law against her mother in law.

Jesus' death by crucifixion, though it is *the Greatest Mercy ever offered to mankind*, became **the dividing line** between all human beings. It divides the human race into two classes – those who receive that Mercy, and those who do not. The division lies in the WILL.

The teaching about mercy has the same effect. It divides people, because some are willing to walk in the Mercy of God, and some are not.

You say, "But it is in the nature of Mercy to agree with the disagreeable and to reach out to one's enemies." Yes, absolutely. The whole world should fall at the feet of Jesus, the Merciful Savior. His crucifixion should unite everyone in reverence and brokenness before that Cross. BUT IT DOESN'T! Unless we acknowledge our sinfulness and repent, the Mercy-

---

‡ Personally, it gives me the chills to think about this incident, for it was NOT an angel from God that appeared to her, though she did not recognize the deception.

of-Calvary cannot be received. And unless our hearts become Thrones of Mercy, as His is and was, we deny the Lord who bought us. The Parable of the Unforgiving Servant ends with these sobering words:

> *So likewise shall my heavenly Father do also unto you, if ye from your hearts forgive not every one his brother their trespasses.* (Matthew 18:23-35)

Hatred against Christians is rising tremendously in the world right now. Those who love the mercy of God, who understand it and walk in it, are likely soon to become targets of enormous hatred, terrible hatred. Those who love mercy and grace and compassion will weep over the spiritual condition of their enemies. The example of Richard Wurmbrand's reaction to lengthy persecution in Romania inspires us to do likewise.[1]

But the "household of faith" also experiences its share of animosity. The lines of division reflect the condition of our hearts. In the course of Rex Andrews' life, the emphasis on *What the Bible Teaches about Mercy* caused a breach even among Faith Home adherents, just as Elder Brooks had prophesied two months before Rex Andrews came back to the Lord. His testimony and teaching caused a large breach; people challenged him to his face with the awful words, "You teach mercy, but you don't do it." I myself have seen the animosity in faces red with anger. I could make a list of twenty individuals who repudiated his words, though he tried to help them. (I could make a longer list, thankfully, of people who DID receive his mercy-counsel, myself included.)

Why were there such reactions? Because not every believer is willing to do the mercy to other people that God has done to them. The "Mercy Teaching" exposes a person for what he is and what he is not. The Pharisees in the church are the ones that get the most angry. "I never took drugs. I never did anything immoral...", yet their hearts are full of dead men's bones. "You hypocrites, you generation of vipers," said the merciful John the Baptist. "The harlots and the publicans go into the kingdom before you," said God's Mercy-in-the-Flesh to the Pharisees. "They repented at the preaching of John, but you would not." Say that to a Pharisee nowadays and see what happens. Yet Jesus offered the same Mercy to them as He did to the sinners they despised!

What repentance is as an act equals what Poverty of Spirit is as a state. Without that continual response in the heart to the Mercy flowing from Calvary, there is no entrance to the Kingdom.

On the other side of the divide, however, lies God's blessing. "Any group that puts into practice what the Bible teaches about mercy, and does it from the heart, will have the power of increase in their ministry." I heard those words and I have experienced the truth of them.

Sitting At the Feet of Jesus

If the enemy of our souls cannot defeat us one way, he will always try another. By invoking a fear of division, he seeks to pull us back from following the example of Jesus, "whom God anointed with the Holy Ghost and power, who went about doing good, and healing all that were oppressed of the devil; for God was with Him" (Acts 10:38). If that fails, he sometimes attacks by substituting "The Social Gospel" for the authentic "Mercy-ing Heart."

To resist the latter attack, I wish to emphasize the following fact: The secret of remaining in the true Spirit of Mercy is found in one place, and one place only, *i.e.,* at Jesus' feet.

The Faith Homes has stood firmly through the years for the need of believers to spend much time in the Word of God and prayer. Indeed, (as we will see later in this history), the daily schedule contained substantial portions of time set aside for individual seeking of Jesus, what many have called, *Sitting At the Feet of Jesus*. Critics leveled serious charges at that, saying that the young people needed to get out into the Lord's Work, become more active in the ministry, begin doing the Mercy that was taught. Yet things of eternal value transpire when we come daily to Jesus' feet to be taught by Him through the written Word and by "waiting on the Lord."

I am reminded of the story of the Chinese pastor who was invited by leading ministers in the United States to see how greatly the work of the Lord was growing here. For two weeks they showed him large church buildings and vigorous programs of ministry. Finally he was asked, "Well, what do you think?" He replied, "I am amazed at how much you have accomplished without God."

So often we force God, as it were, into the position of having to bless us when we are not in the center of His will. The center of His will is for us to be at the feet of Jesus in a broken and contrite spirit, partaking of

His mercies daily, and to carry from that place a divine passion to pour out those mercies where He directs us to do so. If the life of mercy is disconnected from that sacred place, one leaves the center/Jesus, with a resultant decrease in the Spirit's anointing. It happens gradually without one realizing it, like the gradual surrender of Samson's head into Delilah's lap, until the source of the anointing is cut off by her.

In the Faith Homes, we frequently sang treasured hymns to maintain the sight of our need to occupy Mary's place of hearing Jesus' Word at His feet. There is a hymn with the title, *Sitting at the Feet of Jesus*.[2] We sang it often.

> *Sitting at the feet of Jesus, O what words I hear Him say!*
> *Happy place! So near, so precious! May it find me there each day.*
> *Sitting at the feet of Jesus, I would look upon the past;*
> *For His love has been so gracious, It has won my heart at last.*
>
> *Sitting at the feet of Jesus, Where can mortal be more blest?*
> *There I lay my sins and sorrows, And when weary find sweet rest.*
> *Sitting at the feet of Jesus, There I love to weep and pray;*
> *While I from His fulness gather, Grace and comfort every day.*
>
> *Bless me, O my Savior bless me, As I sit low at Thy feet.*
> *O look down in love upon me, Let me see Thy face so sweet.*
> *Give me, Lord, the mind of Jesus; Make me holy as He is;*
> *May I prove I've been with Jesus, Who is all my righteousness.*

Another hymn that still pulls on my heart whenever we sing it is *Sweet Will of God*.[3]

> *My stubborn will at last has yielded;*
> *I would be Thine, and Thine alone.*
> *And this the prayer my lips are bringing,*
> *Lord, let in me Thy Will be done.*
>
>> Chorus: *Sweet Will of God, Still fold me closer,*
>> *Till I am wholly lost in Thee;*
>> *Sweet Will of God, Still fold me closer,*
>> *Till I am wholly lost in Thee.*

> *Thy precious will, O Conq'ring Savior,*
> *Doth now embrace and compass me;*
> *All discords hushed, my peace a river;*
> *My soul a prisoned bird set free.*
>
> *Shut in with Thee, O Lord forever;*
> *My wayward feet no more to roam.*
> *What power from Thee my soul can sever?*
> *The center of God's Will my home.*

I'm speaking of a simplicity that is easily lost. As mentioned earlier, the greatest power there ever was in the Faith Homes, was a simplicity so great that if you didn't know it was God, you wouldn't think it was He. When Jesus produces a Mercy-ing Heart in a disciple who sits at His feet, no recipient of the Mercy given retains a strong impression of the agent; instead, he retains a strong impression of Jesus Himself, the Source of all true Mercy.

An exchange of letters between the well-known Evangelist John G. Lake, and Elder Brooks, illuminates this subject beautifully. I include it as an appendix to this book.§

Addendum

The substance of this chapter was presented to a group of workers involved in a ministry of mercy. Because of the Lord's sweet presence as we closed, a prayer and a message in tongues with interpretation came forth at the end, which was recorded. Perhaps some reader will find blessing in it. It is edited very slightly.

Prayer:

> *Lord, we thank You for Your anointing and help in this hour. I am so conscious of Your help. This is not about us or the Faith Homes. This is about You, Jesus, and learning to love You. You said, "Come and learn of Me; sit at My feet." That's what started all this. "Learn at My feet. That's where you are going to find the truth and the balance, and everything that you need."*

---

§ See Appendix D.

> *I hear you, Lord, calling this staff and calling every one of us here to Your feet. I can hear you calling us because there we will all get the proper word for what and how we should do everything. Instead of You having to accommodate Yourself to us all the time, because of our flesh, our willfulnesss, and our ideas, and instead of You constantly adjusting to us, it would be so wonderful, wouldn't it, Jesus, if we would all accommodate ourselves to You? If we would adjust ourselves to You, and all just be and do what You reveal to us there at Your feet? Then, Your work would be done properly.*
>
> *Jesus, we surrender. We acknowledge You are right; You are right; You are right. I thank You for helping us to express a little bit of the truth of Your heart. I pray that You will continue to help us to understand You. In Jesus' name. Amen.*

Tongues and Interpretation:

> *You have heard but a small part of My heart. You don't know Me like I want to reveal Myself to you. Do you hear Me pleading with you to come and put your ear on My breast and hear My heartbeat and partake of My wisdom instead of your own wisdom? Do you now understand how many times you substitute your own wisdom for Mine? You force Me to go according to your plans?*
>
> *If you are hearing, if your ear is open, you will do something about it. But, if your hearing is dull, you will go on the way you have been. I'm calling you to My feet. Will you please come there every day?*

Before we continue this history to speak of *The Resurgent Years,* an interlude in the form of a testimony may be helpful. It is from the pen of a delightful South African missionary whom we came to know and love, a personal friend. Her name was Miss Dorrel Healey. Her words are inspiring even now, though she left us for Heaven some 35 years ago.

INTERLUDE ONE

LIVING ON CHARITY
BY DORREL HEALEY

Nearly seven years ago, I lay tossing from side to side on a bed in the Zebediela Mission house. My sleepless eyes stared out into the darkness, yet before them, one disconcerting vision after another would pass by. All was still in the house. While others slept, I was the pawn in a conflict between my own PRIDE and the Will of God for my life.

I had been on a motoring trip to the beautiful Victoria Falls in Rhodesia, South Africa, and had traveled with two missionaries and two school-girls from the High School in Johannesburg where I was teaching. During that trip, my call to full-time service for the Lord was renewed. The original call had come about six months after my conversion, and very soon before I had begun to study for the teaching profession. Now by this time, I had been teaching for eight and a half years, and the sound of the call had grown dim.

Now, this night, the Voice I heard was insistent, and was asking if I would be willing to give up my substantial salary, and "go out in FAITH." Here was my struggle! SURELY it would be far better to go out under some Mission Board, I argued, and have SECURITY. How gently Jesus led me on to the admission that there could be no more SECURE security than all the promises in God's Word, which are "Yea, and Amen, IN HIM." One financial prop after another, which I could suggest to the Lord, had been knocked out from under me, until I felt I was dangling in mid-air, not realizing, of course, that His arms are underneath, always UPHOLDING, even if there would seem nothing to stand on.

"Lord," I had asked, "Do you want me to become a BEGGAR, and live on CHARITY?" That would be an absolute DISGRACE, I had thought. How black a picture was presented to me – would drab cast-off clothing and scanty fare become my lot? The PRIDE within me revolted against such a thought, until the Lord graciously met me right where I was mentally, and pacified me by reminding me that "the workman is worthy of his hire," if I WANTED to be a hireling. Well, that could certainly ease the embarrassment, and I would be able to say to my critics, "Well, I WORKED for what I've received, didn't I? Am I not WORKING for the Lord? I'm NOT living on charity."

So I felt I was going to be deserving of everything He would send my way. I would be able to hold my head HIGH and be unashamed – unless, of course, I WERE actually given drab "cast-offs" (but PERISH the miserable thought, for if I were going to live by FAITH, it would be my faith that would set the limits to what God would be able to get me to receive!)

At last, I said "Yes" to my Lord. After all, the Zebediela missionaries did not look as though God is not able to keep His promises and look after His children. I was yet to learn that God gives BEYOND what the worldling would even call a "reasonable hire." Even Peter had wanted to know what the disciples were going to GET for following Jesus (Mark 10:28-30; Matthew 19:27-29). Let us not look askance at Peter, dear ones, for we bear the same covetous make-up, whether we acknowledge it or not. We've given up, or forsaken or left all – or maybe just a part – and followed Him, and we want to know, "What shall we HAVE therefore?" There is always the desire to know what we are to GET FOR "ME" out of anything we do. Jesus' reply to Peter is breath-taking in its immensity. In effect, He says, "You will get WAY BEYOND what you DESERVE – HUNDRED-FOLD – NOW, in this time (but with persecution, sometimes, take note) – AND you shall inherit Everlasting Life." That is CHARITY; it is MERCY; it is beyond HIRE. We can't keep up with God! Hallelujah!

I, too, have tasted of this bounty – houses, brothers, sisters, fathers, mothers – all, it seems, have been received in hundred-fold measure. Even though I am a stranger to this great land of the U. S. A., SEE how much love is lavished on me by relatives in the Spirit, and how many homes I can feel at HOME in – as was the case in South Africa, my home-land.

In the 20th Chapter of Matthew's Gospel, we read that Jesus tells the parable of the house-holder hiring labourers into his vineyard. He starts with the word "FOR" and links this parable in a very beautiful way to the conversation with Peter, that has just been under consideration in the 19th Chapter. Those labourers who first went to work, AGREE with

Interlude One:
Living On Charity, by Dorrel Healey[1]

the house-holder as to what their wages would be – a penny for the day's work. Even though the penny was worth more in those days, it would seem to us little enough reward for their labour, but they had AGREED to work for that. At the end of the long hot day, they would straighten up their tired backs, and feel they had REALLY EARNED it. They could not DEMAND more, for that is what they had agreed upon – they could not expect more. The house-holder hired others to join them. He made no agreement with them as to what their wages would be, but simply said, "Whatsoever is RIGHT, I will give thee."

Some had stood idle even until the eleventh hour, "because no man hath hired us," they said. Other employers had probably taken their choice from the labourers early that morning. They had chosen the young and strong. These who were left were the undesirable, the old, the weak and possibly sick, the crippled, the maimed, the foolish, the illiterate, unskilled, unintelligent – but how much GREATER was their need than the ones who were able to work from morn to night. The house-holder saw their NEED, and met it.

Pay-time came and these last received that which was RIGHT, as he had promised – one WHOLE penny – and FAR more than they DESERVED for the hour's work they had done. They had trusted their employer to do that which was RIGHT, as he had said, and we can imagine their JOY when they received what they did. They had thrown themselves on his MERCY, and what did they get? MERCY – and beyond their wildest hopes. The first labourers were not in the same relationship with their employer – they were hirelings, working for what they had agreed upon – and then their eye was evil because he was good to the needy! May the Lord deliver us from that kind of evil covetous eye, and help us to rejoice over those our GOOD God blesses with His lavish GOODNESS – His charity – His MERCY.

Six months after I had said "Yes" to the Lord, it began to be clear that it was TIME to go into the vineyard of the House-holder, and I knew He would give me only that which was RIGHT. I made application to Ruth Williamson to become, as it were, an "apprentice-faith-missionary" – and though at that time, I did not even have the Baptism of the Holy Spirit to recommend me for such a position, she graciously took me on her Mission Station at Zebediela, when she returned from furlough in 1948, and I have had the privilege of working with her ever since.

When I broke the news to my family, one horrified relative exclaimed, "Well, I certainly would not want to live on CHARITY." I believe I blushed to the very roots of my hair, for had I not been through all that agony of pride before? Had it not been settled that I was going to WORK for the Lord, and DESERVE all I got? I couldn't bear the ignominy of being thought of as a BEGGAR, living on the proverbial coldness of charity. I pocketed my pride, however, and then entered into happy, thrilling years of FAITH-LIFE with Ruth Williamson. We've had our lean times, to be sure, but these were but blessings in disguise, as they proved to be challenges to our faith. The Lord has never let us down, and He always does that which is RIGHT, for He is GOOD.

In December 1949, the Lord sent us one of His servants from the Zion Faith Homes, and he came with an emphasis on a few simple words, that made chapter after chapter of the Bible spring into LIFE. We, who by nature, live in PRIDE and COVETOUSNESS, were being called to a love of LOWLINESS AND MERCY, the opposites of what we live in. We began to WANT the mind of Christ, Who thought it not robbery, or a thing to be grasped at for Himself, to be equal with God, but humbled Himself, and was willing to HAVE NOTHING, BE NOTHING, KNOW NOTHING, WANT NOTHING, be able to DO NOTHING, apart from God. From my mind began to slip even the cursed thought that because I thought I was DOING something for God, I had a right to EXPECT good wages. Everything I received came from His heart of love – my food, clothes, my strength, my health, yes, and my very breath, too. I DESERVED NOTHING – miserable proud creature that I was! I was living on CHARITY – living on His pure MERCY, and learning to know Him as the "Father of Mercies" (II Corinthians 1:3). How could I ever DARE to hold my head up HIGH again, and look into His face and tell Him I deserved anything?

Now, in 1955, my Father of Mercies has planned for me this lovely visit to the States, and to Zion Faith Homes in particular. Could I ever have dreamed of such a thing when I was working for a salary? Money seemed to go out faster than it came in, and the more I received the more had to be spent. Even the dear ones in my family, who hated the thought of my "living on charity," cannot fail to appreciate such bounty. God is not a JUST PAYER, for He pays way beyond any HIRE. He is a GOOD GIVER. He LOVES to GIVE – His LOVE GIVES (John 3:16). He gives

Interlude One:
Living On Charity, by Dorrel Healey[1]

so that not only our needs be supplied, and our lives completed in Him, but that our JOY might be FULL. He gives ALL for OTHERS, ANY others, undeserving others, and He longs to make our hearts GIVING HEARTS too. He wants us to learn to give, Give, GIVE instead of to get, Get, GET something for covetous self all the time. When we GIVE as He gives, to anyone, without exception, we begin to be united with Him, IN THE GIVING OF ALL.

One morning here in Zion, we were considering the story of the blind beggar Bartimaeus. He HAD nothing; WAS nothing (but a nuisance to contemptuous, heartless people, hurrying by); could DO nothing (for he had no sight); he KNEW nothing (except that he NEEDED MERCY and lived on such "charity" as would be condescendingly tossed at him, by way of a coin or a crust of bread); he WANTED nothing but the MERCY that would restore his sight. OH, dear ones, what did he DO when Jesus passed by? He cried for MERCY. What did he get? MERCY! His sight was restored. Hallelujah! Who wouldn't want to live on such MERCY? It is God's light-giving, need-supplying, life-imparting mercy.

Suddenly there crept into my soul the desire to take the attitude of a beggar at Jesus' feet – the LOWLY attitude of recognizing the whole of myself as just a NEED-FOR-MERCY, then to call for mercy to supply that need, and marvel at the way He would GIVE mercy and fill the need. Who are the ones that get mercy, but those who are lowly enough to acknowledge they need it and cry out to God from their own self-INsufficiency for it? In the bright light of what HIS MERCY is, how could I ever again blush at the thought of living on charity? What a rest and a comfort just to look up at Him and know that I don't DESERVE anything, and that I am simply living at His hand.

God's MERCY is the kind of charity that maketh not ashamed, but makes the life FULL, for it is FULFILLING MERCY, FILLING all the emptiness and worthlessness of the life. Why have we made the poor wince at our organized social charity? How has it come about that they talk bitterly about charity being COLD? It is because for centuries, we have not GIVEN as God GIVES, *viz.*, with compassion and an earnest desire to DO GOOD to the needy one, without exception. We have given "to be seen of men," and because of the wicked PRIDE in our hearts, we ENJOY the feeling over being so much SUPERIOR to the one to whom we are giving our alms; we have given "to be seen of men" because of the wicked COVETOUSNESS of our hearts that covet acclamation for what we do, and a reputation for generosity, maybe. PRIDE and COVETOUSNESS have robbed our CHARITY of the warmth of love, because it has to a large extent become self-love. That is why it is COLD now. We need to revise our vocabulary, though, and see what charity really IS.

Because of the perverted use of this once very beautiful word, some translators of the Bible prefer to use the word "love" in First Corinthians 13. Here is Webster's definition of *charity*: "The good affection, or love or tenderness, which men should feel towards their fellows, and which should induce them to do good to, and to think FAVORABLY of others; benevolence (WELL-WISHING); liberality in thinking or judging; liberality in giving to the poor; whatever is bestowed GRATUITOUSLY on the poor for their relief; any ACT of kindness or benevolence, *etc.*"

The foremost quality of charity is LOVE and tenderness, but in addition to this quality, DOING something specific to RELIEVE others and NOT doing it for self at all. It is "Love Doing" – but, dear ones, this is MERCY, isn't it? Those who are poor in material things; those poor in well-wishers; those poor in favour toward them – the poor needy ones, can all have ALL their needs met at all times – and WITHOUT EXCEPTION. These needs can be met by CHARITY when we let it mean what it really means. It doesn't depend on any MERIT at all; the only condition for it to go into action is the sight of a NEED, and the more truly beggarly the beggar may be, the greater the charity to meet the need. Why, THIS IS MERCY!

It would be so refreshing to read through that blessed chapter, First Corinthians 13, with the word "MERCY" replacing the word "charity," instead of the word "love" being the substitute. In our modern conception of things, the beautiful word "love" has also lost much of its true meaning. We LOVE so differently from the way God loves. We love the lovable – God in His MERCY loves ALL, without exception; we love the ones who do something to DESERVE our love – God in His MERCY loves the undeserving, the ugly, the unlovely; we love those who return our love – God, in His Mercy, loves with no hope of any other reward or return, but that of the sheer JOY of filling a need and of watching a life completed.

Interlude One:
Living On Charity, by Dorrel Healey[1]

YES, I AM indeed living on charity – I see it now. I'm living on God's charity, His pure Mercy – and I am not ashamed to let the WORLD know it. On the contrary, I WANT the world to know it. I want them to know and appreciate the RICHES of His MERCY. "The same Lord over ALL, is RICH unto ALL that call upon Him" (Romans 10:12). What must they call? "Jesus, have MERCY on ME." What will they get? MERCY – FILLING the need, whatever it might be. If the need is for salvation, they will get salvation when they call that way (Romans 10:13). If they need healing, that is the MERCY they will get. If they need to be taken out of a "strait place," He will do it for them when they call. When they call, He hears and answers with the charity or mercy that will make the life complete and restore the peace.

The ones who have no need, or self-righteously do not KNOW they have a need, are the ones who do not "LOWER their dignity" to call on God, and they are the ones who get nothing – and then HAVE NOTHING TO GIVE to someone else in need. I see it all now. So, I am happy to be just a little know-nothing, undeserving lamb fed by the Good Shepherd. Yes, I repeat it, so all can understand, that I have no more struggle saying it, "I AM LIVING ON CHARITY."

"Oh, that men would praise the Lord for His GOODNESS and for His wonderful works to the children of men." (Psalm 107:8)

CHAPTER ELEVEN

THE RESURGENT WORK
1949 – 1996

Although I have said little about those who responded to Rex Andrews' ministry in a positive way, I must state clearly that MANY needy souls drew comfort, help, and life-changing influences from his messages. In fact, in a few years' time, many newcomers to the Faith Home meetings chose to make it their church home. There is nothing like NEED to make the word MERCY come alive!

Gradually a good-sized congregation formed again and the partially divided front rooms of the Meeting House had to be remodeled to accommodate the influx of regular members, especially on Sunday mornings. The entire south and west sides of the old house had a make-over, so that the meeting space became a small chapel seating about 120 people. The Monday Night Service became "visitors' night," as scores of pastors and missionaries wanted to participate in the *Showers of Blessing* that had returned to the Faith Homes. Young people who had heard Rex Andrews speak applied to become trainees to prepare themselves for full-time ministry.

We might describe the resurgence as *A Sparkle of Divine Life and Hope*. "God is making Jesus available to anyone who NEEDS Him and will BELIEVE that He will give Himself FREELY to you," was a constant theme. The phrase "fulfilling mercies" lifted the sense of failure that had hung over the Work. Rex Andrews embodied his message, for there was a love-fire in his words, in his voice, in his face, that was contagious. "If the Lord has restored HIM, of all people, then there is hope for me!" It seemed like the words of Isaiah soaked into every heart:

> *...to comfort all that mourn, to appoint unto them that mourn in Zion, to give them beauty for ashes, the oil of joy for mourning, the garment of praise for the spirit of heaviness... For as the earth bringeth forth her bud, and as the garden causeth the things that are sown in it*

to spring forth, so the Lord GOD will cause righteousness and praise to spring forth before all the nations. (Isaiah 61:2-3, 11)

By the time my wife and I came to live in the Homes in early 1967, this resurgence had established itself in a wonderful way. We really felt the Presence of Jesus, not only in the meetings, but even in each of the three homes. "This place is filled with peace," I remarked to my wife after spending one night at the Guest House. "These people are not in confusion; they know what they are doing; there's a taste of Heaven here."

This is a good place to ask the question, "What was it like to live in the Faith Homes after the Lord resurrected the Work?"

My answer to this question frames itself around the basic elements of the life as my wife and I knew it personally for nearly three decades. Other residents might describe it differently if they had the opportunity. From 1949, until mid-1963 (when Rex and Beulah Andrews took up the final period of their residence in the Homes), the Work was supervised primarily by Rev. Earle Pottinger, Miss Hilda Nilsson, Mrs. Marie Robinson, Miss Ruth Jackson, and Miss Ruth Brooks. The trainees of those years would remember life in their particular Home, under the House-parents or Housemother at the 2736 Eschol Home, for example, or the 2820 Meeting House, or the Home at 3002 Enoch Avenue. Please remember, as well, that so much happened every day that a complete chronicle of those years is necessarily impossible to create.

Yet you, as a reader, deserve an account that brings you into the atmosphere that prevailed during those resurgent years. Many times I have referred to it as "heaven on earth." When we all lived in Jesus' Presence, and practiced what we heard about "doing Mercy to others," we tasted the life of Eternity, and it was WONDERFUL.

We will follow a simple outline, looking first at Meetings and Classes, then the Faith Home Schedule, and lastly, Frequently Asked Questions. In the interest of balance, we will include at the end a short summary of "the good and the bad," and "the easy and the difficult."

Meetings and Classes

From the beginning of our stay, the meetings stood out to us more than anything else about the Homes. All the meetings were held in the largest of the three Homes, at 2820 Eschol Avenue, where the downstairs had been re-modeled into a chapel-like room. There were no pews, just chairs arranged in rows. The larger part of the L-shaped room had a center aisle from front to back, while the shorter leg of the "L" held four rows of chairs arranged against the wall on one side with access to an aisle on the other side. The "platform ministers" (as they were usually called), sat in the corner where the two legs of the "L" met. Approximately 125 people could fit comfortably into the meeting space.

The meetings were "Spirit-led," but in such a simple way that it could easily be overlooked that God was directing them. They could be termed "Quaker-style" meetings because, as was mentioned before, anyone was free to participate and there was no "order of service." The meeting might begin with a sermon, or a prayer, or a hymn, or simply with a testimony. Anyone was free to ask for a particular hymn for the whole congregation to sing. Usually there were two or more major "talks" during the service, plus several "testimonies." The ministers were in charge, but order was maintained most of the time simply by their "faith for the meeting," which meant they would pray inwardly for God to maintain the smoothly flowing direction of the service.

Everyone was encouraged to "look to the Lord for His leading" as to what they might share, either by testimony, or by reading a passage of Scripture, or by praying aloud a general prayer. It was not uncommon for someone to rise from his seat and lay hands on another person who needed personal encouragement or prayer. The meetings were "Pentecostal," that is, the "gifts of the Spirit" (as described in I Corinthians 12) were frequently in evidence, all of them, but in an unobtrusive way.

The meeting room resounded with audible praise throughout the services, usually spontaneous praise arising from hearts that had been touched by the truth of a song just sung, or by a message just preached. To describe those times of praise as "beautiful" hardly does justice to the way it was. Much of the praise was "singing" praise, which, when everyone present put their hearts into it, was like the incense offered by fire to the Lord in the ancient Temple in Jerusalem each morning and evening. Jesus was PRESENT, and to refuse to acknowledge His Presence by withholding audible praise was unthinkable. Many times the organist (Ruth Brooks for most of those years) would play the organ "in the Spirit," and I repeat what I said earlier, that no one who heard her play like that could gainsay the unusual and powerful musical expressions that would come through her by that means. Depending on the "theme of the meeting," one could hear armies marching in victory, or souls longing after God, or the worship by angels in heaven, for example. Occasionally the anointing would fall on someone to "dance in the Spirit," often during the times of praise.

Something wonderful happens when people enter into praise like that. It is *a simplicity* which is hard to describe adequately. The powers of darkness become uncomfortable when people truly worship God out of a heart overflowing with gratitude to God for His mercy, when they forget their surroundings and with a loud voice simply praise Jesus. The devil cannot remain when God "inhabits the praises of His people" (Psalm 22:3).

On some occasions the congregation would stand with hearts and hands and voices given over to adoring our King for thirty or forty minutes. I recall one occasion when the praise – entirely unforced – lasted an hour. Jesus was personally present, and oh, so WONDER-FULL and worthy to be PRAISED.

The worship was "inward," not "outward." We were "*lost in wonder, love, and praise,*" as Charles Wesley wrote in his grand hymn, *Love Divine, All Loves Excelling*. It was an acceptable thing to God, because it came from broken but grateful hearts. It was kept pure by the prayer lives of the ministers and by their willingness to be living sacrifices to God.

To summarize a bit: The meetings were almost deceptively simple. It is not so easy to hold open public meetings four times a week, year after year, without disorder and confusion, especially when most meetings were attended by visitors from various types of ministries. As I look back, I consider it a miracle how smoothly things went. As you might expect in an "open" meeting, occasionally things happened that were "out of order," but the ministers always knew how to handle such occurrences. Most of the time such things affected the meetings but slightly, as though a small pebble had been dropped into a large pond, creating a few ripples that soon disappeared. If the ministers sensed the enemy was trying to take over, the offending person would be firmly but kindly confronted and silenced by one of the Faith Home leaders, and we learned much about discernment and discipline by their example.

Sometimes the disruptions were almost humorous!

One Sunday morning, about midway through the service, a newcomer to the services rose to speak. He had purchased the house next door to the Faith Homes, and this was his new church home. He was an adherent of "British Israelism," as taught by the late Herbert W. Armstrong, who believed that all the promises to natural Israel in the Old Testament referred to the United States and England. The doctrine was built on some half-truths about "the ten lost tribes of Israel." Anyway, this man arose from his seat near the back and in a super-spiritual tone of voice said, "Folks, do you know what the middle three letters of the word 'Jerusalem' are?" He paused for effect, then intoned, "U...S...A." I suppose he felt we should all capitulate to this astounding revelation and adopt his doctrine immediately, as though every time the city of Jerusalem is mentioned in the Bible it is a prophetic code-word for the United States of America!

His statement did slow the meeting down a bit, but some brave saints began praising the Lord out loud and gradually the meeting continued in the direction the Lord intended. For the record, Rex Andrews confronted the man privately in hopes of straightening him out, but he passed away some months later without changing his mind, although he did agree to keep quiet in the meetings.

Some disruptions to the meeting were not humorous at all.

One Sunday morning, near the close, a gentleman came to the front to address the congregation. He was well-known to everyone, having been associated with the Homes since his youth. He began to rebuke us in strong terms, and I remember so well one of the expressions he used. "You're all a bunch of reprobates!" he practically yelled into the microphone.

At that point Miss Brooks, who was seated at the organ, said, "You should say, '*We* are all a bunch of reprobates' and include yourself." He turned to look at her, then turned back to the audience and said again, "You're all a bunch of reprobates!"

At that moment Mr. Andrews, listening in his room (partially immobilized, but far from incapacitated by a stroke he had suffered), loudly rang the bell he used when he needed something. "Usher!" he called out from his room above the chapel. The usher ran up the stairs. "Open my door." Then in the most authoritative voice I've ever heard, he shouted so loudly the entire congregation could hear him without the benefit of amplification.

"STOP IT! SIT DOWN!"

The offending speaker tried to mumble a few words more, but simply couldn't get going again and retreated to his seat. After some days he received a letter, a portion of which I quote:

> *...You are forbidden to get up and speak at the end of a meeting. A few Sundays ago, you got up at 10 minutes to 12 – when the service was about to be changed to "prayer requests." You took over, and read and talked FOR THIRTY MINUTES. You held the meeting till 20 minutes after 12, on a Sunday morning – 30 minutes...You are NOT a minister here.*
>
> *You have, for many years, spoken AGAINST This Work in different places. Now, you need to prove your repentance by your words and works. We believe that you mean what you have said, with tears of repentance. God bless you. But that does not mean that you are suddenly being a Big I AM THE ONE. Not at all. You are required to "Be under authority" and in "Obedience."*
>
> *Today, Sunday, December 29, you got up at 10 minutes to 12 again, and put on one of your SHOWS, and I had to ring for an usher to tell you to stop it and sit down. We want no more of such nonsense in these meetings, which are devoted to the Word, and love, and worship of Jesus. So, you are forbidden to speak into the end of any meeting.*
>
> *If you have a real testimony of love for Jesus, you can have 3 or 4 minutes somewhere in a night meeting, but NOT on Sunday morning...*
>
> *I PRAY for you; and ask God to bless you, and give you light.*
>
> *In the Unfading Love of Jesus,*
>
> *(Bro. Rex)*

Thankfully, such disorder didn't happen very often, but when it did, swift and decisive action on the part of the leaders ended the confusion that such behavior had injected into the services.

Often the protracted seasons of praise were followed by another remarkable feature of the meetings, which was SILENCE. Many have testified to the things God did for them during those *silent times*. "Be still and KNOW THAT I AM GOD!" (Psalm 46:10 emphasis added). Let me insert here my notes from things said by Rex Andrews at various times about the silences in the meetings.

Special Point – Silence in the Meetings

It is apparent that we are in the time of a moving of God when we need to understand the silences that occur sometimes in our meetings. I am referring directly to last night's meeting.

That silence is the power of God.

So many times people get tremendously blessed in a glory meeting, and then dissipate what God has done by going back to the natural, talking, laughing, jollying around – when God's purpose is for you to go home quietly, shut the door behind you, and wait a little on God so He can keep you in that; and you would wake up in the morning in the power of God.

Last night the silence didn't last quite long enough. That silence is the POWER OF GOD.

In the tent-meetings the Vessels had before the Homes were organized, they frequently had such quiet times, often lasting as much as a half-hour. Mrs. Judd, (just converted), complained about it, as if they (the Vessels) had nothing to say. MWR said, "That quiet time is just about the greatest thing we have."

Last night it lasted about a minute or so before somebody felt they had to make a noise, start a song, say, "Amen," or so. But the world is trapped in this matter of ACTIVITY.

That silence that settled down over the meeting last night was part of The Power Work.

If we didn't have the 8-10 Period [a daily time set aside for personal devotions], *and the Friday night tarrying meeting, I could feel you don't understand this. But you have those times, and so you ought to be at home in such quietness.*

A Rule of Action: If and when such a quiet time comes, you leave it to the ministers to decide when it should be broken. That will develop in you the ability to hold your peace, keep your mouth shut. You'll need this in your relationship to the world.

Nobody can produce such a silence but God. It is part of the Power Work. That Power goes right down into your body.

Leave it up to the ministers to break that silence. They are trained in the unity of the Spirit, and that's where the Presence of Jesus is in This Work.

When it came last night, that Power of God came down through my body right to my toes, and it was so delicious and wonderful, and so simple. At such a time you have a power to pray that you don't normally have.

Psalm 46:10 and context describes this silence. This is a most importantly tremendous thing.

I will discuss this matter of silence more publicly.

The Power of God in that silence is even greater than the Power of God manifested in the time of the meeting preceding that, the praise and the glory and the ecstasy.

Again, from notes taken in 1968, this time by Ruth Lade [Schleicher]:

One of the remarkable things about Sunday night's meeting was the sustained silence after the great praise. God wants us to learn when God silences us... That silence in the meeting, when it comes, is the presence of the Lord. There is a stillness of God that takes the place of everything else. We want to recognize that when that silence comes, it is God. Read Psalm 46. Our world is facing an earth-shaking, and the heavens as well. The sea will roar in that shaking – a great Light is coming. The wise will understand. We are teaching how to be wise. We need to know the refuge of God. That silence is a refuge.

The Monday Night Meeting was "visitors' night" because so many missionaries, pastors, and other workers who had responsibilities on Sunday could fit the Monday night meeting at the Faith Homes into their schedules. For the trainees, it was inspiring and educational to hear speakers from differing denominations and backgrounds share their experiences in the work of the Lord. If you were a visiting missionary, for example, you were expected to sit in the front row facing the "platform." (That was about the only "honor" allowed in the Faith Homes!) The "platform ministers," usually four or more, always sat facing the congregation, but there was no raised platform; everyone sat on the same level. The Faith Home leaders were deeply interested in the work of the Lord around the world. "Please come and take your liberty, Bro. So-and-so," Miss Brooks might prompt by way of encouragement.

We were required to keep notes of all the meetings during the initial two years of our training, so I have a notebook full of talks that various people gave, and even now the memories come flooding back as I read them. God sent us some of the finest workers in His Vineyard to inspire us. I honor them by this brief recollection.

The next public meeting was the Wednesday Morning Missionary Prayer, held from 8 a.m. to 12 noon. The first two hours always began with a plea for God to "Send forth laborers into the harvest field," as Jesus commanded us to do, but most of the time was spent praying by name for a long list of missionaries who had either been sent out by the Faith Homes, or who had visited and asked for prayer support. It was an introduction to selfless intercession, learning that "men ought always to pray, and not to faint." If a missionary asked for prayer, he was sure to get it. Each missionary was mentioned by name and prayed for. After several years, as one and another took furloughs in the States, we were able to associate names with faces. Their work took on special significance to us, for it is almost impossible to pray by name for people and not be interested in them!

At 10 a.m. we had a short break (10 minutes) for water, tea, *etc*. The prayers resumed with a short portion of Scripture, perhaps a chorus, followed by intercession for the work of the Lord in general. The so-called "Kingdom Prayers" were the highlight of the second two hours. Under the direction of the prayer leader (chosen from the Faith Home congregation), every week the following prayers were lifted up to God:*

Pour out Your Spirit on all flesh, according to Joel 2:28ff.
Thy Kingdom come! Thy Will be done on earth, as it is in heaven!
Let the Word of God arise!
Unveil the Cross!
Let Your peace come to Jerusalem.
Complete the Body of Christ.

This type of praying demanded spiritual discipline beyond anything most of us had ever known prior to coming to the Faith Homes. Week after week, month after month, year after year – with very few cancellations – we interceded. Truly God alone knows how far-reaching the answers were!

On Wednesday nights, Rex Andrews or Ruth Brooks taught a Bible Class open for anyone to attend. Various topics and/or books of the Bible were covered, as well as *What the Bible Teaches about Mercy*, or *Meditations in the Revelation*. After a hymn or special song, the study began and lasted

---
* These prayers are described in detail in Chapter 18, *Kingdom Praying*.

for one hour. I do not remember a time when the teachers failed to observe that one-hour limitation. The studies were rich and deeply rewarding.

On Thursday nights there was another open meeting, commonly called "Trainee Night." Each student/trainee delivered his prepared sermon, or "talk," during the Thursday night service. Frequency depended on the number of trainees enrolled in the Homes.

That service was precious because it was so *simple*. Few visitors attended on Thursday nights. The trainees "preached" in rotation as part of their training. We were all nervous for each other. We had to face the people and give meaningful talks in a meeting room where more than 100,000 talks had been given since 1910! It was intimidating! What could a trainee say that was new?

But the Lord would touch people, and as I mentioned previously, one trainee was baptized in the Spirit while he was speaking. We did our best. We knew Mr. Andrews was listening along with the other ministers; we were under scrutiny for every word we said (though we were seldom confronted; we received much mercy). To this day I remember my first "trainee talk" and the sense of being upheld by Jesus Himself.

The Thursday night meetings were precious because they tended to be "inward" services. That means, everyone was "turned toward the Lord" inside, as opposed to an "outward" meeting where the focus is on people, the program, and what is taking place. In the Faith Homes, the Lord wanted inward meetings where He would be the CENTER and everyone would be concentrating on Him. "Turned to the Lord inside" – that is what inward means. You can praise the Lord with all your might *audibly* and still be inward.

You can *dance* and be inward. Occasionally Miss Brooks danced in the Spirit like a sylph, so sweetly and beautifully, as though she were a long-stemmed flower bending gracefully in the wind. *Dancing in the Spirit* took place in the small open area in the front of the room, between the congregation and the ministers. But when people danced in the Spirit, you could only glance at them; you did not want to look at them out of curiosity. You knew they were worshiping the Lord and their worship touched you. "Dancing in the Spirit is God's harmony in the body," we were taught. If you were the one dancing, your aim was to fit in with what the Holy Ghost was doing in the meeting.

We learned so much on Thursdays nights.

Friday night was prayer meeting night, a tarrying service that lasted two hours. We were taught to wait on the Lord to be filled and refilled with the Holy Spirit. "Waiting on the Lord" meant ministry to Him. The term was used frequently by old-time Pentecostals to describe what the disciples were doing in the Upper Room prior to Pentecost – "tarry in Jerusalem until..." (Luke 24:49). It simply means sitting or kneeling in the presence of God, quietly worshiping Him, rehearsing His promises, and expecting Him to speak into one's soul.

When the situation demanded it, some of the Friday Night Prayer Service was given over to prayer for specific needs. For example, beginning six months prior to a national election, half the meeting would be spent in intercession for God's choice for President. Here is an excerpt from a "Faith Home Bulletin" on the subject:

> And what result, particularly, should we look for and aim at? WHOM should we seek to be elected? What choice do we desire? To those who have surrendered, and resigned, their lives and their wills to God, there is but one choice – GOD'S CHOICE. It is the Pathway of Peace-of-Heart to have no choice but God's choice. The true PRAY-ER wants that, seeks that, and finds faith-rest, in GOD'S CHOICE – always. Your prayer counts infinitely more than your vote.[1]

Before national elections, we spent an hour every Friday night praying in words like these: "God, get Your will done, put Your man in the office; we've got to have Your will, we've got to have Your choice." For me it was tough praying; I had to battle it through when I didn't feel anything. But we did it, and we knew God was hearing.

Saturday night was free, in preparation for Sunday.

The schedule on Sunday started with Sunday School at 9:15 a.m. for all age groups. Trainees taught many of the classes. In 1967 when we arrived at the Homes, Sunday School attendance was nearly 100 and the congregation numbered 125 or so. Our first Sunday School teacher was Mrs. Marie Robinson, and her subject was *The Gospel of John*.[†] She came fully prepared and we learned much from this woman whose training came from the Lord, not man.

The Sunday Morning Service was the main meeting of the week. Until she waned in the late 1970s, Miss Ruth Brooks was the usual Sunday morning

---

[†] Mrs. Marie (Wegman) Robinson was not related to Martha Wing Robinson, but they did share the same initials, MWR.

preacher. (The Lord always expected a substantial full-length message on Sunday morning.) She was on fire. Many a time I felt like crawling under my chair as she spoke, convicted by my lack of mercy for others. Her words made us feel absolutely miserable on account of our selfishness.

"You aren't willing to lay your life down for someone you don't like," she would thunder, "and you pick on them in your heart. You look at their nature and you don't like their personality, so you won't do mercy to them," *etc.* Her words cut us to the heart, and we knew we had to repent.

"How do you expect the blessing of God on *your* life when you don't want it on someone else's? 'Oh,' you say, 'They annoy me.' What kind of a worm are you that you would think that way? And why should God bless you when you won't let Him bless somebody else?" So often we felt shredded by the end of her sermon.

When she was anointed like that, she was totally *un*-self-conscious. In the Faith Homes that lack of self-consciousness was called "abandonment." Each speaker was encouraged to abandon himself to the Holy Spirit. That meant that any speaker whom God was using did NOT always sound the same. Most of us preachers sound the same all the time, and then we have a reputation based on the way we sound. But Miss Brooks could be pleading and sweet and broken-with-weeping in one meeting, and in the next meeting she was John the Baptist in female form: "REPENT!"

And yet, it was always balanced. I remember one sermon where she said, in the course of her preaching, "People make me so angry, that I pray the 'mercy prayer' this way: 'Lord, you flood that bird with fulfilling mercies.'" At the house-meeting that month, Rex Andrews referred to her words and admonished Miss Brooks publicly! "That's the last time anyone will use language like that in their mercy prayer. If you have to say, 'Flood that bird with fulfilling mercies,' you're not in the spirit of mercy." And it was Miss Brooks who had said it! But she took the rebuke sweetly and never said it again.

This illustrates a unique arrangement between the individual ministers of the Homes. They were all under a voluntary covenant that every word they spoke in public could be scrutinized by their fellow ministers for false statements or for failure to express things properly. Every one of us was under that discipline. No matter if the emotion of the moment got into your preaching and you said things in the heat of your message that were a little "too much"! The others could come to you afterwards and say, "Brother, what you said wasn't right."

Any one of us is quite prone to swing off into the flesh, though we may be ever so spiritual in our own eyes! We're like Peter, credited with divine revelation one moment, and rebuked the next: "Get thee behind me, Satan! You savor the things of men, not the things of God!" (Matthew 16:23). Though Peter had spoken well in the first instance, the Lord didn't let his wrong words go unreproved. And that's the way it was in the Faith Homes. You could be blessed and used by the Spirit in one meeting, but the next time you could be out of order and require correction.

But it was wonderful anyway, because there was no animosity in that correction. In lowliness and mercy each minister upheld the other without condemnation. There were no emulations, no desires to get ahead of the other one. If you were the one speaking, you felt the prayers of the ministers sitting behind you. You might be saying things that could make them wince – it is all too easy to "paint yourself pretty" when you are the one preaching! – but you knew they were asking the Lord to help you and to anoint you.

When you are "The Pastor" leading a congregation by yourself and living in your own home, it isn't always the best arrangement. It's a blessing to live with others who see you every day in the ordinary situations of life. When you live in a "glass house," your life is an open book. It will keep you on your toes spiritually! I used to say, only partly in jest, that you couldn't have a decent argument with your wife in the Faith Homes, because someone would hear you. Besides that, if you'd had a little spat, you still had to appear at the breakfast table the next morning and face the people who heard you arguing!

During the Sunday Night Service, Rex Andrews customarily gave the main message. He had a good habit which I admired. He said, "I will speak only for one hour." And he kept his word, almost to the minute. No matter how absorbed he was in his message, he never went "overtime."

But in that one hour, as I've said often, *time stood still* and we were in eternity. That's just the way it was when he spoke: *timeless*. There was something about his words and the wisdom with which he spoke, if you were listening carefully, that made you realize you were hearing Jesus speak. I'm not saying he spoke "the word of the Lord," as Mrs. Robinson did. But he had a tremendous ability to communicate God's truth with few extra words.

Because of that fact, you would think that people came to hear him by the hundreds, but they didn't. Many people angrily resented his ministry and stopped coming. In fact, attendance on Sunday nights gradually diminished. That's amazing, when I think of it now. And some day in the judgment, people are going to have to face the fact that they heard the truth but did not want it, choosing instead to protect their flesh. I don't know how people will face their actions when they see them in judgment-light.

I've described the *public schedule* of meetings, but there were monthly meetings restricted to the residents of the Homes, referred to as *House-meetings*. They were similar to a family conference where any member might need reminders and occasional discipline. Here is a typical sample, taken from my own notes in March of 1972, condensing remarks from three speakers:

> *Pull up the window shades in your room during the day, and turn off your lights (to save electricity).*
>
> *Be careful to be neat. It is not worldly to be neat; in fact, it's worldly today to be slovenly. Dress neatly, especially when you go to minister at the nursing home or the Youth Home (detention facility for youth).*
>
> *Watch your manners – when eating, serving, acting.*
>
> *Be friendly to the outside young people (part of the congregation). They need your encouragement and interest. There may be a longing in their heart for your attention.*
>
> *Keep all matches in covered jars. Same for oily rags and paint rags. Don't let them lie in wastebaskets where they are spontaneously combustible.*
>
> *Unplug the iron before you leave the room; don't leave it up on end on the ironing board (where someone might accidently knock it off).*
>
> *Do not turn water on full force when rinsing dishes.*
>
> *Cooks must wear hairnets. Waitresses must wear tea-aprons.*
>
> *Chipped dishes must be replaced and paid for.*

Rex Andrews concluded that House-meeting with a short talk of his own:

> *What have you said INSIDE to these three remarkable talks? Are you just going to let them slip by and NOT OBEY? If you do, later you will say, "WHY, O Lord Jesus, WHY did I not obey?"*

You should say, "Lord Jesus, I will obey those things that were said."

The point is not whether you WANT to wear a hairnet, or an apron. The point is, someday you will be an example somewhere, facing a group of people whom you are asking to do what you say. And what you will be able to do then, will be affected by what you say to Jesus now. In fact, your whole relationship to the Lord Jesus then will be affected by what you say to Him now.

"Whosoever is faithful in the least will be faithful in much; and whosoever is unfaithful in the least will be unfaithful in that which is greatest."

Anarchy is rising in the world tremendously. Rebellion is in the very air you breathe.

As far as the world of mammon is concerned, we're headed right into a dictatorship, where you will be KILLED IMMEDIATELY if you don't obey them – no jury, either. Why, China alone has been guilty of killing 50 or 60 million people who wouldn't do what the Communistic dictators said to do!

The eye of God's knowledge is perceiving your heart. In the name of Jesus, "What did you do in your heart when you heard these three excellent talks?" Did you say, quietly and humbly, like a little child, "Lord Jesus, I will obey"?

During one House-meeting we were admonished at length on how to close a door. "You are not ready to be a missionary anywhere in the world until you know how to close a door," we were told. "In your hurry to get where you are going, you thoughtlessly slam the door behind you – WHAM! It is because you are so unmerciful that you do that, not realizing someone else is hearing that door close! And you don't have the grace to turn around, put your hand on the handle, and close it properly and reverently."

Such talks are etched into my memory. I can't forget them. But it was the Lord getting at something in us. Most of us were monsters of incivility. We had to be taught to observe etiquette, politeness, courtesy, and respect for one another, at a time when those things were disappearing from the youth culture of the '60s and early '70s. Many of today's young people still carry that "hippie mentality" with them and they don't even know it. So easy it is to imbibe unconsciously the spirit of our generation!

Anyway, those were the things that were dealt with in the monthly house-meetings. We might seem spiritual in the regular services – "These trainees are so consecrated," people would say – but we were all in need of correction. We were, after all, trainees.

Allow me a word of personal testimony. I was raised in a basically Christian home. My dad was not a believer, but my mother more than made up for that. I have attended church all my life. My very first memory is of kneeling at an altar, watching the feet of the pastor as he paced the platform during the Sunday night altar service. I've been in thousands of meetings. I went to Bible School, then to Brooklyn Teen Challenge. At age 24, when I landed in the Faith Homes, I became a student, a trainee, for six and a half years. And even at that, it was daring of the Lord to put me into the ministry at age thirty. It takes years for God to wear down our flesh so that we are somewhat yielded to the Spirit of Grace.

In one of our earliest house-meetings, I heard the following words: "It takes two years for most of you to realize what's going on here, and five years to make a fundamental change in your nature." Inside I was thinking, "I'll be 90 before I'm ready for ministry!" But the statement was absolutely true.

So we had monthly house-meetings and we got scolded and "paddled" and corrected in those house-meetings by kind, loving ministers. We knew they loved us and were laying down their lives for us; that is why we could take it. We were making the lives of the ministers difficult, just by virtue our very natures. Yet they would tirelessly pray for us, work with us, smile at us, correct us.

Once in a while, maybe twice a year, we'd be sitting in a house-meeting when Rex Andrews would start to whimper – he had the most unusual way of crying – and he would say through his tears, "Well, saints, it's so nice that you let me talk to you. You're the nicest group of young people we've ever had here. You're all so consecrated; you're doing so well." And I would cry too, but inside I wished he would go back to correcting us. We preferred the whipping. "How could you be so kind?" we were thinking inside. "You know what we're like." But he loved us, individually and collectively. He had no personal favorites, no respect of persons that I ever saw. I don't mean he was perfect; I know of instances where the other ministers confronted him.‡ But he did what God had told him to do:

---

‡ I don't say that lightly. I have in my files a series of notes he wrote in response to a corrective word from the other ministers. The final note reads, "I AM WRONG... THANK YOU for helping me to see it."

"Do the mercy to others, all others, that I have done to you. That is all I will ever ask of you, in time or eternity." He did that for us. I know it is so.

The Classes

Weekly classes were held only for the trainees, most often taught by Miss Brooks, but sometimes by Mr. Andrews.

The classes with Rex Andrews showed us our need to be real. We had to recite Scripture in every class. "And what does this verse mean, Brother Douglas?" Mr. Andrews would ask. He could tell where we were spiritually by the quality in our voices. "I don't even have to see you. All I have to do is hear you testify and I know where you are by your voice." He could tell if we were honest in our testimonies, or "faking" it, merely by the quality of our voices. He had been through the mill himself, of course. He knew what it was to be obedient and he knew what it was to disobey, but after the Lord restored him, he had no use for hypocrisy. "What do I care what men think? I've already lost my reputation. I don't care what men say and I haven't the slightest interest in what they think of me. All I want is to do the Lord's will."

Because there were no semesters to observe, all material was covered thoroughly. For example, when we arrived in 1967, Miss Brooks was teaching a class on "Patience." All students were required to study every reference in the Bible on patience. Every reference! Later we studied every verse in the Bible on "Judgment," all 960 of them. We didn't have computers in those days to help us search out those references in Hebrew and Greek. "Find them in Strong's Concordance, use his numbering system to track down the references in the original languages, then type them all out. When you finish you will begin to grasp a little of the Biblical teaching on 'judgment.'" That was our assignment from Miss Brooks.

Then we went through all the scriptures on "faith," followed by classes on "Divine Healing," the Book of Jeremiah, and many other subjects. Miss Brooks taught and preached on the Major and Minor Prophets like no one I've ever heard.

In Mr. Andrews' class we studied Galatians verse by verse, then Peter's First Epistle the same way. That was a real Bible School in my estimation, taught spiritually, without omitting any needed "scholarly" insights. Rex Andrews knew Greek and Hebrew thoroughly, though he never made much of it. I've even seen the notes of correction he entered into his personal copy of Gesenius' *Hebrew Lexicon.*

"Do you understand what this verse is telling you? Are you incorporating what it says into your daily life?" That was the thrust of all the meetings and all the classes.

What we did with our time when we weren't in meetings and classes is the subject of the next section.

The Faith Home Schedule

The Faith Homes operated on a schedule that seemed more certain than the sun rising each morning. Prayer times, meals, work duties, meetings – all at certain times – became part of one's life to such an extent that even now, forty years later, I think of my daily schedule in those time-terms!

For example, the daily prayer hours, from 8:00–10:00 each morning except Wednesdays and Sundays, were labeled "The Eight-to-Ten Period." Instituted in 1948, this time alone with God became the backbone of the schedule. It was a modification of the "Morning Prayers" conducted by the presiding minister in each Home, where residents gathered round the table after breakfast for reading of the Word, and for prayers. It became necessary to change the pattern because the Morning Prayers had become somewhat of a ritual, and residents tended to favor one minister over another. The Eight-to-Ten Period also commenced after breakfast, but each resident was required to seek the Lord alone, dividing his time between the Word of God and prayer. No magazines, no helps, no Christian literature were allowed during that time.

For almost forty years the residents of the Homes observed that quiet time faithfully, with much blessing attending. As I look back now, I can see the immense strength that came into my life because of The Eight-to-Ten Period. We were given a basic prayer in three parts that became the backbone of our prayer life. The wording was very simple.

Father, please make me Poor in Spirit. Fill and possess me with the Holy Spirit, and make me like Jesus.

The ministers set the example, each of them spending four hours per day in the Word and Prayer, and Rex Andrews six hours a day. How can one repay the debt to them, except to carry on as they did?

Continuing with the daily schedule: The women took turns baking all the bread, preparing and serving all the meals, learning in the process how to cook efficiently for substantial numbers of people. In all of the Homes, the noon meal was always taken together. In the Guest House, breakfast and supper were also eaten at a common table, in the interest of serving the guests with godly hospitality.

The men of each home washed the dishes and cleaned the kitchens after the meals. They also performed the heavy vacuuming and routine dusting in each home. One trainee said, "The Faith Homes is the only place I know of where they practice 'preventive dusting.' I never see any dust on my cloth!" Spring and Fall cleaning kept everything in tiptop condition.

Rex Andrews would say, "Do you know why we do that? It is because some missionary will come to visit us, God bless him or her, and when you aren't watching them, they'll go over to the window sill and run their finger along it, and say, 'Aha, they don't dust like they should.' Therefore you dust for their sakes, so that when they put their finger on the window sill, they don't find any dust."

(It takes no effort to remember such things; he had a way of saying things that just stuck with a person.)

In the summer months there were vegetables to freeze and fruits to preserve, and we all spent countless hours preparing corn, beans, strawberries, blueberries, apples, peaches, squash, and tomatoes. Most of those items we picked ourselves at farms and orchards far and near.

The men also had work detail, both morning and afternoon, on days when classes were not held. That's where we learned to do routine maintenance, besides carpentry, plumbing, and electrical work. There were thirty-three bedrooms and eleven bathrooms to maintain! We learned lawn-care in the summers, and removed snow in the winters from the long driveways and sidewalks, as well as from the large parking lot behind the Meeting House.

That was the schedule. There was a value in it, because it taught discipline. Discipline is always good, and doubly so when it is administered by people who themselves have been disciplined. The hardest thing is to be under someone who isn't disciplined.

We learned Daily Grace, as it was called. If you didn't learn to be nice to the people around you, life in the Faith Homes could become unbearable; people's personalities and idiosyncrasies grated on you. It was vital to learn to be gracious in the daily life. In fact, the subject of Daily Grace formed a background for everything we did together.

The Faith Home schedule also taught us the value of time. "The most precious commodity you have is time," we were told. "You better learn now to make the best use of it. Redeem it; buy it back."

Many practical things we learned were expressed in a series of seven talks entitled, *What Are You Here For?* They are included in a later chapter (Chapter 19), but for the record, here are the subjects of those seven talks:

1. To Dwell in God's Presence
2. To Redeem the Time
3. To Live and Walk in the Spirit
4. To Learn Daily Grace
5. To Learn The Faith Life
6. To Bear the Cross
7. To Be an Offering unto God

Anyone wanting to "learn of Me," as Jesus invited, finds himself involved sooner or later in each of these topics.

Frequently Asked Questions

What were the people in the Faith Homes like?

In one word, diverse. People from widely differing educational and cultural backgrounds were thrown together and expected to be one family in Christ. No one kept a record of who they were; their number is known only to God. We do know in the early part of the Twentieth Century more than 30,000 people came to visit the Homes or to live in them. Probably the grand total exceeds 50,000. In my view, many whom I knew will surely be reckoned as precious jewels in God's sight.

How were the Homes organized?

The ruling body was called the Faith Home Council. It adhered to the principle of plural leadership. For many years Ruth Brooks was the chairman of the Faith Home Council, but that simply meant she chaired the discussion and led the Council prayer meetings. It was understood that decisions had to be unanimous or they would not be implemented. The faith of each one was, "God is God; He doesn't have two wills." If someone disagreed with the majority, the Council would pray until that person changed his mind, or until the entire group came to see that the minority opinion was the right one. Prayer, followed by discussion, brought agreement. The pattern was Acts 6 and Acts 15.

It worked beautifully for very many years and lent enormous strength to the Work. The degree to which the Presence of the Lord Jesus was manifested in the Homes depended greatly on the unity of the Spirit among the Council members. Private reservations about decisions made were not allowed; disagreements must be stated, and why. "An honest and a true heart" became the basis of respect for each other. It was a powerful way to lead.

The Faith Home Council was self-perpetuating, meaning vacancies (by death or otherwise) were filled by appointment from the remaining members. Not everyone in the Council was a "platform minister" who sat in front and led the meetings. Some were house-parents, administering supervision in each home, or perhaps the wife of one of the platform ministers. Some functioned as Treasurer, or Secretary, or Missions Secretary. Much prayer went into such appointments until there was a strong united sense, "This is God's choice." That is how I was brought into the Council.

Who oversaw the day-to-day schedule?

Between the house-parents and the trainees were the *house-keepers,* the "middle people" between the upper and nether millstones, it seemed. Above them were the House-parents, generally members of the Council; below them were the trainees, the ministers-in-the-making. Mr. Andrews had great compassion for the housekeepers. "It's the most difficult position in the Homes," we were told. They endured the rough edges of the trainees, while carrying out the wishes of the House-parents. Yet the position was essential to keep things running smoothly.

When did a trainee graduate?

There were two levels of trainees – juniors (in training for two years or less) and seniors (more than two years). It was a slight accommodation to the difference between newer ones and older ones. You may remember that it took a new trainee two years to begin to grasp the purpose of the Faith Homes, and five years for the Lord to make a fundamental change in his nature. An applicant thus understood he was making a minimum commitment of two years' duration; in five years he expected to be sent out into the Lord's Work. No one took vows or made promises as is customary with many Christian communities. The leading of the Holy Spirit was paramount in such matters.

What buildings constituted the actual Faith Homes?

Three large homes accommodated all the residents and activities of the Faith Homes.

The largest was located on a double lot at the northwest corner of 29th Street and Eschol Avenue in Zion, Illinois. Its usual name was "The Meeting House," because the first floor functioned as a small chapel seating perhaps 125 people comfortably. First rented in 1910, it was purchased from the heirs of the owner during the Depression. It was remodeled twice to make it more suitable. The balance of the first floor contained a large kitchen and a sizable dining room. On the second floor were seven bedrooms (after the final reconstruction), and two bathrooms; the third floor had four bedrooms and one bathroom. During the final thirteen years of their lives, Mr. and Mrs. Andrews lived in this home.

The "Guest Home" was located one block north of the Meeting House, at 2736 Eschol Avenue, also on a double corner lot. The leaders of the Homes purchased it in 1916, I believe. There were eleven bedrooms on three floors, and four bathrooms, plus a good-sized kitchen and dining room, and a small living room. Miss Brooks presided over the Guest Home for more than thirty years; when she could no longer do it, my wife and I became House-parents of the Guest Home.

The third home was located one block south of the Meeting House and a block east, at 3002 Enoch Avenue, and it was always called the "Enoch Home." Mrs. Robinson herself undertook the faith-responsibility for purchasing that home in 1923. It was the smallest of the three Homes, but still there were nine bedrooms on three floors, and three bathrooms. Most of her years from 1923 until her death in 1936 were spent in that home.§

What were the living arrangements?

The living arrangements were very simple: one room to a married couple, and a shared room for singles of the same gender. From 1916 to 1968 no children were allowed except to couples who were on permanent

---

§ The Enoch home was sold in 2002.

staff. Later, trainees who had children stayed on, and where possible the children were provided their own rooms. Residents customarily used the facilities (toilet and shower or bath) on their own floor. Meals were eaten at a common table, the food having been prepared in a common kitchen. Privacy was limited, but when all residents lived in the unity of the Spirit, no one seemed to mind.

What about visitors?

There were almost always visitors in the Homes, especially in the Guest House. In 1967, our first year in the Homes, I tallied how many days visitors were present: 359 days! Only six days without visitors that first year! Generally that meant preparing and serving meals to a dozen or more people three times a day (for the ladies), and washing all the dishes used in the process (for the men). It was a test for this writer, to be sure! Memories of those days would fill another book. But we learned much from each visitor, and we learned more from Miss Brooks, who took pains to make the table conversation lively and profitable.

The Good and the Bad

The **good** included life-long friendships, and vital prayer support for each other when everyone was living properly in the Spirit of Mercy. For example, Hodgkin's Disease struck our oldest daughter when she was 17, and I will never forget the support of the residents as we went through that horrible ordeal. I offered to move out because I knew the pressure would be heavy on everyone; whatever we were going through, the others would have to bear it with us. Every resident in our home willingly walked through that experience with us. My debt to them is unpayable. In the end the Lord answered prayer. Our daughter has now been cancer free for twenty-eight years.

We received solid training for ministry. We learned to pray. We gained a sense of what it was like to live in the presence of the Lord, in what the Bible calls *the beauty of holiness*. As the Bible uses the term, it includes living, working, and praying together in the spirit of lowliness and mercy. That opened my eyes to something I had not witnessed before. Holiness blossoms where hearts are knit together in love, and in the love of the truth.

We also learned to live by faith, trusting God for every need to be supplied. The Homes charged no one for tuition, or room and board;

residents depended on God alone for personal needs, for everything from postage to transport. None of the ministers ever received a salary – they too lived by faith. We were thankful for training in "the faith life," giving up our demands for everything we needed and our expectations for having everything we wanted. We saw that God never fails those who trust Him.

What was the **bad**, then? We saw examples of people who resisted the work of the Lord in their lives, who did not want to go God's way. That was always difficult. We occasionally saw serious failures. It is painful to recall such things, but the record is not complete without them. For example, a married woman in the Homes seduced one of the trainees. That was one of the hardest things we ever went through. To the glory of God, they both repented and were restored. Moral failure was extremely rare and God protected the reputation of the Homes as a place of integrity. Living in community requires extra caution in all relationships between men and women. God granted much grace in that area, but there were occasional spiritual failures, too, when selfishness replaced mercy in someone's life.

Incidentally, the married woman referred to in the previous paragraph sent a letter to the Council some months later, and I quote from it now:

> *In the past recent weeks I have felt a strong impression to write the Council and ask for your forgiveness. I waited this long so that it would be more established, and myself stronger. At times I have wished that I could go back and undo so many things, but since I cannot, I do humbly repent before and to all of you.*
>
> *I've had to face everything, my sin, and rebellion in the light of all that God has done for me, and needless to say it's been painful. I feel as though I truly did deny the Lord, and did weep bitterly. The Lord's mercy has held me up, and I feel that now I do understand the definition of God's mercy.*
>
> *I'm very thankful for all of your prayers and wisdom. I love each one of you, and do deeply love the Faith Homes.*

There existed, at times, a lack of unity, and that became one of the factors which precipitated my wife and me leaving the Homes in 1996.¶

¶ This indicates the reason for closing my narrative of *The Resurgent Work* with the date 1996. The Faith Homes still exists, but in a much smaller form. As mentioned, one home has been sold. As of the date of this writing, the Council numbers three individuals (a fourth is caring for an ailing friend and no longer lives in the Homes). There are currently no young people enrolled as trainees.

Sometimes financial pressures made life difficult, and yet I recount many instances of God providing for us and for others supernaturally. There were times of deprivation, especially when friends and relatives of the trainees expected them to go the way of "the American dream." Many times the pressure to "get out and get a job" would come when we were trying to believe God for postage stamp money!

The Easy and the Difficult

The **easy** centered in the actual presence of the Lord Jesus Christ in the Homes. Any task, no matter how mundane, became a lovely thing when it was done for Him. It took the drudgery out of the work. Every day was an adventure with Jesus. We were required to read Brother Lawrence's classic, *The Practice of the Presence of God*, ten times, until the truth of his testimony took hold of you. Then each morning you knew the day's activities would be with Jesus. It can only be known by those who have experienced it. Some days were truly Heaven on Earth. It seemed I couldn't imagine anything better than the simple life we were living, all because of His Presence so wonderfully manifested.

Living in "The First Love" truly *eased* the natural pressures of living in community. The definition God gave of The First Love opened up our hearts to him.

The "First Love" is not a great desire to go to work [for Jesus]. The First Love is the awakening of the heart to the wonder of just Jesus Christ Himself.

Similarly, there came a special pleasure when we did all our work for Him, whether it was washing dishes, hanging laundry, or wrestling in prayer for the long four hours on Wednesday mornings. The Lord had said,

The "First Works" are: Doing everything for Jesus.

We were taught that Jesus would do any task we were assigned to do. No duty would be too lowly for Him. His was a servant's heart, "The Servant of all the servants," lowlier than all His creatures. "The Son of Man came not to be ministered unto, but to minister, and to give His life a ransom for many" (Mark 10:45). We were to follow in His steps. In fact, Charles Sheldon's best-selling story, *In His Steps*, was required reading. "The first time through, you read the book," we were told. "The second time through, the book will read you."

The **difficult** included resolving conflicts between people, sometimes very deep conflicts. None of us living in the Homes could honestly say our wills were completed crucified. Our natures, our flesh, our selfishness – they all became factors in every conflict. "Only by pride comes contention," wrote Solomon (Proverbs 13:10). Of course, as in most conflicts, blame is not always equally shared. A good heart-to-heart talk with one of the ministers helped clarify one's responsibility in a conflict. We learned that if people consecrate completely to live out the truth of lowliness and mercy, they will eventually work through their conflicts. *But Christians have a tendency to love one another... until they get to know one another.* In the Faith Homes, it didn't take long to get to know each other!

A second **difficult** thing was facing the darkness and despair that comes against any serious seeker of Jesus. I don't think there are any exceptions to that. When we follow Jesus, He will eventually bring us to Gethsemane and Calvary with all the darkness associated with those places. To me, at times, it seemed the darkness would be my permanent home. I like to be a happy person, and most people think of me as a happy man, but I have faced *the dark night of the soul* more times, and for greater lengths of time, than I care to tell about. It almost killed me. I'm thankful for the ministers who prayed for me during such times.

Ruth Brooks was one who did that for me. Without my saying anything she would sense it. As the Council gathered for prayer on Monday mornings from 10 till noon, she would say, "We have to pray for Douglas today." She and the others would lay hands on me as I sat on a chair surrounded by them. "We're not going to let him suffer like this without praying for him, are we?" she asked. She would pray her heart out for me with such understanding. I don't know how she could understand, but she did; she knew exactly what I was feeling and stood with me and worked with me until God's power came to deliver. I am eternally grateful.

Raising children in the Homes was **difficult**, as it can be for any family living in community. It was especially hard for my wife and my children. I honor her for sticking with me through all those years of raising children in a communal environment with no home of our own and very little privacy. It was not easy. Thank God for His help.

Another **difficult** thing is *losing spiritual vision.* Communal life is overwhelming when the goal disappears from view. It was a battle to stay focused on the vision. There's nothing so difficult as thinking you're going through a pointless spiritual exercise. The position must be held, even against strong opposition, that God believes what you are doing is important. Faith is the victory!

A last **difficulty** to mention is the danger of *spiritual delusion*. "You have to have a cleansing of your heart by God to keep you from the revelations of the devil," said Rex Andrews on my birthday in 1970.

Mrs. Marie Robinson shared with me something that happened to one of the young people way back in the early 1920s that illustrates this extremely important matter. A certain young man – I won't state his name, but I met him as a returning missionary many years later came to the Faith Homes for training. Seeing God's power at work and hearing the Lord speak so directly in the meetings, he zealously sought to have the same anointing on his life. He was especially impressed by the teaching on "death to self." He decided to get hold of Colossians 3:1-4 and "pray it through."

> *If then you be risen with Christ, seek those things which are above, where Christ sitteth on the right hand of God. Set your affection on things above, not on things on the earth; for you are dead and your life is hid with Christ in God. When Christ who is our life shall appear, then shall you also appear with Him in glory.*

"I see others around me who are truly 'dead' like that," he said to himself. "I'm going to pray through to my death-to-self."

He fasted and prayed for a week. And at the end of the week he went to Elder Brooks, that venerable saint of God, and said to him, "Brother Brooks, I fasted and prayed over Colossians 3:1-4 and I'm now 'dead.'"

Elder Brooks looked at him and replied, "You are not!"

"Oh yes I am," he replied. "I've taken it by faith. I've prayed it through. I'm dead."

Elder was not impressed and told him it was a delusion, but the young man didn't believe it.

The young man went on in the Lord and made some progress, but the strength of his delusion became woefully apparent in later years, causing him and others much heartache. He never acknowledged the terrible trap into which he had stepped by his arrogance. By the end of his life he became what the world would call "a pathological liar." Amazing! I repeat: *"You've got to have a cleansing of your heart by God to keep from the revelations of the devil."*

In the Faith Homes we were never allowed to think that we — individually or the Homes corporately — were the main part of the pie. Every believer is a piece of the pie, thank God, but no one is the whole thing. No individual, no ministry, no place is the whole thing. Christ is the Head of the Church; we are members of His body. It is a difficult thing to grasp, if and when God chooses to bless a place, a ministry, or an individual.

God raised up the Faith Homes to defeat that unjust love of the preeminent place that belongs to Jesus Christ alone. Chapters 16 and 17 touch on that issue.

Mrs. Martha Wing Robinson, early 1930s.

The Brooks family. Elder Eugene Brooks, son Eugene, Jr., Mrs. Sara Brooks and daughter Ruth Brooks. Photo taken in front of Faith Home at 2736 Eshcol Avenue early 1920s. Ruth would have been in her twenties.

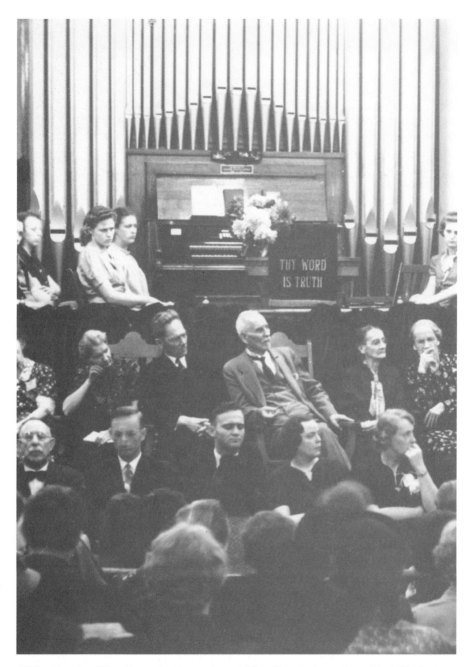

Elder Brooks (directly under banner) and Mrs. Brooks (seated on his left) during Special services at Rev Joseph Wannenmacher's church in Milwaukee, Calvary Assembly of God. Rev. Wannenmacher helped to establish over 15 Assemblies of God churches in that city. Rev. Wannenmacher lived in the Faith Homes for several years and trained under the Faith Home "vessels." A probable date for this photo is the late 1940s.

Ruth Brooks, Hilda Nilsson, Marie Robinson (no relation to Martha Robinson), Rex Andrews. Probably around 1958.

Ruth Brooks. Date is unknown, but probably in her early to mid-eighties.

Helping with the John G. Lake Meetings in Milwaukee, left to right, Rex Andrews (with guitar), Rev. Cornelius Ulrich (Milwaukee pastor), George Finnern (Faith Homes trainee), John G. Lake (healing evangelist).
Names of ladies not known.

Rex Andrews in Kenya around 1951 holding a native child named after him.

Rex Andrews at the Zion Faith Homes around 1961 (before his stroke).

Doug & Millie Detert 1986.

Meeting House at 2820 Eshcol Avenue. Looking northwest 1985.

Guest House at 2736 Eshcol Avenue.
Looking west at front of house 1985.

Guest House at 2736 Eshcol Avenue. Looking northeast, at side and rear of house 1985.

3002 Enoch Avenue. Looking northwest 1985.

Doug & Millie Detert 2005.

CHAPTER TWELVE

A COLOR SKETCH OF RUTH M. BROOKS

In the "Guest House" of the Faith Homes, located at the corner of Eschol Avenue and 28th Street in Zion, a typical day begins at 6:30 a.m. The morning cook prepares breakfast for a dozen people, including guests. The trainees and guests freshen themselves early in order to be downstairs at the dining room table by 7:15 sharp. At the last minute, a cheerful, tiny lady appears to preside over the meal. She's 68 (in 1971), but does not appear to be that old.

At her direction someone prays, and then "Miss Brooks" sends the food around the table from a tri-level serving cart. She leads the conversation, perhaps by soliciting comments on the meeting last night, or by reporting a pressing need phoned in late. She easily shares and listens and keeps the talk flowing while passing the food around a second time.

At 7:45 we are excused, and she lingers for a second cup of coffee, answering questions and making sure everyone is back in his room in time for the two-hour "alone with God" period, from 8 to 10 each day. If it is Tuesday or Thursday, she has no morning obligations, and we won't see her again until noon, because the Lord insisted some years ago that she, as one of the main ministers in the Faith Homes, needs not *two*, but *four* hours in the Word and Prayer daily. Frequently, though, she must be summoned to the phone to counsel and pray with someone in need. No residents have a phone in their rooms, not even Miss Brooks.

Miss Brooks reappears promptly at noon for the main meal of the day. With amazing deftness she turns the lunch hour into a spiritual class without it seeming to be one! For the most part, guests are impressed by her ability to answer questions, discuss trends (spiritual and political), relate Faith Home history, and interpret the Bible, all with an original and delightful sense of humor. She draws from an enormous reservoir of experience, and her remarks remain free of boredom, criticism, or bias.

Outwardly she is small in stature, never weighing more than one hundred pounds, yet inwardly Miss Brooks possesses immense strength and faith. Her dark eyes flash with passion when the occasion demands it. Quips abound. "That woman had the nerve of the Methodist preacher's horse." "When Adam fell, he fell on his head." "My hair looked like last year's birds nest." And once, when I urged her to hurry home from a trip to California, she wrote in reply, "Don't kill the goose that is laying the golden eggs," – a reference to the fact that everywhere she went, friends gave offerings for the Faith Homes!

Four hours a day in prayer and the Word – yes, and frequently more. Her best praying took place in the hours preceding midnight, after any of the four evening meetings a week that we all attended. We cannot forget the messages that incubated during those hours and hatched on Sundays. In our minds she rightfully earned the title of "Sunday morning preacher" for many years. Who could forget her message on, *Ephraim is a cake not turned, and Moab has not been poured from vessel to vessel?* Or, *Living in Mercy is a fire so hot it will burn the hell out of you!*

Ruth Brooks played the organ for all the services for at least 30 years. God gave her a great gift of "playing in the Spirit." Frequently (and I do mean frequently), during times of praise and worship that engulfed the entire congregation, the Spirit produced, through her flying hands on the keys and both feet on the pedals, unparalleled music of triumph, of pleading, of marching armies, and of singing angels – all of it original, and sometimes in chord sequences so breath-taking, that when she finished, the only appropriate response was SILENCE. My wife and I are living witnesses of hundreds of such Spirit-generated musical productions on the organ. She would do it with both eyes open, yet completely absorbed in the flow of notes. The congregation was divinely held spell-bound by the authority behind the music. If you think it is hard to *comprehend*, it is even harder to *describe*. It opened for us an insight into the music and worship of David's time, with trumpeters and trained singers all making *one sound* (II Chronicles 5:13), one great praise to God, *For He is good: for His Mercy is forever*. The modern, pre-planned, humanly generated "worship" is painful to watch, when once you have been exposed to the kind of worship I am describing.

Was Miss Brooks "normal" in everyday life? The short answer is, absolutely.

My mental picture of her after a simple exchange of letters prior to visiting the Homes, turned out to be completely wrong. Such a spiritual person, I reasoned, would dress like a "Pentecostal nun," so to speak – high collar, hair pulled back tightly in a bun, no jewelry, long skirt, *etc.* My wife and I drove to Zion on Friday, January 20, 1967, to "check things out." Miss Brooks, we were told, was not there, but would return the next day. Indeed, Saturday right after lunch she came home, and without even removing her coat or tending to her luggage, she came into the kitchen to chat with us where we were sitting at the table. She was all smiles and graciousness, wearing a stylish hat with a feather, a lovely necklace, and a fashion ring on one of her fingers. Conversation flowed, the love of Christ radiated from her, and the Lord did an "end run" around any latent bias about "women in the ministry." The next morning she preached a powerful and convicting message. We could not gainsay the genuineness of her ministry. We found out later that she wore jewelry only when traveling or on special occasions – which often made it easier for her to witness to others – because her appearance was "normal." She spoke of the Lord freely and easily with strangers; in the Lord's eyes she truly was an "evangelist," and Rex Andrews always referred to her by that title.

Out of respect, we called her "Miss Brooks." Her authority in the Lord demanded it. While cheerful and easy-to-be-around, when occasion demanded she turned into a "lioness" in prayer. Shortly after entering the Homes, news came to all of us that the four-year-old son of neighbors who attended the services at the Faith Homes had tripped while running and hit his head on the sidewalk, resulting in a serious concussion. Miss Brooks stopped everything going on in the house, even meal preparation, and called us to prayer. She insisted that all of us cry out to God for young David to be healed, and she "led the charge" – not for five or ten minutes – but for one solid hour! By her passionate example, she brought out the best prayer instincts in the rest of us. Soon word came that David was responding normally; only then did the prayer cease.

Such a scene was also "normal" for Ruth Brooks. In later years, when dealing with people who either were ill, or in serious spiritual need, we saw her intercede for others with the passion of Christ, even to the point of casting out demons (the ministers always called them "enemies" instead of demons). On days of fasting and prayer, when all Faith Home residents assembled for prolonged intercession, again it is correct to say she "led the charge" and showed us by example how to "wrestle in prayer" until the answer was "prayed through." Those memories are not only unforgettable, but also serve as patterns for present ministry.

In the Spring of 1967, out of respect for four guests staying with us, one of whom spoke nightly at a nearby church where some members were interested in the Baptism of the Holy Spirit, Miss Brooks led us as a supportive delegation to the meeting on a free night. Since the church was less than two blocks away, we all walked there. During the presentation, the speaker asked for everyone who was "filled with the Spirit" to stand up (in an effort to encourage others, I suppose). I was almost on my feet when I realized that Miss Brooks, who was sitting next to me, made no motion to rise. The speaker asked again, "Will everyone who is filled with the Spirit please rise?" Again, no movement from Miss Brooks. I thought to myself, "If *she* isn't going to get up, there's no way *I* will do it." I had already seen how gifted she was by the Spirit.

On the way home, walking next to her, I brought up the subject.

"Why didn't you stand when the speaker asked all Spirit-filled believers to rise?"

"He used the word *filled*," she responded. "I would never say I am *filled* with the Spirit. When the Scripture says that Peter, for example, being *full* of the Holy Ghost, spoke to the crowd on the Day of Pentecost, that represents an infilling I am not prepared to say I have."

That reply demonstrated a degree of understanding about the things of the Spirit that I certainly lacked. I didn't say much, but the impact of her actions stayed with me. "Be realistic about your true spiritual condition," was the maxim imprinted on my heart.

In reading this, please remember that I am not trying to "deify" Miss Brooks, or anyone else, for that matter. There is nothing so unique as Jesus indwelling one of His own. All ideas of human "greatness" fade when Jesus is seen in the majestic splendor of His Presence shining forth through human personalities.

Perhaps this is a good place to insert something Rex Andrews wrote concerning the very human tendency to idolize a spiritual person. Pay close attention to the following quotation from a letter he wrote to Faith Home co-workers in 1961:

> The great difficulty seems to be that practically no one has any clear idea of how to describe the work-of-God IN a person without tending to glorify that person. These days the glorification-of-"man" is reaching its utmost heights in the world. The glorification, near deification, of some of the modern "miracle workers" seems

to approach the ultimate in the OPPOSITE to what the Scriptures record of Jesus and of Paul, to say nothing of the prophets of ancient times, (regarding their "poverty" life), most of whom have never even been recorded by name.[1]

And consider this excerpt from a public talk given in July of 1961:

> Mrs. Robinson considered herself to be just nothing. She considered herself to be so ungreat that any ideas of greatness in the human sense at all were preposterously scandalous, almost. How do we know these things? Because she demonstrated it through her entire life to the absolute end that she laid down her life for those around her... Throughout her life she took the place of being a servant of all the rest of the servants. She tried all her life to put the others AHEAD.[2]

Those last few sentences could be applied to Ruth Brooks just as well. I am an eyewitness and I testify to the truth about Miss Brooks' laid-down life.

As intimated earlier by my deliberate choice of the word "normal," Ruth Brooks was "normal" both outwardly and spiritually. When we became co-workers in August 1973, my knowledge of her life in both areas increased, and I had to learn more thoroughly to respect her spiritually, even as I came to know her personally on a daily basis. One example may serve to illustrate what I mean.

When delivering her sermons on Sunday Morning, Miss Brooks tended to incorporate events from the past week in the Guest House as illustrations of her points. Sometimes *you* were the unnamed example! At the very least, often the residents of the Homes knew to whom she was referring. That irritated me. It obviously wasn't the best source of sermon illustrations. I became frustrated and angry with her. One day during my two-hour quiet time, the Lord impressed me with the need to visit Miss Brooks and to say three things to her: 1) how much I appreciated her life and ministry; 2) that I was repentant for harboring criticism of her in my heart; 3) that I was to ask if I could pray for her. The third point was accompanied by a clear instruction from the Lord about HOW to pray for her. "You are not worthy to pray standing over her; you get on your knees next to her chair, lay hands on her shoulder, and lead out in a pure *Prayer of Mercy* for her."

I did as the Lord bade me. Afterwards, in openness she said, "Douglas, you don't know what this has meant to me. I've been struggling lately with the thought that my messages are not successful in the Lord's eyes. Thank you for being obedient today."

Conversely, some years later, after a tumultuous discussion in the usual business meeting of the Faith Home Council on a Friday morning, I had no sooner reached home (3002 Enoch Ave., not the Guest Home where she lived), than the phone rang. It was Miss Brooks calling for me.

"Did you hear what I said this morning in the Council about (and she named the topic)?"

"Yes," I replied.

"What I said was pure flesh. I am sorry and I apologize."

Stunned by her humility, I forgave her.

After working with her for several years, one day she turned to me and said, "Douglas, when are you going to call me 'Ruth'?" I had never called her anything but "Miss Brooks." It dawned on me that she no longer looked at me as a "trainee," but as a co-worker, though I was almost forty years her junior in age. Difficult as it was to make the switch in my mind, I did as she requested, and we worked together for more than twenty years. That was a God-given opportunity for me to learn things about the ministry that I could never have learned from books. Though the words may sound trite to some, "I am forever grateful" for that opportunity.

Frequently I drove Miss Brooks to Chicago, either to Union Station to catch a train or to O'Hare Airport for a flight. Those were special times of conversation and a chance for me to see how she handled herself in public. On one such trip we were sitting in the waiting area at O'Hare Airport (in the days before strict security) and watched a Hare Krishna devotee sell one of their books to a young man sitting alone.*

"Are you going to let the devil get away with that?" she remarked to me. "You need to talk to that man who just bought their literature."

What could I do but act? While she prayed, I shared with him the truth of Jesus, as compared with what he had just heard and was about to read. I easily answered the young man's objections to Jesus' Divinity, because of the good teaching I had received in the Homes, and because Miss Brooks was praying for me. I kept at it until I was satisfied I had made a dent in his understanding.

---

* In America, especially in the '60s and '70s, the Hare Krishna branch of Hinduism openly and brazenly promoted their pernicious teachings. They teach a fanatical devotion to the Hindu 'god' Krishna.

Another thing I learned by example involved support for younger ministers who needed encouragement to develop their skills, especially preaching skills. For several years following my ordination, I gave occasional "talks" in the meetings, but seldom on a Sunday morning did I share. Without directly saying so, I knew – as did the other ministers on the Faith Home "platform" – that Ruth Brooks was the Sunday morning speaker. And none of us were envious of her, for we knew it involved serious prayer and preparation to bring forth a Spirit-birthed message for the main meeting of the week.

My seat on the platform was to the left and a little forward of the organ, where she generally sat; next to the organ was "her" chair. In my peripheral vision, however, I could always see her. Once in a while, and mostly during the less-attended Monday night or Thursday night meetings, I would see her out of the corner of my eye, (with her hands below the organ keyboard so no one in the congregation could see them), giving a "thumbs up" signal, signifying that I needed to rise and speak at an appropriate time. Despite my reluctance, and encouraged by her repeated insistence, I would get up "by faith" (hers, not mine), and share with the congregation a morsel or two from my "loaves and fishes." This happened many times.

One time in particular it seemed to me useless to obey her. I had nothing to share. She would not, however, stop giving me the signal to rise and speak. It was a case of sheer disobedience vs. meekness, so I did as she requested. I stumbled for a while, then seemed to say something that might bring a little blessing. After the meeting she cornered me. "I'm glad you got up to speak," she began. "It took a little while for you to say what God wanted, but I kept praying for you until you got on track." What could I say? What would you have said?

Another time I simply could not find the strength to rise when she motioned to do so. I saw her gesture time and again, but I pretended not to see it. In a stage whisper (hers were pretty loud, though), I heard her say, "Mr. Detert, get up! You need to speak!" Still I refused. Finally, clearing her throat, she announced to the congregation, "At this time Mr. Detert will get up and speak to us." I'm ashamed now that I was not compliant at first, but <u>she was dogged if she knew it was something God wanted, and would not give up until I obeyed.</u>

God used Miss Brooks to cast "enemies" out of many individuals who suffered from the encroaching presence of darkness personified in their inside worlds. As I matured in ministry, she often included me in laying hands on such persons, or in speaking to the enemy directly. I can hear her now, with a God-backed voice of authority, saying, "YOU GO! IN THE NAME OF JESUS, LEAVE!"

One day we were praying over a woman who battled half a lifetime against certain oddities in her behavior. We were praying earnestly, and it was evident this lady needed deliverance. Clearly the moment had come for the enemy to leave, and I waited for Miss Brooks to speak. Without warning, she turned to me and whispered, "You do it!" Although I felt *my* lack of faith, I spoke with the knowledge that I was being upheld by *her* faith. Jesus set the lady free.

Recently I was looking through old papers and found this note from the woman just mentioned, and I quote it *verbatim*:

12-8-80

Please accept my deepest gratitude for your time, & also your intense effective prayers yesterday afternoon.

All those years in the Faith Homes I was so "high & mighty" it scared me, & I wondered what calamity God was going to use to "bring me down."

But it didn't work out that way - instead, God brought me to the point of being willing to face myself & the evil in me.

Thank you for your kindness & patience & LONG suffering toward me during all those years I was so blind. And your honesty with me when it fell on deaf ears.

I could not experience or realize God's Mercy until I saw my need.

What kind of nature is it that requires 47 years to wake up, especially after being in the light of this teaching for 35 years? God, help!!!

But He has, He does, & He will.

I thank my God upon every rememberance of you all.

God Bless you.

I love you.

Gail

To the Council

2-8-80

Please accept my deepest gratitude for your time, & also your intense effective prayers yesterday afternoon.

All those years in the Faith Homes I was so "high & mighty" it scared me, & I wondered what calamity God was going to use to "bring me down."

But it didn't work out that way — instead, God brought me to the point of being willing to face myself & the evil in me.

Thank you for your kindness & patience & LONG suffering toward me during all those years I was so blind. And your honesty with me when it fell on deaf ears.

I could not experience or

realize God's Mercy until I saw my need.

What kind of nature is it that requires 47 years to wake up, especially after being in the light of this teaching for 35 years? God, help!!!

But He has, He does, & He will.

I thank my God upon every remembrance of you all.

God bless you.

I love you.

Gail

I never took a course in "How to Cast Out Demons" – Ruth Brooks gave me "hands on" experience. Am I grateful?!

As it turned out, when Miss Brooks reached her mid-seventies, the time came for me to take her place as the Sunday morning speaker. I know the year, because of an unusual incident that took place in 1977, involving both Miss Brooks and myself. In the middle of my usual morning prayer time, I received a strong impression from the Lord that I should immediately leave the house on Enoch Avenue and pay a visit to Mrs. Henrietta Klein, who lived on Eschol Avenue between the Meeting House and the Guest House, and who was obviously nearing death from cancer.[†] It was such a strong leading that I did not delay in obeying it.

As I approached Mrs. Klein's home, coming toward me from the opposite direction, was the slight figure of Miss Brooks, unmistakable because of her light step. We met in front of the house. "What are you coming here for"? I asked. "To see Mrs. Klein," she said. "The Lord told me to come now."

Together we were ushered into Mrs. Klein's bedroom by her daughter Beverly. It was obvious Mrs. Klein would not be with us much longer, and though we tried to pray for her and comfort her, clearly we were downcast and she was cheerful! When we finished praying, Miss Brooks stepped out of the room to speak with Beverly, allowing Mrs. Klein the opportunity to speak to me alone. "Ruth is losing her strength," she began, "and she won't be able to keep preaching on Sunday mornings like she has always done. You must step into her shoes and become the Sunday morning preacher. God will help you. It's time." Within less than a week, Mrs. Klein was gone, but what she said to me came to pass exactly as she said it. I ministered the Word most Sunday mornings after that for nearly twenty years.

Miss Brooks herself passed away on Easter Sunday, April 7, 1996. My wife and I were temporarily living in Jerusalem, Israel, at the time and unable to fly home for the funeral. For a long time I had been assembling anecdotes to share about her when she died, as I knew it would be my responsibility to conduct her funeral service. It still grieves me somewhat that I could not be there, although, as was the case with "Judy" (see chapter 16 on *What Is Mercy?*), perhaps the Lord spared me extreme grief. However, I want to relate now one of the stories I would have told about her had I been able to share back then.

[†] Mrs. Klein led the second half of the Missionary Prayer on Wednesday mornings.

Earlier I referred to her gift of "playing in the Spirit" on the organ during times of sacred praise and worship in the Faith Home meetings. One night she began to play in the Spirit, but while doing so she kept looking in my direction. I was seated in front of the reel-to-reel tape recorder as the assigned "tech person" to record the main message for the night, or perhaps an unusual "Word from the Lord" that might come through the gift of prophecy or by tongues and interpretation. My position put me about 30 degrees right of dead center, as far as Miss Brooks' view was concerned. She turned her head toward me as though trying to communicate something, and she kept it up all the while she was playing. It unnerved me so much, that I eventually refused to look at her any longer. I could not imagine what she wanted from me.

After the meeting ended, she confronted me.

"Didn't you see me looking at you tonight when I was playing the organ?" she asked.

"Of course I saw you," I replied, "but I had no idea what you wanted, and it was unsettling to me."

"Mabel Fisher" [one of her friends in California] "wrote to me saying she would like to hear me playing in the Spirit," she explained. "I was trying to get you to turn the tape recorder on."

To this day I cannot imagine how she could play like she did, yielding her hands and feet to the Spirit, while simultaneously thinking about her friend's request, and on top of that, seeking my attention to turn the recorder on!

The likelihood of someone writing a biography of Miss Brooks is very small, but I am glad to share with readers this "color sketch" of a woman who was truly known in Heaven in her lifetime, and who now shares in the glory of her Beloved Jesus.

~~~~~~

Special Addendum

At the request of a friend, I previously wrote a very brief summary of Ruth Brooks' life, along the lines of "just the facts." I insert it here with minor editing for the sake of clarity and non-repetition of things told above, but with an interesting addition about her many potential suitors that I did not include in the sketch.

A Color Sketch Of Ruth M. Brooks

Ruth M. Brooks
Born: May 13, 1903
Died: April 7, 1996 (Easter Sunday)

She was about one month short of being 93 years old when she passed into glory.

She basically grew up in the Faith Homes, being only 6 years old when the meetings started in Toronto in 1909. Her mother and father (Elder Eugene and Sara Brooks) were associated with Mrs. Robinson at least 6 years prior. She was 4 years old when Jesus came to Mrs. Robinson so greatly in early November, 1907, and age 10 when she met Rex Andrews.

She attended elementary school in Zion, Illinois but went to public high school in nearby Waukegan when she was 14. She never took any college courses, but she was well-educated and possessed an enormous vocabulary. Talented in many areas, she excelled in music, especially the organ.

She had a brief period of rebellion (though she never got into drinking, immorality, *etc.*), but God had called her in an audible voice when she was about 11 or 12. She heard her name being loudly spoken, "Ruth! Ruth!" and she was sure it was her father. But being a bit saucy, she waited until the call came a second and a third time. Finally she went up the stairs to his room and asked, "Yes, father, what did you want?"

"I never called you," was the startling answer.

God renewed that call when she was in her twenties.

She and Gertrude Smith pioneered a church in Hebron, Kentucky during the 1930s. On a visit to Zion from Hebron, the Lord moved her father to lay hands on her and ordain her to full-time ministry, something she really didn't want, but God did it anyway.

Eventually she returned to the Homes and helped out in various ways. She was living in the Homes when the Lord restored Rex Andrews in 1944, and she was greatly blessed by the teaching he gave on Mercy when he began sharing it in Zion in 1947. When Mr. Andrews wondered if he should continue teaching it (some people got tired of it), she (and Matthew Eaton) strongly encouraged him to keep speaking about Mercy. If it weren't for their support, Mr. Andrews likely would have left Zion long before the *Mercy Message* had a chance to take root.

In the mid-1950s, Mr. Andrews invited her to join him and Mrs. Andrews in Tiberias, Israel for a time of intense training and discipline that would enable her to become the Housemother at the 2736 Eschol home. He dealt with her quite strongly and required her to spend 4 hours per day in prayer and the Word. That is when the Lord began to anoint her as the Sunday morning speaker in the Homes.

She became the Housemother at the Guest Home sometime in the late 1950s or early 1960s, and she was in charge when my wife Millie and I arrived in January 1967.

She had an unusual way of dealing with guests. Many visitors came with the idea (unconscious idea, hopefully!) that the table conversation should be led by, and centered around, themselves. Pastors and missionaries, especially if they headed up a particular ministry, were used to "being the one," so to speak. Miss Brooks had a way of graciously deflating their self-importance and drawing everyone's attention to Jesus instead of to them. The conversations at the table were directed by the Lord through her, and countless visitors were helped by her ministry at the meals.

As you know, God gave her the ability to play the organ in the Spirit in a most unusual way. Mr. Andrews told me, "Ruth has the gift of glory." Whenever she encouraged the congregation to enter into praise more fully, it always happened.

As a speaker and preacher, she was outstanding, even when compared to male preachers. People who knew her mother and father told me she was a wonderful blend of both. "My father (in his preaching) would flail the flesh," she told me, "and then my mother would get up and pour oil and wine on their wounds." Ruth could do both in the same sermon.

Without minimizing the clear evidence of her inward beauty and walk with the Lord, it should also be observed that she was outwardly attractive. Her friend Gordon Gardiner, author of *Radiant Glory*, documented all of Ruth's known suitors – not just pursuers, but suitors who had asked for her hand in marriage. The total? Ninety-six (96)! No one has ever disputed his tally; in fact, Ruth's sister-in-law, Dorothy Brooks, once told me that all the single girls in the Faith Homes back in the 1930s and '40s despaired of finding a husband among the hundreds of eligible bachelors who visited the Homes during those years. "They all wanted Ruth," she recounted, "and the rest of us had no chance."

Obviously, *Miss* Brooks never said "yes" to any of them, although there was one single pastor, very musical and a talented pianist, to whom she was much attracted. During his visits she would pull up a chair next to the piano bench while we watched with delight as he "wowed" her with chords, arpeggios, and music theory. I will leave him unnamed. He passed away before she did.

For more than twenty years, Ruth Brooks presided over the Faith Home Council meetings, both on Mondays (the prayer day), and on Fridays (the business day). I took that position after she could do it no longer. Similarly, Ruth invited Millie to take her place at the organ when old age prevented Ruth from playing as well as she used to play.

After 1987 (age 84), she slowly eased out of leadership, but she continued to attend the meetings until 1995, when her health declined.

When Millie and I left for Israel in early January of 1996, she was comatose in Victory Hospital in Waukegan and the doctor did not expect her to live. However, she had a physical resurgence and lived another three months with full consciousness. She died on Easter Sunday, April 7, 1996, while living at the Crown Manor Nursing Home on 27th Street in Zion, Illinois.

She entered Heaven having "kept the faith" and I am sure she is being well-rewarded by the Lord.

~ written by Doug Detert on April 9, 2011

Ruth Brooks. November 1979 at 76 years of age.

CHAPTER THIRTEEN

A BLACK & WHITE SKETCH OF REX B. ANDREWS

PART 1

With fond and delightful memories of Ruth Brooks to draw upon, it was easy for me to compose a *color sketch* of Ruth M. Brooks. I knew her well, spent much time with her, and observed her interaction with people in both public and private settings.

In comparison to making a *color sketch* of Miss Brooks, however, I can create only a *black and white sketch* of Rex Andrews. Yes, I knew him well, not only from his messages (I heard him speak at least four hundred times) and his writings (voluminous), but also from many private and semi-private classes and conversations. However, I never saw him outside of the home where he lived the last twelve years of his life. Remarkable as it may seem, he never left 2820 Eschol Avenue from the day he entered it until the day his body was removed by the undertakers!

As you will soon read, in 1963 a stroke rendered his left side (arm and leg) weak and useless. He could walk with a crutch or move about in a wheelchair, but he chose to stop traveling and to remain in his room on the second floor of the Faith Home "Meeting House." With the help of a catheter and two wonderful ladies whom he called "my angels," who rolled him to the bathroom when necessary, he preferred to continue his ministry without leaving the house.

Later I will explain how his ministry actually expanded during those years of voluntary confinement, but I am not able to write from personal observation of him in public settings. This lack is offset somewhat by remembrances of others who knew him when he was fit, and by a journal he kept of his travels to Africa and Europe during the two years, 1949-1951.

The first strokes of the broad-tipped pen making this *black and white sketch* are three sample quotations taken from his writing and speaking, one early in his restoration, one half-way through, and one taken from the close of his life.

1946

And so, feeling sort of like a worthless bungler...

That was the way Rex Andrews closed a letter to Miss Hilda Nilsson, written in 1946 from Santa Cruz, California two years after Jesus restored him to the faith. In that letter he said to her,*

> *Jesus raised me up in PURE MERCY. That is where I live, and the only place in which I can live. But that MERCY slowly turns out to be THE SWEET ETERNAL WILL OF GOD. All I could have ever asked for, imagined, dreamed of, is there in it. But in me there is no desire to "BE" anything, nor to "HAVE" anything, but just to be led along one day at a time. And I would not for the world try to take a position of being over you, nor of trying to teach you, or anyone else.* **BUT TO COMMUNICATE G O D! To communicate a little of God, it seems to me that I would go through any agony or torture.** *And He has let me have enough of that in these two years so that I know I am not just saying something for the dramatic effect it might give...*
>
> *He has shown me what NOTHINGNESS REALLY IS... For two years He has carried me through with Death standing like a devouring Beast ready to pounce upon me at any opening. HE has taken me well through the awful stratum of False Knowledge – so far through, that He is going ahead with whatever plans He has.* **I would rather eat the bread of suffering and tears for a thousand years and KNOW THAT I WOULD BE KEPT IN THE LOWLINESS OF THAT INCOMPARABLE LAMB, than to have all the happy experiences in the world without that one knowledge.** *To be kept in His LOWLINESS. Ah, there is a Shelter in God. There is a "shelter from the storm when the blast of the terrible ones is as a storm against the wall." (Isaiah 25:4)*

1961

In July of 1961, during an extended visit to Zion from his home in Israel, Rex Andrews gave a three-part series on the history of the Zion

---

* I have purposely bolded certain sentences because they convey essential spiritual truth that characterized Faith Home life for so many years.

Faith Homes. It was recorded and transcribed. Toward the end of Part One, referring primarily to Martha Wing Robinson, but secondarily to all the workers of those early days, he said,

> ...*There is a singular characteristic to this Work*† *which is almost the opposite to most places, even "deep life" places. I will bring it out more as we go on, but the characteristic of this Work has been* ***a giving Work, a faith-life Work, where you give, you give, you give all the time.*** *It is a crucifixion Work, to go ON to crucifixion of your will. It is a giving Work. To some favorable degree we have kept that principle alive here, to just go on by faith. The characteristic of the Work has been, from the beginning,* ***to pour out, to give out.*** <u>*You can be reasonably safe, you can feel reasonably safe, that you are not in some kind of a radical fanaticism,*</u> <u>*when the life is GIVING,*</u> *when that is the characteristic of it.*

In Part Two of that series, speaking of what was termed "The Power Work," and referring to that working of the Holy Spirit by which the Faith Home ministers were enabled to pour out their lives for others, he says,

> *[They were in] the working of the Holy Ghost by which... God began to speak out of their mouths, and by which He gave them power from heaven to go and do wonderful works, and* ***supremely, by which He gave them power to lay their lives down.***
>
> *My position here in 1947 was one of a little one who had been a rebel and a traitor and had forfeited everything. I had been IN that experience [of laying down his life] as far as I was myself, and I was a traitor and a rebel and had forfeited everything of my life – but the Lord recovered me and restored to me all that I had; and I have been fighting it out alone for 17 years, but in a pathway that in some respects is a little different. But there is one feature about it – and I have not hesitated to express it from the time I first came back in 1947 – I said, "Well, it is all mercy, and I have not one thing forever I can ever say, not one thing I can ever point to, just mercy." But God has done it. But in it all He did one thing for me.* ***He gave me power to lay down my life.***

---

† Rex Andrews always capitalized the word "Work" when referring to the Zion Faith Homes.

1974

The following words were taken down by this writer during a Wednesday night Bible Class. They are not a *verbatim* record, but they give a fairly accurate picture of the subject that night, "The Lord's Prayer." Everything is just as I wrote it down in longhand, including underlining and bold emphasis. The prophetic sentences are italicized for emphasis.

> The Friday prayer for our government is very important. *What happens now will affect the freedom of God's people. We should pray for God to strengthen <u>the courts</u> and the government.* Believe God to get His Will done.
>
> Scripture for tonight: Luke 11:1-4, the Lord's Prayer.
>
> We're in desperate need in the world right now, desperate need of God's people praying! Nothing at all but prayer will **avail**. The **times** are upon us. The anti-Christ is at the door... *Magnetic; intrusive – everybody in the world will believe that liar.* His purpose will be to imitate the Son of God. The destroyer will claim (thusly) to be greater than the Creator. The prince of <u>liars</u>!
>
> We will have to believe that God is **literally** our Father; BORN of GOD. And that He is the Creator; creating NOW. God doesn't stop working. He hears your prayer. <u>He'll do what you say IF you obey His Word with all your heart. Why IF? Because if you don't obey, you won't be able to believe that God will answer your prayer.</u>
>
> It's very important that many of God's people believe that God has been answering "the Lord's Prayer" for over 1900 years!
>
> Fires; murders; rolling coffins [automobiles]; plane crashes. You're a big fool if you get into anybody's rolling coffin without committing yourself to God.
>
> We need to be living in, actively, every one of these words and lines of the Lord's Prayer. It is fundamental to all prayer. One of the supreme facts in all the Gospels is the fact of Jesus' prayer. He felt the need of it, if not the way we think of need, at least the need just to be with God His Father. He made the most amazing statements about His relation to His Father.
>
> **"Father"** – You need to be in His arms. He wants you to sit on His lap and let Him put His arms around you. How do you stay there? Pray, "Our Father," "my <u>own</u> Father."

"**Hallowed be <u>Your</u> name.**" --- hallowed, as opposed to, "hallowed be <u>my</u> name"; (the whole intellectual world is in this). (Did you ever stop to think that this earth is in <u>heaven</u>? We're not off in a corner of space somewhere. The only thing stopping heaven from being on the earth is the will of God NOT being done on earth like it is in heaven.)

"**Thy kingdom come**" – if you pray it, you'll know it's coming.

"**Thy will be done, as in heaven, so in earth.**" – If you pray that, is there any greater position than that before God? If you pray this way, you'll have the ear of God.

"**Give us day by day our daily bread**" – <u>Are you on those terms with God? You're going to have to depend on God this way.</u> We're right there. *Something could happen to turn this nation into a socialist nation, in which you can't have any property, not even your children.*

This verse is mainly what I took this passage for tonight.

~ Rex Andrews, (notes by DDD), February 6, 1974

As this is being written in 2013, surely his words are more poignant than they were thirty-nine years ago.

A Brief Summary of Rex Andrews' Life

Who was this "worthless bungler"? Where did he come from? What was his Christian testimony? How did he become connected with the Zion Faith Homes? What was his role in the development of those Homes over a span of 62 years? Why are his writings and testimony an inspiration to so many, nearly 40 years after his death?

To my knowledge, no one has attempted to write a biography of Rex Andrews. Shortly after he died on Feb. 1, 1976, the Faith Homes compiled a memorial to his life and ministry as a special issue of its quarterly newsletter.[1] It seems important to me that a longer record be preserved as a testament to God's Mercy.

Rex Andrews spent his boyhood in Rockford, Illinois where his mother practiced a godly life as a Methodist, but his father pursued an ungodly life. Early on, Rex gave a lovely testimony in the Methodist young people's group, affirming his love for Jesus. But there was another force at work in his life: his father's propensity for evil.[‡] When he was about nine years old, after his father had passed away, his mother said to him, "Rex, sometimes you're so naughty that I pray the Lord will take you." And he was naughty, but that was a terrible thing to say. "You have no idea the effect my mother's words had on me," he told me. "They were almost fatal for me."

Around age 12 his mother threatened him (like so many parents do) with these words: "As long as you're under this roof, you're going to obey me." And the response of his heart was, "All right, and as soon as I'm old enough, I'm getting out from under this roof." And that's what he did, running away from home when he was only fourteen. At age fifteen he ran away again, this time for good, riding freight trains westward until he reached Greeley, Colorado where he obtained work loading box cars in the days of "the Wild West." The devil threw temptation at Rex Andrews in the form of sexual immorality during those tender years between 14 and 17, and having enjoyed "the pleasures of sin for a season," he discovered that the devil had planted a hook of evil inside his heart that would not be easily removed.

During the first week of June 1907, he came under the conviction of the Holy Spirit to such an extent that he sought out the local Methodist minister at 11 p.m. on Friday of that week.[§] The minister had already retired for the night, but in his nightshirt he answered the knock at the door, invited Rex in, and led him to Christ the Savior. (That became an example to him of the kind of consecration one needs for the ministry.)

The Lord did a good work in him that night. The next day his hand got caught in one of the box car doors. Normally he would have uttered curse words when it happened, but (in his words) "I waited for the curse words to come, but they never came, and I knew I had been saved!"

Shortly thereafter he decided to return home to his mother and live for the Lord. He began working for The Salvation Army in Rockford and participated in their evangelistic street meetings. He always looked back on those days fondly and retained a love for reaching out to the lost in public meetings for the rest of his life.

[‡] In a private conversation with this writer, he referred to his own struggle with sin as being related to his father's nature and personality. "But we are not prisoners of our parents' natures," he added, "because of the blood of Christ."

[§] No doubt his mother's prayers were being answered.

1907 was the year of the Holy Spirit's outpouring on the Azusa Street Mission in Los Angeles, California and waves of blessing swept across the country from west to east, touching the churches in Rockford along the way. His mother shared with him the testimonies of others who had "received the Spirit." He searched the Scriptures to see if the experience was valid (much like Martha Robinson had done earlier that year), and concluded that it was. He was particularly impressed by Matthew 3:11, where John the Baptist said, "and He [Jesus] shall baptize you with the Holy Ghost and with fire." Rex determined to seek the Lord until he was baptized in the Holy Spirit. He began to wait on the Lord after work, and eventually took time off from his employment, giving up his pay for the day to spend the time praying and waiting on God to be filled with the Holy Ghost. One night he resolved to spend the whole night in prayer, "tarrying for the Spirit," as it was called in those days. He fell asleep on his knees, but when he woke up in the morning, he felt the pleasure of the Lord upon Him.

If you have ever tried to "pray through" for anything you want from God, you know a barrier comes up in front of you, and you feel as though there's no use to keep on praying. That happened to Rex, and he felt as though he could never break through to the answer he was seeking, namely, to be baptized with the Holy Spirit and fire. However, as was taught in those days quite strongly, he kept thanking the Lord for the promised gift of the Holy Spirit and persisted in it.

On December 11, 1907, while on his knees in prayer, he suddenly felt as though someone was pouring a bowl of warm oil upon his head. It wasn't *tangible* oil that one could touch or collect, but it *felt like real oil* pouring down from his head and flowing over his face and body. "I knew at that moment that I had broken through," he recounted. He didn't speak in tongues at that time, but for two weeks, every time he knelt down to pray, the same thing happened.

On Christmas Day he and his mother attended a "cottage prayer meeting." (Yes, a group of earnest saints had gathered for prayer on Christmas Day, 1907. Almost unthinkable in our day!) "It was one of the driest cottage prayer meetings you could ever imagine," he said. It was far from exuberant or glorious. As he began once more to wait on the Lord for the Baptism, he expressed himself by saying repeatedly, "Glory to Jesus. Glory to Jesus." He had been taught, (as I was taught forty years later), that the way through to the Baptism in the Spirit was to praise and thank the Lord for the Promise and the Gift of the Holy Spirit.

As he prayed, the words came faster and faster, and he was saying, "Glory to Jesus, glory to Jesus, glory to Jesus, glory to Jesus," quite rapidly. In his mind he realized that it was impossible to articulate those words as fast as he was speaking them. The instant that awareness came to him, his words turned into another language. He continued to speak in tongues for an hour and a half, and the lady praying next to him kept track of how many times the language changed. She said that he spoke clearly and fluently in fourteen different tongues that afternoon. Truly it was a mighty Baptism in the Holy Spirit. But the tongues were not the greatest thing that happened to him that day. The greater thing was the Spirit's granting him THE GIFT OF THE WORD OF WISDOM, according to First Corinthians 12:8.

Going back for a moment to a statement made earlier that *there were to be three "wisdom teachers" in the Faith Home Work*, you may remember that the Lord had named Rex Andrews as one of the three. Such a statement reflects a gifting, not an achievement. In fact, when Rex Andrews was brought into the circle of Vessels in 1914, as they were praying together, Martha Robinson began to dance around the chair where Rex was sitting, and she said, "He's got Wisdom! He's got Wisdom!" Jesus had revealed to her that God had given Wisdom to him at his Baptism in the Holy Spirit.

Inspired by the strong evangelistic efforts of the Salvation Army, Rex joined their ranks and participated in street meetings in Rockford. He was zealous, enthusiastic, and anointed.

In the course of time, Brother Andrews met Beulah Benedict, a young friend of his mother. He and Beulah enrolled as students in a Bible School for a year in Rochester, New York, and were married at the end of that year. The Holy Spirit anointed his preaching, and his ministry became recognized by several early Pentecostal leaders; two pastors in Chicago officially ordained him. Through a series of divinely appointed circumstances, he was led to Milwaukee and attracted the notice of some leading Pentecostal ministers in that city, the most notable being Rev. John G. Lake, who was mightily used of God in divine healing in the United States, but especially in South Africa. Brother Lake invited Rex to sit on the platform with the other ministers during those wonderful meetings in Milwaukee.

In Rex's words,

> That year, 1912, the Lord brought me – by means of a simple tarrying plan – into the anointing and light of The Work in Zion City. In the Spring of 1913 I was "ordained" to the ministry – with

no particular ability for it except call, anointing, and street-meeting inspiration. In October, by a series of dovetailing events, He got me to The Faith Homes. And I knew that I was "home."

That winter was spent in tarrying as much as possible while having to sleep in the front room used for meetings. The Lord quietly brought me into the beginnings of "power," and into use in the meetings. Mr. Brooks gave me a message that I was called into the Homes, and it was confirmed by Mrs. Robinson. I returned to our home for my family, and in April 1914, we moved into the Faith Homes with two small children.

Within a few months The Lord, by Mrs. Robinson, called me and placed me into the ministry among the Vessels, and gave me a place on "the platform." Though I have not always known it, appreciated it, or remained in the light of it, or even within the basic righteousness of it, <u>my life was cast in THAT Work. And The Lord has maintained the path</u> through what seems to me impossible turnings, backslidings, unwillingnesses, rebellions, and sins. It is my testimony that for 47 years – 1912-1959 (date of this writing July 1959) – for 47 years <u>The Lord has kept me involved in</u> "THIS ONE THING."[2]

On July 4, 1914, The Lord designated him to be one of the Vessels in the Faith Homes, just twenty-five years old, the youngest among them. He was the twelfth of what finally became thirteen Vessels in all.

Thus were the steps by which he was called into the Faith Homes and put into the ministry there. The first "message" he ever received from one of the Vessels came at the end of the first conference in which he was included as a member, just as the meeting ended. One of the ladies followed him to the door and said, "Rex, the Lord says you need to come down!"

God gave him four wonderful and glorious years from 1914-1918. There were battles to be faced, of course, and one of the severest battles was with his own struggle mentioned earlier. Omitting the details, suffice it to say that he found an unwillingness to come down under "the Word of the Lord" through Mrs. Robinson, saying "I will not obey what the Lord is asking of me." Mrs. Robinson called the other Vessels together for an entire day of fervent intercession for the unbroken young vessel.

Their prayers were answered or he would have perished. He later called it "the most terrible and destructive experience of my life," even worse than his falling away from the Lord in 1937. In answer to their prayers, he DID come down and DID give up his will, resulting in the words and music to a song that has often become a favorite wherever it has been introduced and sung, namely, *The Best Friend I Have Ever Known*.

> *When Jesus sought me, and found me, I was way down deep in sin;*
> *He called me forevermore His own.*
> *Now He has given a fountain of sweetness within,*
> *He's the best friend that I have ever known.*
>
>> Chorus: *Oh, I love Him, yes, I love Him!*
>> *He's the best friend that I have ever known!*
>> *Oh, I love Him, yes, I love Him!*
>> *He's the best friend that I have ever known!*
>
> *And oh, the joy that is waiting the soul that trusts in Him,*
> *Trusts all it has to Him alone;*
> *He will not fail it, nor let it be thrust away from Him;*
> *He's the best friend that I have ever known.*
>
> *Soon in His Glory I'll see Him, Coming down from Heav'n above,*
> *Coming to take His loved ones home.*
> *So I'll keep shouting His praises and singing of His love,*
> *He's the best friend that I have ever known.*

That is the background of the *In Memoriam* dedicatory page at the beginning of the *Meditations in the Revelation*.

During those four years, he became fully acquainted with the true history of the Faith Homes. My knowledge of this history comes through him and his writings, together with what I learned from Miss Ruth Brooks, who, having been born in 1903 as the first child of Elder and Mrs. Brooks, practically grew up in the Faith Homes and became one of its long-standing ministers. Those two things – Rex Andrews' spoken word and writings, together with Miss Brooks' oral history recounted to me – are the reason why I am able to pen this narrative with any assurance of "getting it right."

Mr. Andrews was plunged immediately into the conflict raging in the Work over the New Body.¶ He was put into the New Body on many occasions; thus he knew what it was by experience. He testified that there were times when it became unnecessary to breathe. So great is the power, beloved, of the New Body of God, that it is possible for one to live without breathing.** In such a state, Mr. Andrews testified, it was impossible, literally impossible, for him to think of anything he would ever desire than to do the Mercy of God to others. He was in the power of the New Body on different occasions and for different lengths of time.

A terribly fierce conflict arose against him (and against all the Vessels) on account of their calling. The point in relating these highlights of their conflict is not to exalt any of them, but rather to fix in your heart an indelible impression of what Jesus accomplished in the Faith Homes, and also to show a little of how Jesus gets done what He in His Wisdom wills to do, despite fierce opposition.

Years before, the devil had tried to destroy Rex Andrews as a youth. Once he nearly drowned, going down for the third time, when a boyhood chum rescued him. Another time, as he swung under a box car in a slow-moving freight train, to his frightful surprise the bars underneath on which he usually hung were spaced farther apart than usual, bringing him within a hair's-breadth of losing his hand-holds, falling down on the track, and having his body severed by the moving wheels. The devil had an inkling of God's purposes for his life and endeavored to kill him, or, failing that, to corrupt him so completely that he would be shut out of God's plan.

But the greatest onslaughts of the enemy were hurled at him at the time when God's call was made known to him. The Lord spoke His Word through all the Vessels on occasion, and it was vital to the success of what God was doing that they *hear the Lord in each other.* Mrs. Robinson was herself the most able and most willing to detect and to obey the Word of the Lord, no matter which Vessel Jesus used to speak His Word. (The devil's supreme "specialty" is to break down, render void and useless, the WORD OF GOD.)

One day Mr. Andrews gave a "word" that the Vessels were to meet

---

¶ This term will be more fully explained in Chapter 20, *To What End Is God Working?* For now, it is sufficient to say that the term "New Body" was God's choice of words for the experience He gave to Mrs. Robinson and the other Vessels. The Lord, however, did not want the term used publicly in those days, but subsequently allowed its use in later years. (For a Scriptural comparison, note that Jesus expressly forbade Peter, James and John to mention His Transfigured Body until after His Resurrection.)

** Consider how Moses survived without food or drink for 40 days in the presence of God on Mt. Sinai, where God's fire physically sustained him and left him with a glowing countenance. Consider also the three Hebrew children in the fiery furnace, where all oxygen was consumed by the flames.

together on such-and-such a day, at such a time. He was young and "green" compared to the others, and most of the Vessels simply didn't like him. Whatever the cause, the fact is that none of the Vessels believed that "word," and consequently did NOT come to the meeting that day – except for *Mrs. Robinson!* As Mr. Andrews waited at the appointed place and time, somewhat crestfallen that no one was appearing, suddenly into the room walked Mrs. Robinson. Those next few moments became eternal in their importance, for Jesus spoke through Mrs. Robinson and created a link between her work and his work which HAD to be fulfilled or the devil would have won in the Faith Homes. It is sufficient to understand that Mr. Andrews' work and gifts would not be realized without Mrs. Robinson's work and gifts, AND, her work and gifts would never be understood and put within reach, without his work and gifts.

> *For who hath known the mind of the Lord? Or who hath been His counselor? ... For of him, and to him, are all things: to whom be glory forever and ever. Amen.* (Romans 11:34, 36; see also the context of these verses).

The events described in Chapter 6, The Rising and Falling Work, 1914-1921, exerted a negative influence on Rex and on his walk with God. His strong desire to pass out tracts and hold street meetings came into conflict with his need to stay still long enough for God to pull up the deep-rooted "weeds" in his nature, as mentioned briefly above. He pled with the Lord to let him go to nearby Waukegan, Illinois to engage in evangelism; Waukegan was larger than Zion, and as the next city south of Zion, it was an ideal place to establish a thriving church. That was the Lord's plan, but not for him alone; God put together a group of young-people-in-training who responded to His call to be soul-winners in Waukegan. God desired "branch works" to be established as well in Kenosha, Wisconsin to the north, and even in Racine, still further north. Such branch works of the Faith Homes would serve as places where the young people in the Homes could put into practice what they were learning. The churches thus established were intended of the Lord to be "large, evangelistic, and deep life."

Unfortunately, the enemy used the natural tendency of Rex Andrews to be "active" to pull him away from the Faith Homes and from the supervision of the other Vessels, ever so slowly but ever so definitely. In 1918 or 1919, Rex Andrews and his family moved out of the Faith Homes and into the rear quarters of a church building in Waukegan.

The building itself had been constructed by the Navy during World War I as a library for the Great Lakes Naval Training Center, just south of Waukegan. Rex Andrews purchased it from the government after the War, disassembled it with help from the men of the fledgling church, then rebuilt it on a small plot of land he bought a few blocks from downtown Waukegan. He was ambitious, zealous, and determined. But he was not carrying out God's best will.

Mrs. Robinson wrote to him in May 1919, and again in September of that year, offering God's wisdom for his efforts and suggesting a plan for keeping in touch with her and with the Faith Homes. Years later he commented on those two letters as follows:

> The background to these two records is this: Toward the end of World War I, a little mission was started in Waukegan. During that time I was working in the YMCA Bible classes at Great Lakes Naval Station, and had about a hundred "conversions," which means boys that wanted prayer and made a surrender to God. It was on my own, but a few of the YP [Young People] from the Homes came down for street meetings on Sunday afternoons. But I started to work [gainful employment, he means] to "help support" it, and lost my inspiration and gave up. However we still kept up a cottage meeting each Sunday afternoon. That was in 1918.
>
> That winter Mrs. Robinson had some talks with me, seeking to encourage my "broken faith," and the Lord indicated that He was not wanting to give up the opportunity for a work there – "Branch Work" He called it. Later He began the effort which is recorded in the May 7, 1919 letter and the letter and instructions of September 26th. But I jumped ahead, always, rented a mission, and finally bought a Naval Station Library building and moved it to Waukegan and rebuilt it on the Philippa Avenue site. The Lord, however, thru Mrs. Robinson, kept the group of YP interested and they remained with us until one and another gradually went to other places. We worked there for 10 years, from 1918 to 1928.

Tragically, his anointing gradually faded and his ministry showed no signs of fruitfulness. And, most importantly, in his own words, "I never completed the prayer I had begun years ago for Poverty of Spirit."

Mrs. Robinson's heart was broken. She knew his calling. She knew his place in the Work and she knew he was running from the Lord's call. She was sweet to him, keeping up as much contact as she could. She tried to help him and bring him out of his willful resistance to the crucifixion of his flesh, but all to no avail.

He pastored the Waukegan branch church until 1928, then moved with his family to California for a year. He returned to pastor a small church in Sterling, Illinois a year later, but, finding no fulfillment, traveled here and there as an evangelist until 1933 when he returned to Zion and moved back into the Faith Homes. His heart was far from God's original call over his life. It was during this time that he asked for an appointment with Martha Robinson to talk with her – but she knew, of course, that he was only pretending to be doing the Lord's will. I will never forget his chilling account of that failed attempt to see her. She sent only one sentence in reply to his request: "I have nothing to say to a liar."

On June 26, 1936, Mrs. Martha Robinson departed this world for the world above, having filled up the sufferings of Christ that He required of her, not the least of which was her long and difficult intercession for Rex Andrews. Her death was a terrible blow to Rex, for he had been kept from serious sin primarily by her faith for him. He fell into a deep depression and had no success in surmounting it.

He had been giving guitar lessons to interested students, presumably to help with the family's financial needs, but the devil seized the moment to make a horrible attack against God's chosen vessel. He brought a young woman from California directly into Rex's view. Her parents had lived in the Homes previously. She was 16 years old, but wise in the ways of destruction. While visiting the Homes, she requested guitar lessons, and he willingly but unwisely agreed. He liked the guitar, played well, and had some talent for composing music. She wanted lessons, but it was a ploy of the devil, and he went like a lamb to the slaughter – but not the good kind of lamb to the good kind of slaughter. She used her knowledge of evil to tempt the 48-year-old guitar teacher, and he succumbed to her – how fully I do not know, but far enough so that the guilt he carried exploded his façade. Unable to face anyone with what had transpired between them, he simply packed up and left his family, his calling, and his twenty-three years of ministry, departing without a word to anyone – gone, vanished, unreachable. In his words later, "The Lord allowed me finally to fall into that trap because I wouldn't let the

Lord deal with my nature; when the trap was sprung, I was powerless to resist. I threw my life away for a 16-year-old girl."

After a time he reached California, where he was swallowed up by that horrible, immoral, ungodly lifestyle for which California is still notorious. He lived "in the pig pen" morally for seven years. He was as far gone as you could possible imagine, although sometimes when inebriated, he would find himself talking to people about their need for Jesus.

But in truth he was lost, without hope, and without any desire to make a U-turn. "I went so far, that I didn't even care anymore," he said. Mr. Andrews' anointing, and everything he knew to be true, was gone. He had "tasted the powers of the world to come," and still fallen away. He often said, "I'm the worst sinner here," and he meant it, because he had strayed from the Lord, despite being part of a glorious and deep work of God. There wasn't a shred of hope left for him. "Not only was I blind," he said later, "but I had put out my own eyes." It's hard for me to put into words the hopelessness of the situation.[3]

In the spring of 1944 he found himself living with a woman who was not his wife, and a child which was not his, but hers. To make a living for the three of them, he did interior painting and wallpaper hanging. All attempts by friends and relatives back in the Midwest to reach out to him had met with adamant resistance.

And yet!

In the late spring of 1944, two amazing things took place in Mr. Andrews' life. One morning as he sat down to breakfast, there was a Bible on the table open to Isaiah 53. He never could explain how it got there. He began reading, and when he came to the words in verse 6, "All we like sheep have gone astray; we have turned every one to his own way; and the Lord has laid on Him the iniquity of us all," the words shot through him like an injection of life. It was the first time in seven years that any portion of the Word of God had been made real to him. In fact, for seven years he had not read the Bible at all. Now he felt a desire to read Isaiah 53 all the way through.

The second thing happened sometime during the first week of June. In the middle of the night he heard his name being called: "Rex!" It was the Lord's messenger sent from Heaven to call that lost sheep back to God. The messenger was invisible, but the voice was unmistakable: it was Mrs. Robinson's voice! He said later that nothing could ever erase from his memory that voice and its quality. He knew it was Mrs. Robinson's voice.

And she called his name! In a burst of divine illumination, beloved, he grasped what had been missing from his understanding all those earlier years when he had begun to pray for poverty of spirit, but failed to pray it through. He understood in a moment that ***the will of God is Mercy.***

From that point on, every night he was awake at 11 p.m. or thereabouts in order to feed his hunger for the Bible. It was involuntary, almost; later he said to us, "Don't ever give me credit for praying through the night all these years. The Lord started it and made me able to keep it up until it became a habit." Sometimes the Lord shook the bed until he arose to pray and read the Bible.

One of the things Mr. Andrews had fallen into was drinking, "the painter's addiction," as it is sometimes called. Not only that, but there were many temptations that accompanied the life of an interior house painter. The West was still wild and California was in the beginning stages of what it is now – a virtual greenhouse of lust and cupidity and loose living and lasciviousness. He had to continue working under those conditions and still arise every night at midnight when the Lord awakened him to pray.

He was living as yet with this woman who was not his wife, and his wage supported her as well as her daughter who also lived there. The first thing he did was to move out of the bedroom to sleep elsewhere in the house. He had an obligation to them which he met and kept up as long as it was necessary. Insofar as he was able to repair the damage he had done, and to provide for those who were dependent on him, he did his best to meet those obligations. He also prayed for two years for all the people whom he had hurt in his fallen life.

His heart began to hunger for Psalm 119 and he would find himself praying it through every night. The Lord said to him that he was not to read the Bible to make a sermon. He had no thought that he would ever preach a sermon again in all his life, nor had he the desire to do so. He simply ate the Word of God. The Lord made it real to him: "You must read my Word to have it form your mind. That's why you are reading it. Your mind needs to be reformed by my Word." And to his amazement, beloved, to his utter amazement, in those first months of his restored life, God began to give back to him all the gifts he had had before he fell. The Lord began to perfect the Gift of Wisdom he once had. He also opened up to him things that were long since forgotten and lost to view, things that had been said in the

Vessels' Conferences he had attended with Mrs. Robinson for four years. The Lord also gave him the understanding of why the Work had failed, and why the Vessels had failed, and what the trouble was. God showed him how to proceed, and what God was now doing, and the place of the New Body in the earth now – the "whys, and wherefores, and hows" – in such amazing and vast detail that even what we have written down is not half of what he saw. And he understood that all of it was mercy, just Pure Mercy.

As you might expect, Rex Andrews was now tested on all the things that had overthrown him in his backslidden life, in the same circumstances, the same environment, the same temptations, the same pressures, for more than two years. God preserved his integrity and kept him also in the all-night prayer and taught him to walk with God right in the midst of all that had defeated him before. And by means of that, *God has opened a way of victory in this Work. The door is open for any one of us to go through into God.*

Now as strange as it may sound, Mr. Andrews was also conscious that Mrs. Robinson was working with him. From her place in the heavens, she was working with him. It was heart-breaking, and it was humbling. It was hard for him to accept and grasp that she would do that. She was the holiest woman that one could imagine; he was the vilest, filthiest sinner he had ever heard of or known about, not only by virtue of what he had done, but by virtue of what he had done *with the light that he had*. And yet he knew that she loved him.

Mrs. Robinson understood Rex Andrews. It's hard to take in, isn't it? You who have struggled with evil (and there's hardly one of us who hasn't struggled with evil), you need to know that God is like this. The Lord has brought many people to us in the extremes of their condition. They are representative of various types of problems. The Lord brings them and deals with them and wins in them. All of us are like that pretty much.

In addition to that consciousness, he experienced the Presence of Jesus in an unusual way. "For nearly two years I had a running conversation with Jesus while I was working," he told me personally. "I felt as if He were right there next to my shoulder. I would ask Him questions, and He would reply in words." Everything he had learned about "inwardness" now became REALITY to him. He was lost in "the wonder of just Jesus Himself" – it was The First Love. He found the ability to "do everything for Jesus" – it was The First Works. Holiness is not merely freedom from sin; holiness is the ability to mix and mingle with sinners, even to "to participate in another's ills, evils and faults,"†† and to inject love into their lives without becoming corrupted yourself.

The point is, beloved, Jesus understands where you've been and what you fight. He *understands* it. He has Himself actually been there. That is something that many people do not grasp about God. He understands wickedness. There are times when I felt I would expire when that thought was made real to me. I felt I would die, considering the things I had done, and why I did them – but realizing that Jesus had actually been there with me and understood me. It's more than I can take in. But Jesus is holy, and He has no other purpose in that understanding than to give you His love and make you know HIM and His holy love.

That is what Mr. Andrews discovered in those years. All the talk about "praying through for love" in those first forty years of the Work suddenly became illuminated to him. He saw what love was. He understood it and could explain it. Everything began to make sense.

When I speak of "a large gift of wisdom," that is what I am talking about. It is, of course, WHAT THE BIBLE TEACHES on the subject, but it is presented in a way that makes you face God, and face life, and face others, in the knowledge of what HE is and what HE does in a world of lost sinners.

The Lord led Mr. Andrews to write to Elder Brooks in Zion, but no reply was received, so he wrote to Mrs. Judd, who was about the same age as he was and had also been one of the original Vessels. They had been the two youngest ministers in those earlier days, and they were good friends, "chums," he once told me. He wrote to her, opening his heart about God's new work in his life. He wanted to come back to Zion to repent, but he was afraid that nobody would have him, because he (mistakenly) assumed that Elder Brooks had rejected his return (not knowing that Elder Brooks had never received his letters).‡‡

I should mention that his son Charles, who never lost faith for his father to be restored, prayed for him daily and wrote to him weekly for seven years. Many in the Faith Homes prayed for him as well. One of the members of the congregation made a trip to California to visit Mr.

---

†† Mercy NEVER commits the sins others are in. It "participates" in the sense of "eating and drinking with sinners," as Jesus did. For Jesus, that participation would mean that He *became* sin for us, that we might be made the righteousness of God in Him (II Corinthians 5:21).

‡‡ It is not proven, but evidence exists that someone in the Faith Homes intercepted his letters to prevent his return.

Andrews and offer help and encouragement. Mr. Andrews cursed at him and pushed him out the door. Others also prayed, including his wife Beulah, who remained faithful to him during those awful years.

Anyway, he now wanted to come back to repent publicly for all his sins, after which he planned to travel to Kenya, East Africa where his wife had gone to live with their daughter and son-in-law (they headed a mission station there). He did come back to Zion at Mrs. Judd's invitation, found out that Elder Brooks welcomed him "home," and he did repent. In a public meeting he knelt in front of Elder Brooks and asked forgiveness for his sins, from all his former co-workers, as well as from the entire Faith Home family. He said, "I know you all have heard about the terrible things I have done, but I was ten times worse than anything you heard."

At this point it is time to make some observations, before we complete this *black & white sketch* of Rex Andrews' life and ministry.

Observation #1. The purpose for which God raised up the Zion Faith Homes, and the call of God on Rex Andrews' life, were inextricably bound together.

In later years, he admitted that he should have never left Zion in the first place in 1918. God in His Mercy brought him back to Zion in 1946 for nearly three years, and again in 1963 until his death in 1976.

Observation #2. The Zion Faith Homes stood for a complete and utter surrender to Jesus Christ, of spirit, soul, and *body*. As related in Gordon Gardiner's biography of Martha Wing Robinson, *Radiant Glory*, Jesus demonstrated His power to accept such a surrender and to possess His Vessel to a degree that few have imagined possible.§§ After her death in 1936, the Faith Homes struggled to maintain the purity of that example, and no one knew what to do to move the Work forward, except Jesus.

In His Mercy, Jesus resurrected the Work by restoring Rex Andrews to his intended ministry, especially as it related to the Gift of the Word of Wisdom. "I have never seen a work go so low and then be recovered in its strength and power," a visiting missionary who was in a position to know, told me. I am deliberately saying that the purpose of God in raising up the Faith Homes in those early years of 1907 to 1936 was not defeated. This

---

§§ In other words, God will make her experience normative, not exceptional.

book is in some ways a sequel to *Radiant Glory*, because it must be known that God's intended plan did not cease with Martha Robinson's death.

Observation #3. I have it in writing that the Faith Home history would be divided into two 40-year periods: 1907 to 1947, and 1947 to 1987. Those periods have come and gone, but the second period was just as important as the first. Rex Andrews' ministry formed the leading characteristics of that second period in the life of the Homes, and my own ministry is a testament to what Jesus did during those years.

Observation #4. God never meant the Faith Homes, or Rex Andrews' life, to diffuse an atmosphere of exclusiveness or elitism. Those who say so do not understand the divine goal toward which God is taking His people. Speaking of her experience, Mrs. Robinson said, "It is not meant for one, but for many." Rex Andrews said, "I abominate the use of my name. If what I say about God is true, it doesn't need my name to prop it up. And if what I say is not true, then you shouldn't be repeating it." To some extent, I have reservations about writing a chapter or two about him. What helps me is the thought that his words of wisdom will be a help to seeking souls.¶¶

The next chapter will finish this biographical section of *A Vast Simplicity*. Of necessity it will include a more personal testimony of the influence Rex Andrews had on this writer. But I hasten to add, what I have received was the direct result of Christ-in-the-man.

¶¶ "God told us once that He was going to establish 12 places on the earth in which He would do more or less what He is doing here. *And He will.*" From this writer's notes taken down (not *verbatim*) during a talk by Rex Andrews on August 27, 1972.

CHAPTER FOURTEEN

A BLACK & WHITE SKETCH OF
 # REX B. ANDREWS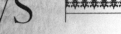
PART 2

The restoration of the Faith Home Work took place along the lines of the light which was opened up to Mr. Andrews. As mentioned, no one else knew what to do.

After his public repentance, the days of his stay lengthened into weeks, and the weeks into months. The old-timers met frequently to be corrected, yes, but the Lord gave them much more than that. Hope sprung up in the desert of their hearts. Jesus' majestic Presence dominated every session. Miss Brooks told me the message of Mercy thrilled her through and through. False foundations of self-righteousness crumbled to pieces and the Cross appeared in its Glory.

Elder Brooks welcomed the Prodigal Son's return the way "the elder brother" in the parable SHOULD HAVE welcomed his younger brother. He invited Mr. Andrews to share about repentance, lowliness, and mercy in the general meetings, held now four times a week. By word of mouth the story of Rex Andrews' restoration spread outside of the Homes, and hungry souls crowded the meeting room. Soon he was speaking daily.

Not everyone was pleased, however, and some attributed Elder Brooks' openness to Rex Andrews to his advanced age, or even senility. The thought of a "new work" taking the place of the "old work" did not sit well with many, especially among those who felt they were spiritually advanced because "we knew Mrs. Robinson and her teaching. We learned all we needed to know about Love through Mrs. Robinson's ministry," they said.

Elder Brooks had given a prophecy in 1944, however, and it was being fulfilled. By way of recalling the essence of what was previously shared, here are a few excerpts from that prophecy as they were taken down in shorthand:

> KNOW ALL MEN BY THESE PRESENTS: that I, God Almighty, have spoken and will speak again. Let your scribes take out their scroll. I want these words taken.

I want my people to understand a mystery. I want them to know that this Work is set for the rise and fall again of many in America, for a sign, which shall be spoken against. There are many that are now your friends and your praisers who will be otherwise before they finish their course...

And to some who are sitting in this place today, I will announce that <u>unless you get into the Word of God and on your knees more definitely and constantly</u> than you have done, you will become a persecutor and an opposer of this Work, for as the breach grows wider, it will be because there is a neglecting of The Book and of prayer, and you will be among them...

I would not have you suppose that the present condition of this Work is God's ultimate. I want you to understand that you must arise out of this self-life and out of this flesh and seek the Lord more definitely, or you will be classed among the dissenters.[1]

Nearly half of what could be called "Faith Home adherents" never accepted the Word and Testimony that God gave Rex Andrews at that time. In fact, the truth of Mercy nearly died out (and the Homes would have closed down), had not Ruth Brooks and Mr. Eaton urged Mr. Andrews to continue speaking it. Much has been written about that period in the history of the Faith Homes, but we must return to the *black and white sketch* of the man God used to restore the power and spiritual vigor of the Homes.

After two and a half years, enough had been said and done to put the Homes back on track. Mr. Andrews kept up his *Night Watch*, and yet found the strength and time to visit people in the congregation, to take the noon meal alternately at each of the three Faith Home households, and to share frequently in conferences and meetings. He deliberately turned down most invitations to minister elsewhere, though the passion and fire of his ministry attracted attention, especially in the Midwest.

At last he felt released to leave America and rejoin his wife and family in Kenya, stopping in South Africa on the way to visit several mission stations staffed by missionaries sent out by the Faith Homes in previous years. He kept what he called the *Log of a Testimony*, during that long journey which ultimately took him beyond Kenya, to Europe, and finally to the recently established State of Israel, covering a span of three full years. In this interesting *Log* of eighty-eight pages, one is able to see him in all kinds of settings, interacting with unbelievers and believers alike. Several passages strongly impressed me. It is worthwhile to review some of them here. Where needed, I have made minor edits and added comments to set the scene.

Leaving Zion, he went to New York City, where he boarded a freighter headed for Durban, South Africa. Missionaries often went to their appointed fields via freighter. Rooms were available on board for a dozen passengers who simply wanted a ride, not entertainment; meals were taken with the ship's captain and crew. Here is Mr. Andrews' description of his first opportunity to witness for Jesus onboard:

This morning at breakfast Mr. Holman, big lawyer from Seattle, offered a cigar to the Captain, who started to refuse, but Mr. H. made some joke about smoking old communistic cigars and not capitalistic ones. Then I said, "I knew they were rank, but not that rank." Laughingly, of course. And then added that I used to smoke them all day long, but not anymore. Then Mrs. McLeod, widow from Los Angeles (elderly, Congregationalist) said something about my being an example of those who decide to quit and do it. My answer was, "No, The Power of God. I tried to stop, but couldn't. Then I prayed, and it was taken away." The Chief Engineer, Mr. Wilkinson, said, "You wouldn't take that away from us, would you?" Then my mouth said, "I'm not taking anything, I'm GIVING. Took me about forty years to find it out. When you GIVE, then everything begins to come to you." Mrs. Holman nodded. Mr. H. looked touched. The Captain's face kind of halted in mid-air, so to speak. The Engineer couldn't think of anything for that, AND I had gotten my first testimony into the conversation, at the table without any forethought or worry. With me, The Lord seems to arrange unexpected things that work out nicely. The point is to keep in touch and in worship INSIDE, and then you are always ready. But you can't do it if you are getting mad inside at this and that which you don't like in other people. You have to stay centered in GOD no matter what "they" are like. And The Mercy-ing Heart does it. Beautiful Life! Wonderful, wonderful Father.

Four weeks after he left New York, he finally reached "Bethesda Mission," remotely located 150 miles north of Pretoria, the capital of

South Africa. (I visited this Mission myself in 1978.) The welcome he received prompted the following comments on "smiling":

> *We got over to "Bethesda" about 5:30, just before dusk. The missionaries came out to meet us, smiling big broad smiles that made you feel glad that you were alive and had gotten where they (the smiles) are. It's a wonderful and blessed thing to smile. I heard once someone say that Jesus, The Man of Sorrows, NEVER smiled. The truth is that <u>no one</u> ever smiled like Jesus. The OT speaks much of a Lord who is "our Joy and Song"; who puts laughter in our mouths; who was worshiped with songs of Joy, and with dances of Joy. He promised JOY. One of the First manifestations of Joy is smiling eyes and smiling countenance. The NT is full of Rejoicing in God, both on earth and among angels. Jesus looked up to Heaven "rejoicing in Spirit," and said, "Father, I THANK Thee that Thou hast revealed these things to BABES." He brought Joy everywhere He went, joyful release from sin, sickness, troubles, disease, devils. Joy swirled around Him like leaves in a wind. Children shouted for Joy in the temple. No one ever smiled like Jesus. Maybe He would give you part of His sweet smile too, if you would forget your self-important ideas, and feast with The Lowly One in His outflowing Love. Paul says, "Rejoice always, and I will say it over again: REJOICE." People are not spiritual because they hold their face like a mask, and don't relax its muscles into smiles.*
>
> *Why, the OT calls out for the "light of Thy Countenance." What is the light of the countenance but smiling – radiant smiling eyes – with the features arranging themselves accordingly? Smiling and rejoicing are taken for granted in the Bible, as the accompaniment of a happy, joyful heart. A joyful heart is the direct result of cleansing and victory over sin. The most "inward" person I ever knew had one of the most radiant smiles I ever saw. She could smile through sorrow. It was still there through heartbreak. She knew what it was to have a broken heart, but she could still smile. She taught us to have a "Glory Heart." She could teach it because she had it. She had a Glory Heart because she had a lowly, mercying heart, which is: Abiding in Jesus. That was The Founder of The Faith Home Work. She had a most charming laughter. Inwardness made her smile, because Inwardness is FINDING GOD AND KNOWING JESUS. Smile folks, SMILE!*

Those paragraphs qualify as a spiritual gem.

As one might expect, he had a few bouts with physical affliction, particularly where insects abounded and personal hygiene was difficult to maintain. In the following quotation, Mr. Andrews records his need for healing from spider bites:

> *At Zebediela, the day before, a bunch of 7 or 8 bites had appeared on left leg above the ankle, on inside. I thought they were tick bites, but later, all agreed that they were spider. They were very red ... except the big one and two others which were brown. The number had increased to 20, which looked also like incisions. Some fever started in mouth and head, but I thought it was the heat. Had prayer in the nite meeting, and claimed the victory. Next morning there looked like more tick stabs, counted 38; and on Friday 47. (They weren't bites, however, but poison coming out, I guess.) By Friday nite the fever was definitely taking hold. Then, about 2 a.m. it suddenly changed and became cool and free. I had awakened about 11 p.m. in some kind of a dream where the way was continually blocked; and just at the point where it seemed that overwhelming collapse was imminent, The Holy Spirit quickened my whole being, body and soul, with a surging Word, "THIS is The Victory that OVERCOMES" – "Faith is The Victory, O Glorious Victory" – that OVERCOMES. The chorus of that hymn swelled out in Glory and Praise within, as the Word repeated itself over and over: "This is THE Victory, even our Faith." And there was a flow of wonderful abundant Life glowing sweetly thru the whole body.*
>
> *O God of all comforts! We have come now to the life of naked faith in God's WORD. <u>"Our Faith" is to CEASE from our reasonings, and love of own intellect, and simply LET GOD'S WORD LIVE.</u> O Glorious Victory! For six years now, my whole life has been just THAT, viz.: seeing God's WORD triumph over the world, and the flesh, and the devil. It is The Holy Spirit who does it, and who keeps THE WORD. O Sweet Spirit of The Lamb. How lovely, how wonderful you are.*
>
> *At 2 a.m. the fever LEFT. All nice and cool. The ankle swelled quite a bit and became a pink band about 4 inches wide clear around, itched a trifle. A streak of blood poison, red, and wide as a little finger, started racing up the leg inside. It reached to exactly 4 inches above*

the knee. And there it STOPPED. Right there. It remained visible for over three weeks. But no pain at all. God had demonstrated to me again that He was THERE. "Thus far, and NO FARTHER." I love my Father. The Name of the Lord IS a strong tower. We run IN and ARE SAFE. Glory to God in the highest, and on Earth, PEACE.

In 1978, I spent a full month in South Africa, visiting several places where Rex Andrews had been 28 years before. Providentially, I met Rev. John Bond, who was considered an "apostle" in South Africa; he pioneered over fifty churches for the Assemblies of God in that nation. After speaking at the Sunday Morning Service in his church in Johannesburg, I accepted his kind invitation to share Sunday lunch with him and his wife in their home. After the meal I asked them, "Do you remember when Rex Andrews came to South Africa?"

Mrs. Bond immediately responded, "How can I forget? The conviction of the Holy Spirit in his meetings was very strong. I saw that I was not a very loving person!"

Mr. Andrews spent ten wonderful months in South Africa before taking another boat up the African east coast to Kenya, where He rejoined his wife

Mrs. Beulah Andrews and Rex Andrews at the equator with their three grandchildren and a native boy.

and youngest daughter and family. Many opportunities to share opened up to him. At one point, he was invited to be a guest speaker at a conference of the Anglican Church in Kenya. After his first talk, the presiding Bishop came to him and said, "Brother, please take all of my allotted speaking times at this Conference." Such a response came because of the intense reality of the messages Rex Andrews spoke. Mrs. Andrews told me, years later, "Douglas, you have no idea the fire that my husband was in during those days! It was a blaze of truth and its effect on people was enormous."

While in Kenya, still keeping up with his *Log of a Testimony*, he wrote a short paragraph on the need for the Word of God that has become one of his most oft-quoted comments.

> *The most foolish person in the world is the one who has the opportunity to read, absorb, digest, live in, be immersed in worship-reading the Bible, but doesn't do it because of PREOCCUPATION with other things of this world. It gives me the creeps and the chills, almost, as it becomes plainer to me the immense, incalculable LOSS which even the children of God are incurring for one thing, viz., WASTING their time on the flesh-desired and mind-desired things of the modern world, instead of being immersed in the Bible as the very HOME of the soul.*

To that I must add another quote about the Word of God.

> **It is the Love of The WORD which is going to wipe Satan from the Earth like a little dust removed by the cloth.**

As his time in Kenya came to an end, he felt the Lord "was pressing me in spirit to turn toward Palestine," he wrote in his *Log* in February 1951. Although the War of Independence made it difficult to enter Israel as a tourist, God opened the way. By the end of March he took a room in Tiberias, near the Sea of Galilee, experiencing "a sense of GOD'S FACE LOOKING DOWN," as he put it in his *Log*. God led him into contact with Finnish missionaries to Israel, and, to make a long story short, he followed the Spirit's leading to Finland, where he ministered in 23 different places in ten weeks; to Switzerland, ministering for nearly three weeks in 16 places; and to Germany, where he ministered for a month.

However, before 1952 ended, he traveled to Israel once again, this time to stay for eleven years. "Our work in Israel," he stated in his Log, "will be centered in a Prayer Ministry which seeks God for everyone to find Him more, and FULFILL THEIR CALLING WHERE THEY ARE, to the very utmost of His power and blessing upon and in them."* As it turned out, he did that, but God used him in other ways as well. All of the things he had been teaching – beginning with the Bible Classes and meetings in Zion, continuing as he ministered in Africa, Europe, and Finland, and bearing fruit among God's workers wherever he went – developed into the in-depth study of What the Bible Teaches About Mercy. The 35 chapters as we now have them were all written in Israel.

Returning to Tiberias, he discovered that R. G. Letourneau, Christian inventor and philanthropist, had built a small neighborhood of one-story homes in the village of Poria Elit, located on a plateau about 8 miles west of Tiberias, with a lovely view of the Sea of Galilee to the east. He purchased one into which he and his wife Beulah moved in 1953, fully expecting to remain there for the remainder of his life. In order to make it easier to keep up his *Night Watch* without disturbing Beulah, he added a second story to the house. They developed a garden for flowers and planted fruit trees. He reached out to his Jewish neighbors, whom he invited to his home for a simple prayer service each evening as the old day closed out and a new one came in (by Jewish reckoning, "days" begin at sundown, of course).

From time to time the Lord led him to various population centers in Israel, where he would take a room simply to intercede for the fulfillment of God's promises to The Land and its People. Sometimes he would pray without interruption for as long as 17 hours with just one plea in his heart: "Mercy, Father, Mercy!" How could it be otherwise, when he knew by experience the Mercy that drew him back to God after seven years of rebellion? Would not God fulfill His promise to His People as expressed in Isaiah 54:7-10?

---

* Along these same lines, Mr. Andrews also wrote: "In dealing with the missionaries, individually, The Lord gave me to try to help them to see where they needed to be different. But SECRETLY, i have to confess that i always had a deep and vigorous admiration for them, each one: because i could see what they were up against merely to keep their heads above water, so to speak, and make any headway at all. ALL the missionaries are REGAL people to me. I love them all, no matter what organization they belong to. An almost impossible thing has happened within me: i long to see every one fulfill in God, and that entirely apart from any desire to make them disciples to me, or to any organization." (Often he used the lower case "i" instead of an upper case "I".) Rex B. Andrews, *Log of a Testimony*, unpublished journal, p. 78.

For a mere moment I have forsaken you, But with great mercies I will gather you.

With a little wrath I hid My face from you for a moment; But with everlasting kindness [hhesed] I will have mercy [rahham] on you, says the LORD, *your Redeemer.*

For this is like the waters of Noah to Me; For as I have sworn that the waters of Noah would no longer cover the earth, so have I sworn that I would not be angry with you, nor rebuke you.

For the mountains shall depart and the hills be removed, but My kindness [hhesed] shall not depart from you, nor shall My covenant of peace be removed, says the LORD, *who has mercy [hhesed] on you.*

In Poria, the Lord impressed on his heart the desire to write out some *Meditations in the Revelation,* as they came to be called. He completed 15 chapters sometime in 1955, covering the first three chapters of the Book of Revelation, but found no inspiration to continue writing after that. Jesus revealed many things to him during the quiet hours of the night, things which would emerge later in his teaching. He traveled to the States two or three times during the eleven years he lived in Poria Elit, blessing the saints in Zion, but stating that he had no intention of returning to the Homes or of assuming a leadership role in them. Jesus had in mind, however, a further work of purification of Rex Andrews and a fuller crucifixion of his will, but did not reveal it to him until it happened.

God continued to restore divine touches of "the Power Work" on his physical body. One night in the early Spring of 1963, the Enemy appeared before him.[2] "You will not proceed any farther on the pathway you are walking. I will block you."

Shocked, but not deterred, Rex Andrews replied, "No, you are mistaken. In Christ's strength I will keep going forward."

"No, you will not," replied Satan. "You are not going this way any longer."

"Yes, I am," replied Rex Andrews.

Not long afterward, a sudden and debilitating stroke left him paralyzed from his neck down! He could only open his mouth and blink his eyes, nothing more. His wife Beulah could only do so much for him. A British nurse came to help temporarily, whose brusque bedside manner ordinarily would have unsettled him, but in God-given lowliness Mr. Andrews called her "an angel from God." He and Beulah sent out other pleas for assistance, but no one agreed to provide long-term care.† God partially relieved their plight by healing him completely on his right side, but it soon became clear they could not continue living in Israel.

The following notice appeared at the end of the July 1963 newsletter from the Faith Homes:

> Mr. and Mrs. Rex Andrews arrived at O'Hare field from Israel on June 6. We are very happy to have them here and their ministry is a real blessing to us.

Such a simple notice, not even mentioning the stroke as the reason for their return to Zion! But I will never forget what one of the trainees told me about the welcome he received from the large number of friends who drove to O'Hare Airport to meet them. "As the attendants wheeled him to the gate where we were gathered to greet him, when we saw him we all broke into that beautiful chorus, *A Fountain Has Been Opened*. It was unforgettable!"

Let me put in all the words here, as we sang them frequently in Zion.

> *A Fountain has been opened, In Jesus' side;*
> *A healing stream it flows, My sins to hide.*
> *O let me bathe my spirit, Within its flow;*
> *I know that it will cleanse me, Whiter than the snow.*

Recalling that incoming passengers in those days could be met right at the gate, can you picture the effect of that on the bystanders? Many times, we as trainees and staff gathered round arriving or departing missionaries that way, singing with them and praying for them. It's a shame, isn't it, that we can no longer do that?

And so it was that God brought Rex Andrews full-circle, back to the place from which he had withdrawn 45 years earlier! Jesus, the Patient One, had "waited to be gracious." Now He could bring His fulfilling mercies into His loved-one's life for the next 12 years to make them "the best years of my life," as Rex said to us not long before he passed away; "all the pieces have fallen into place." That was true, not only in his own life, but also in the everyday life of the Faith Homes.

---

† While on a visit to Israel in 1975, my wife and I met a missionary in Israel who was a trained nurse. She was one of those whom the Andrews had contacted for help. She related that the Lord told her specifically NOT to assent to their plea to nurse Brother Andrews. Upon hearing "the rest of the story" from us, that it was God's will for him to return to Zion, she was greatly relieved, for she had long wrestled with guilt over saying, "No."

Miss Ruth Jackson, long-time resident of the Homes, and housemother of the home into which Rex and Beulah had moved, told me, "Douglas, you have no idea what a blessing his presence in the Homes made at that time." Loose ends were tightened up. Rules were enforced. The young trainees found much comfort, instruction, and encouragement from Mr. Andrews. To everyone's surprise, he never let his semi-invalid condition prevent him from carrying out a full schedule of ministry: speaking in the meetings; conducting Bible classes for the trainees; counseling people individually; and maintaining correspondence with pastors and missionaries. His *Night Watch* continued as usual.

I suppose in reading these sentences the reader may be forgiven some latent or overt skepticism, but I am a witness to the truth. For nine years my wife and I observed these things and know firsthand whereof we speak. **It was Jesus-in-the-man that made it possible. We were enabled to see a Great Jesus, not a great man. God is making Jesus available to His people now in the same way, and to the same degree. That is why this book is being written.**

Gradually the daily life in the Homes steadied measurably, and young people who completed their training were sent out into the ministry, both in the States and abroad. My wife and I arrived when the resurgence in the Faith Homes had swelled considerably. The first time I heard Rex Andrews share a message, it seemed to me I was hearing a voice from Eternity. His messages, though normally limited to one hour, went by like ten minutes. Jesus' Presence came through his voice, as it were. It is hard to express the authority and power in his voice. My understanding began to open to the Truth of God's Love.

During my daily quiet times (the Eight-to-Ten Period), questions arose that I could not answer. In the next meeting where Mr. Andrews spoke, the answers came as part of his message, as though he were giving answers to specific questions I had submitted in writing. "His sermons are like a tree," Miss Brooks explained to me. "There is always a trunk to them, but as he climbs the trunk, he explores each branch in detail before heading back to the trunk." "That happens," she continued, "because unwittingly the Spirit guides him to meet the differing needs of his listeners." I was not the only one, then, who testified of having my questions answered as he talked.

The leaders of the Homes required us to take notes of the various talks, special music, and testimonies that filled all the meetings. For two years I did that faithfully. Actually, after each service I had to rewrite all of my notes in more legible handwriting because Mr. Andrews asked us to submit our notes to him for inspection. What a treasure I now have!

The Sunday Evening Service was Rex Andrews' night to speak. We would sing, praise the Lord out loud, and testify for about half an hour, followed by special music (he always wanted that before he shared).‡ Customarily, two strong men carried him in a chair from his room on the second floor to the front of the meeting room where, from a sitting position, he addressed the people using a microphone set on a small table in front of him. After several years, he decided it was "too much trouble" for the men to take him back and forth, and instead he both heard the meeting via a loudspeaker in his room, and also shared his messages from his room using a microphone, without seeing anyone, of course. Somehow it worked, and nothing was lost by his not being visible.

I kept taking notes of his messages for more than six years. In 1994 the Lord led me to put them in digital form, typing them into the computer – a massive undertaking – but many interested souls have been blessed by reading them. Even now those notes bring me back into the atmosphere of the services in which they were shared.

Personal Remembrances

In a sketch of this nature, it is impossible to include all the instances of personal interaction between Mr. Andrews and myself. Some things are best left unsaid, being private and sacred. Nevertheless, I must confess that I studiously avoided seeing him for the first two years of our residence in the Homes, mainly because I knew he "could see right through me." Later I broke through that barrier of fear and self-preservation and spent many hours in his room seeking and receiving both counsel and correction. I will reproduce enough of his words and notes to give the flavor of our relationship, with a simple qualification: He made *all* of us feel "special" and gave us *all* equal attention. No one had a privileged place in his circle of friends.§

On his birthday, Miss Brooks rounded up the trainees to sing "Happy Birthday" to him in his room. He seemed uncomfortable, and when we

---

‡ The late Evangelist Leonard Ravenhill did the same. If the pastor wished to introduce him to the people, Len insisted on special music between the introduction and his sermon, so that the atmosphere of the music, sung worshipfully by skilled musicians, prepared the way for his message. My wife sang that way at his request many times.

§ The one exception may have been Miss Ruth Brooks, to whom he had entrusted a great deal of responsibility for oversight of the Work. "He told me I never needed to make an appointment to see him," she said to me after he died. "I wish I had taken greater advantage of his offer." Of Miss Brooks, Rex told this writer in 1975 that "the Work could not go on without her at the present time." She outlived Mr. Andrews by 21 years.

finished he raised his head and said, "Thank you, I really appreciate it. But if you knew what a sinner I've been, you might not be so eager to sing to me." We all assured him of our appreciation for his life, of course, but his obvious lowliness stunned me.

For five years I did the ordinary grocery shopping for the households of the Faith Homes, a responsibility that took several hours to complete as generally 30-35 people ate three meals a day in the three separate Homes. Mr. Andrews at that time decided to resume a class for the male trainees. He sent word that he did not want to interfere with my shopping responsibilities and left it up to me what day, and what time, the class should meet. Why should he care about *my* convenience? I could hardly understand it.

One day, in 1970 I believe, I received a call from the pastor of a church in a neighboring town, inquiring if my wife and I would be willing to join him as full-time staff members. It seemed like an open door for us; after all, were we not being trained for an opportunity like this? I went to Mr. Andrews to tell him about the offer and to solicit his prayers for us. The next day I received a handwritten note on a small 3x5 piece of paper. It read as follows:

Shalom, Brother!

This is to urge one thing re your decision, <u>and</u> stating it to Bro. H_____.

It is this:
Cut all words and explanations down to ONE THING – don't even mention me at all. Let your answer be the complete simplicity:

The LORD leads me to accept.
or
The LORD leads me not to accept.

There needs to be no "explanations." Either God does, or does not, command you to accept the invitation. "In all thy ways ACKNOWLEDGE HIM – the Lord – and He will direct thy paths."

In case your answer is, "Yes," you may be sure that we will love you and remain interested in your Work and in your Future.

In His Unfading Love,

Saba¶

¶ *Saba* is the Hebrew word for Grandfather, and many Faith Home residents respectfully and lovingly referred to him that way.

> Shalom Brother!
> This is to urge one thing re your decision, **and** stating it to Bro. H_____.
> It is this:
> Cut all words and explanations down to ONE THING — don't even mention me at all. Let your answer be the complete simplicity:
> "The LORD leads me to accept."
> or
> "The LORD leads me to not accept."
> There needs to be no "explanations". Either God does, or does not, command you to accept the invitation. "In all thy ways ACKNOWLEDGE HIM — The Lord — and He will direct thy paths."
>
> In case your answer is "Yes", you may be sure that we will love you and remain interested in your work and in your future.
>
> In His Unfading Love,
> Saba.

My wife and I prayed for a day or two more, with a clear word coming to us: *The answer is "No."* I called the pastor and told him – without any explanation – that the Lord had led us not to accept his offer. I thanked him, and he was gracious.

That afternoon I went to the Meeting House where Mr. Andrews lived, not wanting to bother him, but just to leave word that I had declined the invitation. I found Miss Violet van Hellen, who helped care for him, and asked her to convey the message. On my way out of the house, Violet came running after me and said, "He wants to see you." I went upstairs to his room, and as soon as I entered, he thrust out his hand to shake mine and said, "Congratulations! You made the right decision!"

As I stood there speechless, he continued: "Did I say or do anything to persuade you one way or the other?"

"No, not at all," I replied.

"I left you in the Lord's hands," he said. "But I want you to know that if you stay here five years, the Lord will give you a ministry." I thanked him and left the room.

Not every encounter turned out like that one. One day I received word that he wished to speak to me alone as soon as possible. At the appointed time I knocked on his door, waiting for the usual response bidding me, "Come." Instead of shaking my hand, though, he motioned to the empty chair in front of his little desk, and said sternly, "Sit down, brother. You are in trouble."

For the next 30-45 minutes he exposed my need for Poverty of Spirit in a way that left me completely stripped, undone, with no excuses to give. When he finished, he asked, "What do you have to say?"

"Thank you."

"That's good," he said, and prayed for me before I left the room.

On the way back to "the Enoch home" (3002 Enoch Avenue) where we lived, my head was swirling and I could barely hold myself together. My memory said, "What did he tell you to do?" I replied to myself, "He said that I should pray a three-word prayer, 'Bring me down'." "Right," said my memory. "Then start now."

That was a life-line for me into a "coming down" that continues to this day. I prayed that simple prayer hundreds, if not thousands of times. *I am grateful for that day of confrontation and correction.*

Five years came and went. The impression deepened that my ministerial call was to the Faith Homes, not elsewhere. In February of 1973, Millie and I met with Rex Andrews to tell him we wanted to stay in the Homes, "even if it means washing dishes and mowing lawns for the rest of my life," I said. He smiled, thanked us, prayed for us, and dismissed us. Although I meant what I had said, Mr. Andrews offered no position, no promises.

That summer I drove our family to Boston, Massachusetts for a vacation/visit with my wife's relatives, returning to Zion on July 29th, a Sunday. Miss Brooks informed me that Rex Andrews wished to see me and Millie the next afternoon. There were two chairs waiting for us in his room. He greeted us and we sat down.

"Do you know what you've done wrong?" he asked me. I cringed. "No," I managed to say.

It was the only time he ever teased me!

"God wants you to be a minister in the Faith Homes," he continued, smiling. "We all have been praying while you were away, and we know this is God's will. You will be ordained two weeks from today in the Monday Night Service. Rev. Jack Rettinger (a friend of the Homes and pastor of a nearby church) will officiate. I like the dignity he brings to such a service."

Thus on Monday evening, August 13, 1973, the Lord put me into my life's calling.**

At his request, Millie and I went up to his room for prayer after the meeting. I said something about "feeling at home since the day we came here." His head shot up as though he had seen a snake! Instantly I realized what I had done: exalted myself, as though God was obligated to honor me as "a good fit." I deserved another dressing down, but instead he gave me advice that has stayed with me all these years.

"There are two temptations that come to a new minister," he said. "First, the almost unconscious thought that 'I am special'; second, the feeling of holding back because 'I'm new at this.' Both are wrong. Instead, simply follow the leadings of the Spirit." Those are not his exact words, but close enough to convey the sense of it.

The next day I received another note, this one related to the new dress suit (with a plaid pattern) I had purchased especially for the ordination service. The note reads:

> *Shalom! It would be nice for you to have a dark suit, coat and trousers, for all year wear. Being in the front, it is wise to have on something which does not attract the gaze of the audience, nor cause any to stare. Then your words will not be lost in the working minds. Avoid modern "sports wear" – colors and mixed suit. Just a dark all year suit of good material, <u>Dark</u> blue, or gray, always good. Gray is good in several shades.*
>
> *If your clothes are just a part of the general view – then your <u>WORDS</u> will receive proper attention.*
>
> *In His Name, Saba*

** My father, who was not a believer at the time, came to that service of his own volition, with my mother. To my knowledge, it was the only time he attended a church service in more than 30 years.

> Shalom! It would be nice for you to have a dark suit, coat and trousers, for all year wear. Being in the front, it is wise to have on something which does not attract the gaze of the audience, nor cause any to stare. Then your words will not be lost in the working minds. Avoid modern "sports wear" — colors and mixed suit. Just a dark all year suit of good material. Dark blue, or gray, always good. Gray is good in several shades.
>
> If your clothes are just a part of the general view — then your WORDS will receive proper attention.
>
> In His name, Baba

Douglas Petert
3002

His words stung a little bit, but out of the envelope fluttered two $100 bills to cover the cost of another new suit! As I recall, I picked out a suit that matched his recommendations, and the bill came to just over $198. What lessons I learned from that experience!

Now I had to find the balance line between the two temptations he had outlined for me. As the youngest (by ten years) of the ministers on the "platform" of the Faith Homes, I wondered what I could share that had not been preached by the others many times over. I had no natural speaking gifts. Only by prayer could I find out what, and how, to share anything fresh, bringing forth "treasures both old and new," as Jesus put it.

Barely three months later, I gave a message from the latter half of Luke 21, trying to show the beauty, as well as the meaning, of the key words in verses 28, 30, and 31, *Redemption, Summer,* and *Kingdom of God.* I still was not comfortable speaking in front of the older ministers, including Mr. Andrews, who listened from his room.

The next day my heart rejoiced at the note handed to me by his assistant, Ruth Lade ("Ruthel"). It said,

> *Shalom!*
>
> *You were very much on the Right Path, in your talk Sun. morning Dec. 2.*
>
> *That kind of truth and teaching fits right into – meshes in – the fundamentals of the F H Work of those "other years."*
>
> *If this Work, now, can get the full grasp of the Supreme truth that God <u>wants to</u> "give Jesus for free" – even as He desires to give – pour Himself – into His children, then the Tree of Life is <u>blooming</u>, and "summer" is at hand: Luke 21:28-29-30: "Redemption – Summer – Kingdom" Context 24-33-36.*
>
> *Saba*

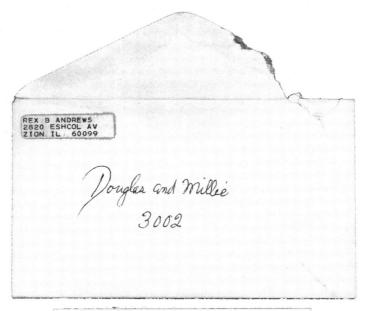

Envelope:
REX B ANDREWS
2820 ESHCOL AV
ZION IL 60099

Douglas and Millie
3002

Note:
Shalom! You were very much on the Right Path in your talk Sun. morning Dec. 2.

That kind of truth and teaching fits right into — meshes in — the fundamentals of The FH Work of those "other years".

If this Work, now, can get the full grasp of the Supreme truth that God wants to "give Jesus for free" — even as He desires to give — pour Himself — into His children, then the Tree of Life is blooming, and "summer" is at hand: Luke 21:28-29-30: "Redemption — Summer — Kingdom" Context 24-33-36.

Aba

My final personal remembrance for this sketch took place in 1975, just before his health and mental strength began to ebb. Millie and I were making plans for another summer trip to the Boston area, and I wanted to follow that up with a solo stay at a summer place my brother owned in Minnesota. The entire vacation would span six weeks, a normal length of time for staff members to be away, to relieve the stress of communal living. The Faith Home Council had approved the plan, and Mr. Andrews always read the minutes of those meetings.

This time the Lord intervened, as the following note indicates:

4:15 AM

Precious Bro. & Sister Detert, Shalom.

After several hours of leaving it before the Lord, I am presenting a question to you:

What is God's Work going to do with one of the Main Ministers gone away for six weeks?

You are not Trainees. You are Leaders. The minutes of the F. H. council inform that you plan to be away for six weeks. There seems to be something missing. For 60 years things have been differently: We have "the Word of The Lord" here still, by which VITAL things are decided. And it is a vital question: What is God's F. H. Work going to do with you away for six weeks!

Perhaps you could meet with this Old Saba Thursday afternoon after 2 p.m. so we can discuss the matter of the Faith Home Work and meetings.

If convenient, please let Ruthel know when you can come. Scuse writing. 4:30 am. now. God Bless you.

Old Saba.

P. S. If some other day and hour is best for you, please let Ruthel know. Thanks

MEMO

4:15 A.M.
Scribbles from
Brother Rex

Precious Bro. & Sister Detert, Shalom.

After several hours of laying it before The Lord, I am presenting a question to you:

What is God's Work going to do with one of the Main Ministers gone away for six weeks? You are not Trainees. You are Leaders. The minutes of the F.H. Council inform that you plan to be away for six weeks. There seems to be something missing. For 60 years things have been differently. We have "The Word of The Lord" here still, by which VITAL things are decided. And it is a vital question: What is God's F.H. Work going to do with you away for six weeks?

Perhaps you could meet with this Old Saba Tuesday afternoon after 2 p.m. so we can discuss the matter of The Faith Home Work and meetings.

If convenient, please let Ruth know when you can come.

Tense writing. 4:30 a.m. now. God Bless you

Old Saba.

P.S. If some other day and hour is best for you, please let Ruth know. Thanks

We kept the appointment, which turned into two appointments. The Lord laid the groundwork for accepting more responsibility as leaders in the Homes, a necessary thing in light of the soon passing of this beloved *Saba*. We discarded our plans to be away for six weeks.

Strangely enough, two months later, a member of the Faith Home congregation offered Millie and me a 10-day, all-expenses-paid, trip to Israel! Instead of approving our small vision of a vacation, the Lord gave us a much more important trip, sending us to Israel in November 1975 to attend the *Second World Conference on the Holy Spirit*, and to tour His Land from north to south.

As the young people say, "Go figure!"

The *Meditations in the Revelation*

The library of every conscientious minister contains hundreds of good books written by a variety of saints down through the centuries. Leonard Ravenhill's collection lined all four walls of his office. My colleague here at Evergreen Center, where I have ministered since leaving the Faith Homes, possesses an even larger library. Using the new techniques of digital storage, my computer can carry thousands of volumes to any place I may travel. I have read hundreds of them and am familiar with hundreds more. Certain books I have read multiple times. Rex Andrews read *The Autobiography of Madame Guyon* at least 48 times. His copy of her book was given to me after his death, and I found the hash marks inside the back cover that kept track of his readings. As trainees in the Faith Homes, we were required to read slowly through *The Practice of the Presence of God* by Brother Lawrence ten times. Oswald Chambers' daily devotional, *My Utmost for His Highest*, continues to bless God's people by the millions since it was first put together for publication by his wife not long after his death.

I do not know how many times I have read through *What the Bible Teaches about Mercy*, though a conservative estimate might be 20 times. Why? Because the words bring Jesus near to me, and in His Light I see more clearly my need to be like Him. Are those *Studies* equal with Scripture? Of course not, but they do bring the sincere reader into the Bible teaching about Mercy in a powerful way. Why? Because they are written by one whose giftings included "The Word of Wisdom." What is the Wisdom of God? "Wisdom, God's Wisdom, is the understanding of the Love of God as the Law of Life." The *Mercy Studies* fill out the understanding of Jesus' Spirit-Word in Matthew 5:7, "Blessed are the merciful: for they shall obtain mercy."

In 1954-55, the Lord began to inspire Rex Andrews to meditate on the next Spirit-Word in verse 8 of the Sermon on the Mount: "Blessed are the pure in heart: for they shall see God." The results became the first fifteen chapters of *Meditations in the Revelation*. The ability and the fire of inspiration to continue past the third chapter in the Book of Revelation dried up, however, and the *Meditations* stopped.

Unexpectedly, in the early months of 1971, the fire rekindled! I was there when it happened. Night after night he wrote by hand, chapter after chapter. Often, when considering the next passage in the Book of Revelation, he had no idea what to write; the Lord would inspire him and the words would flow. He experienced what David did when preparing the plans for constructing the Temple that Solomon would build: "All this, said David, the LORD made me understand in writing, by His hand upon me, all the works of these plans."* By June of that year, he wrote twenty-five more *meditations*, covering the remainder of the Book of Revelation, Chapters 4 – 22. Rex Andrews spoke about it publicly and I took notes on what he said (please accept my disclaimer that I put down what I think he said; my notes are not a *verbatim* record):

> *It has taken 7 years here in this room to get me down enough to write these last 25 Meditations without getting my natural reasoning mind into them <u>at all</u>. They were practically DICTATED TO ME. I have only seen that fact (about the 7 years' preparation) in the last few days.*[3]

That became the final puzzle piece in his life, coming back to Zion to complete what God had begun in him so many years before – *and* to get him "down enough" to finish the *Meditations in the Revelation* which he had begun writing in Israel fifteen years before. In some ways it was the climax of his life.

I have no record of how many times I have gone over the *Meditations*, but I am confident it exceeds 15 times. Each time I sense the urgency of the Lord in them: GET READY FOR MY COMING! THERE'S NOT

---

* Commentators differ on the meaning of the phrase, "by His hand upon me," confused perhaps because there have been many counterfeits of the real thing. It's best to understand this phrase essentially as, "dictated writing"; Madame Guyon experienced the same thing I am attributing to Mr. Andrews here.

MUCH TIME LEFT! I AM COMING "IN SUCH AN HOUR AS YOU THINK NOT!" Those who have attended the classes where I have read through the *Meditations* and commented on them, can attest to that same urgency rising in their hearts as we considered these things together. I trust the reader will hear the same call of God as you wait on Him to give you a pure heart.

His Passing into Glory

About a year before he died, Rex Andrews informed Ruth Brooks that he would no longer be sharing a message each Sunday night as he had done for ten years. He also removed his name on the Trust Deed in which the Faith Home properties were held, replacing it with two younger ministers. Slowly he closed down his outward ministry of teaching, holding classes, and corresponding with numerous workers and friends. We all knew his time had come, but we kept up earnest prayers for him, knowing how dependent we had become on him for spiritual leadership and advice.

Late in the summer of 1975, our beloved missionary friends from Argentina, Ken and Annie Schisler, came to visit the Homes for the third time. Annie's walk with God was well-known, because the Lord had opened the heavens to her from the time of her conversion (1970) and thereafter.[4] On previous visits to the Homes, Annie and Rex had conversed about the things God had revealed to both of them concerning the end of this present Age, and they found their experiences dove-tailed perfectly.[†]

On this, their final visit, I had the privilege of driving Ken and Annie to their next destination. From the back seat, Annie suddenly said to me, "Why are you holding on to Brother Andrews? Don't you know that he already has one foot in heaven? Hasn't he suffered enough? Besides that, the Lord wants to develop the rest of you."

That night at 11 p.m. she called Ruth Brooks to repeat the same message. It truly was the Lord's time to take him, and we could not deny it.

Meanwhile, his mind began to weaken to such an extent that we hardly knew how to take care of him. He called for a special meeting of the Faith Home Council to be held in his room at 12:30 p.m. during the normal lunch hour. Dutifully we all came, but he was unable to communicate what he wanted. In other ways his behavior became strange, and sometimes he

---

† This was stated publicly by Rex Andrews on more than one occasion. Though not usually given to promoting anyone's "visions," he stated emphatically that Annie's visions were "authentic."

would issue orders in a loud voice with no one around. Finally the Lord spoke very specifically to us in prophecy through one of the members of the Faith Home Council. I remember one phrase in particular, "You mean well and you want to serve him, but his mind is weak… When he hollers, shut the door."

I could hardly bear to witness the changes in him. One Sunday afternoon I cried out to the Lord in a time of private prayer, "Lord, why can't you give him a glorious home-going, like you did for D. L. Moody, or Elder Brooks, or many other great saints?" All I heard was, "He is going to die like any ordinary person in a nursing home." It was a hard word for me to accept. My wife, with greater understanding, said, "It is part of his crucifixion."

As it turned out, Mr. Andrews passed away when three of the older ministers were either sick or away from Zion. At about 8:30 a.m. on Sunday, February 1, 1976, Ruth Lade phoned me to say, "I think he is leaving us soon. What should we do?"

"Call each of the three Homes," I replied, "and gather all the residents together. Let us all take the answer to the many, many months of prayer for him."

This was done, and at 10 o'clock he was seen to raise his hand, then sink down on the pillow – and into the arms of Jesus. No trumpets blowing audibly, no angels appearing, no unusual presence of Jesus in the room. Simply gone, like any ordinary person in a nursing home might go.

At 10:30 that morning it became my sad duty to announce to the saints assembled for the usual Sunday Morning Worship Service that our beloved brother had passed into Glory. His funeral took place the following Wednesday, February 4th. He was 86-years-old/young. I close the sketch this way, deliberately using the expression "old/young," because of my love for a favorite quotation from his writings:

"You can be young and fresh with Jesus' arm around you."

CHAPTER FIFTEEN

PARTICULAR EXPRESSIONS OF GOD'S WISDOM

Introduction

Several times in this book, I have mentioned the Gift of the Holy Spirit which Paul calls *the Word of Wisdom* (I Corinthians 12:8). From its inception, the Faith Homes operated under the direct control of the Holy Spirit as manifested in that particular gift. Though little was said about the "gifts," their influence on the Work was large. The Lord spoke His wisdom through His servants, called *Vessels*, bringing help and blessing to many needy souls. The "word of wisdom" gave unusual and effective counsel to individuals by the hundreds. Lesser known is the fact that the "word of wisdom" created a schedule that could bind a communal household together in an orderly and balanced way. The work duties, the times of prayer, the daily meetings, distribution of responsibilities, and even room assignments, were all given directly by God's wisdom. Had it not been so, the Faith Homes would have been a chaotic place in which to live!

It would be a mistake to think of this gift as a natural ability to see into matters with insight that comes from experience and age, even if the person so used is "sanctified." There is a marked difference between human wisdom and God's wisdom. Solomon obviously possessed God's wisdom, given to him as a gift, because he asked for it instead of asking for riches or wealth or honor or the life of his enemies. "Wisdom and knowledge are granted to you," God told him (II Chronicles 1:12 NKJV).

Paul the Apostle received that same gift from God, as Peter affirms in his Second Epistle: "…according to the wisdom given to him, has written to you, as also in all his epistles" (II Peter 3:15-16).* To this day scholars and

---

* Jamieson, Faucett and Brown's comment is, "Supernatural and inspired wisdom 'GIVEN' him, not acquired in human schools of learning."

laymen alike still study his letters and struggle to understand "some things hard to be understood." Nearly half the "books" in the New Testament are his work, and they are quite correctly accepted as being "the Word of God."

"Wisdom is the principle thing: therefore get wisdom," said Solomon (Proverbs 4:9). All through the Book of Proverbs, "wisdom" stands out as the most valuable possession a man can have. At least 50 times the word "wisdom" appears in Proverbs.

Most of us are very familiar with the verse, "The fear of the Lord is the beginning of wisdom" (Proverbs 9:10). If *fear* is defined as, "a sense of being overwhelmed by anything, whether good or evil," then the beginning of wisdom is a sense of being overwhelmed by God's goodness, *i.e.*, that "He is good, for [because] His Mercy is forever."

As mentioned earlier, the Lord appointed three of the Vessels to be "wisdom teachers" in the Faith Homes. They were: Mrs. Robinson, Mrs. L. M. Judd, and Rex Andrews. That meant that each of them had to stay in a continual awareness of the overwhelming nature of God's goodness, especially as it related to the Cross of Jesus Christ.

Mrs. Robinson expressed such an awareness even before Jesus took complete possession of her. She wrote,

> *I asked God to show me myself as He saw me, and in answer to that prayer He gave me a glimpse of myself such as I shall never forget. For the first time in my life I felt the need of Christ's atoning blood. I saw the meaning of His death for our sin. I saw that all my consecration and obedience – if it were possible to be PERFECT in this – were not sufficient to cleanse my heart. I saw that what I had regarded as an upright and even Christian life, was very dark in God's eyes.*[1]

Rex Andrews testified that,

> Mrs. Robinson considered herself to be just nothing. She considered herself to be so ungreat that any ideas of greatness in the human sense at all were preposterously scandalous, almost. How do we know these things? Because she demonstrated it through her entire life to the absolute end that she laid down her life for those around her; laid down her life for the Work; and she laid it down in intercession, which if God could only get a few like that in the world, a lot of things would be done, and He is going to have them, I am sure. Throughout her life she took the place

of being a servant of all the rest of the servants. She tried all her life to put the others AHEAD. She took the club on her for their mistakes. She had to pray them through and she took it, but she was always trying to push the other ones ahead and ahead and ahead and forward to be the ones who could stand and hold the positions. I know that, because I was one of those who in 1914 was designated for a certain position here, but it broke down for certain reasons and never was carried through.²

The Lord Jesus kept Mrs. Robinson in the exercise of the *Word of Wisdom* from 1907 until her death in 1936. All who knew her well gave testimony to that fact.

Mrs. L. M. Judd found herself in a terrible contest over her call to be one of the "wisdom teachers" in the Homes. Within a year or two of joining the Work when it moved to Zion in 1910, the enemy endeavored to block her from advancing into the place to which God had called her. He did it by catering to her desire to "be the one who would obey the Lord perfectly" – a noble desire, to be sure, but one that had to be founded completely on the awareness of her absolute nothingness, on the one hand, and a large sense of being overwhelmed by the Mercy of God to her through Jesus crucified, on the other hand. The spirit of emulations surfaced to interfere with her calling.†

The Lord worked and worked with her, both before and after Mrs. Robinson's death, but she never "saw" that she had been wrong or self-seeking in her pursuit of a place in God. Please understand that she was a true warrior for God, and fought valiantly as she thought best. However, her "wisdom" became tainted and never benefited the Work as it should have.

The enemy of souls also targeted Rex Andrews, as related in the biographical sketch of him, who battled "the lust of the flesh." The devil also induced him to back away from the Work before God could strengthen him in his gifting. The Lord planned to give him "ten teachings to establish him in the Gift of Wisdom," but for various reasons, all attributable to the enemy, he never received them. Having withdrawn from the sources of help in the Faith Homes, his ministry waned and the operation of his gifts all but disappeared, until "God in His fabulous wisdom let me fail," as he stated later. After his recovery, he never strayed from that sense of being

---

† "Emulations" is defined as "ambition or endeavor to equal or excel others." It is named as a work of the flesh in Galatians 5:20.

overwhelmed by the Mercy of God. (This sentence hardly does justice to the depth of that overwhelming sense of Mercy.) Even during the weeks when his mind was failing just prior to his death, his son Charles remembers him saying,

> "I am the worst sinner in the world." He also quoted the verse, "I am the Lord. I change not." And several times he quoted this and then he seemed to be saying that the pearly gates would "creak" open for him because the Lord does not change, because His mercies do not change or fail.‡

That understanding is the setting in which the Gift of Wisdom could flourish, and it did.

A few years ago, I composed an *Ode to Hidden Wisdom*. It fits in here.

> *You stagger on in human wisdom's light,*
> *Your ersatz joy erases not the night;*
> *You only have a hollow boast to bring*
> *Before the piercing eyes of Christ the King.*
>
> *Were you created but to think and move*
> *Inside the tiny house He calls 'self-love'?*
> *Behold expansive Love! Behold His hands and feet!*
> *Who opes his heart tastes something more than sweet!*
>
> *Stand still before His Cross, your ears and eyes*
> *And heart entranced! A spectacle behold, and cries!*
> *Ask now to understand! Eternal verities*
> *Bespeak the Father's love beneath grey skies.*
>
> *Love has spoken! Have you heard that Voice*
> *Which pleads for you the right to choose a choice*
> *To follow in His steps, alive, ablaze,*
> *And free, yet pris'ner of His Sacred Gaze?*
>
> *With one accord let us allow the Dove*
> *To move us far away from sin, with love*
> *To speak into a lost soul's night a word*
> *That draws him into heaven's glist'ning world.*

---

‡ Shared at Rex Andrews' funeral by his son Charles Andrews.

The secret of life's joy yields not to human ken;
God's inside world transcends the minds of men.
O seek not wisdom on a mundane plane,
But let God's love-tipped arrows find their aim.

With the above explanations in mind, we can briefly introduce five expressions of that Gift of Wisdom that remain with us in Rex Andrews' writings. The five, which will be taken up in the next chapters, are:

1. What Is Mercy? - *What the Bible Teaches About Mercy*
2. Poverty of Spirit and Lowliness
3. The Missionary Prayers - *Kingdom Praying*
4. Seven Talks to Ministerial Trainees - *What Are You Here For?*
5. In What Manner Will He Come? - *The Meditations in the Revelation*

First: What Is Mercy? - *What the Bible Teaches About Mercy*

I will discuss the subject of "Mercy" more fully in Chapter 16, but I want to relate now my first reaction to the *Mercy Studies*. On the second day of our visit to the Faith Homes in early 1967, as we were about to start our prayer time, the Assistant House-mother at the Guest Home handed me one of the chapters. In those days the *Studies* had not yet been bound into a book; they were just loose-leaf chapters. The heading was, *Chapter 14, A Glimpse into the Prophets' Lives, Isaiah 55, 57, 58.*

"Read this," she said, "and it will bless you."

I tried, but the words made no sense to me! It sounded like "gobbledygook," very repetitious, and super-spiritual. The sentences did not connect in my mind. What I read I promptly forgot. My background told me I needed something more orderly, scholarly, academic. I was not the type to get emotional over spiritual-sounding treatises.

How little did I know my need at the time! No wonder Paul prayed for the Ephesians, that "the God of our Lord Jesus Christ, the Father of glory, would give you the spirit of wisdom and revelation in the knowledge of Him..." (Ephesians 1:17). Only gradually did I come to appreciate the fact that God speaks "not in words which man's wisdom teaches, but which the Holy Spirit teaches, comparing spiritual things with spiritual" (I Corinthians 2:13). When I heard Mr. Andrews reading from and teaching the *Mercy Studies*, they slowly opened up to me; the wisdom in them began to break down my "natural mathematical reasoning mind." Having been a math major in college, that phrase jarred me a little (and he used those words often, but dropped the word "mathematical" later on), and I presumed he was anti-intellectual. The Lord slowly confronted me with verses such as,

For the mind of the flesh is death, but the mind of the Spirit is life and peace; because the mind of the flesh is enmity toward God; for it is not being subjected to the Law of God, for neither can it be. (Romans 8:6-7, Literal Translation)

...to the acknowledgement of the mystery of God, and of the Father, and of Christ; in whom are hid all the treasures of wisdom and knowledge. And this I say, lest any man should beguile you with enticing words. (Colossians 2:2b-4)

*Trust in the L*ORD *with all your heart, and lean not on your own understanding; in all your ways acknowledge Him, and He shall direct your paths. Do not be wise in your own eyes; fear the L*ORD *and depart from evil.* (Proverbs 3:5-7)

*Let no one deceive himself. If anyone among you seems to be wise in this age, let him become a fool that he may become wise. For the wisdom of this world is foolishness with God. For it is written, "He catches the wise in their own craftiness"; and again, "The L*ORD *knows the thoughts of the wise, that they are futile."* (I Corinthians 3:18-20)

In my early Christian life, I thought the "carnal mind" meant the "unsaved mind." Only later did I grasp that Paul called the Corinthians "carnal," though he stated clearly in the opening of his first epistle that they were "sanctified in Christ Jesus, called-out saints" (I Corinthians 1:2)! And the words quoted from First Corinthians 3 (above), implied that their worldly wisdom had caused the divisions which split them!

The definition of wisdom, God's wisdom, helped me: **"God's wisdom is the understanding of the Love of God as the Law of life."** Our lack of power to affect people for Christ traces to our love of human wisdom, our reliance on the "natural reasoning mind," instead of relying wholly on the Spirit of Wisdom.

After all these years, my conviction grows stronger that the book entitled *What the Bible Teaches About Mercy* quite clearly expresses the Wisdom of God. We were taught, "The Mercy teaching falls flat unless one is willing to DO it."

Jesus said, "If anyone wills to do His [God's] will, he shall know concerning the doctrine, whether it is from God or whether I speak on My own authority." (John 7:17). Are you willing to "do His will"?

Second: Poverty of Spirit and Lowliness

No one document by Rex Andrews summarizes the light God gave him concerning the vital truths of Poverty of Spirit and Lowliness, although he wrote about those fundamental issues frequently. I have devoted an entire chapter to them, because "mercy," and "Poverty of Spirit and Lowliness," must needs go hand in hand, *viz.*, they are inseparable. The words God gave Mr. Andrews to define the terms "Poverty of Spirit" and "Lowliness" are evidence of the Gift of Wisdom operating in his writings. Those definitions did not come from "study" or "academic inquiry"; they are not the product of intellect-at-work. They were revealed to him by the Holy Spirit, exactly as the Holy Spirit had given him the definition of "Mercy" in 1944.[3]

Unless one accepts this explanation, the meaning of Poverty of Spirit, or of Lowliness, is lost. The mind of man, even with the best of intentions, will miss the point I am making in this chapter about the Gift of Wisdom. Consider the following words:

> The natural-reasoning-mind is the fortress of the world and self. The idolatry of "mind" is the most wicked worship in the world. It is Self-worship. And the worship of Self and Mind is "flesh" in its vilest form.
>
> We cannot cross over into the fullness of God unless we are willing to give up that which is opposite to it: the natural-reasoning-mind, which is the palace of Self. Self-worship and Mind-worship is distinctly what God is fighting against. The great world issue today is not merely in some nation which champions atheism and communism, but in the State-of-Mind which loves, and reveres, and exalts the nature-mind rather than the Mind of Christ Jesus.[4]

I have witnessed first-hand the kind of reaction people, even Christian people, have had against the truths of Poverty of Spirit and Lowliness. You see such reactions in the Book of Acts – against Stephen, then against the disciples, and especially against the Apostle Paul. "The off-scouring of all things," they called him (II Corinthians 4:13), as well as "babbler," *i.e.,* "seed-picker" (Acts 17:18). That ridicule arose primarily in Greece, where the culture prized their so-called "wisdom," but despised the preaching of the Cross as "foolishness." There is no blindness equal to the self-darkness of pride. Listen to this quotation:

> The Holy Spirit would guide us in simple, but triumphant ways of prayer if we weren't so important in our own eyes. One of the devastating features of the natural-reasoning-mind is the uncrucified Self-importance, which will hardly cease from constantly "thinking" – ON self – while we try to concentrate on our Heavenly Father in prayer. "Let THIS MIND be in you which was also in Christ Jesus." That is a trysting place WITH GOD. Jesus was crucified at "The place of a skull." "He bowed His HEAD and gave up the spirit." And we must follow HIM.
>
> Jesus had to wear the crown of thorns because of our pride-mind, self-mind, natural-reasoning-mind. The understanding, with its true reasoning, works properly in the Light of God. You have to look at CALVARY in faith, or your reasoning goes astray, and the Cross-of-Christ is "made of NONE EFFECT." "For Christ sent me not to baptize, but to preach the gospel, NOT WITH WISDOM OF WORDS, LEST THE CROSS OF CHRIST SHOULD BE MADE OF NONE EFFECT." (I Corinthians 1:17).[5]

As you read the chapter summarizing the teaching about Poverty of Spirit and Lowliness, I trust you will understand I am not simply lashing out at some imaginary opponent. The opponent was not imaginary: it was ME! I needed to come down, as Martha Robinson said so eloquently – and publicly – in 1934:

> You need so many times to come down. Jesus has the life and love and faith you need. He wants you to come down, down, down, down, and find Him. Don't be so important. Don't advertise yourself. Why don't you let Jesus who is your keeper, keep you down? Then there is a chance for you to rise. You can't find your place [yourself]. He wants to show you that you have only begun. And He would prove you had been down, if you would only let yourself come.
>
> And now another little word for you who say, "I suppose I must come down." Why don't you see that Jesus is so low down

and it is delightful to come down to find Him – down in the valley at His feet. Don't get a picture of yourself coming down; get a picture of Jesus who is so lowly. God Himself will show you the way down. You do not come down just to come down, but to see Jesus meek and lowly; and to want to follow Him, *where He is*. Learn to let yourself come down. God will say, "Come down, my child, just come down and rest at Jesus' feet. I really want to have my way with you. Why will you not come down?"[6]

Beloved, that also was spoken by the Gift of the Word of Wisdom! Do you have "ears to hear"?

Third: Missionary Prayers - *Kingdom Praying*

Through the years, and even recently, sincere and praying people have remarked how powerful the *Kingdom Prayers* are, if prayed earnestly and regularly.

It needs to be stated simply, that they were given by the Word of Wisdom. From the myriad of possibilities, God chose what pathway the intercessors in the Faith Homes should follow, when it came to praying against the powers of darkness. That does not mean He has not assigned other prayers for other ministries! God's wisdom is infinite, and He always has a remnant throughout the world that does His bidding.§ If you are reading this, then you may assume God invites you to join with others praying in the same Spirit.

As with the previous two topics, I have devoted an entire chapter to the *Kingdom Prayers*.¶

Fourth: Seven Talks to Ministerial Trainees - *What Are You Here For?*

When my wife and I enrolled as trainees in the *Ministerial Training Faith Homes,* as it was called, we had very little idea of the "what, where,

---

§ For example, during WWII the Lord directed Rees Howells and his Bible College students in Wales to pray specifically that Hitler would open an Eastern Front against Russia – which Hitler eventually did, against the advice of his generals. It was a great answer to long and fervent praying. Yet Leonard Ravenhill visited two other ministries, one in Canada, and one in the United States, to whom the Lord had given the same assignment in prayer! Each ministry supposed it had been the only one to pray it through!

¶ See Chapter 18, *Kingdom Praying*.

when, why, and how" as God was leading us. We filled out no applications and signed nothing. Miss Brooks had disarmed me by asking, on that memorable Saturday (January 21, 1967), "What day are you moving in?" I stuttered the reply, not realizing I was making what would be a 30-year commitment, "Uh, uh… a week from Tuesday." We knew nothing about a training program, or that the suggested minimum stay was two years.

In September of that year, Rex Andrews started a series of talks for all the ministerial trainees on Wednesday evenings. Someone recorded the talks, and after seven weeks, Mr. Andrews asked if I would be willing to transcribe them from reel-to-reel tapes to written form. My Royal electric typewriter and the reel-to-reel tape recorder were all the tools I had. Push the play button for a few seconds; type what I thought I heard; rewind the tape and check for accuracy. Each talk became 14-18 type-written pages, double-spaced. It took a while to complete!

Mr. Andrews edited my transcription of his talks, paring them down to half or less of their original length. I still have the originals, with his corrections, because I also had to re-type the edited versions for him to approve. When the time came for the seventh talk in the series, he simply wrote it out instead of speaking it. To our surprise, he stated publicly that they were "as near to the Word of Wisdom in the early years as we now have." As time passed, I realized that the truths expressed in those talks are indeed the Wisdom of God, not *word-for-word*, of course, (as evidenced by the fact that they were reduced from their original length by 60 to 70 percent), but *in substance*. Not only that, but it also became clear to me that *anyone* would benefit from that Wisdom by putting into practice the life-changing understanding contained in the answers to the question, "What am **I** here for?"

The Faith Homes bound those talks into a booklet entitled *What Are You Here For?*, which I include as one of the chapters in this book, editing and adding comments where necessary to explain remarks that belonged to Faith Home life and would not be understood otherwise.**

Do these talks help you understand "God's Love as Life's Law"? You be the judge.

** See Chapter 19, *What Are You Here For?*

Fifth: In What Manner Will He Come? *The Meditations in the Revelation*

This last expression of Divine Wisdom combines both the words of Martha Robinson and the words and writings of Rex Andrews.

My background in eschatology ("study of future things") grew out of annual visits from Rev. John Hall to the church near Chicago which I attended from 1949 until 1956. Rev. Hall taught Dispensational Theology based on Clarence Larkin's well-known charts of the end-times. The Assemblies of God sanctioned Rev. Hall's ministry, and he was considered to be the foremost prophecy teacher in the denomination. I attended the week-long series every year until I almost memorized the presentation. The Rapture of the Church preceding "Daniel's 70th week" became Gospel truth to me. I knew how the Great Tribulation would be broken into two segments of 3 ½ years each; that Israel would rebuild its Third Temple; that the Anti-Christ would deceive the Jews (and the world) until the "middle of the week" (3 ½ years), when he would put an image of himself into the rebuilt Temple and declare himself to be "God"; and that this act would be the "abomination of desolation" prophesied by Daniel and referred to by Jesus. Of course, it all mattered little to the Church, which would be waiting in Heaven for the dust to settle from the conflict raging on Earth. All believers would return with Jesus for the destruction of the Anti-Christ and his hordes and help to usher in the Thousand-Year Reign of Christ.

In Bible College in 1964-65, I learned there were other views, mainly "Mid-Trib" and "Post-Trib" Raptures, as opposed to the majority view, *i.e.*, the "Pre-Tribulation Rapture of the Church." I also had the unpleasant memory of viewing the first movie about "the Rapture"; it was called *The Missing Christians*. Something about that depiction struck me as being childish, but what were the alternatives? I had no idea.

One day while passing Leonard Ravenhill in the Teen Challenge office building, he posed a question to me: "Doug, in the Parable of the Wheat and the Tares in Matthew 13, who goes first? — the wheat or the tares?"

"The tares," I answered correctly.

"Then why do you say that the wheat is taken out of the world before the tares?"

He walked away and left me standing there to absorb the shock of his words. "Does he mean the Church will *not* be removed before the wicked are harvested?" I scarcely knew what to think. Looking back now, it seems to me the Lord was preparing my heart to embrace a fuller – and less childish – understanding of His Return.

The point, however, of this introduction to the subject of "In What Manner Is He Coming," is to present to the reader a possible readjustment of his thinking about the Lord's Second Coming. Consider the following words spoken by Mrs. Martha Robinson during special meetings in the Faith Homes in November of 1934:

> Open thine eyes to see the King. You do not see The King – Jesus. Behold what it is The Lord has sought for thee: it is to have Jesus. He is waiting for everyone. He has not meant it for one, but for many. God is going to take you soon, but not at this time; and if you will be wide awake and open your eyes, you will behold The King. Get ready and meet The King. He is very near. Just look at Jesus. Do not look at it as you have planned. He wants people to take steps just as He plans. It is a lesson that can only be learned by those who have found The King, have seen Jesus in their soul. Open your eyes. Be comfortable with Jesus. It is God and He wants His people to be prepared for His Coming. He is coming, but in a different manner than most people suppose when they study out this subject.
>
> Command this people to know it in a greater way: When is God coming? And unto whom is God coming? It is not yet found out in this world, not yet taught. And the people who are so ready to argue about it are those who are the most ignorant on the subject. Hold your heart open, and when He calls He will not be unknown to you. Jesus knows and will not leave us ignorant.[7]

By 1934, the major evangelical Protestant denominations in America had standardized their end-time positions, adopting a "Pre-Tribulation Rapture" view, as mentioned above. Now, in 2013, those positions remain the same. Yet the Lord in His Wisdom (and I don't use that term lightly) said, "When is God coming? And unto whom is God coming? It is not yet found out in this world, not yet taught." Could it be, then, that our understanding of Jesus' Return lacks something? Is the Church at large adequately prepared, should events *not* unfold as they suppose they will?

Mrs. Robinson *added very little* in her writings that gave answers to those questions. I have a copy of the barest outline of a Scriptural study she made about Jesus' Second Coming, but it only hints at the possibility of His Coming "in a different manner than most people suppose when they study out this subject," as quoted above.

In the *Meditations in the Revelation*, however, Rex Andrews *added a great deal* that gave answers to those questions raised in 1934. I will devote two chapters to the emphasis he put on "The Opening of the Sixth Seal," for example – a topic hardly addressed by the usual views of the end-times.†† The *Meditations* also bring us face-to-face with the seven-times-purified Word of God in the "Messages to the Seven Churches," in a way that confronts our childish notions about "The Rapture" and convicts us of the absolute necessity of a *pure heart* as essential preparation for the Lord's Return.‡‡

The more one reads the *Meditations*, the more one realizes their origin lies not in the reasonings of a man, but in "the light of the knowledge of the glory of God," as seen in the face of the Transfigured Jesus, we might say. You may question the correctness of what I am saying, but I hope you will not reject it out of hand. I believe the *Meditations* are an expression of the Biblical gift of the *Word of Wisdom*. If they are, you will be blessed with a greater appreciation for "the understanding of the Love of God as the Law of Life."

As Philip said to Nathanael, *Come and see!*

---

†† See Chapter 20, *To What End Is God Working?* and Chapter 22, *The Opening of the Sixth Seal*.

‡‡ John says, "Beloved, it does not yet appear what we shall be; but we know that, when He shall appear, we shall be like Him, for we shall see Him as He is. And every man that hath this hope in Him PURIFIES HIMSELF, even as He [Jesus] is pure" (I John 3:3).

CHAPTER SIXTEEN

WHAT IS MERCY?

The young graduate from Harvard College, now working for Teen Challenge in New York City, had reached his limit.

Things were not being run in a business-like way. Bad decisions were spoiling the effectiveness of the ministry. One of his favorite co-workers came under fire for alleged improper behavior with a lady staff worker, when clearly he was not guilty, just disliked. The schedule was hectic – "They don't even give you time to go to the toilet!" one older worker once remarked to me.

The last straw became "night shift" assignments, requiring the young man to work a four-hour shift from 10 p.m. to 2 a.m., or from 2 a.m. to 6 a.m., even after a full day's work during normal hours. It was "normal" for ex-drug addicts to be awake during those hours, and they had a tendency to roam around the Teen Challenge Center at night, as they had done before being converted; thus the need for night-time supervision. The young worker, however, needed his sleep and couldn't keep up with the pace.

For this, as well as other reasons, the young worker decided it was time to go over David Wilkerson's head and expose these grievances to a leading pastor who sat on the Board of Brooklyn Teen Challenge. The appointment was made and kept. For an hour and a half the worker denounced Brother Dave and urged the Board to take action against him. He was satisfied he had done "the right thing."

Less than a year later, the young worker found himself in the *Wednesday Morning Missionary Prayer Service* in the Zion Faith Homes. To him it was the weekly *prayer marathon,* lasting four long hours from 8:00 a.m. until noon. He had never prayed so much in his life! He knelt at his chair on his right elbow for 15 minutes, then switched to his left elbow for another 15 minutes. Then he would kneel on both elbows for 15 minutes, before sitting up on the chair for another 15 minutes. Still only one hour had passed!

From 8 a.m. until 10 a.m., most of the prayers focused on individual missionaries, none known to the young worker. The prayer leader read the names and each Faith Home resident took turns praying for the mission worker so named. "How can any of this be meaningful?" the worker thought to himself. "This is like Group Think!"

After a ten-minute break half-way through the morning, another lady* arrived to lead what were called *Kingdom Prayers*. (After thirty years of praying them, it is still easy to remember each section):

- *Send forth laborers into Your Harvest Field,* according to Matthew 9:38
- *Pour out Your Spirit on all flesh,* according to Joel 2:28ff.
- *Your Kingdom come! Your Will be done, as in Heaven, so in earth!* according to Matthew 6:10
- *Let Your Word rise,* according to Isaiah 40:6
- *Unveil the Cross!*
- *Let Your peace come to Jerusalem,* according to Psalm 122:6
- *Complete the Body of Christ,* according to Ephesians 2:21-22 and 4:12-16

At various points during the second half, the Holy Spirit guided the prayer leader to concentrate on a specific ministry, or a specific man, that needed special prayer and intercession.

On this particular Wednesday morning in the Spring of 1967, Mrs. Klein opened the session with an announcement.

"Dear (v)ones," she said in her German accent, "in my prifate prayer time dis morning, da Lord told me vee must pray for Brudder Dafid Wilkerson. He is such a younk man with such heavy burdens. He needs God's help to run such a bik ministry as Teen Challenge. Let us take de next fifteen minutes to intercede for him."

In a flash of understanding, the young worker suddenly realized that not once had he ever prayed that way for David Wilkerson! At the same time he saw his utter lack of mercy in the light of his own selfishness and glaring inconsistencies. All he could do was weep before God in humiliation and brokenness while the others called on God to bless Brother Dave and his ministry. During those 15 minutes of agony, a crack opened and a sliver of light shone into his self-righteous heart.

---
* Mrs. Henrietta Klein, mentioned in Chapter 12, in the sketch of Ruth Brooks.

As the weeks turned into months, the word "mercy" took on new meaning for the young worker. He began to see that "mercy" was a name for something REAL. Encouraged by the instruction he received in meetings and classes, and more so by the examples of mercy he saw in the lives of his teachers, he delved into a study of mercy as taught in the Bible. The Hebrew word *hhesed*, translated most often as "mercy," "steadfast love," or "loving-kindness," took on a luster he had never seen before. He studied all the passages in the Old Testament that contained that word and its derivatives. He read with astonishment the little booklet entitled *The Will of God*,[1] and saw for the first time that "God's will" did not refer primarily to *a geographical location, or to some great choice in life.*

He had been taught that "God's will" must be sought for: Where should I go to college? What career should I pursue? What woman should I marry? To what country will I be sent as a missionary? It never occurred to him that God had a WILL OF HIS OWN, a DESIRE, as expressed, for example, through Hosea the prophet, "For I desired mercy (*hhesed*) and not sacrifice; the knowledge of God, more than burnt offerings" (Hosea 6:6). Like the Pharisees, he needed to "Go and learn what this means, 'I will have mercy, and not sacrifice,'" as Jesus urged them to do (Matthew 12:10).

As he looked back, he saw the Lord may have been nudging him toward a comprehension of the word "will" (as a noun) in his final year at Harvard. To fulfill his requirements for a liberal arts degree, he took a course called *Introduction to Psychology*. Having been exposed to various schools of thought in the field of psychology, he and his classmates were assigned to write a major paper at the end of the term. He chose to write on the topic, "What Is Will?"

To his surprise, he could not find a good "working definition" of the word "will" in any of the literature! He also discovered major disagreements between the various schools of thought regarding a scientific approach to such a crucial matter as "the will." At least one of his professors, Dr. Jerome Bruner, who became famous for his work in Cognitive Psychology, was realistic: he wrote about "The Black Box" (which turned out to be "the will"), into which went stimuli, and out of which came behavior; but no one knew what happened inside the Black Box! The young student actually thought that was humorous, if not admirable![2] It troubled him, however, that psychologists were trying to modify human behavior without a solid understanding of what constituted the human will. Nonetheless, he got an "A" on his paper, with the professor urging him to write more on the subject.

Shortly after he entered the Faith Homes as a trainee, the Lord drew him into Psalm 136 and asked him to write down why each statement in that psalm should be followed by the words, "for His mercy is forever." He still has that study (and will attach it – updated, after 45 years of experience! – in the Appendices of this book).†

Gradually a realization seeped into his conscious thought. "I have a will of my own. I know what I want, and I pursue my desires deliberately and eagerly. Most of them are selfish in nature, but I do have an overall "will" that has nothing to do with my geographical location or life's big choices. Therefore, it follows that God Himself has a will, and His will has a name: MERCY, or *hhesed*. I need to DO what Jesus said and LEARN more about God's will."

Phrases to describe what he was learning came into his mind, such as:

- **Mercy is to daily life what blood is to every cell in the human body.**

    The means by which each cell receives fresh nutrients continually is called the Circulatory System. It is vital to life. Similarly, mercy provides the physical and non-physical needs of every human being, and the means by which this happens is God's "Supply System" of Mercy.

- **Mercy is a like a river that nourishes life near its banks and tributaries.**

    As the Nile River is to Egypt, and as the Amazon River is to Brazil, so is Mercy to all that live near its banks. Living plants need water! Living beings need Mercy!

- **Like daily sunlight on plants and animals, so is mercy to the inner and outer existence of human beings.**

    Plants need sunlight to survive, because without sunlight there is no photosynthesis. Mercy is God's sunshine, and without its nourishment and sustenance mankind is not able to meet life's demands.

---

† See *Appendix A: Studies in Psalm 136*.

- **As the laws of physics govern the orderly behavior of planets, similarly the laws of mercy govern society, preventing mutual self-destruction.**

    In our solar system, Earth is one relatively small planet held together by an almost infinite number of intricate biological, ecological and meteorological systems. Furthermore, its place in the solar system is maintained by an amazing, harmonious dance of spinning, whirling, fast-moving planets held in their places by a perfectly-sized star called the sun, and a force no one has seen called "gravity."

    Similarly, human society is held in a righteous balance, even under the curse of Genesis 3, by Mercy and Truth, without which we would all destroy ourselves. A very small illustration would be the laws governing vehicle traffic (much observed in the United States, somewhat observed in India!): If no driver yields to another, or stays on the proper side of the road, death reigns!

He began to study in earnest the wording of the *Definition of Mercy* as given to Rex Andrews by the Holy Spirit (a claim the young worker immediately questioned):

MERCY is God's supply system for every need everywhere.

Mercy is that kindness, compassion and tenderness which is a passion to suffer with, or participate in, another's ills or evils in order to relieve, heal and restore.

It accepts another freely and gladly AS he is and supplies the needed good of life to build up and to bring to peace and keep in peace.

It is to take another into one's heart JUST AS HE IS and cherish and nourish him there.

Mercy takes another's sins and evils and faults as its own, and frees the other by bearing them to God.

This is the Glow-of-love. This is the ANOINTING.[3]

He decided to see if these statements were Biblical or not (and that study can be found also in the Appendices of this book).[‡]

[‡] See *Appendix B: The Definition of Mercy*.

His mother's oft-repeated words played in the back of his mind, "Son, don't ever go to a church where they don't preach *Jesus Christ and Him crucified.*" He listened attentively to the messages given in the Faith Homes; he observed carefully the lives of the leaders, most of whom resided in the Faith Homes with the staff and students. His conclusion? "This is REAL and you need to take heed."

The "young worker" was, of course, this author. Years later the words of Frederick Faber's hymn would become very precious to him.

> *I worship thee, sweet will of God! And all thy ways adore;*
> *And every day I live, I seem To love Thee more and more.*
>
> *I love to kiss each print where Thou hast set Thine unseen feet;*
> *I cannot fear thee, blessed will! Thine empire is so sweet.*[4]

What the Bible Teaches About Mercy

Sometime during our second year of training in the Homes, I decided to read all 35 chapters of *What the Bible Teaches About Mercy*. When the schedule of classes and work assignments permitted, I found an empty room and read the *Mercy Studies* on my knees with my Bible open. I read out loud to keep my attention from wandering; I read every Scripture referred to in the *Studies*; I prayed all the prayers recommended, including Psalm 119.

When I finished, I read through all 35 studies a second time in the same manner. As best as I can recall, I covered about three chapters a week, finishing the first read-through in three to four months, and taking just as long for the second read-through.

God met me during that year in a life-changing way. I began to pray *The Mercy Prayer* for those around me. I began to understand the truth of the Hebrew couplet (a well-known characteristic in the Old Testament),[5]

I desired mercy	and not sacrifice
The knowledge of God	more than burnt offerings

implying that "mercy" = "the knowledge of God"; just as "sacrifice" = "burnt offerings." I found and copied the following words from the *Mercy Studies,* and they are now posted in my office where I can see them every day:

> **The knowledge of God is always right before your face.**
> **It is the NEED OF HUMAN LIVES.**[6]

The needs of others around me superseded the self-vision of my own need. I slowly began to know the Creator in His lowliness, revealed in His *Servant-of-All* Son. Though I hardly realized it then, God was preparing me for a ministry of more than 40 years, which continues to the present day.

Love and Mercy

The supreme word in Christian practice is *love*. "God is love," said John so succinctly (I John 4:8). Martha Robinson taught *love* in such a way that many were inspired to pray earnestly over the phrases in First Corinthians 13 until their lives reflected the words of that unparalleled chapter.

Why then was there a need for additional teaching in the Faith Homes on the word *Mercy*? Because the devil had perverted the meaning of that precious word *love*.

At Teen Challenge David Wilkerson had taught us that "love is something you do." I liked the sound of that, though I did not understand it very well. By the time I was born in 1942, Satan had mutilated the word "love" to such an extent that the expression, "I love Jesus," could be used in the same way as saying, "I love my dog," or "I love McDonald's hamburgers." In fact, in my days of summer employment, while working in a paper warehouse in downtown Chicago, my boss played "The Top 40" on radio station WJJD every day, and for weeks I heard Elvis Presley sing songs that clearly confused *love* with *lust*.

In my generation, we needed to know the *components* of love, not the *counterfeits* of love. I am certain this present generation needs such knowledge even more desperately than ours did.

Anyone reading this can obtain a copy of *What the Bible Teaches About Mercy,* where the understanding of Mercy in relation to Love is clearly spelled out.[7] For the purposes of this chapter, I offer the following summary of *love's components*. I hope it is as helpful to you as it is to me.

Grace is the **Face of Love, or Love Looking**. In the Hebrew language, grace (*hhen*) is often used with the word *eyes*, as in Ruth's exquisite words to Boaz, "Then she fell on her face, and bowed herself to the ground, and said unto him, '*Why have I found grace in thine eyes*, that thou shouldest take knowledge of me, seeing I am a stranger?'" **Grace is the welcoming, smiling Face of Love.** It signifies acceptance in the presence of the one looking. The wording of the priestly blessing in Numbers 6:25 expresses it perfectly, "The LORD make His face to shine upon you and be gracious unto you."

Compassion is the **Fellowship of Love,** or **Love Choosing to Share**. In Hebrew, the word for compassion (*rahham*) also means "womb," because the expectant mother's life is bound up with the child in her womb. *Rahham* is also the Hebrew word for "stork," because of the well-known devotion of that bird to its young.

Mercy is the **Action of Love,** or **Love Acting**. It is what love does, in grace and in compassion. The word appears nearly 300 times in the Old Testament, but we find it most frequently in the Psalms. For example, Psalm 86:5 reads, "For thou, Lord, art good, and ready to forgive; and plenteous in mercy unto all them that call upon thee."

The revelation of God to Moses on Mt. Sinai, so basic to knowing God's will, became embodied in Jesus Christ. Compare the wording of Exodus 34:6§

> *And the LORD passed by before him, and proclaimed, The LORD, The LORD God, merciful [Heb. rahham, compassionate] and gracious [Heb. hhen], longsuffering, and abundant in goodness [Heb. hhesed, merciful] and truth...*

to the description of Jesus in Matthew 14:14.

> *And Jesus went forth, and* **saw** *[blessed Face of Love!] a great multitude, and was* **moved with compassion** *[Love's choice to share in their sufferings] toward them, and he* **healed their sick** *[Love acting]. (Emphasis added)*

The Bible itself defines love by pointing to the Cross of Christ and its obvious meaning. For example, hear John again, from First John 4:9-11,

> *In this was manifested the love of God toward us, because that God sent his only begotten Son into the world, that we might live through him. Herein is love, not that we loved God, but that he loved us, and sent his Son to be the propitiation for our sins. Beloved, if God* **so** *loved us, we ought also to love one another. (Emphasis added)*

---

§ Bible scholar and translator, Joseph B. Rotherham, calls this passage *the refrain of the Old Testament*. In this *refrain* I find the three words which together describe *what love is*, at least in the language and atmosphere of the Old Testament.

What power there is in the word "so," meaning, "in such a way"! This is not a treatise on "love in the New Testament," however, but an introduction to the word "mercy" as it is used in the Bible.

God has made these things REAL to me, not as "teaching," but as "life." In the atmosphere of the Discipleship Program at Evergreen Center, where my wife and I now minister, this kind of love is worked out daily in the lives of the interns and staff. This is a very real way to put Christian love into action in the daily life of believers. It includes what we do with our face and eyes, the decision whether or not to allow someone else's sufferings to "touch" us, and the willingness to DO the things that will fulfill their need.

It all spells C-A-L-V-A-R-Y, does it not? How beautifully the following hymn expresses what God's love is, and what it has done:[8]

> *Down from His glory, Ever living story,*
> *My God and Savior came, And Jesus was His name.*
> *Born in a manger, To His own a stranger,*
> *A Man of sorrows, tears and agony.*
>
> Chorus: *O how I love Him! How I adore Him!*
> *My breath, my sunshine, my all in all!*
> *The great Creator became my Savior,*
> *And all God's fulness dwelleth in Him*
>
> *What condescension, Bringing us redemption;*
> *That in the dead of night, Not one faint hope in sight,*
> *God, gracious, tender, Laid aside His splendor,*
> *Stooping to woo, to win, to save my soul.*
>
> *Without reluctance, Flesh and blood His substance*
> *He took the form of man, Revealed the hidden plan.*
> *O glorious myst'ry, Sacrifice of Calv'ry,*
> *And now I know Thou art the great "I AM."*

The Cross absolutely affirms the TRUTH of our sinfulness, our rebellion, our rejection of God's Will, and our guilt. It also absolutely affirms the MERCY of God to any and to all who WILL (to) repent of their sins and embrace the Covenant in Jesus' Blood, called "The New Covenant." "For I will be merciful to their unrighteousness, and their sins and their iniquities I will remember NO MORE" (Hebrews 8:12, emphasis added).

The importance of the word *mercy* in the Bible, in both the Old and New Testaments becomes more evident if one reads the Hebrew translation of the New Testament. It is startling to discover that in most instances where the Greek word *grace*, (*i.e., charis*) is used, the translators have chosen the Hebrew word *hhesed* as best expressing the meaning of *charis* to a Hebrew speaker or reader![9] To any Hebrew-speaking reader, therefore, the God of *hhesed* in the Old Testament is the God of *grace* in the New Testament. Jesus Christ truly is "the same, yesterday, today, and forever" (Hebrews 13:9)!

The Mercy Prayer

What effect does the discussion about "mercy" and "love" have on us? The understanding of mercy changes the way we treat others.

Where does the *teaching* intersect with *behavior*? In the "inside world." What happens at the intersection point? The choice appears, either to *judge* the one I "see" in my inside world, or to *pray* for him or her. This may not be obvious at first. It appears as a *choice* when one is faced with some person who is "seen" in the heart, especially a person who does not delight the imagination of the *look-er*, or who inflames one's heart into anger, or lust, or indifference, or distaste.

We are not aware of how frequently during the day we *judge* others inwardly.

Each day an endless stream of people parade past our inside "view." In that view, we sit on a judgment throne or perch, deciding (*i.e.*, making a judgment) who we like, or don't like; or who is worthy of our attention; or worse yet, who will fill our need (lust of pride) to be honored by them, or our desire (lust of anger) to abuse them with words, or our passion (lust of flesh) to take advantage of them. The inside judging takes place almost instantly, and almost unconsciously. We are habitual judges by nature. Even "saints" who appear *quite kind* on the outside, eventually discover they are *quite judgmental* on the inside, if God shines His light into their hearts.

It is easy to be defensive about this subject. Various objections constitute the defense:

- Only the naïve don't make judgments.
- Jesus not only said, "Judge not," He also said, "Judge righteous judgment."

- If one is not discerning, he will easily be deceived by people with wrong motives.
- In my job, I simply have to make judgments about people.
- *Etc.*

From long experience we have discovered that the main reason people discount or trivialize this matter of "mercy," is their unwillingness to do to others the "mercy" God has done to them.

However, for anyone who earnestly desires to follow in Jesus' steps, the basic question remains to be answered: How did *Jesus* think *inside* while here on earth? How does He think right now, looking down from Heaven? What are His thoughts about YOU, at this very moment? What is His basic, instinctive reaction when He looks at YOU? Is it "judgment," or is it "mercy"? *Selah* – pause and think calmly and meditatively about that. Does Jesus Himself keep "The Golden Rule"?

"With some of us it takes a lifetime," we were told, "to give down that the Will of God is actually mercy." The expression "give down" means, a willingness to CONSENT from the heart that something is so.

What would happen to YOU if you agreed that you needed to pray for everyone you looked at, not only in the outside world, but also in the inside world? Especially if you did so precisely because Jesus prayed for you when you were living in sin, as an alien from God, a rebel against His call, rejecting His Grace? Not to mention what He prays for you now? Would it make a difference in how you "saw" people?

What would happen if your heart became a *throne of mercy*, instead of a *throne of judgment*? What if the love of Jesus for all persons poured through you onto them? What if *the passion of mercy* became your daily life, even as it is the daily life of God?

PRAYER is the intersection, then, of the <u>teaching about</u> mercy and the <u>life of</u> mercy in the heart of a believer. All other acts of mercy flow out of prayer, as the Holy Spirit takes possession of one's inside world.

The wording of *The Mercy Prayer* precludes self: *Father, please flood him/her with Your fulfilling mercies, meeting his/her need as You see it.* Not, *Help me to love them,* or, *Make them treat me better, etc.* Other unselfish prayers flow out of a *Mercy-ing heart,* such as:

Father, make him/her to be what they were born to be, and born-again to be.

Father, make them succeed spiritually, regardless of what happens to me.

Father, cover their sins and mistakes with Jesus' precious blood, and restore them to full and sweet fellowship with You.

Father, as far as possible, let blame fall on me, not on them. Let me bear their reproach.

This is testimony, not theory. It has taken years for the teaching to intersect with my living, but God has subdued me, at least to some extent, so that I truly want *His* will to be done, not *my* will.

In his Bible class, Rex Andrews said to us students, "Don't go out into the ministry waving a green book (the cover of the *Mercy Studies* was green) and tell the people, 'This is what we are going to study.' No, you study what the Bible teaches about mercy, make it part of your life by doing it, and then teach it straight from the Bible." Of course, if people were interested in studying the "green book" on their own or in a Bible class, there was no objection to doing that. But it was never taught as a private doctrine, a "Faith Home teaching," or any similar thing. "It either is the truth, or it isn't," we were taught. "It doesn't need my name to make it stand, or the Faith Home name," said Rex Andrews. "If it isn't the truth, don't preach it. If it is the truth, then teach it as the truth, but live it before you preach and teach it."

Judy – A Difficult Case

I want to tell you the story of *Judy*. Yes, that is her real name, and some of my older Faith Home friends may recall who she is. She passed into Heaven about ten years ago, so I feel free to share her testimony. My wife and I hold her in precious memory now, but it was not always so...

Judy entered into the Faith Home training program about the same time we did, in early 1967. She arrived from England, newly saved and newly anointed, and under the influence of the British evangelist Harry Greenwood. She had been told by well-meaning friends that she possessed ALL the Gifts of the Spirit. Yes, ALL of them.¶ She was, however, difficult to handle, and even more difficult to live with. Acquaintances in the States had suggested she enroll as a trainee in the Faith Homes.

¶ Unfortunately, it soon became evident that their assessment was not correct.

In my view at the time, Judy was insufferable. She was everything in a woman that I did not like – aggressive, overly "loving," way too "spiritual" in her talk and actions, pushy. In a matter of weeks we all knew she was a "problem." In classes she was a "know-it-all"; in meetings she became extremely emotional, almost screaming praises; in relationships, domineering. I did everything I could to avoid Judy. I did not like her at all. The thought of *praying mercy for her* was unbearable. I wished she would just LEAVE.

Gradually her unconquered nature began to show. She once broke a mirror over her roommate's head in a fit of anger. She used the fire escape ladder from her third floor room to sneak downtown at night. Her mind started to play tricks on her, and toward the end of her two-year stay in the Faith Homes she "fainted" several times. Once, while still in her nightgown, she threw herself down the large staircase leading from the second floor of the Meeting House – an episode I know happened because I was one of two men asked to carry her back to her room while she was still (supposedly) comatose. To say she was a "trial" would be an understatement.

And yet...

I did not know at the time that Judy's parents were alcoholics; that she had been living on the street since age 14; that she had earned her living by prostituting herself; that she had recently survived a broken engagement. BUT GOD REACHED DOWN AND SAVED HER, literally!

She was terribly vulnerable to anyone who gave her attention, but hardly anyone knew how to train her to become a godly woman. But God found four people in particular who LOVED her and SAW HER DIFFERENTLY than I did. Those four were Rex Andrews, Ruth Brooks, Mrs. Henrietta Klein, and Mrs. Zella McNutt (Mrs. Klein and Mrs. McNutt were members of the Faith Home congregation). In the words of one of my favorite modern hymns, they *looked beyond her faults and saw her need.*

Rex Andrews worked with Judy on a personal level more than he did with any of the rest of us interns. He taught her what mercy was by the way he treated her, in a perfect blend of mercy and truth. Once (as she related to us later), when she had broken the rules, he began by saying, "Judith, did you do what I heard you did?" "Yes," she admitted. "Get down on your knees and repent." She complied, and repented. She told us later, "It was almost impossible to disobey Saba [Hebrew for Grandfather]. I *wanted* to refuse obedience, but something about the way he spoke made me *want* to obey, despite my resistance." It seemed to us who were looking on, that Saba had infinite patience with her.

Ruth Brooks became Judy's friend, not simply her housemother and teacher. I could not understand why she did that. She took Judy shopping, often sat and just chatted with her, spoke to her sweetly instead of curtly. As long as Judy lived, Miss Brooks treated her that way.

Mrs. Klein interceded for Judy before the Throne of Grace (as did the others), but with a good grasp of Judy's needs. Mrs. Klein, having gone to Rex Andrews for counsel on how to help Judy, quoted him as saying, "Henrietta, every inch we gain with Judy is a great victory." As I look back, I can see what a heart of compassion Mrs. Klein had for Judy.

Mrs. McNutt frequently invited Judy to her home to counsel and pray with her.

> [Story within a story: Mrs. McNutt lived in deep depression for many years. When I became a Faith Home minister in 1973, she often called for prayer. I gave her virtually no help; no matter what I said, it made no dent in her shell of darkness. One day in desperation she asked Rex Andrews to pray for her. He simply spoke to the enemy and quietly commanded him/it to depart from her. She was instantly and permanently delivered and became an enormous blessing to all the needy people who came to her for spiritual help. Mrs. McNutt LOVED Judy deeply, and Judy knew it. Later I will recount how Judy in turn blessed me so greatly at Mrs. McNutt's funeral, which I conducted.]

After the incident when Judy threw herself down the stairs, Mr. Andrews knew it was time to make a change. He arranged for her to transition from the Faith Homes to a Salvation Army facility in Chicago, Illinois. He even gave her a *Certificate of Graduation* from the Faith Homes! When it came time to tell him good-bye, she fell on his neck and they cried together for twenty minutes! Talk about *grace, mercy,* and *compassion*! At the time, I simply did not understand it well enough to make a much-needed change in my inner view of her.

Judy more or less bounced around after that, eventually marrying a widower whom she had met when he visited the Faith Homes. It wasn't an ideal match, but she accepted his proposal. Millie and I attended the wedding in Michigan. Their marriage produced two sons, but the boys grew up in a home with too much strife and misunderstanding for them to develop fully in their Christian faith. Divorce lay ahead, causing much grief. Judy's mental condition deteriorated to the point where she had to be hospitalized in a psychiatric facility on Chicago's South Side. Some years later, after I had been ordained, she called from there and solicited my help.

I did *not* want to visit her, but I felt the Holy Spirit would be grieved if I didn't. The memory of that visit remains vivid even as I write. Judy was rational, but terribly needy. She reached out to me for *compassion*, and Jesus-in-me responded. I gave her a small New Testament I had used during my days in New York City, when I was in charge of visiting prisoners on behalf of Teen Challenge. I said she had "lost her moorings" and needed to re-establish them. She asked me what the word "moorings" meant and together we talked about how to find them again. Something was changing in my inside world. I found that I actually CARED what happened to her. In an unspoken way, I felt the Lord was asking me to pick up Judy's "case" where Rex Andrews had left off (he had passed away by then). The *prayer of mercy* enabled me to bless her both in my heart and outwardly.

After Judy's release (indicating she was normal in the eyes of the authorities), she returned to live in the Zion area. She started coming to the meetings again. Another widower befriended her and she felt it was right before the Lord to marry him. (In deference to my thoughts on the matter, she said to me, "I know you have convictions about my re-marrying, and therefore, as much as I would like you to perform the ceremony, I have asked a non-denominational reverend in town to wed us; this way you won't struggle over what to do about me." I was taken aback by her thoughtfulness toward me.)

Her life began to mend and she and her husband drew closer to Jesus, much closer than I at first realized. They attended the Faith Home meetings regularly, even after my wife and I left Zion in 1996. She often drove to Wisconsin to see us, and whenever we were in the Zion area we visited her. When her husband died, she gave me the privilege of giving the main talk at his funeral. She spoke frequently of Rex Andrews and what he had done for her, as well as what Ruth Brooks, Mrs. Klein, and Mrs. McNutt had done for her. Now, we actually looked forward to seeing her! She was a true friend.

On the occasion of Mrs. McNutt's funeral, the Lord opened Judy's eyes to the unseen world. I had been away from Zion when Mrs. McNutt passed away, but I returned in time to conduct her funeral service. We were all singing the hymn *Great Is Thy Faithfulness*, when suddenly Judy saw Jesus standing next to me with His arm around my shoulder, and an expression of appreciation on His face. He didn't speak, but just looked at me as though thanking me. Then He turned and looked at Mrs. McNutt's body in the open casket, with the same expression of gratitude toward her, before He faded from Judy's vision.

I had no idea what had happened until the next morning. Just before the Sunday Morning Worship Service in the Faith Homes, Judy beckoned me to talk with her privately, and she shared what she had seen the day before. I was totally shattered by her account and simply could not recover my composure during the entire service, weeping quietly the whole time, not able even to preach. (At such times, one is thankful for plural leadership.) Though Judy was not conscious of the blessing she had been to me, God had brought about a complete turnaround in our relationship, so that any *mercy* I had done to her came back to me multiplied. Many times I have wept in recalling that incident.

Gradually Judy's health deteriorated, and while we were away on a missions trip to India, she passed over into *Immanuel's Land*. What a victory for Jesus! What a demonstration to me, *not simply of teaching,* but of *teaching put into practice*. Among her possessions was the New Testament I had given her years before, with a note about "you have lost your moorings" in it, and it was returned to me. In looking back, I suppose the Lord spared me from excessive grief by taking her when I was absent. *Judy, I will see you again, precious sister!*

To her applies the words of one of my favorite hymns, *He Looked Beyond My Faults and Saw My Need:* [10]

> *Amazing Grace will always be my song of praise,*
> *For it was Grace that brought me liberty;*
> *I do not know just why He came to love me so -*
> *He looked beyond my faults and saw my need.*
>
> *I shall forever lift mine eyes to Calvary,*
> *To view the Cross, where Jesus died for me;*
> *How marvelous, His grace that caught my falling soul -*
> *He looked beyond my faults and saw my need.*

The Ministerial Association in Zion – Another Tough Case

Sharing my testimony of how God continues to soften my hard heart to give His mercy freely to others would be a distinct pleasure, but unfair to those still living who would be part of the story. Instead, I'll share how the Lord broke down my prejudice and self-righteousness toward others in the ministry.

Newly ordained, and now the youngest member of the Faith Home Council, I was told to obtain membership in the local Ministerial Association. With roots reaching back into the evangelical foundation of the City of Zion, the pastors in Zion preached the Gospel clearly, with few exceptions. The Methodist church had swerved a bit toward the liberal side, and the priest at the only Roman Catholic Church in the area attended the meetings, but as a whole the group could agree on the basics. I did NOT want to become a member, however, and protested to the Council that I considered membership in the group to be a waste of time. Of course I never considered that my presence in their meetings might be a trial to them!

My protest went unheard. I reluctantly obeyed the wishes of the Council and began attending the monthly meetings. I had learned a good deal about Mercy by this time, but found a residue of prejudice in my heart against other denominations, especially those who were openly anti-Pentecostal. One day, for example, we were discussing the need to hold a united evangelical outreach in the park, and whether or not to take an offering. "Well," said the Baptist pastor, "the way I see it, you haven't had a meeting unless you take an offering!" On another occasion, the pastors decided to invite a guest speaker for an Easter Sunrise Service. I knew the man, and he had taken a public stand that it was rude to refer to Jesus Christ as "Jesus" – "His real name is Jesus Christ," he stated emphatically. Still another brother, pastor of one of the larger churches in town, had preached publicly against Pentecostals and charismatics. After a few years in the Association, he said to me once, half in jest, "Doug, sometimes I can almost forget that you are Pentecostal!"

What to do? Pray mercy for every pastor in attendance, asking God to give them success in their ministries, to make His Word REAL to them, and to assist them by His Spirit whether they believed in the Baptism in the Holy Spirit or not. Gradually my heart softened and I began to truly LOVE them. In time they elected me to various offices in the Association, including President.

The man who could "almost forget that you are Pentecostal" faced a deep trial when his 18-year-old son developed leukemia, not long after my own daughter was diagnosed with Hodgkins Disease. I knew I should pray *with* him, not only *for* him. I called his office and asked for an appointment, which he granted. We prayed. His son recovered, as did my daughter. One day he said to me, "Doug, a lot of pastors in town called to say they were praying for me, but you were the only one who came to my office to pray in person with me."

Another pastor in a non-Pentecostal church, Rev. Earl Minton, went into a similar deep and very dark valley when his daughter, who had graduated from Moody Bible Institute in Chicago, left the faith and married a Jewish man who had converted to a fanatical branch of Hinduism, leaving her parents heart-broken. This happened at the very time that our daughter was fighting for her life. Rev. Minton and I shared our sorrows and turned toward the Lord in our grief, and I met with him frequently to pray for our girls. God knit our hearts together. He became one of my best and truest friends in the ministry. In 2001 he invited me to accompany him on a month's missionary journey to India, which I accepted; as a result, a new door of ministry opened that changed our lives forever. Now in his upper 80s, he has asked me to conduct a memorial service for him in his former church in Zion when he passes away.

Only by embracing what the Bible teaches about Mercy have I been able to obey Paul's commands to "let each esteem others better than themselves" (Philippians 2:3), and in honor to "prefer one another" (Romans 12:10). Who am I anyway? What do I have that I have not received? I do not want what I deserve; do you?

Nothing speaks so loudly as what you do. You can protest with your mouth all you want, but it's what you do that counts. If your mouth matches your heart, people will believe you. But if there is a discrepancy between the outside and the inside, nobody will believe you.

The Parable of the Talents

This brief introduction to the subject, *What Is Mercy?*, would not be complete without a fresh look at *The Parable of the Talents*. We will use the account in Matthew 25:14-30, although Luke's account could be studied just as well.

As a young person growing up in the church, I heard the "talents" in the parable explained as special giftings, such as playing a musical instrument especially well, or singing beautifully, or simply being unusually "smart." It was drilled into us that it was "a shame to bury your talents," meaning,

I suppose, that such giftings had to be shared with others, not hidden and thus unused.

Many years later, at a financial conference in Florida, I heard the late Jim McKeever speak of the talents as "money," and that God fully expects you to multiply your wealth (hopefully for the benefit of others), and that He would scold you in the judgment if you failed to do so.[11]

Both interpretations fall far short of the parable's meaning, however. The Greek word for *talent* refers to money, but particularly the wealth inherent in bars or coins of silver and gold; the English word *talent* is a measure of weight, and has nothing to do with "giftings" or "unusual abilities."** When we consider that the servants received the "goods" of their master, surely Jesus' words portray the *riches* of the "God who is *rich in mercy*" (Ephesians 2:4), which every servant of His receives. "What hast thou that thou didst not receive?" asks Paul of the Corinthians (I Corinthians 4:7). "As we have received mercy, we faint not," he tells them (II Corinthians 4:1). "For unto whomsoever much is given, of him shall be much required," said Jesus (Luke 12:48). As a guest in Simon the Pharisee's house, having accepted Mary's poured out love at His feet, He concluded his remarks by saying to Simon, "Her sins, which are many, are forgiven; for she loved much: but to whom little is forgiven, the same loveth little" (Luke 7:47).

Thus, if we view the talents as being the Lord's mercy-money, so to speak, then the servant who was given five talents had received much mercy. Is that not the same as saying he had been forgiven much? Similarly, the servant who was given one talent had received a little mercy (only little in his own eyes, as it turns out). Is his failure to multiply his mercy-money traceable to his sense of having been forgiven little?††

** "A talent was 6,000 denarii or about a thousand dollars or 240 British pounds [in 1940s dollars or pounds!]... A talent represented a considerable amount of money at that time when a *denarius* was a day's wage." (Taken from A. T. Robertson's *Word Pictures of the New Testament* in comments on Matthew 18:24 and Matthew 25:15, as cited on *e-sword*.) If we update these amounts to 2012 wages (~$120/day; or 75 British pounds), then each talent equaled $120 x 6,000 = $700,000 dollars, or £450,000! Thus the man who was given 5 talents received $3.5 million, the one given 2 talents received $1.4 million, and the servant who was given 1 talent received "only" $700,000 in today's money.

†† For those to whom the talents seem to represent earthly money, consider the contrasting way in which the word "rich" is used in the messages to the Smyrna Church and the Laodicean Church, as well as the way the corresponding words "poverty" and "poor" are used: "I know thy works, and tribulation, and poverty, but thou art rich..." (said to Smyrna in Revelation 2:9). "Because thou sayest, I am rich, and increased with goods, and have need of nothing; and knowest not that thou art wretched, and miserable, and poor, and blind, and naked..." (said to Laodicea in Revelation 3:17).

The master's desire, however, was the same for ALL the servants, no matter how much of their lord's money they had received: they were to multiply the wealth he gave them. In Matthew's account it is said they *traded* with the money, and multiplied it. The word *traded* simply means *worked with it*. In Luke's account, they were told to *occupy* (Greek, *do business*) *until the Master's return*. Jesus' parable depicts what His servants are expected to do until He returns: **multiply the mercy that has been given to us**. Work with it! Do business with it!

When Jesus returns, He wants to know if His investment in us has benefited the Kingdom. His commendation of the two servants who doubled His investment is exactly the same, regardless of *the amount* of "mercy money" he had given them – "Well done, thou good and faithful servant; thou hast been faithful over a few things, I will make thee ruler over many things: enter thou into the joy of thy lord" (vv. 21, 23).

Why was the lord displeased with the man who *digged in the earth, and hid his lord's money* (vv. 18, 25)? Because the man put so little value on the master's investment, and because he accused his master of being a "hard man, reaping where thou hast not sown, and gathering where thou hast not strawed" (v. 24). He did not appreciate the mercy he had received! Jesus' response shows what he should have done, even if he did not want to *work with it*. In my own words, "You should have given it to someone who would have at least made some interest from it" (v. 27).

This response is very personal to me, because on several occasions I was tempted to leave the Faith Homes, feeling angry that I had ever heard about *mercy*, wishing I could get away from it all. The Lord seemed to say to me, "All right, you may leave if you wish. But before you go, please tell someone what you *do* understand of My mercy, someone who will make interest for me from what you tell them." That crushed me inside! I knew I had received many talents, *i.e.*, much mercy. My desire to leave stemmed from an unwillingness to do to others what God had done for me, and *not* because God was "a hard man," asking me to do a hard thing.

If we compare this parable with the Parable of the Unforgiving Servant in Matthew 18:23-35, we see the link between them is, simply, *doing the mercy to others that God has done to us*. If you make exceptions, or refuse to let the mercy of God pass through you to others, you demonstrate your lack of appreciation for the work of Redemption which God wrought through Jesus' crucifixion. It is never a question of *earning righteousness by doing mercy*. It is a question of *our willingness to do to others what God has done to us.*

Surely this is the meaning of James' pronouncement in his Epistle: "Even so faith, if it hath not works, is dead, being alone... I will show thee my faith by my works" (James 2:17-18).

The question Jesus will ask each one of us at the Judgment Seat is, *What did you do with the mercy I gave you?*

He that saith he abideth in Him ought himself also so to walk, even as He walked. (I John 2:6)

Blessed are the merciful: for they shall obtain mercy. (Matthew 5:7)

INTERLUDE TWO

TAKING MERCY FOR FREE

The following allegory was written by one of the young interns at the Evergreen Center. It is included here to emphasize the importance of taking God's mercy for free.

THE CONUNDRUM OF MADAME FREELY-GIVE

In the woods, a good distance from the city of Self-Sufficient, was a tiny cottage where Madame Freely-Give resided. She was a delightful old woman, full of spunk, charm, and smiles. Her life seemed ever so copacetic, except for one glaring oddity: she always carried on her back a large burlap sack filled to the top with golden brown grain. To an onlooker, it surely must have seemed as if the sack were large enough to crush the little lady; however, not one word of complaint about its weight or inconvenience ever crossed her lips.

Her house was almost as strange as her person. It was a study in contrasts. The roof was beyond dilapidated and covered in moss; picturesque to be sure, but not at all practical. Cracks were visible between most of the log walls, and a little red door hung crookedly at the entrance. Anyone walking by the house would easily think, "Oh, how quaint! But surely no one LIVES there!" Yet, content as ever, little Madame Freely-Give lived there, to all appearances unprotected and vulnerable.

The road passing by the Madame's house was not well-used, branching off another more popular route. For whatever reason, however, every once in a while a thirsty, hungry, or in some other way needy pilgrim would find himself traveling past her cottage, and without fail Madame Freely-Give graciously offered her aid. Despite the lack of frequent visitors, Madame Freely-Give's heart longed to serve others. No effort seemed too great if she could help any sad, suffering soul.

One morning as she was tending her flowers, she heard the faint clippity-clop of a horse. Overjoyed, she made her way to the roadside to see who it might be. The view was impressive – colorful garb and frills nearly obscured the rider from her sight. It seemed as if he might pass on without so much as a glance, but her persistent waves caught his attention and brought him to a halt. With a warm smile she addressed him. "Please sir, is there any way I might assist you?"

With a haughty cough, the man took stock of the landscape and chuckled rudely. "It looks as if YOU are the one needing help from a proud citizen of Self-Sufficient! Do you not know who I am? I am Sir Know-It-All," he continued without pause, "and knowing all is what I do best! Come now, don't be silly going about shouldering that ridiculous bag. Put it aside and I KNOW your life will be much brighter!"

"But sir," she replied kindly, "this sack brings me much joy and happiness. I could not think of putting it down. Would you like some grain from my sack to aid you on your journey?"

"And what might you give that I don't already possess?" he answered scornfully. "I will waste no more time. Good day!" With a snort of contempt he spurred his horse on toward the horizon.

Madame Freely-Give turned away sadly and resumed her work. Later that same day the sound of horse and harness was heard again, and the lovely little lady gazed expectantly down the road. The figure accompanying the sound was not nearly as impressive as the last traveler, more ordinary looking. Eagerly hurrying forth, Madame Freely-Give caught the gentleman's attention and inquired if he needed any assistance.

"Oh, my dear sweet lady," replied the worn itinerant, "I am near dead with thirst from my travel from yonder city of Self-Sufficient. However, I see the burden you already carry, and I would be grieved to add even one ounce of trouble to your load!"

"But you are greatly mistaken, sir!" the Madame hastily cried. "Believe me when I say the pack is but feather-light, for the burden is not one of heaviness by nature. Here, take this grain, for it fills all needs of body and soul!"

Interlude Two: Taking Mercy For Free

His eyes lit up for a moment with a glow of hope, then quickly resumed their sad stare. "Many thanks for you felicitous offer, but I cannot, will not, ask you to lift so much as a finger. My name is Sir No-Inconvenience, and I desire to cause no one trouble on my part. After all, I am strong, and even though I could indeed use some relief, I will strive on and forge ahead."

It looked as though the Madame might cry as she stated her plea, "But Sir No-Inconvenience, I love to help. My only pleasure in life is to relieve, heal, and restore others! Indeed I cannot force you, but I beseech you yet again. Will you accept my offer of grain?"

Holding out a hand he took the kernels and eyed them skeptically. After a moment of consideration, he shook his head and answered, "No, I cannot," and returned the grains gently to her hands. Then, with a slight backward glance, Sir No-Inconvenience nudged his mount forward and disappeared.

Madame Freely-Give cried to herself, "My, oh my! Is there no one left on this earth who can simply accept some grains of mercy given willingly and freely?"

At that moment a young boy fell into view, and fall he quite literally did, for his poor little foot caught a tree root which sent him tumbling head over bruise. He was filthy from head to foot, completely out of sorts, and unable to tell up from down due to the recent tumble. The Madame ran to his side with a cry of pity and carefully helped him to his feet. When she inquired after his name he replied, "I am Matthew Not-Wanted from the city of Self-Sufficient. I don't seem to belong there, so I headed out to find a place where I do belong."

Quietly and timidly the Madame asked, "Would you like to belong here?" Her heart raced, hoping with all her might that she would not be rejected again.

"Really? You mean it?" the boy whispered back with wide, unbelieving eyes.

A slight nod of her head gave the answer. With a delighted squeal the boy jumped into her arms. "Oh, how wonderful! You don't even know me! How ever could you be so kind?"

Throwing back her head with a laugh, the little lady led the way to the cottage. Upon entering the cottage, the boy exclaimed, "How does the rain not come in, and the wind not rearrange everything within its grasp, for this house is full of holes and cracks?"

"Oh, dear child," she replied, "true treasure is usually found in cracked vessels. Though it looks as if the elements of the world will tear this quaint place to pieces, it is held together and protected by my Father, because it serves His purpose and shields me completely from wind and rain, as I do His bidding and delight in His ways."

"And what is the burden you carry?" Matthew inquired.

"This is my biggest joy," the Madame replied, "for in here I store grains of mercy which are always ready to be dispersed whenever a need arises, for they have the power to fill, cover, and restore if simply taken for free. Would you like some?"

"Yes please!" he cried. And for the first time in his life, Matthew Not-Wanted felt loved. Time passed quickly, and the boy gratefully ate from the Madame's table and thrived under her watchful, tender care. As weeks and months passed there were many storms accompanied by wind and rain, but the little cottage, true to the Madame's word, never leaked and was always warm and dry.

One day, Matthew approached Madame Freely-Give and inquired, "I feel this strange pull to find another place to live. But there is something clouded in my mind and beyond my grasp, a stronger pull and desire. Do you know what that might be?"

A smile crept over the Madame's face. Setting down her ever present sack, she reached in and drew out an identical burlap bag. "This," she explained, "is all the mercy you have allowed me to bestow on you. I gave it willingly, and now it is yours. This burden is light, and it will not tire and break you like other worldly burdens will. Sometimes it will bring you physical and mental pain, but it also contains a renewing strength. The pull you feel is a call from my Father to give what you have received. Please, answer that call; you will never be sorry you did."

Matthew gathered his things from the cottage. As he prepared to leave, Madame Freely-Give placed the precious mercy bag on his shoulders. With a proud smile she announced, "Now, I give you a new name, for you are no longer a child Not-Wanted. From now on, you shall be called Matthew Mercy-Heart, for you have accepted my mercy freely. But now you must give that mercy to others, for there is a special

Interlude Two:
Taking Mercy For Free

need somewhere in the world that only you, with the mercy in your bag and the strength and guidance from our Father, can fill."

With a grateful and loving glance back, Matthew Mercy-Heart strode off, to fulfill the call in his heart.

A few years later...

One fine afternoon as Madame Freely-Give sat reading her favorite book, she was heralded by a voice from the road. Looking up in surprise, she beheld a group of young people waving to her. She returned their salutations, and inquired if they were in need.

"Oh, no!" one replied, "We are blessed beyond measure! Our only goal was to meet the little lady in the woods and send her greetings from Matthew Mercy-Heart." She laughed and thanked them for their message as the group turned to leave. But Madame Freely-Give could not help but notice as they turned and started off, that each of them had, perched high on their shoulders, a little burlap sack.

Now the moral of the story (all good stories have a moral, don't they?) is this: that mercy rejected causes sorrow, and mercy not shared even greater sorrow, but mercy freely received and imparted to others is joy beyond measure, and true heavenly treasure.

THE END

Does not wisdom cry out, and understanding lift up her voice? (Proverbs 8:1)

And the LORD passed before him and proclaimed, "The LORD, the LORD God, merciful and gracious, longsuffering, and abounding in goodness and truth." (Exodus 34:6)

But we have this treasure in earthen vessels, that the excellence of the power may be of God and not of us. (2 Corinthians 4:7)

...And He [Jesus Christ] died for all, that those who live might not live for themselves, but for Him who died and rose again. (2 Corinthians 5:15)

CHAPTER SEVENTEEN

POVERTY OF SPIRIT AND LOWLINESS

Introduction

For years I have marked places in the writings of Rex Andrews where he defines and discusses both Poverty of Spirit and Lowliness. Those terms are Biblical terms. Words are names for "things," *visible* things, and things *not so visible*. Poverty of Spirit, and Lowliness, are divine things; their meaning opens up to the worshiping reader. They are part of what the Bible teaches about Mercy, which is to say, they belong to what Jesus is and does. That is not readily apparent if one reads the Bible without loving and worshiping Jesus as the Word of God made flesh. It is too easy to *analyze* the Word, leaving out the One who wrote it. As Rex Andrews once wrote to me in a note:

> ...*Psalm 1:1 is a Red Danger Signal Blinking in the night of darkness in which the world is engulfed. Doubt, and Questioning, and reasoning is a slippery chute into Hell for many "unstable souls." For the many poor weak mortals, the thin-edge-axe of doubt splits the log of reasoning sufficiently enough to let in a flood of questions as to: The Certainty of The Authorship of The Word. And with many that is enough to drown them in the perdition of Unbelief.*[1]

Partly in an attempt to keep myself from falling into such a "slippery chute," I memorized half of Philippians 2, and all of Philippians 3. The words in 2:5-8, especially, guarded the entrance to that chute. "Let this mind be in you, which was also in Christ Jesus..." Paul left no doubt about the nature of that Holy Mind. We know how Jesus "thought" about Himself, and about His relationship to His fallen creatures. In a way, Paul also shows us in the Epistle to the Philippians how God brought him down from the height of Pharisaical pride into the "same mind" of Christ. Philippians is his testimony. God brought Paul down to the place where he counted all his previous attainments as "dung," compared to "the excellency of the knowledge of Christ Jesus my Lord, for whom I have suffered the loss of all things." What a life story is condensed into the phrase, "that I may win Christ, and be found in Him, not having my own righteousness"! Paul's fire-desire is to "know Him, and the power of His resurrection, and the fellowship of His sufferings" (Philippians 3:8-10).

How can anyone produce such words apart from the Spirit of God making it real to him, not only mentally, but also by experience? And how can any of us appreciate what Paul is saying unless we long for Christ's mind to be in us and allow our Teacher-Spirit to explain it to us? The natural man knows only the things of man, and "no one knows the things of God except the Spirit of God" (I Corinthians 2:11).

Paul uses a word in Greek to describe the "mind of Christ" that requires three words in English to translate it. The Greek word is *tapeinophrosunē*. The King James Version renders it "lowliness of mind."* But what words adequately convey the way Jesus thought of Himself? The phrase given (by Wisdom) in the Faith Homes expresses for me the essence of the meaning of *tapeinophrosunē* as Paul uses it: "a self-emptying mind." The Spirit led me to construct a pictorial of "Seven Steps Down into the Knowledge of God." It pictures Jesus' self-emptying mind, which is what I want.[2]

Stand on each step for a while in your prayer time, and ask God to give you a sense of Jesus standing next to you, so that you can grasp what propelled Him to descend from the top step to the next lower one, and the next one, until He reached the Cross at the bottom. No being has ever been so high who went so low. Is that the way you think?

Without realizing it when we entered the Homes in 1967, this was the staircase we needed to descend.† I'm quite sure I haven't reached the lowest step, but I want to go there – with Him.

---

* Various other renditions include: "having a humble opinion of one's self; humility; modesty; a deep sense of one's (moral) littleness." It is used by Paul in Ephesians 4:2 and Colossians 3:12; by Luke in Acts 20:19; and by Peter in I Peter 5:5.

† Not starting out "Equal with God," of course, but self THINKS it is equal with God!

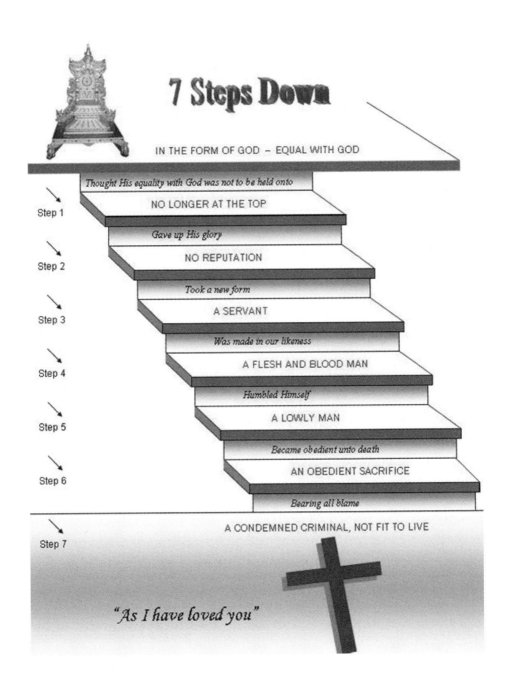

POVERTY OF SPIRIT

Turning now to Scripture, and to the comments made in Wisdom on these two exceedingly important "things," we begin with Jesus' startling declaration to his disciples in Matthew 5:3 –

Blessed are the poor in spirit: for theirs is the Kingdom of Heaven.

Jesus' words convey what He Himself is: Poor in His Spirit. Such a state of heart/mind is rightly called *Poverty of Spirit*. It is one of the branches of the Seven-Fold Knowledge of God as expressed in this and the next six "beatitudes," as they are commonly called. It is "the doorway into all the rest of the *Blesseds*," as Martha Robinson once remarked.

Rex Andrews defined it this way:

"Blessed are the poor in spirit." This is the Spirit of Poverty. The word "poor" means: afflicted, pauper, beggar. It names those who have nothing in themselves. Especially does this mean: no riches of self-ability or intellect, in addition to the love of wealth. In "poverty" all self-ability of will and intellect has to die. The "poor-in-spirit" are paupers, beggars, afflicted. Their knowledge is to "ASK." ...It is the knowledge to be utterly indwelt and ruled by God. That is the poverty of God: an inability to lust-covet; an utter lowliness of knowing how to give all; and the knowledge of having NOTHING AT ALL of one's own, apart from God ...Poverty of Spirit is the knowledge of self-nothingness.[3]

This is easy to swallow if one is a "babe," to whom Jesus referred when He thanked the Father that "You have hidden these things from the wise and prudent and have revealed them to babes" (Matthew 11:25); it is difficult to swallow if one basks in the light of self-accomplishments and self-esteem.

Repentance as an ACT, is the same thing as Poverty-of-spirit, which is the permanent STATE of it. Both Repentance and Poverty-of-spirit describe that turning to God, in which the soul of man has come to NOTHINGNESS. Nothingness, as a mystery of God, is the place, or power, or condition, in which one KNOWS he has no power or knowledge IN HIMSELF, by which to save himself.[4]

What a light shined into my soul when I first comprehended these words! *Poverty of Spirit is the permanent state of repentance.* From sad experience I knew the helplessness of failing Jesus again and again, and turning to Him for a glimmer of hope and a longing for restoration. But to live in that helplessness as a permanent thing – without feeling condemned! That was something new to me. To know that Jesus would meet me gladly in my helpless condition – and to come to Him that way every hour, nay, every moment! It seemed too good to be true. I had not known as yet the need to "despair happily," as Madame Guyon put it.

Here is another quotation that I find helpful:

Chapter One in the knowledge of God, is: The Spirit of Poverty. It is the knowledge of The First Love. In the first love is the knowledge of self-nothingness, repentance, will-breaking, turning to God, conquering the world-spirit, eating of the Tree of Life which is in the midst of the garden of the pleasures of God. In that divine poverty is the knowledge of innocence.[5]

Innocence! God Himself is innocent, I discovered. He Himself is free from coveting in all its horrid forms. He is "poor" in His Spirit, wanting nothing for Himself, but only the blessing and perfection of His loved ones. Could He restore my innocence?

I had memorized all of Jeremiah 31 in my desperate need to appropriate the New Covenant personally, especially the promise to "put His law into my mind, and write it on my heart." I saw in verse 3 that God called Israel a "virgin," yet her innocence had been lost by spiritual fornication, as described by the Prophet Ezekiel and even by Jeremiah himself.

> The LORD hath appeared of old unto me, saying, Yea, I have loved thee with an everlasting love: therefore with lovingkindness have I drawn thee. Again I will build thee, and thou shalt be built, *O virgin of Israel:* thou shalt again be adorned with thy tabrets, and shalt go forth in the dances of them that make merry. (Jeremiah 31:3-4)

How could it be? Surely a Holy God saw Israel's sin and hated it! And He hated my sins, too! The answer lay in the understanding of Poverty of Spirit. The explanation of such truth got through to me, as I pondered words like this next quotation, surely given by the Wisdom of God.

The "holiness" of God can never be accurately known or gauged, apart from this primary of all knowledge. Because GOD is not only "HOLY," He is also the INNOCENCE of all purity. No one has ever really "known" God – as He IS – without entering into that "INNOCENCE." Neither is God holy, as humans consider "holiness" – even though they themselves be in a state of hating, and condemning, and killing, and despising. There is NO HOLINESS IN HEAVEN APART FROM INNOCENCE. You may fight for a sectarian doctrine of "justification," or of "sanctification," but if you depart from the simplicity and divine innocence of the first love, then you are not describing the God and Father of our Lord Jesus Christ, nor can you perceive what "holiness" is apart from that love.[6]

God in His Holy Love "uncorrupted me" through the death of Jesus, just as He will "uncorrupt" Israel and turn her into the prophesied "virgin." I love Him because of what He is. I trust I will never get beyond *the wonder of just Jesus Christ Himself.*

It might be well to "state the obvious" – especially since it is *a simplicity so vast* it can be easily taken for granted – that **Poverty of Spirit is not an achievement, not even a spiritual achievement. No one attains it.** To be poor in spirit is to be united with The Poor One, Jesus Christ Himself. Paul states it in words that can never be excelled for clarity:

> *For you know the grace of our Lord Jesus Christ, that though He was rich, yet for your sakes He became poor, that you through His poverty might become rich.* (II Corinthians 8:9)

Jesus was both outwardly and inwardly "poor" (though it does not seem so to our modern-day preachers of prosperity).

Outwardly:

- He had no certain dwelling place. "The Son of man hath not where to lay His head," He said to one who wanted to follow Him. (Matthew 8:20)

- He entrusted the offering bag to Judas, who stole from it repeatedly. (John 12:6)

- A coin retrieved from the mouth of a fish paid the Temple tax for both Peter and himself. (Matthew 17:27)
- He, being "the greatest in the Kingdom," was the "slave of all" (Mark 10:44-45). Bondslaves had no rights and few, if any, possessions of their own.
- In Luke 8:3, we get a look at how he was supported financially, at least partially: "And the twelve were with Him, and certain women who had been healed of evil spirits and infirmities – Mary called Magdalene, out of whom had come seven demons, and Joanna the wife of Chuza, Herod's steward, and Susanna, and many others *who provided for Him from their substance.*" Yes, He lived on charity, but His own! He never charged anyone for His services, though countless numbers were healed and delivered.
- He did not ask "the rich young ruler" for any of his possessions or money, not even for one shekel of his wealth. He did ask him to give it ALL away, but not to Him, only to "the poor."‡

Inwardly:

- "Verily, verily, I say unto you: The Son cannot be doing, of Himself, a single thing – save anything He may see the Father doing; for, whatsoever, He, may be doing, these things, the Son also, in like manner, doeth." (John 5:19, Rotherham)
- "I, cannot be doing, of myself, a single thing." (John 5:30, Rotherham)
- He refused to satisfy his natural hunger when Satan urged Him to do so. (Luke 4:2-4)
- He refused to call for angelic help at the time of His arrest. (Matthew 26:53)
- He remained voluntarily helpless when taunted by His crucifiers, "Save yourself and come down from the Cross, and we will believe you."(Matthew 27:42)

Both outwardly and inwardly (in one of the most shocking revelations about Jesus in the entire Bible):

- *"But I am a worm, and no man."* (Psalm 22:6)

---

‡ Many have given away great portions of their wealth for good causes, but few have given it ALL away.

Jesus said of Himself, "I am meek and lowly in heart" (Matthew 11:29). The word "lowly" means "not rising far from the ground." I will repeat a quotation of Martha Robinson's remarks in 1934, because it fits in here:

> You need so many times to come down. Jesus has the life and love and faith you need. He wants you to come down, down, down, down, and find Him. Don't be so important. Don't advertise yourself. Why don't you let Jesus, who is your keeper, keep you down? Then there is a chance for you to rise. You can't find your place [yourself]. He wants to show you that you have only begun. And He would prove you had been down, if you would only let yourself come.
>
> And now another little word for you who say, "I suppose I must come down." Why don't you see that Jesus is so low down and it is delightful to come down to find Him – down in the valley at His feet. Don't get a picture of yourself coming down; get a picture of Jesus who is so lowly. (God Himself will show you the way down.) You do not come down just to come down, but to see Jesus meek and lowly; and to want to follow Him, *where He is*. Learn to let yourself come down. God will say, "Come down, my child, just come down and rest at Jesus' feet. I really want to have my way with you. Why will you not come down?"

This is Wisdom, beloved reader, God's Wisdom. "Don't get a picture of yourself coming down; get a picture of Jesus who is so lowly."

In Poverty of Spirit, I am nothing, I don't have anything, I don't know anything, I can do nothing, without Jesus, and I am learning to WANT NOTHING but Jesus – **but if I HAVE HIM, I have everything I need.**§

Jesus said, "BLESSED are…" Living in Poverty of Spirit is truly BLESSED! If you ask Him to make you poor in spirit, He will do it, and you will know then just how blessed you are! You will walk through life yoked with the Lowly One in unspeakable bliss, giving Mercy to all!¶

---

§ I am well aware of the unbalanced and misinformed teaching commonly known as "Worm Theology." It is, however, a poor counterfeit of the REAL thing.

¶ There are many more references to Poverty of Spirit in what could be called "Faith Home Literature." Please see *Appendix E: Letter to a Brother Seeking Forgiveness*. It is one of the best and clearest descriptions of Poverty of Spirit and Lowliness that I have ever read.

LOWLINESS

Have you sung the hymn, *God in Heaven Hath a Treasure?*[7] Are you familiar with the words? If not, here they are. Pay special attention to the words of stanzas three and four.

*God in heaven hath a treasure, Riches none may count or tell;
Hath a deep eternal pleasure, Christ, the Son, He loveth well.
God hath HERE on earth a treasure, None but He its price may know—
Deep unfathomable pleasure, Christ revealed in saints below.*

*God in tongues of fire descending, Chosen vessels thus to fill
With the treasure never ending, Ever spent—unfailing still.
God's own hand the vessel filling, From the glory far above;
Longing hearts forever stilling, With the riches of His love.*

*Thus though worn, and tried, and tempted, Glorious calling, saint, is thine;
Let the Lord but find thee emptied, Living branch in Christ the Vine!
Vessels of the world's despising; Vessels weak, and poor, and base,
Bearing wealth God's heart is prizing, Glory from Christ's bless-ed face.*

Oh to be but emptier, lowlier, mean,* *unnoticed, and unknown,
And to God a vessel holier, Filled with Christ and Christ alone!
Naught of earth to cloud the Glory; Naught of self the light to dim,
Telling forth His wondrous story, EMPTIED—to be FILLED WITH HIM.*

Does the hymn attract you, or repel you? Do you prefer to think about "who we are in Christ," or, "who He is in you"? I hope you want to be "EMPTIED—to be FILLED WITH HIM."

I can promise you that "Lowliness" is not something the Devil wants, nor does your flesh want it. Yet, in words I can never erase from my mind, "Lowliness is the PURE LIGHT of God."[8] I am certainly not lowly in my natural personality! I am thankful Jesus invited us to "learn from Me" (Matthew 11:29 NKJV).

Let's take a further look at the way the Lord expressed this matter in His Wisdom.

** "Mean" in this hymn carries the older definition of "average."

> Lowliness is the very quality of God's Form, by which He is all-in-all TO all. In other words, the amazing lowliness by which He serves all, and can approach every one of His creatures on the level of their own existence. Not to consume, but to impart LIFE... In all our teaching we use the word "lowliness" to name the love of having-nothing-of-one's own.⁹

That last definition still chafes me: I understand the value of "having-nothing-of-my-own," but to "LOVE" that??? To be absolutely content to possess NOTHING but Jesus??? That is so opposite to everything I know about "making it" in this world.

At the same time, there's something inexpressibly beautiful about Paul's testimony to the Corinthians,

> As sorrowful, yet always rejoicing; as poor, yet making many rich; as *having nothing, and yet possessing all things*. (II Corinthians 6:10)

His statement reflects an admirable balance for saints who easily put their weight too heavily on one side or the other. If we acknowledge the literal truth of his testimony in Galatians 2:20, then we must admit that Paul expressed the life of Christ perfectly. This describes the Lowliness of the Creator, suffering with us and for us, becoming nothing that we might have everything, the "Man of Sorrows and acquainted with grief" (Isaiah 53:3), yet the happiest being that ever walked this planet.

We find this balance prophetically in Isaiah, especially in the amazing Chapters 57-60 (not meaning to confine our amazement to those chapters alone). Does not this balanced life of Jesus fulfill the exquisitely worded passage in Isaiah 57:15-18?

> For thus saith the high and lofty One that inhabiteth eternity, whose name is Holy; I dwell in the high and holy place, with him also that is of a contrite and humble spirit, to revive the spirit of the humble, and to revive the heart of the contrite ones. For I will not contend for ever, neither will I be always wroth: for the spirit should fail before me, and the souls which I have made. For the iniquity of his covetousness was I wroth, and smote him: I hid me, and was wroth, and he went on frowardly in the way of his heart. I have seen his ways, and will heal him: I will lead him also, and restore comforts unto him and to his mourners.

Yes, Jesus' life DOES FULFILL such words. As Peter put it in Cornelius' house: "How God anointed Jesus of Nazareth with the Holy Spirit and with power, who went about doing good, and healing all that were oppressed by the devil, for God was with Him." (Acts 10:38)

The case of blind Bartimaeus illustrates the Lowliness of the "High and Lofty One."

"What do you want me to do for you?" asked <u>the Servant of Beggars</u>. "Lord, that I may receive my sight," said the poor blind man. "Go your way," said Jesus, "your faith has made you well." (Luke 18:41-42)

This story is dealt with at length in the *Mercy Studies*, but I will quote a few sentences of it.

> And Jesus answered and said unto him, "What wilt thou that I should do unto thee?" The blind man said unto him, "Lord, that I might receive my sight." "What WILL YOU that I do?" A note here in my Bible says, "GOD asking for orders from a blind beggar." And that is what is called in the Bible: "The Mystery of God." If it ever truly dawns ON you, you will be IN the Dawn of God's DAY. I said those words in a meeting one time: "God asking for orders from a blind beggar"! And one of my – what shall I say, correctors, challengers, setters-right? – well, whatever it is, one of them arose, rather straight and stalwart, to defend God from me. He said, "GOD taking orders from a man! I guess not. Not by a long shot! God isn't taking orders from anybody!" BUT HE IS. And that is "the Mystery" of Him.[10]

<u>The Mystery of God is His lowliness, by which He gives Himself to all His creatures, even to the lowest of them.</u> That is why men cannot "see" Him, as my dear late friend and former Sunday School teacher, John Collins, shared in a service one time. <u>They look "up" for Him, when they should look "down" to find him – washing their feet!</u> That is why the Pharisees could not "see" who Jesus was, while another blind man (in John 9) saw Him clearly! That is why Jesus so easily revealed to the Samaritan woman at the well WHO HE WAS! She was lowly – practically an outcast, having had five husbands, and living with a sixth man not her husband – but sensing that Jesus was the answer to her hunger for love. "Come and see a man who told me all that I ever did!" Why didn't that repel her? Because the "High and Lofty One, who inhabits eternity, whose

name is HOLY" had <u>bent down lower than</u> she was, to "revive the heart of the humble, and <u>to revive the heart of the contrite ones."</u>

May I sing to you, from my own broken heart,

> *Hallelujah! I have found Him, Whom my soul so long had craved! Jesus satisfies my longing, By His blood I now am saved.*[11]

Before we close this too-brief chapter with another quotation from a talk Rex Andrews gave entitled, *The Prophet Abraham*, let us look at one more Scripture passage. That passage is Luke 15:11-32.

We like to call this story, "The Parable of the Prodigal Son," although more accurately it was "The Parable of *Two Prodigal Sons*," if it is a parable indeed, and not a true story ("A *certain man* had two sons..."). It is the lowliness of the father in the story that is "mysterious" to those who know not God.

Quickly going over the main points: The younger son could hardly wait to get his hands on his father's money. He wanted his inheritance *before* his father's death. The power of that money overcame him and lured him away from home into a dissolute life. It was his father's hard-earned money that he wasted on harlots and riotous living!

When all was gone and pigs' fare his food, he "came to himself" and decided servanthood in his father's house was better than serving swine. He turned his face toward home with a speech of repentance on his tongue, "I have sinned..." His father was *not* "surprised by a knock on the door, and upon opening it, saw the disgusting, emaciated shell of the son he once knew." No, no! *"He saw him coming from a great way off, had compassion on him, ran to meet him, and fell on his neck and kissed him."* IF IT WERE NOT SACRED SCRIPTURE I AM QUOTING, I *WOULD* NOT, I *COULD* NOT, BELIEVE THOSE WORDS! Talk about Lowliness! And the father spent still more of his hard-earned money to throw a banquet celebrating the return of his lost son! Nothing said about "Son, you will pay me back when this is over, by years of 'hard labor'; I cannot accept the way you spent MY money."

But it wasn't only the younger son who had humiliated his father – <u>the older boy hurled insults into his father's face and ears that were worse than the filth his younger brother had lived in.</u> To this day, when I read the older boy's words, I feel the depth of scorn and despising coming out of his heart and through his mouth. He was hot with anger. If I had been his father, would he have finished his tirade without serious injury?

I can hardly bear to quote the elder brother's words — so full of venomous anger — but they are part of the account.

> So he answered and said to his father, "Lo, these many years I have been serving you; I never transgressed your commandment at any time; and yet you never gave me a young goat, that I might make merry with my friends. But as soon as this son of yours came, who has devoured your livelihood with harlots, you killed the fatted calf for him."

I hear myself in these words! That is why I don't like quoting them! They seem so *right*, so obviously *true*. It is the voice of self-righteousness. Wouldn't most of us have said the same thing?

What "mystifies" me is the father's answer, void of anger, tender, lowly:

> "Son, you are always with me, and all that I have is yours. It was right that we should make merry and be glad, for your brother was dead and is alive again, and was lost and is found."

All that I have is yours. My mind reels at those words. Is there any question that the father went *beneath* both his sons? Can anyone doubt that he *loved* them both, equally? Did the brother who left home and returned in repentance, know his father better than the brother who stayed at home?

Who suffered the loss incurred by the younger son's fling? His father. Who suffered when he was reviled by his older son's tirade? His father.

Is not this man a type of Our Heavenly Father? Is not this *what God really is*, in His nature? Does this not shed light on Peter's description of Jesus, "Who, when He was reviled, reviled not again? When He suffered, He threatened not? ...Who His own self bare our sins in His own body on the tree"?

Are we not all either Prodigals — taking the Mercy of Life that God gives us, and spending it selfishly to enjoy the pleasures of sin — or Elder Brothers, building up anger against God because we are not receiving what we think we deserve?[12]

Now for the quotation from *The Prophet Abraham*. It is transcribed from a talk, with minor editing. May its truth strike home to your heart.

We come into the FIRST Love at Calvary. That First Love can be first in sequence, but it distinctly means, "chief" – the ruling love, that which controls and rules everything else in the life. That is what First Love is. What was it that happened to us when we came to Calvary? We found a position – we were in repentance. That repentance was never anything of our OWN. We had nothing LEFT. We had nothing at ALL. There we were stripped and helpless and hopeless. We had nothing but the blood of the Lamb. That brought us to repentance, and that was poverty.

There we stood before the Lord. And, we SAW something. We saw the love of God in Christ crucified. We entered into our first love, because our hearts awakened to the wonder of Jesus. That was the first love: "Wonderful Jesus. God loves me." That is the Lamb of God.

There were two things – word-names of Spirit – two word-names which we saw there: Lowliness and Mercy. Utter Lowliness, and Pure and Complete Mercy. The LOWLINESS was the form of God. The MERCY was the eternal flowing love and resource of God to supply every need. There could be nothing more lowly than that DEAD form on that Cross, which seemed not even human anymore. He was taking the place of a SNAKE. He WAS a snake. He was YOUR snake. He was DEAD there because that was you. That was YOUR sin, there. Nothing could be lowlier than that, for the King of Glory to take the form of your sin, and BE that sin, and expire there, nailed helplessly, spiked helplessly to the Cross – that is LOWLINESS. That is poverty of spirit. You just keep looking at Calvary and see what that means – that form hanging there. That is Poverty of Spirit. He will make you see by LIGHT what you would not get in a hundred years by the natural processes of the mind.

So, you see two things there: one is The Free Mercy of God; the other is an extreme lowliness. LOWLINESS is God's form, or His Light, by which any creature can see Him. They could not see God, ever, except by the light that shines from Him. Whatever that Light is, is what God looks like to anyone who is looking at Him. That light is the LOWLINESS that does not put your eyes out. It is perfect LOWLINESS. It is the shining of the ESSENTIAL quality of God by which He can BE in fellowship with His creatures. If He were not lowly like that, there could not be any fellowship with Him at all. It is the mystery of God, the mystery which is going to drive the devil from the earth.

The knowledge of that simple truth is going to put Satan off the earth – just bind him right up. Bind him with bands of LIGHT. Nobody is going to go around and try to hit him on the jaw. You can never touch his jaw. Nobody is going to go around and yell at him. You cannot get him by yelling. He just lets it echo back and mocks you. No, no. What is going to BIND Satan is the KNOWLEDGE of the GLORY of the LORD – the LIGHT of it, the LIGHT of that knowledge. The light of the knowledge of the Lord IS: that the Most High God is the Most Low. He is lowlier than ALL His creatures. And that quality in Him makes Him to be the Light of LIFE to His creatures so that He can FILL them, and be just what they NEED all the time. He is Lowlier than they are. He does not condescend to do that. He IS that.

When the Lord showed me this simple point, in answering the prayer for Poverty of Spirit almost eight years ago, it completely changed my whole being. It changed my outlook on theology – changed it from the root OUT. I had to change my idea about the HORRIBLE, TERRIBLENESS of God – almost a monster at the end of things there, just waiting to destroy everything and everybody.

The DESTROYER is the devil, not the Lord. The devil is the DESTROYING angel. His kingdom is the kingdom of darkness that tears down what is past its use and usefulness. He has a right to that because he is false. His knowledge is false. AND, his WISDOM is false. It is a mathematical science. It is an intellectual process by which he understands the knowledge of ripping things to pieces, tearing them apart, and lopping them down, and sucking out the vitals of whatever is in them, to perpetuate his own glory. The adversary is everlastingly trying to get some self-glory. He is trying to steal it from everybody who has a little glory; what he does is to make the child of God want a little glory of his own and, lo, it is gone. The adversary then has the little robe of light worn by that one. It is his now. He can step in where the child of God WAS and say to God, "Well, here I am, Lord. Are You GREATER than I am? I have got the GLORY. I stole it. YOUR witness just gives in as easy as can be, to anything I do, because he LOVES himself. It is like I say, I can condemn Your followers before You, and tell You where all their points of weakness are. I can kill them. I can destroy them. I can take away from them whatever light You give. I can take away from them the glory You give to them."

Somewhere, somehow, somebody has to arise in this present evil WORLD and DEFY and REFUTE this evil statement. It will have to be those who come to the knowledge of the Lord. They come into the light of the knowledge of the glory of God. They do not have to go UP to bring it down. They do not have to go down to bring it up. WHERE is this knowledge? HOW will we ever get it? It is right in your mouth, in your heart – the Word of Faith which we preach. If you believe in your heart that God raised Jesus Christ from the dead, and confess Him with your mouth as Lord, you shall be saved. That knowledge is in the SAVING quality of the truth of God, and it is Light – the Light of Life.

What we have been saying is, that those two simple qualities describe what the love of God IS by which we STAND in this present evil age: it is a love of Lowliness and Mercy. That is the first opening of the knowledge of what the love of God is. You see those two qualities at Calvary: Utter Lowliness, and Pure Mercy.[13]

When "the eyes of the understanding" are enlightened by the Spirit to see that Lowliness and Mercy, the same passion expressed by Rex Andrews rises in the heart. It has in mine, and I trust in yours also.

Listen again to the words from his letter to Miss Nilsson, written in 1946:

I would rather eat the bread of suffering and tears for a thousand years and KNOW THAT I WOULD BE KEPT IN THE LOWLINESS OF THAT INCOMPARABLE LAMB, than to have all the happy experiences in the world without that one knowledge. To be kept in His LOWLINESS. Ah, there is a Shelter in God. There is a "shelter from the storm when the blast of the terrible ones is as a storm against the wall." Isaiah 25:4.

"*THAT INCOMPARABLE LAMB.*" There seems to be no end to what could, and should, be said about Him. Someday we will hear voices raised in worship of Him, grouped in circles around Him and His Father –

The twenty-four elders...

    Millions and millions of angels...

        All creatures...

and this is part of what we will hear (Revelation 5:1-14):

Thou art worthy to take the book, and to open the seals thereof: for thou wast slain, and hast redeemed us to God by thy blood out of every kindred, and tongue, and people, and nation; And hast made us unto our God kings and priests: and we shall reign on the earth...

Worthy is the Lamb that was slain to receive power, and riches, and wisdom, and strength, and honour, and glory, and blessing...

Blessing, and honour, and glory, and power, be unto him that sitteth upon the throne, and unto the Lamb for ever and ever.

Amen!

CHAPTER EIGHTEEN

KINGDOM PRAYING

Introduction

Have you ever wondered whether you are praying the right thing or not?

Peter and John once asked Jesus for the wrong thing! "Lord, do You want us to command fire to come down from heaven and consume them, just as Elijah did?" "You don't know what manner of spirit you are of," was His reply (Luke 9:54-55).

"Bid my sister that she come and help me," requested Martha, upset because Mary was sitting at Jesus' feet instead of helping her prepare a meal for thirteen guests. "Martha, Martha," said Jesus lovingly. "You are worried and troubled about many things. But one thing is needed, and Mary has chosen that good part, which will not be taken away from her" (Luke 10:52). Martha asked for the wrong thing, and Jesus refused to grant her request.

"Father in heaven, please give us victory over the Yankee armies," prayed Confederate General Stonewall Jackson repeatedly during America's Civil War. Eventually he heard God's answer. "No, please stop making that request. It is not My will for the South to win this war against the North. Don't ask Me anymore."[1]

"Lord, teach us to pray," asked the disciples in Luke 11:1.

"The Faith Home Work was established in long prayers, and many," said Rex Andrews.

One aspect of that fact became known as the *Kingdom Prayers*. The Lord Himself gave the wording of those prayers through the Word of Wisdom. As far as this author can determine, they began in the 1920s and continued to be prayed every week for at least 80 years after that. They were part of this author's life for 30 years. I testify that these prayers are God's will. He will answer every one of them.

They were mentioned in a previous chapter, but only in passing. Now we present them in detail. As we begin, it would be well to consider the following statement about prayer, given to us many years ago:

> *"There is a mystery about prayer...God will get done what He wants to get done, but He must have people on the earth asking Him to do what He wants to do."**

The Kingdom Prayers

Here are the seven prayers once again:

- *Send forth laborers into Your Harvest Field,* according to Matthew 9:38
- *Pour out Your Spirit on all flesh,* according to Joel 2:28ff.
- *Your Kingdom come! Your Will be done, as in Heaven, so in earth!* according to Matthew 6:10
- *Let Your Word rise,* according to Isaiah 40:6
- *Unveil the Cross!*
- *Let Your peace come to Jerusalem,* according to Psalm 122:6
- *Complete the Body of Christ,* according to Ephesians 2:21-22 and 4:12-16

Having prayed them for so long, they are a part of my understanding, and even when not consciously praying them, they lodge in my heart as a continual plea for God to answer them. And He will!

Send forth laborers into Your Harvest Field (according to Matthew 9:38)

No one doubts the importance of this prayer among those who know our Lord's command to take the Gospel to all nations. There are never enough workers for Jesus! "The harvest is plenteous, but the workers are few," He said to His disciples, following that up with "Pray therefore the Lord of the harvest, that He will send forth laborers into His harvest field" (Matthew 9:37-38; Luke 10:2).

---

* Rex Andrews, as recalled by the author, who heard him say it.

Though many things have changed in the Assemblies of God denomination in which I grew up, one thing has not changed: the plea for young people to give up their lives, their homes, their countries, and their comforts, to bring the Gospel to every nation. I know many precious young people who have done exactly that, and I am involved now in training potential laborers for service in God's harvest field. I went forward to the altar many times in my youth in response to some missionary's fervent plea to consecrate my life utterly to Christ.

There is nothing hard to understand about this first *Kingdom Prayer*. What is difficult is to maintain it as an "importunate prayer," *i.e.,* a prayer-position held constantly before God, not only in private prayer, but also in scheduled prayer times with others of like mind *who won't give up*. As with all the *Kingdom Prayers*, it is part of our weekly prayer meeting at Evergreen Center.

But there is even more to it beneath the surface of Jesus' words. In the *Parable of the Wheat and the Tares* (Matthew 13), Jesus refers to the Final Harvest as "the end of the world." Who are the reapers? The angels, God's angels! This means we must include them in our prayer for "laborers to be thrust into the Harvest Field," who reap the tares as well as the wheat.

We get a glimpse of such things in the story of Israel's deliverance from Sennacherib's armies by the hand of angels, when 185,000 Assyrians were killed by the angel of the Lord (II Kings 19:35, with the context). "This passage may have its application in the Last Time," reads the handwritten note I put in my Bible many years ago while meditating on this chapter.

Further, Jesus "could have called for twelve legions of angels" to deliver Him at the time of His arrest and subsequent crucifixion. There is no doubt they would have responded immediately had He so called! The time will come, however, when they will be called forth by the persistent prayers of God's people for "laborers to be sent forth into the Harvest Field."

Are you praying for them to come?

Pour out Your Spirit on all flesh (according to Joel 2:28ff.)

One of the problems connected with "dispensational theology" is a wrong view of what "fulfilled prophecy" actually means. "Fulfilled" seems to imply "over and done with." That is not the complete picture, however. Looking at it from Heaven's standpoint, the meaning of "fulfilled" is closer to "now open for continuous unfolding and ever-increasing fulfillment."

For example, we look at Redemption through Christ's death and resurrection as a fulfillment of all the Old Testament prophecies concerning His First Coming, but we also see them reaching a climax of fulfillment at His Second Coming. All the parables depicting the growth of the Kingdom of God on earth bear this out. So do the repeated references in the Book of Acts to the Word of God increasing, from its beginning in Jerusalem to its dispersion throughout the Gentile world.

Yet, when it comes to Joel's prophecy of the Spirit being poured out "on all flesh," there is a tendency to think of it as being "over and done with" on the Day of Pentecost, especially in the view of our non-Pentecostal brethren. The exact opposite is closer to the truth, I believe. What began on the Day of Pentecost is increasing tremendously in the world now, especially in so-called Third World countries. It will have its climax in a wave of blessing we can hardly imagine, and it must be fulfilled in the Jewish world as well, for it was addressed in the first place to "your (Israel's) sons and daughters."

All right, then, who is praying <u>earnestly</u>, <u>fervently</u>, and <u>repeatedly</u> for that to happen? Have you ever experienced the passion of that prayer, so it almost consumed you with its intensity?[2]

Remember, <u>God WANTS to be asked to do what He has promised He will do!</u> Are you asking?

Your Kingdom come! Your Will be done, as in Heaven, so in earth!
(according to Matthew 6:10)

How many times has this prayer passed through the lips of earth's dwellers? It is estimated that there are one billion adherents to the religion of Roman Catholicism, and perhaps another billion with Christian background and/or teaching. Most have been taught to repeat "The Lord's Prayer" as part of the ritual practice of their religion. Many have prayed it thoughtlessly, of course, but doubtless many have prayed it from the heart, especially those who qualify for the term "poor and needy." Has God heard them? Will this prayer be answered?

For us, as serious (or would-be serious), men and women of prayer, the link into the realm of "praying in the Holy Ghost" is "Reign in me, Father!" We sing a popular chorus by that name, but often we sing it too lightly, with little understanding of its implications. O that the words would become real to us! Only then will we see clearly how God will answer this prayer in the world at large.

It is not enough to have an abstract idea of God's people "taking dominion" in nations, or cultures, or various areas of life, or even to form a concrete plan of action for making it happen. The words of Francis Havergal's hymn, *Live Out Thy Life Within Me*, show us more deeply what it means for God to have His Kingdom come **in me**, and for His will to be done **in me**.

> *Live out Thy life within me, O Jesus, King of kings!*
> *Be Thou Thyself the answer to all my questionings;*
> *Live out Thy life within me, in all things have Thy way!*
> *I, the transparent medium, Thy glory to display.*
>
> *The temple has been yielded, and purified of sin,*
> *Let Thy Shekinah glory now flash forth from within,*
> *And all the earth keep silence, the body henceforth be*
> *Thy silent, docile servant, moved only as by Thee.*
>
> *Its members every moment held subject to Thy call,*
> *Ready to have Thee use them, or not be used at all,*
> *Held without restless longing, or strain, or stress, or fret,*
> *Or chafings at Thy dealings, or thoughts of vain regret.*
>
> *But restful, calm and pliant, from bend and bias free,*
> *Permitting Thee to settle, when Thou hast need of me.*
> *Live out Thy life within me, O Jesus, King of kings!*
> *Be Thou the glorious answer to all my questionings.*†

This is not to say that God won't answer this prayer by raising up another Joseph, or another Daniel, or another Zerubbabel! He may do that as He wills. Yet the New Testament pattern is "the authority of a laid down life," as seen in the martyrdom of all but one of the eleven original disciples, as well as in the death of Paul the Apostle. The Kingdom of God came as they gave their lives to establish it. And the Will of God was done when they lived out the mercy of God which they had received. "As we have received mercy, we faint not," said Paul (II Corinthians 4:1).

In my own life, this earnest prayer of thirty-and-more-years is being answered in ways I never would have chosen had not God enlightened my

---

† It is worth noting that this hymn ranked high on Martha Robinson's list of favorites.

understanding. The effect or end result of my surrender is not yet known, but I can see glimpses of Jesus reigning as King in Evergreen Center, in parts of India, and in Burma. His Will of Mercy is being done by those whom I have been given to train. All glory to Jesus!

Let Your Word rise *(according to Isaiah 40:6)*

"Talitha, cumi!" Those are the exact words Jesus used when he stood over Jairus' dead daughter and commanded her to rise from the dead (Mark 5:41). "Damsel, I say unto thee, Arise!" The Aramaic word *cumi* is akin to the Hebrew word *qum*, as used by Isaiah in the famous verses of Chapter 40:6-8, which read in the New King James Version:

> The voice said, "Cry out!" And he said, "What shall I cry?"
>
> "All flesh is grass, and all its loveliness is like the flower of the field. The grass withers, the flower fades, because the Spirit of the LORD blows on it. Surely the people is grass. The grass withers, the flower fades: but the word of our God shall stand forever."

The Hebrew word translated by the English word *stand* is *qum*, and its fullest meaning involves *rising, arising, going from a sitting or prone position to standing upright on both feet*. When contrasted with the fading and withering nature of all flesh, especially in the weak and transient area of *loveliness* (which translates the Hebrew word *hhesed*), the Word of God is seen as the exact opposite in its inherent nature! Flesh fades, falls down; the Word of God stands up, continually rises, moves easily from an (apparent) sitting position to a stance of standing in authority.

This prayer then, for God to cause His Word to rise, is a plea for God to take authority throughout the earth, as though He were commanding all creation to participate in His Resurrection Power!

I am convinced that many historical events of spiritual significance took place in answer to such praying. How else does one account for the tearing down of the Berlin Wall? Or the success of the Gospel in China after decades of rampant Communist persecution of Christians? Or the unseating of the BJP (Hindu) government in India (to name but a few such events)?

May I recount a personal testimony of God's triumph in answer to the prayer for the Word of God to rise?

In the Fall of 2001, Rev. Earl Minton and I travelled to Nagaland, a remote state in the northeast corner of India. In the early years of the 20th Century, most Nagas had converted from complete heathenism to Christianity,[3] but by the 1960s the wave of revival had waned considerably. Our host, Rev. Anjo Keikung, took us to his boyhood home of Pongo Village, located on a ridge settled by the Phom tribe at least a thousand years ago. We were the first white people they had ever seen. There we met his brother, an uncle, and other relatives. They were eager to tell the story of an unexpected and widespread revival among the Phom people that took place thirty years earlier, in 1971, resulting in a complete spiritual turnaround in the tribe. I actually preached in their new church building, where at least 900 people (the entire village!) turned out at 7 a.m. for a special service with the visiting Americans!

As these precious believers shared their story, I couldn't stop weeping, because it flashed all through me: *This was partly an answer to the "Kingdom Prayers" we were praying every Wednesday morning in the Faith Homes at that very time!* It was so real to me, the unseen but very real connection between our prayers and the move of God that took place on the other side of the world. Minutes passed before I regained enough composure to tell the others what I had seen. To God be the glory, all the glory! But God wants to be ASKED for what He longs to do!

Are you praying for God's Word to RISE? To take authority and dominion throughout the world? Or do you see only man's words rising (see Daniel 7, "a mouth speaking great things")? Do you not sense that Psalm 2 must be fulfilled in its entirety? Do you have a sense of helping to "pray it through to fulfillment"?

Unveil the Cross!

What do the following verses mean to you?

> But we speak the wisdom of God in a mystery, even the hidden wisdom, which God ordained before the world unto our glory: Which none of the princes of this world knew: for had they known it, they would not have crucified the Lord of glory.
> (I Corinthians 2:7-8)

What is *the hidden wisdom* that was *ordained* before the world's creation?

The context gives the answer: The hidden wisdom is "*Christ crucified... the power of God and the wisdom of God*" (II Corinthians 1:23-24). Jesus is the Lamb slain "before the foundation of the world," according to Peter (I Peter 1:19-20). The wise of this world cannot see the wisdom of God; it is foolishness to them. Paul says to the Ephesians, "Walk not as other Gentiles walk, in the vanity of their minds, having their understanding darkened, being alienated from the life of God... because of the blindness of their hearts." In his second letter to the Corinthians, he says, "Whom the god of this world [*i.e.*, Satan] hath blinded the minds of them that believe not" (II Corinthians 4:4). Think of it! "Has *blinded* their hearts! Has *blinded* their minds!"

Hence the need for this tremendous prayer, "Father, unveil the Cross!" The words of a sacred hymn by John Newton fit in with this prayer:

> *In evil long I took delight, Unawed by shame or fear,*
> *Till a new object struck my sight, And stopped my wild career.*
>
> *I saw One hanging on a tree, In agony and blood,*
> *Who fixed His languid eyes on me, As near His cross I stood.*
>
> *Sure, never to my latest breath, Can I forget that look;*
> *It seemed to charge me with His death, Though not a word He spoke.*
>
> *My conscience felt and owned the guilt, And plunged me in despair,*
> *I saw my sins His blood had spilt, And helped to nail Him there.*
>
> *Alas! I knew not what I did, But now my tears are vain;*
> *Where shall my trembling soul be hid? For I the Lord have slain.*
>
> *A second look He gave, which said, I freely all forgive;*
> *This blood is for thy ransom paid; I die that thou may'st live.*
>
> *Thus, while His death my sin displays, In all its blackest hue,*
> *Such is the mystery of grace, It seals my pardon too.*
>
> *With pleasing grief and mournful joy, My spirit now is filled;*
> *That I should such a life destroy, Yet live by Him I killed.*[4]

Undoubtedly, the Cross was unveiled to John Newton, who also wrote the words of the hymn *Amazing Grace*.

I have wept many, many times while offering up this prayer to Jesus. The Roman Catholic Church needs an unveiling of the Cross.

The dying denominations of mainstream Protestantism need an unveiling of the Cross. The four prevalent non-Christian religions of the world need an unveiling of the Cross: Judaism, Hinduism, Buddhism, and Islam. The intellectual world is blinded to Calvary by gross Idolatry of the Mind. Communism wants nothing to do with the Cross. China, with almost one-quarter of the world's population, needs an unveiling of the Cross.

Miss Ruth Brooks once said to me, "Douglas, I must be getting hardened in my heart. I can now read the Gospel accounts of the Crucifixion without weeping." For years, Rex Andrews could hardly speak of "mercy" without breaking down in tears.

Do you long for the Cross to be unveiled?

Let Your peace come to Jerusalem (according to Psalm 122:6)

My comments on this prayer would only echo Rex Andrews' article, "God's Blessing Pact," written for *Feed My Lambs* many years ago, as follows:[5]

> "PRAY FOR THE PEACE OF JERUSALEM; THEY SHALL PROSPER THAT LOVE THEE." Psalm 122:6. It is now "The Hour" for all who love Jesus Christ to unite in God's Blessing Pact and PRAY FOR THE PEACE OF JERUSALEM. Here is God's holy unalterable Word. Here is the Creative Word of God. And His Word not only foretells what shall BE, His Word also PROVIDES what shall be. And whatever God has promised He is able to perform. Before you is a Blessing Pact from God. It contains a Command and a Promise, and LIFE is in God's Command – LIFE is in His Command. So, this Blessing Pact with God is a pact of Life between Him and you – the Believer. You are a believer if you DO your part in the Pact. And the Believer who actually does DO the command is the Receiver of the Promise.
>
> The Command is: "PRAY FOR THE PEACE OF JERUSALEM." And the Promise is: "They shall PROSPER that love thee." That constitutes a Pact between The God of Heaven and His Believer on the earth. It is God's Word, and it is God's Proposal.
>
> NOW The Great Hour has come, for all the Redeemed, TO PRAY. NOW is The Time for all those who have received the

New Birth from Above to ENTER INTO God's Blessing Pact. This Pact is concerning Jerusalem, the City which Jesus Christ wept over. This is the City, the ONLY CITY, of which Jesus said, "IT is The City of The Great King." And of This City it is said, "In Jerusalem shall My Name be for ever."

What is "The Peace of Jerusalem?" The Peace of Jerusalem is: "Loving-kindness and Mercies," Jeremiah 16:5. When God returns to Israel and Jerusalem with "Loving-kindness and Mercies," THEN He restores the Peace which He took away. And That Time is NOW. It is happening NOW. "The Land" of Israel is encircled with nations fired with implacable hatred – cursing and swearing to destroy Israel utterly: and the Northern army of Russia already moving to help them.

NOW "PRAY FOR THE PEACE OF JERUSALEM." Study Ezekiel 36-39. Also Isaiah 2, and also Zechariah 12. It will pay you to read the whole Old Testament through just to see what is said, by God, ABOUT JERUSALEM!!! There is a Prosperity which God promises to those who really PRAY for the Peace of Jerusalem. And that Prosperity can include the triumph in your own life which God has called YOU to. Peace be unto you! Shalom!

Complete the Body of Christ (according to Ephesians 2:21-22 and 4:12-16)

One of the great puzzles for Christianity's skeptics is the multiplicity of denominations. While visiting Israel some years ago, I shared the testimony of Jesus (*Yeshua*) with a Jewish businessman. His response touched a nerve. "Which of the 76 different Christian groups in Israel do you want me to join?"

In 1975, on our first visit to Israel, we attended *The Second World Conference on the Holy Spirit,* held in Jerusalem for three days. Charismatic believers from many different denominations, including Roman Catholics, filled the auditorium. When it came time to close the Conference by holding a sacred communion service, the presiding Catholic authorities refused to let their parishioners take communion with the Protestant believers, choosing instead to hold a separate service in another location.

What can we do about such obvious fractures within the Body of Christ? Simply, PRAY.

This is the gist of the seventh and final request of the *Kingdom Prayers*. Resting solidly on Jesus' High Priestly Prayer in John 17 for His followers to be "one, Father, even as we are one," and on Paul's confident prediction in Ephesians 4:13, "till we all come to the unity of the faith, unto a perfect man, unto the measure of the stature of the fullness of Christ...," the Kingdom Pray-er approaches the Throne of Grace for something impossible, but not impossible with God.

In fact, the more impossible it seems, the greater is the pray-ers' faith, for he knows that no human effort to *complete the Body of Christ* will ever succeed. God has to do it, or it won't be done at all. Nevertheless, **He asks God for what God says He wants done,** and in child-like faith claims the answer.

The pray-er also recognizes that he must conform his own life to the need for the Church to be completed as One Body. He remembers the words which constitute "the great un-used tool of evangelism" described by Jesus in John 13:35, "By this shall all men know that you are my disciples, if you have love one for another." He is conscious that Jesus defined that love as being, "as I have loved you."

The more he prays this prayer, the more he longs for the Lord to answer it personally, and globally.

In Conclusion

Someone has said, "We learn more about prayer by doing it, than we do by reading about it." Prayer has no substitute. Prayer is "the breath and action of desire seeking to gain its object."

I sincerely hope this chapter has inspired you to pray, fervently and effectively, in cooperation with the purposes of God in our time.

CHAPTER NINETEEN

WHAT ARE YOU HERE FOR?

Introduction and Comments

As mentioned in Chapter 15, *Particular Expressions of the Word of Wisdom*, Rex Andrews gave seven talks to the trainees in the Faith Homes in the fall of 1967. Each talk was an answer to the question, "What Are You Here For?" He spoke for approximately one hour on each topic. This writer transcribed the talks, Rex Andrews edited them, and the Faith Homes subsequently printed them in booklet form.

In preparing them for this book, I have omitted some references that pertained strictly to Faith Home life. In a few places I have inserted comments for the sake of clarity. The end result admittedly is a bit choppy, but I am reluctant to smooth it out, choosing, rather, to keep the talks in the same form in which they have been printed and distributed. You will see how often a thing is repeated, and that may test your patience. But as the repeated blows of the hammer are necessary to drive the nail home, so the repetition here serves to embed these truths in your heart. I urge you, therefore, to endure, for you will find your heart opening to God in a way you did not expect.

The principles apply across the board. "What am I here for?" is a good question for any Christian to ask. These seven answers describe the kind of man or woman who hungers for Psalm 119:1 to be made real in the actual living-of-life: "Blessed are the undefiled in the way, who walk in the law of the LORD."

These talks also give the reader a "feel" for the atmosphere that prevailed in the Faith Homes. It is not an exaggeration to say that "Jesus was personally present." We all forgot it at times, but Jesus' love drew us back to Him as the Center of our activities: the quiet times of prayer and the Word; the work schedule; the sharing with each other at meal times;

the meetings; and the classes. There was no strain to it, just the simple recognition of His Presence.

During the time these talks were given, God gave this writer an unusual and heightened sense of Jesus' Personal Presence, in which I seemed to be on earth and in Heaven at the same time. It lasted for ten days. It was a foretaste of "something God is going to do in the last days."

God is still calling His own to come closer to Jesus – to find Him within as the "Lover of My Soul" – the One who offers you all that He is.

> *Jesus, lover of my soul, let me to Thy bosom fly,*
> *While the nearer waters roll, while the tempest still is high.*
> *Hide me, O my Savior, hide, till the storm of life is past;*
> *Safe into the haven guide; O receive my soul at last.*
>
> *Other refuge have I none, hangs my helpless soul on Thee;*
> *Leave, ah! leave me not alone, still support and comfort me.*
> *All my trust on Thee is stayed, all my help from Thee I bring;*
> *Cover my defenseless head with the shadow of Thy wing.*
>
> *Thou, O Christ, art all I want, more than all in Thee I find;*
> *Raise the fallen, cheer the faint, heal the sick, and lead the blind.*
> *Just and holy is Thy Name, I am all unrighteousness;*
> *Vile and full of sin I am; Thou art full of truth and grace.*
>
> *Plenteous grace with Thee is found, grace to cover all my sin;*
> *Let the healing streams abound; make and keep me pure within.*
> *Thou of life the fountain art, freely let me take of Thee*
> *Spring Thou up within my heart; rise to all eternity.*[1]

I urge you not to rush through these messages in one sitting. I can testify that *my "heart burned within me"* during the hour-long sessions as they were being spoken. **Jesus was PRESENT.** He wants to be PRESENT with you as you meditate on these seven guiding principles of our relationship to God and to others. God's goal for us is nothing less than union with Jesus, and Jesus embodied these principles; yes, every one of them.

What Are You Here For?

- To Dwell in the Presence of the Lord
- Redeeming the Time
- Living and Walking in the Spirit
- Daily Grace
- The Faith Life
- Bearing the Cross
- To Be an Offering to God

TO DWELL IN THE PRESENCE OF THE LORD

We are not here just to have a place to live. We are not here to have a place to stay a year or two. We are here to DWELL IN THE PRESENCE OF THE LORD. We are here dwelling in the Presence of the Lord, and to learn to keep adjusted to that Presence. There are quite a number of things which it is important for you to grasp. It takes a couple of years for almost anyone to really come to grips with it in their heart. This kind of training life takes time. Some people are more alert to it, more willing, more open to what the Lord is doing, but it takes several years for it to really change you as God wishes to do.

We are here to dwell in the Presence of the Lord. It takes time to do it. God wants to change you, each one of you, from what you are by nature, and the way you act naturally, and how you do things according to your background, how you grew up, where you grew up, and the way you are used to working, and how you do things. God is certainly preparing in this world a people on the earth who will just let the Lord have His way. And that is one of the features that the Lord has maintained in these Homes for 57 years.

What are you here for? It is to learn to dwell in the Presence of the Lord. It becomes your life. You then come to do naturally what God plans for your life no matter where you are. Wherever you go, if you carry through what God wants you to do in the training in these Homes, you should have learned to dwell in God's Presence. And that is going to be the supreme need in these days.

Sometimes people think there is going to be somebody who will make them to be a minister. But you have to walk with God yourself, and then God makes a place for you. It is up to you. If you are dishonest with your time, if you are not honorable with God, for instance, in the morning during the 8 to 10 period,* when God has arranged that you should have that time in prayer and with your Bible, and do not do it honorably, you are a dishonest spiritual person. And then you are not going to be able to arrange properly your life on the mission field, on the foreign field, or home field, or in whatever might open for you. You have to learn to arrange your life, and it is supremely important that you KNOW HOW TO ARRANGE YOUR LIFE. All of us who have any responsibility of leadership, and teaching, in the Homes, desire to do only one thing: we desire to express the will of God to all. If you do not do it honorably, and truthfully and honestly carry out the things that are made known to you of the life in the Homes, you will not know how to adjust your life.

You are here to DWELL IN THE PRESENCE OF THE LORD. If the Presence of the Lord were not here to be dwelt in, these would be words without any purpose at all. We are not here to be entertained. Sometimes it rises up in people's minds, because it is their nature, "I don't want to be in the meeting tonight unless she's there, or he's there." Well, you might as well pack up and go some place else and not bother to waste your time with us, if such is the case. YOU ARE HERE TO DWELL IN THE PRESENCE OF THE LORD, and that means that the Lord is THE person. You are here to learn to live in the Presence of the Lord. That means, and must mean, that He has the privilege of saying and teaching what HE chooses. He will get your spiritual pride down, so that He has the privilege to change you to know Jesus Christ as your King. He wants to make you to be a blessing anytime, anywhere, no matter where it is or when it is.

It is an act of the Lord - the fact that you are living here. You are led by the Lord to come to these meetings, with the purpose to be fulfilled that you are in the Presence of the Lord. And you want God to bless whoever speaks, whoever reads the Bible, whatever is done. If you are ever going to be a worker for God anywhere, bless your heart, you are going to have to go through hard times wherever God may in His wisdom lead you. And you may say, "Oh, why didn't I learn when I had all that time? If I had only learned then just to be a blessing to everybody. Oh, if I had just been willing to humble myself and take up my cross daily, like

---

* Faith Home residents were required to spend two hours alone with God each morning in the Word of God and Prayer between the hours of 8 and 10 a.m.

Jesus said, and be a vessel of mercy! I wasted my time in the Homes" (I'm just imagining this now), "now I'm out in the Work [of the Lord], and I don't know how to help people. I don't know how to minister to people."

Your training here should bring you to the knowledge of DWELLING IN THE PRESENCE OF THE LORD: that you are in the center of His will all the time. That is a feature of what the Bible teaches about Mercy, but we will not take that up now. To every one of you training in these Homes, whether for a short or a long period, I believe I can safely say that the Lord's direct purpose for you, and His continued working for you, is to establish that very thing in your life: that you dwell in His Presence, you just live in His Presence. For 57 years the Presence of the Lord has remained in these Homes. It has been continuous in this House of the Lord [the "Meeting House," located at 2820 Eschol Avenue, in Zion, Illinois]. The Lord has kept this Work in His Presence. He was considered as PERSONALLY present. We were to worship HIM. The essential feature has remained. It is the Presence of the Lord. I imagine this is the purpose of the Lord anywhere, when two or three gather together in His Name.

But I am convinced that there is a different awareness of the Presence of the Lord, according to the attitude of the individual heart as to the Lordship of our Lord Jesus Christ in their life, and whether Jesus is King of their heart. The highest service there is to God is to worship Him, and praise and thank Him always. If you live so, it is certain you will fit in almost any place He leads you: DWELLING IN HIS PRESENCE. It is an amazing truth, unveiled and unfolded throughout the Old and New Testaments, that we are to seek the Lord and dwell in His Presence. Every feature, everything, work in the kitchen, every phase of life in the Homes, should be training to dwell in the Presence of the Lord. He wants His people to know that *that Presence of the Lord* is the Lord. You should study this topically in The Bible.

With most of us it takes some years to change our ideas about that into permanent reality. We call it "Ministerial Training." If you learn what God can teach you on this line, then wherever you go you will find His Presence; you will bear witness of Him; you will lead others to Jesus; and HE WILL POUR OUT HIS SPIRIT ON YOU AND BLESS YOUR WORK FOR HIM.

God richly bless you.

REDEEMING THE TIME

What are you here for: THE USE OF YOUR TIME; YOU ARE HERE TO REDEEM YOUR TIME. You are here to dwell in God's Presence, but you will not dwell in His Presence unless you know how to USE YOUR TIME. This is a basic thing – that you are here to learn to use your time. We choose for our scripture one that refers to it directly, the 16th verse of Ephesians 5, "Redeeming the time, because the days are evil."

Redeeming the time! You are learning what Redemption is; you are learning to testify to the Redeeming Power of the Blood; but do you realize that some of you do not know very much about REDEEMING THE TIME? It is well to include also verses 15-17: "See then that ye walk circumspectly, not as fools, but as wise, redeeming the time, because the days are evil. Wherefore be ye not unwise, but understanding what the will of the Lord is." You have to learn this, because if you do not learn how to redeem your time, and how to use your time, you are only going to be half a minister anywhere; you will be going after the world in all kinds of ways.

There are many things you can do which waste your time. For instance, television and radio. You have to LEARN HOW TO REDEEM YOUR TIME; AND YOU CANNOT REDEEM YOUR TIME BY SPENDING IT ON TELEVISION OR RADIO. There are some things of value in the radio if you use it with a very great deal of restraint and self-discipline. "Redeeming the time *because the days are evil.*" If you do not know how to use your time, if you do not know how to redeem your time, you are simply building your house on the sand! One of the essentials in overcoming the evil in these days is to USE YOUR TIME FOR GOD.

One of the reasons you are in these Homes is to LEARN HOW TO USE YOUR TIME, to REDEEM THE TIME. Read again the three verses, Ephesians 5:15-17 – "See then that ye walk circumspectly, not as fools, but as wise, redeeming the time, because the days are evil. Wherefore be ye not unwise, but understanding what the will of the Lord is."

The word "circumspectly" is made up of two words; "circum," meaning "around"; and "spect," meaning "to look." So "circumspectly" means "to look around, to give attention to all sides." In order to be circumspect you must be willing to come under. The term "come under" is a vital thing in these Homes. It always has been, and it never can be any different. It means: TO COME UNDER THE WILL OF THE LORD. We do not have so many rules as they have in a monastery, or even in some Bible Schools. But it is important, and very necessary, that you come down, come under, the will of the Lord, sufficiently so that you can look around and see what is going on. "Circumspect": give attention to it so that you will not walk as fools. The word "fool" in the New Testament generally means "a foolish person," and does not usually carry with it the rather deep slur of contempt.

"Walk circumspectly, not as fools, but as wise." Give attention; look around you. And how are you going to do that, unless you learn to use your time? You have to have a firm discipline in these matters. "Redeeming the time, because the days are evil. Wherefore be ye not unwise, but understanding what the will of the Lord is." Ohhh! How long it takes some people to even consent, or to give down, that the Will of God is Mercy, (the consent being necessary because they must not contradict the plain statements of the Scripture as to the value and position and power of the Mercy of the Lord), when it comes to subjecting the will to DO THE MERCY! Oh, how people will halt between two opinions, for years on end, because their natural-reasoning minds cannot work it out logically and mathematically to suit self-will. Mercy-doing does redeem the time.

God is not working things out logically and mathematically, except by HIS logic and HIS mathematics. It is logical with God, and it is Divine reasoning in Heaven, that if you confess your sins, He will cleanse you. "Though your sins be as scarlet, they shall be white as snow." That is Divine Reasoning, not human reasoning. So is this: "See then that you walk circumspectly" (looking around on all sides; giving attention), "not as fools, but as wise, redeeming the time, because the days are evil. Wherefore be ye not unwise, but understanding what the will of the Lord is."

Some day it will dawn on you that we are teaching you the truth. We do not have any fancy fables, or anything like that here. But some day it will dawn on your heart, "Why, that was the Will of God!" But there is a problem about the Will of God, and we are touching one phase of it here: THE USE OF YOUR TIME. You know one reason you do not like the Will of God? It is because He breaks in on your time! He demands, eventually, that you give up ALL YOUR TIME TO HIM. But, bless your hearts, He also says, "But I offer you Eternity." Give up your time – that is about the only commodity you have, except your flesh and your heart – you give up your time to God. And He says, "What I was interested in always, from the beginning of your life in the world, was for you to have Jesus, and to dwell in Eternity." So, what are you in the Faith Homes for? First, to learn to live and to DWELL IN HIS PRESENCE; and second, to LEARN TO USE YOUR TIME.

Now to practical considerations: THE EIGHT-TO-TEN-PERIOD. These propositions are a sort of a Bible Class study. They are not necessarily given in a one-two-three order, one depending on the other for sequence. They are given as they appear, and they fit all together as: Using your time for the Lord.

Now, the Eight-to-Ten a.m. Prayer Period. This involves you in a prayer-life which has some reality to it. This prayer period was started in 1948 here; it was to take the place of Morning Prayers.[†] Instead of having Morning Prayers at 8 o'clock, after breakfast, it was instituted as a new feature of this Work, for EVERYONE in the Homes. Specifically and specially, it means those who are here preparing for the Lord's Work. We call them trainees, and staff members after they have been here five years or so.

The Eight-to-Ten Prayer Period was given by the Lord, to take the place of morning prayers. That meant that everybody was on their honor to be at their place, in their room, kneeling at their bed or sitting at their desk, with Bible open, in whatever way is comfortable, and to be there at 8 o'clock. Then the period runs for two hours, from 8 to 10 a.m. We do praise the Lord for how well it has been carried out through the years. Those who have lived in the Homes, trainees and otherwise, have been GREATLY, GREATLY blessed, and strengthened, and edified, in getting a FOUNDATION for their work for God, by carrying that out as strictly as possible during the period of time they were in the Homes. Too frequently people have a plan, or a hope, or something like that, that they will someday take time to pray. But they do not do it. You can go anywhere among Pentecostal people, and you cannot find many who really have a Prayer-life.

[†] For over thirty years, the residents in each of the three Faith Homes met around the dining room table for Morning Prayers, led by one of the Ministers in that Home. It was essentially a Group Prayer/Bible Study Session, guided by the Lord. At Evergreen Center, the Lord has led us to combine these two types of spending time with the Lord around His Word: each resident must spend one hour alone with God, and one hour together with the others in a group time of Prayer and Bible reading, under the direction of one of the Ministers.

One value of this Eight-to-Ten Prayer Period is that it gives an opportunity for you to develop a basic habit. You need to have a basic habit in which a Prayer time is INVIOLABLE, SACROSANCT, BELONGS TO GOD. In your ministry there might have to be a re-adjustment of that time; or if you should happen to be working somewhere daily, you might have to change the hours that you pray; – but you need to have a HABIT of spending two hours a day in prayer. That does not mean an hour and fifty-eight minutes; it does not mean an hour and forty minutes. It means TWO HOURS. Because if you are not honest with God in that apparently small matter, you will be dishonest with God in all kinds of things! We say this kindly: YOU ARE DISHONEST WITH GOD IN TOO MANY THINGS. You should watch yourself and see how honest you are in your Eight-to-Ten Period.

In this Eight-to-Ten Prayer Period, you are on your honor. Nobody is going to investigate every day to see if you started at eight o'clock and kept on until ten o'clock. It is between you and God. But if you do not redeem your time in this way, the effect in your life will be: a sloppy missionary or minister. And that will become a slippery path to walk on. You will not be able to train other people because you have not disciplined yourself. It is not meant that you get under a strain for fear that you will be one minute late – but if you do not have this kind of discipline, this kind of a habit in your life, how are you going to teach people? Supposing you should go to Africa, what would you teach them? People preach about prayer, but they don't pray! What we are talking about is: you pray first, and then preach about it. And if you do not have this as a basic thing in your life, how are you going to teach about it? This is a very important matter.

The Eight-to-Ten Period is for Bible and Prayer – NO READING BOOKS AND MAGAZINES. You can use that Prayer Period in whatever way your heart dictates. But be sure that you have asked the Lord to direct your heart, so that your heart dictates right! You can spend half of your time with your Bible, and half of your time in prayer. Or, there are times when you might want to spend three-quarters of your time with the Bible. There might be other times when you want to spend three-quarters of your time in prayer. What do I mean by prayer? Mainly is meant, getting down on your knees by your bed or by your chair and WAITING ON THE LORD. If you do that, He will put prayers in your heart to pray, and you will pray in the Will of God; you will pray in the Spirit; "praying always in the Spirit" (Jude 20). The Eight-to-Ten Prayer Period is there to help you to REDEEM YOUR TIME. And if you are honest in it before God, it will bring circumspection into you without you trying to figure it out. You will begin to watch, as well as pray.

Another thing to use your time for: BIBLE STUDY. We talk about Prayer and Bible Study very much in the meetings, and you have heard a lot of it through the years. This is important in how to use your time. If you would rather use your time listening to the radio or looking at television – God grant that we will never have any television in these Homes – much of it is the world, the flesh, and the devil, right in your room, and in your eyes, and in your ears, and you can't get away from it – it is AWFUL!

What we are getting at here is DISCIPLINE. You need to redeem your time because the days are evil. You can redeem your time by being a hungry Bible reader. If you do not study the Word of God, you NEVER WILL KNOW some things that Jesus and the Apostles described about living on God. Jesus said, "As the living Father hath sent me, and I live by the Father, so he that eateth me shall live by me" (John 6:57). DO YOU KNOW HOW TO EAT GOD? You will never know how to eat God, unless you are willing to have a hunger established, a craving established, in your life for the Word of God. That has to mean that you read the Bible through.

How many of you ever did read the Bible through? You ought to aim to read the Bible through at least four or five times. It would be good to read it through once a year if possible. You need to read the Bible. You should have a plan by which you read the Bible clear through, as a consistent plan, so that you gain a comprehension of what is in the whole Bible. Also, vary your reading using the New Testament many times. Also topics, and individual books.

When God returned to me, and returned me to Him, in 1944, after seven years away from God, one vital thing was shown to me at the very outset: it was that I should read the Bible, not to find a text to develop into some kind of a talk, but just read the Bible TO LET THE BIBLE MOLD MY MIND! That is the Word I got in my soul, clear as could be. I was now to read the Bible just to let the Word of God MOLD MY MIND into the shape He wanted it to be. And that has been going on since the spring of 1944. It has brought about blessed and wonderful things in my life. You need a hunger for the Word, which the Lord can utilize to overthrow the devil in your life, who will come against you to try to take you away from prayer, and try to get you NOT to be circumspect, and not to use your time, not to redeem your time, and not to be hungry for the Word of God. The Lord bless you, if you have hunger for the Word of God, Glory to God, then you are a divine astronaut – moving IN GOD. Just be hungry for God's Word!‡

That is one of the features of Redeeming your time: to study the Bible, and read the Bible, and learn to feed on the Word. Be careful not to get the gripe that some get at one time or another when they come here. Don't say, "Oh, I haven't got time! I have so much work to do." You don't either! It is not so! People like to pet themselves, and even lie to themselves, but God sees if you are lying to yourself.

Supposing you were working some place at any kind of a modern job, or trade of some kind; figure out how much time it involves in getting to work and getting back home again. Then reckon the amount of time that you would have to put in on the job, and for the job, and about the job. Then compare that amount of time with the amount of time that you can give God if you REDEEM YOUR TIME in these Homes, without the problem of making your living that way. You are in these Homes to learn to use your time, and to *redeem* your time. One of the means by which you redeem your time is to develop a big habit of reading in the Bible and feeding on the Word.

Another point under utilization of your time, redeeming your time, is: MEETINGS. You are here to learn to use your time in meetings. And that involves you, in this Work, in GENUINE WORSHIP OF GOD IN SPIRIT AND IN TRUTH. It involves you in PRAISE, using your time in Praise and Thanksgiving; using your time in receiving and giving instruction; and using your time in WITNESSING. God wants you to be a WITNESS in the meetings. The Lord wants every one of you to speak. That is God's will. There have been some in the course of the years who felt that the Lord had shown them NOT to speak. But the Lord has NOT shown anyone in these Homes that you are NOT to speak in these meetings. THE LORD HAS NOT SHOWN ANYONE AT ANYTIME IN THESE HOMES THAT YOU ARE NOT TO SPEAK. IT IS GOD'S WILL FOR YOU TO WITNESS FOR JESUS CHRIST! TO PEOPLE ANYWHERE!§

---

‡ My prayer for years has been, "Lord, make Your Word REAL to me. Mold and shape my mind by Your Word. Make Your Word to be BREAD to me the eater, and SEED to me the sower."

§ This strong word exposed and confronted one of the trainees, who felt God had told him not to testify in the meetings for an entire year.

How are you going to give expression, and to get experience, and to develop any kind of facility in speaking, if you do not open your mouth? If you are willing to let the Lord inspire you, you can find a chance once or twice a week to get up, God bless you, and say, "Thank God for Jesus. I love Jesus. I believe on the Son of God," or something like that.

Another point about how to use your time is: YOU WILL USE YOUR TIME FOR OTHERS, OTHERS! We are sometimes considered as a people who are cloistered, and do not do anything for anybody else. Well, we have to do what we are doing or we would not be here! If we did not do what God gave us to do, who would do it? You are here to learn to use your time and redeem your time, FOR OTHERS. And that includes, and has to do with, souls, saving souls, and seeking souls, helping souls. ANYBODY! Save ANYBODY, just ANYBODY. One very valuable feature of this is to have a prayer list. A prayer list is a wonderful thing. You jot down the name of someone who is impressed upon you in one way or another, and you pray for them faithfully; and you will find that God will use you that way to the salvation of souls, and in other ways for God.

And again: you are to learn to use your time in FAITH HOME MAINTENANCE. We have as lovely a group of people in these Homes now as at any other time in the history of them. Practically everyone is trying to do their work for Jesus, and to do it with gladness. Sometimes people get a little overwrought, or maybe they get a little overworked; but then, you will get overworked sometimes anywhere! If you do not know what to do when you think you have too much to do, what will you do when you really do get overworked? A problem of many of God's Workers! You are here to learn to use your time in God's Work, and Faith Home Maintenance is very really God's Work.¶

Through the last 50 years, or more, we have taken a lot of potshots. Sometimes people say we ought to get out! We ought to get out! They do not know that we always have anywhere from 12 to 20 or 25 persons out in the Lord's Work who claim this as their home base. We do not say much about it. We could count at least 20 people right now who consider this their home base and in a very definite degree are sent out from here to various parts of the world. There have been at least 500 people who have gone out into the Lord's Work, either directly from these Homes, or from some church or mission that these Homes have been the root of.

¶ This applies to any ministry with property, be it church building, school, offices, *etc.* Using your time to maintain property can be a great blessing.

Here is a Bible truth which is beautiful to God in heaven, and beautiful for God on the earth: "Whatever you do, in word or in deed, do ALL in the Name of Jesus" (Colossians 3:17) and unto His Glory. If you will do that, and not faint – labor and not faint – you will VERY DEFINITELY find out what God means in the Word: to Redeem your time.

LIVING AND WALKING IN THE SPIRIT

"For brethren, you have been called unto liberty; only use not liberty for an occasion to the flesh, but by love serve one another." (Galatians 5:13)

There have been about 150,000 preachings, teachings, messages and talks in these Faith Homes since 1910.** I suppose the majority of those preachings and teachings and talks and messages would have some relation to this scripture: "Only use not liberty for an occasion to the flesh, but by love serve one another. For all the law is fulfilled in one word, even in this; Thou shalt love thy neighbour as thyself. But if you bite and devour one another, take heed that you be not consumed one of another. This I say then, WALK IN THE SPIRIT, and you shall not fulfill the lust of the flesh. For the flesh lusteth against the Spirit, and the Spirit against the flesh; and these are contrary the one to the other: so that ye cannot do the things that you would." (Galatians 5:13-17)

Quite a subject! "You cannot do the things that you would." Do you like that kind of talk from God? Do you like God to talk to you and say, "Look here, you cannot DO the things that you would, because your flesh is at war with My Spirit." But He is very nice about it. Glory to God! You cannot DO the things that you would because the Spirit is against the flesh, and these are contrary one to the other. WALK IN THE SPIRIT: that is what you are here to learn. You are here to learn to live in His Presence. There is a lot to learn about it. We are here to learn how to use our time. There is a lot to learn about it. One little house meeting talk about it barely nicks the surface of the matter. Now we are taking as our subject, "LIVING AND WALKING IN THE SPIRIT."

Just go ahead and let the Spirit lead you. Glory to God! Isn't that a wonderful way to live? Glory! Praise the Lord! If you are led by the Spirit, you are not under the Old Testament Law; you are in the New Testament

---

** Not willing to accept that tally without checking, I calculated the number myself, based on how many meetings per day were held in the early years and up to the present, and what I knew of the average number of talks given in an ordinary service. His tally is accurate.

Covenant. <u>The New Testament Covenant is the will of God to give you life.</u> The Old Testament Covenant was the will of God describing where sin is, which is the mystery of death; and He described it by that Law. But this is not meant to be a discussion on that point.

"Now the works of the flesh are manifest, which are these..."

- "Adultery, fornication, uncleanness, lasciviousness" – These four things have to do with the sex life and perversions of it in various ways. The thing in hand is: What are you here for? To live and Walk in the Spirit. So, we will pass on.

- "Idolatry" – which is covetousness;

- "witchcraft" – which is a thousand different kinds of superstition;

- "hatred" – which is that vicious, deadly root down in the heart, the opposite of Divine Love; hatred has multi-forms;

- "variance" – which means dissension, discord, argument, debate, controversy, to be against something, or somebody;

- "emulations" – meaning the desire to surpass others; it is a rank, terrible, horrible thing;

- "wrath" – we will not stop now on those things; there are so many kinds of wrath.

- "Strife" – there is so much of strife, and much of it is an effort to justify and exalt Self; just a word will so frequently start a quarrel and then strife appears. Bless your heart, if you would just learn how to pray the Mercy Prayer, and be willing to pray for the person you are looking at, or the person you are thinking about, or the person the devil TAUNTS you with in your MIND – get to praying that the Lord will pour out His Spirit in floods of Mercies, Lovingkindness, fulfilling their need – the strife would disappear.
  God bless you. Everybody is needy enough and needs your prayers. Instead of sparking off in strife by a word or an expression or a look, PRAY, PRAY, PRAY. The Lord has been teaching us here for 20 years what to do. And I believe the Lord has made it clear that such teaching is for the preparation

of the Coming of the Lord, and all that is involved in it. That is what is included in what the Bible teaches about Mercy.

- "Seditions" – well, we had better pass on; we are not bothered with them too much.

- "heresies"

- "envyings" – this murderous thing, this thing that cannot STAND it to have somebody take your place or go ahead of you. In this Work it often takes the form: You are not my boss, I don't have to obey YOU. "Envyings" – you can't say anything terrible or awful enough to really describe the wickedness and the devilishness and the murderousness of that work of the flesh called "envy."

- "murders" – you can study murder in the First Epistle of John, what it says there about manslaughter.

- "Drunkenness, revelings" – I won't discuss those now;

"…of the which I tell you before, as I have also told you in time past, that they which do such things shall not inherit the kingdom of God."

Now we come to the 22nd verse. Let's sing a chorus:

> *I am coming Lord, Coming now to Thee;*
> *Wash me, cleanse me in the blood, That flowed on Calvary.*

That was to give you a little moment to breathe, and shake yourself, and get ready for the rest of it here.

"But the fruit of the Spirit is love, joy, peace…" We want to get enough out of it so that you feel at home in that kind of truth. And you are at home with God when you believe God, that the Holy Spirit will do in you what He has told you to do. God has not told you to do anything at all, in the whole Bible, but what He has given the Holy Spirit to enable you to do it. So, the fruit of the Spirit – that which the Spirit does in you, that which is the result of His possession of you as you are growing up in God – that fruit of the Spirit is LOVE. (I suppose that all the rest of these fruits are part of that word LOVE.) "Joy, peace, longsuffering, gentleness, goodness, faith, meekness, temperance (which is self-control); against such there is no law."

You will find that all of these words in verb form, – verbing the word love, verbing the word joy, verbing the word peace – they are all part of what the Bible teaches about Mercy. That is because Mercy is Lovingkindness, and Lovingkindness-Mercy is Love-in-Action. So all of these words, when you verb them, are the Spirit of Grace and Mercy. You cannot get away from the word Mercy, or Lovingkindness; because there is not any joy, except in lovingkindness; there is not any peace, except in lovingkindness (that is the love-in-action). There is not any longsuffering – you try it! Bless your hearts, you have tried it plenty of times; so have I. How patient are you anyway? We can easily tell each other "to let patience have her perfect work" (James 1:4). You must! Patience is endurance, and it is a very wonderful thing. But you try it! Try to have patience without lovingkindness-mercy.

You know, God bless you, that if you are willing to take such training in these Faith Homes, and to live in the Spirit and walk in the Spirit, and willing to be a fountain of blessing which issues in mercy, and in the Prayer of Mercy, and in feeding on the Word, do you realize what it will do for you, what kind of a training you will be in? Just imagine, having longsuffering, or patience, LONGsuffering, L O N G-suffering. You try to manufacture it, and you will find that you will have to have a breath of God in you praying for other people that they will be blessed of God, and engraced of God, and flooded with His Spirit with fulfilling mercies. Fulfilling mercies means, whatever he needs. "Ohhh, Lord! Just give them EVERYTHING that is necessary to make their need to be fulfilled." If you never learned anything else, and have learned that, you are qualified to go as a missionary any place in the world. You may not agree with that, but you will after some years.

"The fruit of the Spirit is love, joy, peace, long-suffering, GENTLENESS." A beautiful word. I sometimes wish that the Lord had made me gentle, but He has been "gentle-ing" me through the years. Gentleness is the Lord. He is gentle. "Thy GENTLENESS has made me great."[††] The Lord bless you, do you want that kind of greatness? Are you willing to let God train you in His own ways? Are you willing to let Him teach you how to put up with all kinds of things that seem to go against you? You come out with some degree of this fruit of the Spirit, GENTLENESS. What will make you more gentle than to pray for the one

---

[††] Psalm 18:35

you are looking at or thinking about; pray that God will simply FLOOD their lives, God's generosity, God's charity, "FLOOD that one with your SPIRIT, with FULFILLING mercies, whatever they need, fulfill their need." GENTLE. The simplicity of the books of the New Testament is that Heaven is opened *to your soul* in those Words, if your heart and your soul is *opened to the Words*. SIMPLICITY, wonderful.

"Goodness, faith." We won't stop on these words. "Meekness." Meekness, you know, is the willing submission of your mind to somebody else's will. And that is where meekness is: your willing submission. It is an amazing thing, the FRUIT of meekness; which is what Jesus is Himself. HE DIED FOR YOU. He knew you would never be meek in time or eternity. So He died for you. And He wants you to die for Him – in His arms, in His Spirit – to swallow up your will in His. This Work teaches that, and, by the Grace of God, we are not going to swerve either to the right hand or to the left. We are not going to swerve, because it is the MEEK that are going to inherit the earth, and not those who merely imagine they are meek, or those who do not love the Meekness of The Meek One.

Meekness is the surrender and submission of your will and your mind to do the mind and will of another. And what could be more wonderful, than that the Holy Spirit should develop in you, and bring forth in you, *Meekness* as a fruit that belongs to God. These fruits that are borne on you do not belong to you, they belong to God; they belong to the husbandman; they belong to Him. DON'T YOU WANT GOD TO HAVE SOMETHING OUT OF YOU? DON'T YOU WANT TO HAVE SOMETHING THAT GOD CAN PICK OFF OF YOU? FOR HIMSELF? God is looking at your life, and has planned for you, and has worked for you, and is working in you, to bring forth the fruit of the Spirit. Not only to live by the Spirit and preach to other people how they must live, not only to live in the Spirit, but also to WALK in the Spirit.

That is where we have to part company, sometimes, with some who are very blessedly used of the Lord, up to a certain point. But when it comes to that point of MEEKNESS!!! – they do not know what it is. Philip Hanson Jones' book, *Signs and Wonders in China,* describes it graphically.‡‡ It is an amazing thing, an amazing thing: MEEKNESS.

---

‡‡ P. Hansen Jones was a frequent and beloved guest in the Faith Homes. His book is long out of print; however, this writer has a photocopy of it.

"Temperance." TEMPERANCE means self-control. Bless your dear hearts, some of you have a little self-control. JUST AS MUCH AS THE LORD CAN TAKE POSSESSION OF YOUR WILL, GLORY TO GOD! THAT IS HOW MUCH YOU HAVE OF SELF-CONTROL. Of ourselves we can do nothing; through Christ we can do all things. Temperance means, first of all, GOD POSSESSING YOU. <u>You cannot see the ALLNESS, the FULNESS, THE PERFECT COMPLETENESS, OF GOD, in everything that you need, except in the degree in which He has brought you to the perception that you are nothing in yourself.</u> And that is where people part company with us sometimes, because the "OUTWARD" life is simply seeking constantly to BE something. Well, there is a ministry and work of being something, and God anoints, and makes people to be something. <u>But oh, if He starts to perfect them, in the wonder of union with Himself, they find that they have to give up their lives to the</u> "INWARD" path, in which the LORD ALONE IS EVERYTHING.

It is a terrible shock to some people to learn that they are nothing. But there has to be that kind of ministry. Here, the Lord asks everyone to choose which Path they want to follow: The INWARD or the OUTWARD. The Inward Path is a pathway of going into God, where you have nothing but JESUS; and <u>little by little He strips you so that you see it as plain as can be: You are naked, spiritually, and you haven't anything good in yourself.</u> So many Christians, and I mean baptized-in-the-Holy-Ghost-Christians, demand to be entertained; they have to be entertained. The preacher must entertain them, or else they do not feel they have received any blessing. Lust for entertainment! Outward life!

"Against such there is no law." God gives a training here which sifts out people who want to go the Outward way and who want to stay in the life of Being Something. You are taught here how to live and WALK in the Spirit, the knowledge of WALKING in the Spirit. If you are taught that, and trained in that, then you are becoming an inheritor of the kingdom of God.

<u>"And they that are Christ's have crucified the flesh with its affections and lusts.</u> IF WE LIVE IN THE SPIRIT, LET US ALSO WALK IN THE SPIRIT." And the climax is, "Let us not be desirous of vain-glory, provoking one another, or envying one another." So, they that are Christ's, do these things. If you are Christ's, you are a branch in the Vine, and the Father is the husbandman, taking care of you; and He is going to prune you down, to the next-to-last bud, when He prunes you; sometimes, the last two buds. It makes more grapes when you are pruned – the Father is

the husbandman and He knows how to prune you best! He will surely do it, if you are Christ's, and are wanting to live and walk in the Spirit.

That is what this Work is for. That is what the training is for. It is not simply that you should scrub floors when you don't like to scrub floors, or do maintenance work; but it is: "Doing everything for Christ." There isn't a thing you will ever have to do in these Homes, living and walking in the Spirit, but what JESUS WOULD BE WILLING right now to come down off the throne of God and do. He would be willing to take the mop out of your hands, and take the paring knife out of your hands, and the dust cloth. There is not anything you are ever going to have to do, or be asked to do, in these Homes, but what Jesus Himself would be perfectly willing to do. Praise the Lord. Do you believe that?

What have we been talking about? Living and Walking in the Spirit. WHAT ARE YOU HERE FOR? You are here to LIVE IN THE PRESENCE OF THE LORD: and you have to learn it, more than you know. You are here to KNOW HOW TO MAKE USE OF YOUR TIME, AND REDEEM THE TIME for God. You are here to LEARN TO LIVE AND WALK IN THE HOLY SPIRIT. If you will live in what the Bible teaches about Mercy, God bless you, you will learn quite surely in a simplified way, how to live, and how to walk, in the Holy Spirit.

This matter of LIVING AND WALKING IN THE SPIRIT needs great emphasis, and continuous repetition. It is too easy for "Christians" to substitute information-learning for the true knowledge of God that comes into the life by DOING-JESUS'-WORDS. If one reads the Bible much, with an increasing hunger to be like Jesus, they will find that the whole New Covenant (Testament) describes a New Life in The Holy Spirit which is living-in-the-Words-of-Jesus. THAT IS POWER! THAT IS "THE POWER OF GOD!"

You learn the wonder and glory of The Will of God by doing what He has said. And that involves a change of WILL – GOD'S WILL in place of your self-will. He gives you The Holy Spirit to bring that to pass. To Live and Walk in The Holy Spirit is the first and main essential in any true training for the Lord's Work. And, is it not also the true Preparation for The Coming of The Lord? It surely is.

Wherever you may go in the Lord's Service you will need to be able to teach people to Live and Walk in The Holy Spirit. But, how can you teach others unless you live that way yourself? The training in the Faith Homes is intended of God to build you up in that Life and Knowledge of God. It is good to have a good education so as to be able to express yourself well and to impart the Truth to others; but even if your education is deficient, you will IMPART THE TRUTH OF GOD to those around you IF YOU LIVE AND WALK IN THE SPIRIT.

It is your TESTIMONY that God wants to use. For His Work is accomplished by the flow-through, impartation, of The Spirit of Grace.

Blessed Lord, You have heard all these words. They give a good taste in one's mouth. Thank You, Father, for the taste of it; it tastes good. It does not mean that we are good, but it means that YOU ARE GOOD, and Your Goodness is part of the fruition of the union of our will with Thine, by the Spirit of God possessing. We pray that You will bless this word to everyone. Do not let a single one who reads this feel in any way whatever that they have been robbed, or they have been depreciated or anything like that. We pray that it shall be clear to everyone that the opening of Your Word gives Light to the soul. Thank You, Father, for the Holy Spirit. In Jesus' Name. Amen.

DAILY GRACE

What are you here in the Homes for, what are you here for? What does it mean: Ministerial Training?

Our subject is DAILY GRACE. You have come here in a consecration of your life to the Lord, desiring that He mold you as the potter's clay, into whatever form He wants. You are learning to surrender daily, and moment by moment, resigning your life to Him to do with you as He pleases. But the thought may strike up into your mind, that the pasture would be greener across the fence somewhere; if you were just somewhere else than here, maybe you would have it better, and enjoy it more, and get more out of it. The devil tries to disrupt, and confuse, and poison the heart and its affections, and its lovely surrender to the Lord. What are you really here for?

For one thing: DAILY GRACE. The last phrase of each verse of the song, *Sitting at the Feet of Jesus*, portrays really and beautifully, what we mean by DAILY GRACE.

> *Sitting at the feet of Jesus, Oh, what words I hear Him say!*
> *Happy place! so near, so precious! May it find me there each day;*
> *Sitting at the feet of Jesus, I would look upon the past;*
> *For His love has been so gracious, It has won my heart at last.*

Sitting at the feet of Jesus, Where can mortal be more blest?
There I lay my sins and sorrows, And, when weary, find sweet rest;
Sitting at the feet of Jesus, There I love to weep and pray;
While I from His fullness gather Grace and comfort every day.

Bless me, O my Savior, bless me, As I sit low at Thy feet;
Oh, look down in love upon me, Let me see Thy face so sweet;
Give me, Lord, the mind of Jesus, Keep me holy as He is;
May I prove I've been with Jesus, Who is all my righteousness.[2]

"For His love has been so gracious, It has won my heart at last."

He wins your heart at first. Between the first and the last, there has to be a between; and Jesus has to become The Between in every way and in everything in our lives. He fills the space between first and last. So, He wins your heart, God bless you; He wins your heart at the beginning, and that is how you start out.

If you were to think of DAILY GRACE as being YOUR grace, immediately you have plummeted down from the position that you were in, in the First Love, and you have FALLEN from that position. The Grace that we are talking about is not OUR grace; it is the Grace of God. And you are learning to be God-like. You are here to learn to be JUST LIKE JESUS. You cannot be just like Jesus apart from the Grace of God. The DAILY GRACE which we are considering is not OUR Grace. It is the GRACE OF GOD, inter-penetrating the substance of your soul; changing your very heart, and soul, and mind, and bodily strength – changing you into the substance of God. "For His love has been so gracious, It has won my heart at last." He wins your heart at first; then Jesus becomes, Himself, the Grace of God to you, by His Word, and the Gift of His Spirit, and by leading you in the pathway of Prayer and Faith. He is the First and the Last. Glory to God!

Then, in the second verse,

"While I from His fullness gather, Grace and Comfort every day."

This is a problem that many of God's dear children do not seem to comprehend. So many feel that their church life is sufficient. But what the New Testament is describing from the beginning of Jesus' teachings until the climax of the Book of Revelation, is that from HIS

FULNESS we gather Grace and Comfort every day. You are here to learn DAILY GRACE, and to LIVE IN DAILY GRACE. Sometimes individuals have been here who felt very gracious before they came; in fact, they felt that they were almost at the top of it. They seemed to have a lot of love, and a lot of grace, until they got into the daily life in the Homes, and being on schedule, and having people step on their toes, and all kinds of things happened. Then they found that they did not have enough Grace to get through a day without exploding or going into a dump, or fuss, or discouragement. They think it is somebody else's fault that they feel so bad; somebody else said something or did something, or they imagine it.§§

And then they blame their ill feelings on someone else. But the whole trouble is they did not have the Grace of God like they thought they had. People come here sometimes feeling that they are VERY spiritual, out in front of the pack, so to speak. They seemed, in their own minds, to have developed a lot of Grace; they were sweet and gracious. But after they have lived in the Homes a little while, they are tempted, or tested, or tried, in angles and in various ways in which they were never tried much before. Then they find that their Grace has been a bag with a lot of big holes in it, and everything seems to have leaked out. They find that they have to learn the meaning of these words, "While I from His fullness (HIS fullness) gather, Grace and Comfort every day." These verses show what is meant in the background of this subject of DAILY GRACE.

So, in the last verse,

"May I prove I've been with Jesus, Who is all my righteousness."

Rom 12:1

It has to be proved, beloved, and you are here to prove it, with the Lord's help. "May I prove I've been with Jesus, Who is all my righteousness." Yes, it has to be proved. The words, "test," or "tempt," or "prove," are quite synonymous in reference to what the Lord allows to come into your life. He is not tempted by evil, St. James says; and He does not tempt anybody to do evil. But we are tempted when we are drawn up by fleshly desire, or some lust, or working of the devil in some form.¶¶ When we are excited, in one form or another, we are drawn up out of our lowliness and our

---

§§ What he says here about the need for "daily grace" in the Faith Homes applies equally to one's workplace, or even at home.
¶¶ See James 1:12-14

peace of heart, and we carry forth what the devil tries to get us to do. The Lord permits those things, though He does NOT tempt us to do evil; He proves us in order that our faith shall overcome all evil. He proves us by testing, and by allowing us to be tried, in many forms, according to what He is planning our lives to be. He wants you to be what He wants you to be; and He will prove very faithful to you in producing what He aims for you to be eternally. There has to be proof: "MAY I PROVE I'VE BEEN WITH JESUS, Who is all my righteousness."

The Lord bless you! Don't be upset because you did not prove it the first time. God wants proof. He wants you to PROVE that you have been with Jesus, because you are going to be with Him forever. He wants to MAKE you to BE what He plans for you to be forever. That means: to be able, in this world, to stand against the wiles of the devil. We are talking about DAILY GRACE. It is the background in which God forms you into the likeness of Jesus – a wonderful, glorious, unfading life for you to fulfill.

The results in your life, to a large extent, will be what you make them to be, by what you do in the Daily Grace of God. Too frequently, individuals come into the Homes who are expecting results to be made for them like you add something up on a paper; or that somebody will DO something for them. Once in awhile there is somebody who feels that they ought to be EMPOWERED to fill some office, to BE something. And then we say, "Nobody here has any power to make you, or anybody, to BE anything. We cannot anoint anybody with the Holy Ghost. If you are going to be in the ministry, in any form whatever at all, it has got to be GOD that puts you there; it has to be God who anoints you and makes you able to do it. There isn't anybody that is going to make you able or ready for any kind of ministry for God, BUT GOD." People have all kinds of queer ideas. They get queer ideas sometimes on the things that are nowadays so much talked about: GIFTS – as though people give gifts. But it is not people who give gifts. People come here with the expectation that it is going to be wonderful. Well, it is wonderful! They expect somehow or other that they are going to be made to BE wonderful. But with most individuals there is a LONG PERIOD OF DEFLATION from their INFLATION, in which they come down, and come down, and come down, to practically nothing. And when they are "nothing" enough, then God begins to anoint and show what He wants.

One woman, a lovely woman, came here years ago, who felt that she had quite a ministry, was quite anointed of the Lord. Somebody said something to her about coming here to get light from the Lord. She said, "Well, I didn't come here to GET light; I came here to GIVE light." Well, she is still getting light, and I guess still giving light. In the 50,000 of preachings and teachings we have had in these meetings through the decades, and the 100,000 or more of other messages of one kind or another which are important for people's lives, I think about everything that is worth hearing has been spoken in one form or another. Some things we have had over and over and over again, which includes most everything that could be said of value. DAILY GRACE is one of those things. It includes in itself much of what there is to know! But it takes years and years, sometimes, to find it out. But! What do you care: it is all finding and knowing Jesus – forever!

You came here to GET light. The Lord's light has been shining here through long decades. It is a very simple and beautiful light, God bless you. It is as simple as a candle. We used to sing,

Jesus bids us shine with a pure, clear light, Like a little candle shining in the night;
He looks down from heaven, sees us shine; You in your small corner, and I in mine.

Pretty lovely, isn't it? Can you get down there, brother, sister? It is essential that you get down to that simplicity. God has required that this Work remain in that UTTER SIMPLICITY, because that is what it means when we say, "We must have JESUS ALONE." There is a another chorus we used to sing –

Jesus alone, Jesus for me; Jesus alone, Jesus for me;
Jesus through all eternity; Jesus alone for me.

How about it?

And that is it. Supposing you stay here ten years, or five years, or three years, or two years (we hope you stay more than one!); what do you think you will have learned? As you look back, what will show up in your life that you have been here for? That is what we are trying to get at in this series. Bless your dear heart, if The Flower of God's Garden has blossomed in your heart, which is Jesus, so that you can see the BEAUTY of God, THE WONDERFUL SON, the blossom will be, "I have found Jesus. I have come to know that Jesus is my all, and in all." When you have learned it, then whatever God wants of you, God can empower you to be.

You are here to become empowered of God. This is a very, very simple point: for you to be a little candle shining in your corner. If the candlelight is Jesus, and if the fire is the love of God, and you are the wick, and you are burning in the oil of God, IT WILL BE JESUS that actually appears.

There is nothing else that will be important at all, in the long run. We are getting into such a peculiar, mixed-up, devilish, and hellish time in the world; and everything is in confusion; and it is going to be worse; and people's hearts will fail them for fear for what is coming on the earth. And GOD MUST HAVE HIS WITNESSES. He must have His people on the earth who can overcome the world by faith, and who have learned the foundation of it. And DAILY GRACE, the walk in DAILY GRACE, is an important part of that matter.

The results of your training here will be what you make them, by what you do. You see, we put the end of each of those three verses of that song, *Sitting at the Feet of Jesus,* in as a background. I just love it. I must read it again:

For His love has been so gracious, (GRACE, GRACE, GRACE!),
It has won my heart at last (first, and then last; first, and then last).

While I from His fullness gather, Grace and comfort every day (day-by-day, Daily Grace, day-by-day).

May I prove I've been with Jesus, Who is all my righteousness.

I just love those words; they give power to the subject of DAILY GRACE.

We will put in here, before we go any further, a word about Witnessing. We could say that *each one of these subjects has its effect on Witnessing.* Somebody might say, "Well, I thought we were to be witnesses." Yes, you are. But you are to be Witnesses of THE LORD. You need to know the Lord. You are here to live in the Presence of the Lord. You know, God bless you, that you can hardly *live in the Presence of the Lord* without making it known. There will be a witness from your actions and your words. It may be completely unknown to you, but if you live in the Presence of the Lord, you will be a witness of that Lord and of His Presence, without your even trying to do it.

In the same connection: *The Use of Your Time.* Why, God bless you, if you use your time, redeeming your time, and live the Word of God, and live a life of Prayer – you are bound to BE a witness! The fountain will spring up. You will be a witness.

And the next one: *Living and Walking in the Spirit* – as we had it in Galatians 5. Why, God bless you, if you Live-and-Walk-in-the-Spirit, do you think you will have nothing to say? If you live in the Presence of the Lord, do you think you have no witness? If you are Using your Time for God, do you think you have nothing to say? That is what you are learning here.

And we add that Time blends into Eternity, and Living and Using Your Time for the Lord, you will wake up and realize, "I am living in Eternity." And you will have something to say about it. All of these themes have a result in Witnessing. So whether we use the subject of Witnessing for Jesus, or not, as one of these talks, it must become clear to you that every one of these themes will result, or should result, automatically and spontaneously, in Witnessing for the Lord.

God bless you, do you love Jesus? Well, if you love Him, what do you say? Why bless your heart, if you are in love with Jesus, you just want to talk about it; you want to talk about Him. It is a target at which the devil aims his spears and arrows. If he can by any means whatever take out of your heart, and out of your lips, the simplicity that you LOVE Jesus, he is going to put something else in your heart and your mind and your mouth besides that. That is where the potent, life-giving, life-birthing power of God is: the witness of the Word of God in your heart that YOU LOVE THE LORD.

The Schedule Work in the Faith Homes is a very realistic and important factor in living in Daily Grace. In the olden days (we speak of the Old Work), all of the schedules were given by the Word of the Lord. Many people don't know that, and do not realize that these Homes, for many years, were conducted by the Word of the Lord, and all of the Schedule Work was arranged by the Lord's Word. But amazingly, though it was the Word of the Lord, and the individuals were supposed to believe it, and did believe it as far as the nice meeting talks were concerned, yet when it came to the schedule, they sometimes felt they were being unjustly treated, and then they fussed. They would say, "I don't believe that was God!" Now we arrange the schedule, with prayer and trust that the Lord will make it balance out if you keep your peace, and WALK IN DAILY GRACE.***

I don't know that the Lord is going to make a pet out of any one of you. I hope there is nobody in the Work now that wants to be petted; but maybe you do, and maybe you do not know it. I do not think the Lord is going to make a pet out of you that way. But the Lord knows what you NEED, in your life, to make you strong and able to stand, and to withstand the wiles and works of the devil, and, "having done all, to stand." We mention Schedule Work because in most everyone's life, who lives in the Homes for any length of time, the matter of the Schedule can sometimes become a fuss if you do not DO IT JUST FOR JESUS. It is too easy to feel that somebody else is treated better than you, and all that kind of thing. The truth is, the Faith Homes require work done to keep them going. Too many times, through the years, people have said, "You ought to get out, you ought to get out! You ought to scatter! Get the people OUT of there; get them into doing something!" And we say, "They ARE doing something." But what would happen to the Homes if everybody went somewhere? The work has to be done, and it has to be done WELL. And Praise God it is a ministry for Jesus.

We might just add here a little point: The housework has to be done WELL. The baseboards have to be wiped off, and the dust removed from everything. There are all kinds of things that have to be done. It is very important that the housework be done VERY WELL, because visitors come in from all over. They might stay for a night and a day. Visitors have come to stay, but left the next morning, because the room smelled, or there was dust or dirt, or there was something they did not like.

It is exceedingly important that the housework be done well. Some of the visitors don't care, except they do want clean sheets. There are some people who are down-to-earth, and they do not pay too much attention to all the niceties. But there are those who come to the Homes who are unconsciously very critical. They do not know it; they would have to live in the Homes a year or two to find out how terribly critical they are. They want to put their finger on the corner of the table, or along the window sill, or on the piano, and then they look at their finger to see if it has dust on it!

Cleanliness is exceedingly important. Maybe you do not see why it has to be that way! Why, bless your heart, that is where DAILY GRACE

*** It should be obvious that this paragraph, and the following ones, apply to secular employment also.

comes in! There is one thing you may be sure of about Heaven: IT WILL BE CLEAN!!! Glory! After all, wherever you go in your lifetime to work for the Lord, you will find that you need to KNOW HOW to do things right; how to keep a house clean; *etc.*

And say, another little point that we will throw in here. THAT IS, DOING DISHES. You know, dishes are not stones that you dump out of a tray into a pile so they can be washed. Dishes are things to be handled, and be handled with care. Through the years we have sometimes had at the different homes those who did the dishes a good deal. And some of them were clatterers. Talk about an uproar, a noise, a confusion, a clattering! Why, they rattled those dishes, dumped them into the pan, and whished them around, and banged them down and around; an unholy useless noise. And chipped dishes! And sometimes unwilling to take instruction! Sometimes they would rattle those dishes, and clatter those dishes, while the meal was going on, and while people were trying to talk and pray. Now, they do not think of it just like that.

At one time about 20 years ago, I was making the rounds at a noon meal, one day at one Home, and another day at another Home, and another day at another Home, at least the three Homes once a week, for several weeks. This was in order to take up matters which had arisen in the Homes that needed to be talked over. We had little House Meetings at the table, and I had to be the smoother-over of things. And certain fellows would go and do it THEN. One day I went into the kitchen and talked to them about it, and left, meaning to leave the impression that they must wash the dishes in a different way. So, I went out, turned around, and went in again – and there they were, at it just the same – banging, rattling, noising. We had next time a very special table meeting on obedience. And we made the main theme to be: JESUS WOULD DO ANY JOB YOU HAVE, AND DO IT RIGHT!

DAILY GRACE means that you are willing to be TOLD that you are doing wrong! You may THINK you are doing right because you always did a thing in a certain way. But just because you always did a thing in a certain way does not always mean that you are RIGHT. In the Faith Homes, there are many things which have to be re-adjusted, because the situation is different. People who have come from all different types of homes and backgrounds are thrown together in a home like the Faith Homes, and then they find that one wants to be the center-pole, with everyone else swinging around them; they want others to adjust to their likes and wishes. And when you have *several people* like that – well, the problem has to be worked out in Grace, Wisdom, Patience, Love. After 60 years the important things are known to us!

Our subject is: DAILY GRACE. If you are willing to admit it; and if you are willing to be corrected; and not get your feelings hurt; and not get in a dump; and not get into an aggravated state of refusal to get down – THAT IS DAILY GRACE, and what we mean by "Mercy"! There have been those who do not like it here. They do not want to be bossed. They do not want to have anybody over them. They do not want to be TOLD anything. They think they know everything already. And sometimes they humble themselves and "Get Down" – and stay! But these Faith Homes actually run in a beautiful way. Even with any lopsidedness, and any difficulties that arise, these Faith Homes are a LONG-STANDING MIRACLE OF GOD IN THE EARTH, and in the Unity of the Spirit. Living at peace with one another does have a tremendous effect ANY PLACE, where people live in the Spirit and walk in Daily Grace. And it has a tremendous effect on the spirit world.

So we will read four verses here, the end of the Fourth Chapter of Ephesians, verses 29-32. "Let no corrupt communication proceed out of your mouth…" If we stopped to talk about corrupt communication, we would start all over again. What you SAY; what comes OUT of your mouth, God bless you! "Let no corrupt communication proceed out of your mouth, but that which is good to the use of edifying, that it may MINISTER GRACE unto the hearers." What comes out of your mouth! You are here to learn a Life. You are learning to live a Life in which you MINISTER THE GRACE OF GOD TO OTHERS. And if you DON'T, you are no minister. And if you DO, you are a minister, whether you have any title or not. If you MINISTER THE GRACE OF GOD, YOU ARE A MINISTER! And God will use you to destroy the works of the devil.

If you do not minister the Grace of God, you may fall in a heap! But even then, the Lord will lift you up out of that heap if you will repent. "And grieve not the Holy Spirit of God, whereby you are sealed unto the day of redemption." We are in that day; NOW is the day. "Let all bitterness, and wrath, and anger, and clamour, and evil speaking, be put away from you, with all malice." Another sermon there, or two. "And be ye kind one to another, tenderhearted, forgiving one another," (even, even, EVEN), "forgiving one another EVEN as God for Christ's sake hath forgiven you."

You can do that, if you will pray the Mercy Prayer for anyone and everyone around you, with no exceptions; you can DO it. Just pray to the Lord: *"Blessed Lord, the one I am looking at, the one I am thinking about, the one that is in my mind, the one that I think has hurt me, the one I do not like, that one I am thinking about, simply send floods of Thy Holy Spirit in Mercies Fulfilling, Fulfilling Mercies, on their life, meeting and fulfilling every need of theirs."* Just about like that. Do you know, and do you realize, that you will then be in this Word? – "And be ye kind one to another, tenderhearted, forgiving one another, even as God for Christ's sake hath forgiven you."

That is where "ministering Grace to the hearers" comes in so many, many, many times. Little things that bump you; the little things you do not like. Those little things sometimes stab so deep into the heart-life, that the mind becomes a slave to the feelings in the heart. But if you will minister the Grace of God, then you are in His Ministry. Again, "Let no corrupt communication proceed out of your mouth, but that which is good to the use of edifying, that it may minister grace unto the hearers."

This has been a pleasure, God bless you.

Blessed Lord, You have told us to want the milk, the good milk of the Word, and we thank You for it. These things we have been talking about are fundamentals; they are first principles. We pray, Lord, that You will bless everyone here with an increasing awareness of the MEANING of the Word of God, and that the Word of God is not hidden somewhere in the heights or the depths, but it is in the HEART, and in the MOUTH, the WORD of Living Faith which we speak. Blessed Lord, make Thy Word, and these words, this kind of truth, real to every one of us, that we may MINISTER GRACE unto those who hear us, and to those whom we think about. Thank you, Father, for your Presence, and the Wonder of Your Spirit. In Jesus' Name. Amen.

THE FAITH LIFE

What are you here for? What are you doing? What are you in the Faith Homes for? And that does not refer only to those who are more recently here as trainees, but to every one of us; for in a very direct and realistic way, we are all trainees.

First: You are here to learn TO DWELL IN HIS PRESENCE. Second: You are here to learn TO USE YOUR TIME – to redeem the time. Third: WALKING IN THE SPIRIT, to learn to live and walk in the Spirit. These are all basic points. They are Divine factors in your training. Your training here is not so much carrying out classwork, in the ordinary sense of Bible School work, as it is the realization that you are living before the face of the Lord; living and walking in the Holy Spirit at all times. Fourth: DAILY GRACE. This is intended of the Lord to be an INWARD work. The INWARD life means inward toward God, IN God, toward the Lord, turned toward Him all the time. And that means to live in Daily Grace. Fifth: Our subject is, THE FAITH LIFE. What are you here for? What are you training for? What are you doing in the Homes? You are here to learn to LIVE A FAITH LIFE.

To some of you that may seem very simple, as just being part of your consecration to the Lord. But in a very significant way, you will find that in this Work the Lord will lead you to tread a pathway that is in some DEFINITE degree different from the life that you have been in previously. Some of the things that you will have to learn are involved in DEPRIVATION – deprivation of things you have been used to, or want, or would like.

To some this is a frightening day that we are living in, because the natural-reasoning mind, or intellect, is so deeply involved in the belief that you are your own faith – whatever you believe you can do, you CAN do – the illusion of riches, or money, and the life of mammon, the delusion of what money means, and can be. This DELUSION which the world is in makes it almost impossible for some people to see the pathway of FAITH, because there are so many things they think they can provide for themselves. One of the Divine matters which the Lord is undertaking in what we call a Life of Faith, is that THE LORD WILL PROVIDE. But you will find (perhaps you have already found in some degree), that you will be DEPRIVED. It is not a life of covetous getting, but of GIVING GOD.

You must get over squealing and squalling about being deprived of this, and deprived of that; you don't like this, and you don't like that; and you expected it to be different here…! What did you expect? What DID you expect, I wonder? You may find that you are in a pathway in which deprivation appears. You know how to do a thing, don't you? You know how to get money ... you get up and say, "Give us a collection." Well, we only take up an offering for missionaries, and once in a long while what we call a "Dorcas" offering.††† You may find that you are in a process, in the Faith Life, of being deprived of your ability to make ends meet, to MAKE it be done. And one of the things that you are bound to learn is WHAT TO DO WHEN YOU ARE DEPRIVED.

Turning it around the other way, the Lord comes around the corner, God bless you, and He says, "Welcome! Hail, my child! Here, I have what you need." The Faith Life means to have GOD – only God. You are going to be in it all your life long. The Lord is not going to work out your own will – He is going to teach you to walk by faith so that you can do HIS Will.

> *I love to kiss each print, where Thou hast set Thine unseen feet;*
> *I cannot fear Thee, Blessed Will, Thine empire is so sweet.*[3]

There are different ways in which we could say, "This is the Faith Life." You have it expressed in the New Testament very blessedly and very wonderfully. In Hebrews 11 we have it: "All these died in faith, not having RECEIVED the promise"; but they died IN FAITH, they were IN FAITH. The whole New Testament is the illustration of the Faith OF GOD. Through the WHOLE New Testament are the footprints of His "unseen feet." So we can say, the Faith Life means, to walk in the steps of Jesus.

God is not so concerned with what YOU can work out, with all your wonderful knowledge, and with all your ability that you believe you have in one way or another. He is not concerned with what YOU can work out. What God is doing is working out something in you which you do not understand. It is this question of *Understanding* that we are dealing with all the time when we talk about a Faith Life. Paul says, in Second Corinthians 5:7, "We walk by faith, not by sight." We had the beautiful scripture in the fifth chapter of Galatians: "If you *live* in the Spirit," says the Apostle, – and he had utilized the first four chapters to describe that spiritual life, as living in the Spirit – "If we live in the Spirit, let us *walk* in the Spirit."

How are you going to walk in the Spirit? BY FAITH, bless your

---

††† A "Dorcas" offering meant a collection for a Benevolent Fund, used by the Faith Homes to aid the poor and needy in the congregation, privately. No offerings for the General Fund were ever taken; no salaries were ever paid to any of the ministers or staff workers. Once a month an offering was collected for the support of the Faith Home missionaries.

heart. How are you going to walk by faith? Well, you have to follow Jesus; there is no other way expressed in the New Testament that I know anything about. He started right out at the beginning of His ministry by saying to certain ones – fishermen they happened to be – "Follow me." And, GLORY TO GOD, they got out of their boats, and left their father and the hired servants in the boat, and went with Jesus. So that is what it means when He says, "Follow me." It means, "Walk with me; come with me; live with me." We talk about walking in the Spirit, living and walking in the Spirit – that has to mean living and walking with Jesus. We talk about walking by faith – that has to mean living and walking with Jesus. We talk about walking by faith and not by sight. The faith we are in, when we are walking by faith and not by sight, HAS TO BE faith in His Spirit. He gives His Spirit for free. Then, His Spirit will take possession of us according as we obey the words of Jesus. So, the Faith Life is walking with Jesus. The HOLY SPIRIT teaches us to do Jesus' Words.

This is the pathway of faith: to learn to Dwell in His Presence; to Redeem the Time; to Walk in the Spirit; to Live in Daily Grace; so the question of a Faith life is not just a question of getting money enough to live on. It is a question of LIVING UNTO GOD. And so Faith in God is derived into you by the Word of the Lord Jesus Christ, who Himself was the Word which was with God, and was God, and became flesh. He spoke to you the INWARD WORD, the Word of indwelling in God, and God in you. And that creates, or gives birth, to Divine Understanding. And Divine Understanding and FAITH occupy the same place, and they are the development of God in your soul; because as you believe God's Word, which He has communicated to you, you begin to understand it, and you LIVE IN THE TRUTH OF GOD. And that is WHAT FAITH IS. You do not walk by human sight, or mind, or intellect.

Faith gives you a birth of God in you. And faith IS a birth of God in you because of what your faith is IN. If you believe a liar, then you are connected with a lie; but if you believe in the truth of Jesus, then God springs up in your heart. And that is Faith. *Faith is then a Reborn Understanding – a Heavenly Understanding.*

What does the Faith Life involve you in, then? Well, bless your heart, it involves you in LOVING HIM WHO TOLD YOU THAT GOD LOVES

YOU. Faith says, "Well, if He loved ME, and gave Himself for ME, then I will love HIM, and give myself for HIM." Faith says, "If He suffered for ME, then I understand that I shall suffer for HIM." It is Truth that, "If we suffer for Him and with Him, we shall also reign with Him."☨☨☨ Faith makes your understanding alive and open to the truth, "If I suffer with Him, I shall also reign with Him." That is FAITH. You understand by FAITH. You do not understand much about what it is going to mean to reign with Him, but you understand that it is BEING WITH HIM. People substitute human intellect for Understanding. But Understanding is dead unless it is the Word of God that we understand!

Think of it, beloved: *Faith is understanding.* Faith is a living thing. A lie is a dead thing. But Jesus is the TRUTH. And His Words were uttered by a Being, a NEW KIND OF A MAN, who was IN GOD, in the fullest meaning of those words. When He opened His mouth and said, "Blessed ... blessed," for example – in fact, everything he expressed can be put this way – *"I am explaining to you what it is like to be COMPLETELY IMMERSED IN GOD."* The "Faith Life" is exactly THAT: Your whole spirit, soul, and body, completely immersed in God. And it is "Blessed."

And what will you do in the pathway of faith? You will learn TO LOVE JESUS. And thus it will unfold in your life that "faith works by love," and love *loves Him* in place of yourself.

Walking by faith requires honesty. "Provide things honest in the sight of all men," says the scripture (Romans 12:17). Walking by faith means that you are faithful in that which is least. "He that is faithful in that which is least is faithful in much. He that is unjust in the least is unjust in much"! (Luke 16:10). If you are going to walk by faith, you find that you have to be faithful in that which is least.

Unfeigned faith. "The end of the commandment is love out of a pure heart, a good conscience, and unfeigned faith"! (I Timothy 1:5). The world is full of feigned faith. The churches have too much of feigned faith, hypocrisy – something professed that is not possessed. Feigned faith. "Oh, woman," Jesus said to the Syrophoenician woman, "GREAT IS YOUR FAITH. Be it unto you as you have requested" (Matthew 15:28). *Faith is a fight.* "Fight the good fight of faith, lay hold on eternal life" (II Timothy 6:12). *Faith is the Word.* I take up almost the supreme point last, "Faith comes by hearing, and hearing by the Word of God" (Romans 10:17).

☨☨☨ II Timothy 2:12, paraphrased.

Hearing means DOING; it means believing to DO. And so faith grows that way. And JESUS IS HIMSELF THAT FAITH. He is the faith; it is THE LORD that you believe in.

Blessed Lord, this is lovely to talk about. I just enjoy it. You are sweet to talk about, Lord, not because we are sweet to talk, but because you are sweet to talk about. You are the wonder of believing, not because we say, "I believe," but because you are WHAT we believe. God bless you, LORD. Thank you, Lord, for being you. Thank you for ever coming into this world of sin and death and hell. Thank you, Lord, that we do not have to walk by sight, and go to hell, and stumble on our faces all the time. We can walk by faith, and NOT by sight. And YOU are the source of it all, and the end of it all. Bless each one who reads this, and we thank you, Precious, Wonderful Lord, THE TRUTH!

BEARING THE CROSS

What are you doing here? What are you in the Faith Homes for? Why did you come here? That is an exceedingly important matter, because the question may come up in your life. In every one of these now six subjects, the truth of Witnessing is involved in it. One of the primary purposes of your life in the Faith Homes is that you should be a Witness of the Lord. And that Witness seems to appear beautifully and naturally in the discussion of all of these different topics. Especially so in: Bearing The Cross.

First of all, you are here in the Faith Homes to learn: To dwell in the Lord's Presence. That means: You are seeking to dwell that way all the time. And if you live in the Lord's Presence, as I believe He offers it here for you to learn to be in His Presence, it can become, and should become, your life – your normal life. Almost everything else that we would teach on these subjects would be part of that. If you DWELL IN HIS PRESENCE, all the rest of these things are almost automatically a part of it, being part of the truth of the New Covenant. If you LIVE in His Presence, you are going to be a WITNESS to Him. Gradually it works out in BEARING THE CROSS – THE CROSS-BEARING LIFE. Then you are in His Hands; He uses you as His witness.

On your part, you supply the WILLINGNESS TO BE His witness; you are the one who gives over your life to Him. He is the one who asks for it, and takes it, and anoints you with the Holy Ghost and power, and guides you in all that you will say and do. He is The One who initiates, who authorizes, who empowers, who leads into, the witnessing for His name. On your part, you supply the willingness, the obedience. And that is true in each one of these subjects or sub-topics.

Second: THE USE OF YOUR TIME. You are here in these Homes to REDEEM YOUR TIME. You are not here to have a good time in the sense in which the world uses that expression. You are not here just to be comfortable and not have to go across the city somewhere to work every day. You are not here to have an easy time, or to have a hard time, either one, in the natural sense. You are here to give all your time to the Lord. Everything about this life is an OFFERING TO GOD. And these various topics show you quite distinctly how to offer your life up to God and what is involved in it.

It is EXCEEDINGLY important that you know how to dwell in the Lord's Presence. It is exceedingly important that you know what to do with your time. Nobody is going to keep after you every day in the Homes, "Have you got your hours arranged today? Are you redeeming your time?" as a timekeeper for the Lord. But it is one of the things which God will seek to teach you and train you in: What to do with your time. When you are in some other place and have a work of your own, or helping in a mission, or on a mission station, you will be in tremendous need to know what to do with your time. And if you have not learned how to divide up your time, and have not learned how to live for the Lord in all your minutes and all your hours, you will be in a great disadvantage. That is part of what it means to BEAR THE CROSS.

Third: WALKING IN THE SPIRIT. It should be obvious to everyone that you are here to learn to walk in the Spirit. You find a great necessity to walk in the Spirit here. You are not here to live a merely hopeful life that sometime, in some better situation, or some situation which appeals to you as being of more worth to the Lord, that THEN you will walk in the Spirit. "Walking in the Spirit," must have with it the word "NOW." Every single minute of your time in the Faith Homes, you are expected of the Lord to be BELIEVING to walk in His Spirit.

Witnessing works naturally out of it – Walking in The Spirit. If you redeem your time, part of your time will definitely be used in witnessing for the Lord in some way. There are many ways to witness for Jesus.

That truth works out beautifully in the Faith Home life in BEARING

THE CROSS, daily. If you bear your cross daily, then it works out that you are conscious of needing the Holy Spirit in order to bear your cross. So you need to live and walk in the Spirit, and it works out, if you do live and walk in the Spirit, and bear your cross, you are certain to be a witness of the Lord, because HE WILL GIVE YOU THE OPENING OF YOUR MOUTH. Meetings are valuable for this purpose for you.

One of the reasons you are here is to Witness for the Lord. The basis of it is your belief in Jesus. "I believe on the Son of God. I love Jesus." That is the basis of your witness, because you have no witness if you do not believe something; this is what you witness about. The opening of the heart and mouth comes from the Love of the Lord. It is part of your life in these Homes to witness in the meetings more than occasionally. Some of you are very slow, or backward, or lax in this matter. It is true that sometimes the meetings are taken up almost exclusively by talks. But in many of them there is an opportunity for you to open your mouth and SAY with your lips, "I believe in the Lord Jesus Christ, the Son of God." You can sit here in this Work and say nothing. The net effect of it after some years will be that you do not say anything. But God wants you to develop and unfold in the anointing of the Lord so that He can use you to speak. And part of the reason you are here is to get a foundation for speaking. How will you ever speak if you don't speak? But at the same time, we do not want anybody to be under a great bondage and strain about it. It may not take even a minute, in which the fundamental of eternal life is expressed by the mouth, and by the word, "I believe on the Lord Jesus Christ, the Son of God;" or, "I love Jesus." From that base, or from that root, there is all expression, witnessing, teaching, and preaching.

Fourth: DAILY GRACE. We mentioned that this Work is intended of the Lord to be an Inward Work, where your life is oriented toward the Lord. The Inward Life is a life in which He is the Center, and is allowed to be the Center, and is made to be the Center, by the choice of the individual to live before Him and unto Him. And that makes a vast difference in what your life becomes. This is intended of the Lord to be an Inward Life, as contrasted with the Outward Life which so many of God's children live. They do not live in an anointing. They go to meetings, and sometimes it is a sort of a spiritual entertainment. But the Outward life is not living in the Presence of the Lord, is not redeeming the time, is not walking and living in the Spirit; it is not occupied with the matter of Daily Grace, living in the Grace of the Lord.

Fifth, was the FAITH LIFE. That is one of the things that the Lord wants to develop in every one of you, and will keep developing all your life. Here, you have an opportunity to become rooted and grounded in the simplicity of the FAITH LIFE. That is the kind of life by which God is going to change the Ages. The Ages will be changed by those that live in the FAITH LIFE. And that means a resignation of your life utterly to God for Him to do with you as He pleases. The Inward life is a FAITH LIFE, and the FAITH LIFE brings you constantly to the point which is expressed so obviously and markedly by the expression, "I don't have anything but God." That is the FAITH LIFE. You have nothing but God. Turn it over and look at it from the other side, and it is, "I have everything in God." But, you have to LEARN it.

One of the lessons involved in learning the Faith Life is BEARING THE CROSS DAILY – Luke 14:25-33. And to BEAR THE CROSS involves the truth of CRUCIFIXION WITH CHRIST. Crucifixion with Christ, of course, involves you in the supremacy of Love. It involves you in what Love is; it involves you in the learning of the knowledge of the Love of God. And apparently there is no way at all for anybody to comprehend and to come into that full knowledge of God, as your normal life forever, without the Cross, bearing the cross – being crucified with Christ. Luke 14, beginning with verse 25:

> *And there were great multitudes with Him: and He turned, and said unto them, If any man come to me, and hate not his father, and mother, and wife* (of course, in such expressions wife or husband is interchangeable there)*, and children, and brethren, and sisters, yea, and his own life also, he cannot be my disciple. And whosoever doth not bear his cross, and come after me, cannot be my disciple.*
>
> *For which of you, intending to build a tower, sitteth not down first, and counteth the cost, whether he have sufficient to finish it? Lest haply, after he hath laid the foundation, and is not able to finish it, all that behold it begin to mock him, saying, This man began to build, and was not able to finish.*
>
> *Or what king, going to make war against another king, sitteth not down first, and consulteth whether he be able with ten thousand to meet him that cometh against him with twenty thousand? Or else,*

while the other is yet a great way off, he sendeth an ambassage, and desireth conditions of peace.

So likewise, whosoever he be of you that forsaketh not all that he hath, he cannot be my disciple.

Transformed IN LOVE!

This expression, "and his own life also," gives us the clue to the understanding, the spiritual understanding, of what Jesus was getting at when He used the word "hate," because God, when He "hates," does not hate like a sinful human hates. God hates sin, and He hates unholiness, but His hatred is a Divine Love, a desire to include, to enfold the sinner, or the child of God, within the fellowship of His Cross. There the individual, being enfolded in His love and in His Mercy, will have NO GODS BEFORE HIM, NOT EVEN SELF! These words, "and his own life also," define for us what the meaning, and the intention of the meaning is, concerning "hating." When God hates, He hates what will destroy you. When we hate, we hate in the spirit that wants to destroy others. And these are two completely opposite things.

God's Love, for instance, is the combining power of life in the entire universe. God's Love combines everything with everything, according to its existence level, and purpose of creation, to BE SOMETHING FOR OTHERS. And God's Love makes everything fit into its place, to work together in one great and increasing whole – one God, and one Creation, in one Love, combined to give Life, and maintain Life, and perfect Life. That is the Love of God.

But the love of self, and of the world, which is of the devil, is false love; and false love is lust. Self-love seeks to get advantage, and work out advantage and honor and glory and pleasure, to self, regardless of what happens to anybody else. That false love of the world is DIVISIVE. It DIVIDES, it SCATTERS. Our explosive situation in the world today is an exhibition of it, now come almost to the climax in the history of the world. EXPLODE EVERYTHING. And scientists, many of them, without realizing what a false base they are standing on, think of the original creation of the universe, as something EXPLODING, EXPLODING! And that is the exact opposite of God's Love.

This matter of the cross, BEARING THE CROSS, is fundamental. We will not go now much into the subject of what we generally term as CRUCIFIXION. That is spoken of in the meetings now and then.

Crucifixion of your self-love; crucifixion of your life. Here we are using this expression, "AND YOUR OWN LIFE ALSO," to give a grasp of what Jesus means when He says, "hate." Because the Love of God is the exact opposite of the corrupting and corroding and destructive Love of the world. God's Love is healing. It is Divine Union. God's Love makes everything to come into union with everything else, in God's own Presence, and in His own unfolding increase in His creation, and in His purpose for it all. *The word "hate" in God's mouth – and Jesus was God's mouth – was describing what it means to live forever; what the kingdom of God is on the earth; what it means to be full of God now; what is it going to be on the earth in the Kingdom of God*; this it is – HE MUST BE THE CENTER, AND THE FIRST, because that is WHAT HE IS.

All through the Old Testament, as well as all through the New Testament, is expressed that FIRSTNESS of the Lord. So Jesus is saying, "If you want me, I will have to be first in your life. I will have to be first before father. I will have to be first before mother. I will have to be first before wife or husband. I will have to be first before children. I will have to be first before brothers or sisters. AND, I will have to be first before YOUR OWN life – hate your own life also." And He goes on, "He cannot be my disciple otherwise." In the life of God it is THE WAY to really bless and help your own: love them in God – God first. Jesus must be in the place which, in all creation, is occupied, and must be occupied, by GOD, in whatever form or way He has ordained that it be in the creature. Jesus uses the term, or illustration, of a branch to a vine. You are a branch in a vine. A branch in a vine needs the life which the vine itself has. It grows and develops by it. You are joined to Him. You do it by OFFERING IT ALL TO GOD. Cross-bearing becomes TRANSFORMATION IN LOVE!

"Unless you hate your own life also, you CANNOT be my disciple." Now this word "cannot" simply means, in its fundamental power, "NOT ABLE"; you are not able to be His disciple. And it should become apparent to every one of you, that you are NOT ABLE to be a learner of Jesus, to learn His life, to be a disciple, to be a learner, unless you hate and forsake your own life also, because it says you "cannot." You are NOT ABLE to know, or learn to know Jesus, to be His disciple, IN THE NEW TESTAMENT SENSE, UNLESS YOU HATE YOUR OWN LIFE AS YOUR PERSONAL POSSESSION, AND FORSAKE IT. So, "Unless he hate his own life also, he is NOT ABLE to be my disciple," is the meaning there. You "learn" to be transformed in love.

What Are You Here For?

"All power in heaven is yours." You can have the power of God. For what? To be His disciple. What do we mean? He will make you ABLE to follow Him. Where will you follow? Everywhere. This is bearing your cross. You are here to LEARN TO BE JESUS' DISCIPLE. And that involves you in this: "And whosoever does not BEAR HIS CROSS, and come after me, cannot be my disciple."

This is a very wonderful statement, but it is also a very fearful statement. You FOLLOW HIM, WITH THE CROSS ON YOUR SHOULDER. It says in the 9th chapter of Luke, "You take up your cross daily." What for? TO FOLLOW JESUS. What do you want to follow Jesus for? Because you want to BE WITH HIM, don't you? You do not want to live forever in another realm, do you, where Jesus is NOT? But, bless your heart, what will you be forsaking your own life for? That is what He is getting at in all this matter of BEARING THE CROSS. You are forsaking your life so you can learn of Him, can be like Him. He will make you like Himself; you cannot make yourself like Him, like He is. But your job is to LET Him do it.

And all of these things which we are teaching, and will be teaching, and you will be teaching, are involved in this matter of WILLINGNESS, getting people to be willing, to let Him have His way with YOU, whether you understand His way or not. But He GIVES you, in the subject of Bearing the Cross, the wide open and free offer of HIS UNDERSTANDING, so that you can UNDERSTAND GOD. You cannot understand God, and be His close follower or disciple, except you understand the CROSS. And you have to bear it to understand it. Transformed in LOVE.

So we read, verse 28,

For which of you, intending to build a tower, sitteth not down first, and counteth the cost, whether he be able to finish it; lest, haply, after he has laid the foundation (and here is the word 'cannot' in the other form) is NOT ABLE to finish it (cannot finish it, is not able), and all that behold it begin to mock him, saying, This man began to build and was not able (could not, cannot, was not able) to finish. For what king going to war against another king, sitteth not down first and consulteth whether he be able with ten thousand to meet him that cometh against him with twenty thousand? Or else, while the other is yet a great way off, he sends an ambassage and desires conditions of peace. SO LIKEWISE WHOSOEVER HE BE OF YOU THAT

FORSAKETH NOT ALL THAT HE HATH, HE CANNOT BE (IS NOT ABLE TO BE) MY DISCIPLE.

So the Bearing of the Cross is the fellowship of Jesus, to let God have your life utterly. And in that fellowship you learn the lesson of allowing NOTHING in His place. While you are learning those things, you are learning the Power of God. The Power of God has to be in your life, the ability to forsake your own life also. And it will work out beautifully in your own life that God will make you a winner of souls, in the degree in which He desires. He will form you into the beauty of the King. Jesus' Cross-bearing was the ultimate and climax of LOVE.

We want the REALITY OF GOD. The reality of God is made known to us by WORDS – WORDS which have come out of the life and mind and mouth of Jesus, and of those who had the Mind of Christ. Everyone who is living in these Homes has been brought here for a very EXPLICIT purpose, and that purpose, as we see it clearly in the Word, must unfold in the power of this truth, of the CROSS: we are TO BEAR THE CROSS; we are to have the fellowship of His sufferings, and be conformed to His death. We ARE NOT ABLE TO BE A LEARNER OF CHRIST, AND OF GOD, in the Kingdom fullness, EXCEPT THAT CROSS IS THE POSITION THAT WE OCCUPY BEFORE GOD. The climax? Transformed IN GOD.

TO BE AN OFFERING UNTO GOD[§§§]

An offering of a sweet savor unto God; a fragrant offering by Jesus Christ unto God; a living sacrifice; holy, acceptable unto God! A beauty! A wonder! A manifestation of the Grace of God! Christ's offering to the Father.

"I beseech you therefore, brethren, BY THE MERCIES OF GOD, that ye present your bodies A LIVING SACRIFICE, holy, acceptable unto God, which is your reasonable service. And be not conformed to this world; but be ye TRANSFORMED BY THE RENEWING OF YOUR MIND, that ye may prove what is that good, and acceptable, and perfect will of God" (Romans 12:1-2).

[§§§] As it turned out, this "talk" was written down and passed out, but it was never spoken to the trainees in the Faith Homes.

The whole of the Old Testament is involved in this matter of: AN OFFERING TO GOD. The whole of the New Testament describes that OFFERING UNTO GOD. JESUS IS THAT OFFERING! Glory to God! Praise His Precious and Holy Name forever. HE is that holy and acceptable offering OF God, and TO God. He is your offering TO God. And you are Jesus Christ's peculiar, precious, offering to God.

A Living Sacrifice. A Holy Offering. An Acceptable Sacrifice. Your proper, reasonable, true OFFERING. In the process, Jesus TRANSFORMS you – in fellowship with Himself – by the renewing (making NEW) of your mind in the transforming Power of His Love. In that transformation you learn and prove what the WILL OF GOD IS: that Gracious, Glorious, Wonderful, Life-giving WILL. That Will is GOOD; it is Acceptable (Grace); it is Perfect (complete). It is "The Will of God in Christ Jesus concerning you." It is, "Sweet Will of God, still fold me closer, 'til I am WHOLLY LOST IN THEE!" Glory to Jesus, Glory to Jesus!

Our studies in *What the Bible Teaches About Mercy*, to a definite degree, touch that Fellowship with Jesus, and that Transformation in God. An offering to God has to be a HOLY OFFERING. JESUS makes you that. You have to learn to yield to the Truth of His LOVE. An offering to God has to be a Free-will Offering. "Lovingkindness-Mercy" MAKES YOU THAT.

The Offering of all offerings was Jesus on Calvary. That is what Calvary means before God. Calvary, the Cross, they mean the same thing. JESUS OFFERED HIMSELF WITHOUT SPOT UNTO GOD. That is what Calvary means; that is what "The Cross" means. The "Saul" of Tarsus was transformed by the renewing of his mind, when the meaning of the Cross burst upon his soul, as Heavenly Daylight. He saw it. It changed him from the utmost of sin into one "accepted in The Beloved." And Paul never got over witnessing and proclaiming that amazing "Will of God" which became understandable to him in the daylight blaze of the revelation of Grace-mercy in Jesus Christ: IN THE CRUCIFIED CHRIST. Jesus became The Crucified Christ by THE CROSS. It was the ultimate of Love; not a dissertation on "love", but Love-in-action; God's Mercy. AN OFFERING TO GOD BY THE WILL OF GOD.

The Apostle Paul spent his life in that Great Inner Light. He never tired of telling – WITNESSING – the Wonder of Jesus crucified who became within him the "Hope of the glory of God," and of "Christ in you the hope of Glory."¶¶¶ He was transformed in LOVE; what he once hated, now he LOVED. He was transformed IN GOD, for by Grace-mercy Paul could know God and comprehend something of WHAT LOVE IS. No one has ever excelled his good and acceptable and perfect ode-to-Love, describing Calvary's meaning and power, AND THE WILL OF GOD. The WILL of God, IS GOD. And the meaningless crucifixion-death of Jesus became to The Jesus-hater the inextinguishable "light of the knowledge OF THE GLORY OF GOD,"**** in the glorified vision of the Face marred more than any man – the Face of Jesus Christ. JESUS OFFERED FOR HIM!! And the proper and reasonable result of such "knowledge" was the "understanding" to be himself, Paul, an offering of Christ to God – a Whole Burnt Offering. And if you do not do the same thing as a result of reading Paul's words, then you have never understood Paul – nor JESUS – nor GOD!

God bless you, and bless you – to be a blessing! God not only gave Jesus as an offering FOR you; He gave Jesus TO you – ALL of JESUS. God gave Jesus TO you: to be your Life, your soul, your all. Paul says, "It is a NEW CREATION." He was himself a New Creation. But he said, "IT'S CHRIST IN ME – my very life" – "to me TO LIVE IS CHRIST." As an offering-to-God, the blessed Apostle could understand – in part, he said – the Mystery of "The Will of God" hidden from ages past. And, he never could have understood THAT HOLY WILL, except by becoming an Offering to God. And one of his choice expressions describes it as "Fellowship." Fellowship, sharing, partnership, IN THE CROSS and in THE WILL OF GOD. "The fellowship of the mystery. The fellowship of the body and blood of Jesus." "The fellowship of His sufferings" – fellowship, fellowship, fellowship. That is what an Offering to God is.

But it all had to do with: KNOWING JESUS – KNOWING HIM! And at that point Paul affirms: "I do not count myself to have attained." He was not like the modern know-it-alls who are immersed in their own reasonings, interpretations, and self-assurances, sure that they can think-it-out in the light of their own wisdom. No! The apostle only wanted: "To know HIM, and the Power of HIS resurrection, and the Fellowship of HIS sufferings, being made conformable unto HIS death." †††† ALL JESUS!

¶¶¶ Romans 5:2; Colossians 1:27
**** II Corinthians 4:6
†††† Philippians 3:10

Only JESUS! Not having his own righteousness, nor his own wisdom. All his works, and words and sufferings attributed to ONE THING: the Grace-Mercy of God. THAT IS AN OFFERING TO GOD.

Don't mistake it. The New Covenant in Jesus' Blood is not a discussion of opinions and human beliefs and explanations-about-God. The New Covenant is God-offering-Himself in Jesus Christ: not "thinking," but KNOWING JESUS. "God was IN CHRIST reconciling the world TO HIMSELF" – describing God offering Himself to fallen, hopeless man. That is what "Mercy-loving-kindness" IS, isn't it? People who want anything else but "JUST JESUS" cannot advance very far into the knowledge of what it means to be An Offering To God. It is, "The Knowledge of the Holy is understanding"; and the Understanding of Mercy is LIFE. Fellowship with Jesus – that is the Mystery, now, of God and of His LIFE. Fellowship with Jesus – that is the Mystery, now, of God and of His Kingdom. And the Creator has planned that, IN CHRIST JESUS, THE WHOLE CREATION, in Heaven and earth, shall become AN OFFERING TO GOD – Holy and acceptable. Hallelujah! Hallelujah! Hallelujah, Glory to God!

You are in the Faith Homes to be, to become, An Offering to God. God bless you. The lessons before you are not so much classwork, as it is generally understood. God has set before His children lessons to learn in the Spirit of Grace and Prayer; lessons in living and doing His Word, which is His Sweet Will. And His Word is: that JESUS HIMSELF is "MADE UNTO YOU Wisdom and Righteousness and Sanctification and Redemption."‡‡‡‡ JESUS is God communicating Himself to you by His Holy Spirit. Wisdom-understanding in God's Will; Righteousness-faith doing God's Will; Sanctification, holy in God's Will; Redemption, restoration to the Image of God by God's Will.

God will take care of The Offering. You make the offering. In the process of the transformation of the making-new of your mind (into "the mind of Christ") you will be guided into "all truth." And "ALL TRUTH" can be comprehended only by KNOWING JESUS as: The Way, The Truth, The Life, The Resurrection, The New Man, The Beginning and Ending, The Wisdom, The Righteousness, The Holiness, The Redemption – of GOD; each one, and all, OF GOD!

---

‡‡‡‡ I Corinthians 1:30

This is, in brief, WHAT YOU ARE HERE FOR. God bless you! And is not that what every child of God is in the world for?[§§§§]

Our Blessed and Precious and Holy Father, open Thy Word to our hearts; and open our hearts to Thy Word. Let, we pray, the truths expressed in this series of simple instructions, become in us a clear understanding of what Thy Will is. Make us each one a True Offering to God. Make us alive to see and enter into the truth of Thy continual immersion in the Holy Spirit and fire. Grant us to come continually to Him who is meek and Lowly IN HEART, that we may learn the great lesson of offering up, continually, all our will to God. Grant us never to lose the divine vision of the meaning of Calvary. And guide us, Blessed Father, guide us into that fellowship with Jesus which You created this habitable world to bring forth. Thank You, Father. Thank You for Christ Crucified. Amen.

[§§§§] Indeed it is! That is the reason these 7 talks are included in this book. We were encouraged to go over these messages prayerfully at least once a year.

INTERLUDE THREE

JESUS IS COMING IN THE GLORY OF HIS FATHER

For thirty years (1950-1980), the Faith Homes produced a Quarterly Paper called *Feed My Lambs*. Each issue contained various sermons and articles, some by Faith Home ministers, some by well-known authors, even some by the trainees that resided in the Homes and gave talks on Thursday nights during the service. Also included were letters from missionaries either sent out by, or closely associated with, the Faith Homes.

Feed My Lambs is a gold mine of spiritual truth, as well as an interesting historical record of the missionaries' and pastors' lives who looked to the Faith Homes for prayer support.

For many years, Rex Andrews furnished the opening article placed on the front page of each new issue of *Feed My Lambs*. The first time I saw one of those articles, while working at Teen Challenge in New York City, I thought it was over-blown spiritual talk, too lofty for me.* It was difficult not to feel disgusted with it

Now my heart thrills when I read those articles. I have learned to appreciate God's love-language in a way I never thought possible.

The following two articles appeared consecutively in the January and April issues of *Feed My Lambs* for 1963. They express a vast simplicity about the Coming of Jesus, related to the vastness of the astronomical heavens, but in language that allows us to soar to the very Throne of the Father while we read. I believe this Interlude Two will carry us into the spirit of the remaining chapters.

* * * * * * *

---

* My reaction was similar to the first time my brother and I listened to the opera on the radio: We rolled on our beds with laughter at the exaggerated vibrato of the singers (as we judged it), with no appreciation for the artful beauty of classical singing.

THE SON OF MAN SHALL COME IN THE GLORY OF THE FATHER†

Jesus is coming! It can be emphasized in several ways by placing the emphasis on one word or another. To begin with, it is JESUS who is coming. Here He refers to Himself as "The Son of Man." HE is coming IN the heavens and FROM the heavens as is so abundantly declared in many passages: "Whom the heaven must receive until the times of restitution of all things, which God hath spoken by the mouth of all his holy prophets since the world began" (Acts 3:21). "Then shall appear the sign of the Son of man in heaven; and then shall all the tribes of the earth mourn, and they shall see the Son of man coming in the clouds of heaven with power and great glory" (Matthew 24:30).

In these, as in so many other places, there is a great emphasis on the point: JESUS, THE SON OF MAN, IS COMING. Some of us are not able perhaps, to fill out the picture – the glory, and the power, and the reconstitution of all the things which the holy prophets have spoken. And we may not consider ourselves as being able to analyze, and detail, the "signs of His appearing." But we must, we must all of us by all means become thoroughly acquainted with, and fully understanding of, the primary truth offered to us in these two scriptures. It is the plain declaration that JESUS IS COMING. Surely there can be no other phase of the great truth of the Coming of the Lord which is of more importance to you. Emphasize it to yourself: JESUS is coming – Jesus IS coming – Jesus is COMING – Jesus, the Son of Man IS COMING!!!!!

There is a very special reason for you to do this – and to do it often. That reason is this: we have become such inveterate reasoners on various phases of "doctrine" that we easily lose sight of the Great Foremost of a truth. We can so readily become interested in some included truth, that without realizing it we LOSE SIGHT of the great all-encompassing truth itself. For instance, in the passage in Acts quoted above, it is possible to become so interested in, and imbued with the subject of "the restitution of all things" as to lose sight of what is actually said there; but worse still to become fired with a belief over some interpretation of the words, that we find ourselves wandering through the atmosphere of reasonings like a balloon which has drifted away in the air currents. For if we lose

---
† Matthew 16:27

Interlude Three:
Jesus Is Coming In The Glory Of His Father

SIGHT OF JESUS in argument, or in doctrinizing, then we have lost that which no arguments can possibly restore or reconstitute. And when the great wonder which is Jesus, The Son of Man, fades out of its complete domination of the heart AND MIND, then all our ideas, however proudly stated and maintained, become a bag with holes, a framework of speech without meaning, clouds without water. The great truth of the "Coming" of the Lord is that HE IS COMING. He is coming!! Jesus is coming!! The SON of Man is coming! HE IS.

Jesus said, "The Son of Man shall come"!! In these days, with so many human ideas bandied about everywhere – in the pulpit and out – "Let every man be persuaded in his own mind."‡ It has become ultra-imperative that we shall every one KNOW what it is that we really believe; and be so sure of it that no "science" report or discovery can in the slightest degree cause our foundation to shake or tremble. And one of the very foremost means by which we can be so secured is this which we are here pressing upon you. It is to emphasize the scriptures in such a way as to KEEP THE CENTRAL TRUTH in position and to keep it before your eyes. It is all important to you to become fixed – as the Psalm expresses it, "My heart is fixed."§ You need for your everyday life – all the time – the solid, unshakeable word of God ringing through your being. "The Son of man SHALL COME." You need that truth in its utmost simplicity, as the very foundation of WHAT YOU BELIEVE about the "Second Coming of the Lord." That is a personal thing to you. And whatever you may not grasp about the details of that coming, or about the arrangements or listed events or sequences, there is "ONE THING" that is vital to you, and that is the deeply settled knowledge, the final certainty, the shining assurance of the very simply stated fact which GOD has uttered: "The Son of Man shall come."

Say it over and over! Repeat the words often. Don't let the flood of the world's words and ideas blot out the absolute certainty of the knowledge that "JESUS IS COMING." Try to discern clearly that it is not a "coming" that is coming, but that it is JESUS, The Son of Man WHO IS COMING. And whenever you are reading a scripture passage about That Coming, take time to love Him, and give thanks that HE IS COMING.

R. B. A.

---

‡ Romans 14:5
§ Psalm 57:7

IN THE GLORY OF HIS FATHER

"When I consider the HEAVENS, the work of thy fingers, the moon and the stars, which thou hast ordained; What is man, that thou art mindful of him? And the son of man, that thou visitest him?" (Psalm 8:3-4)

Cooped up in our little box apartments, roofed in during our movings about in auto or bus, or train or plane, we consider mostly objects and persons within a very few feet of the end of our noses. Someone may look at a sunset once in a long while, though for the most part that look is only a bare glimpse out of the corner of the eye.

Once in a while we may be caught out under the open skies on a "lovely" night and catch a hasty sight of the myriad lights of the great opera of LIGHT, which is there soundlessly harping forth its nothing-like-it multi-tune and incomparable harmony in which are blended and combined lights of ages; a descent to our vision of expanses which, in a thousand formations, render a chorus of softened star-blazing immensities which sing the wonders of infinity, endlessness, eternity.

Looking full up into the moonless sky on a clear night, we stand in the vision-center of paths of light streaming in from every conceivable direction, as though we were located IN THE CENTER of a limitless, horizonless glory which is beyond all grasp, and which demotes all human knowledge to a mere memorandum, files, as it were, in a pigeon-hole of the desk of memory.

God! GOD! THE GOD OF GLORY! The breath of our spirit murmurs. And if we are wise we will worship and adore, and give some breathless utterance to that which arises within from the EFFECT of such an eternal weight of GLORY.

And, if we are there considering long enough, it may be that the moon will arise slowly from below the horizon, and the glory of the stars will gradually dim in the soft bathing light which takes over the visible heavens – soft moonlight – whitish – REFLECTED LIGHT – not the blaze of the sun's daylight – but the heart-and-mind-bath of GLORY turned down sufficiently to enable us to gaze full-face and open-eyed directly at the great orb of moon.

The sun we are apt to take for granted most of the days of our lives. Unless the weather is too hot, we may hardly notice that there is any sun. We are constantly offered a never-ending shifting of heavenly scenery in which to live our little lives in formations above us and around us which

Interlude Three:
Jesus Is Coming In The Glory Of His Father

endlessly express a glory of GOD. Happy and blessed is the one who has learned to SAY, "GLORY TO GOD The Father, and to The Son of God, who is my Light and my Salvation."

But the expression which issues from unnumbered thousands of mouths is: "IT" – simply, "IT." It is a most terrible effect of the fall of man's soul from its true heavenly state, that the heart is UNWILLING to give that WONDERFUL FATHER any glory at all. The human says, "IT." Humans are so easily shamed from reading The Bible because that amazing volume says, "GOD" – "The God of Glory" – "The LORD of GLORY."

The derangement of that which was created to be the Image of God, is made vivid and utterly empty and void by the endless repetition of the word "IT." And in such a state we are incapable of tasting "goodness of God" in such expressions as we have quoted above, *"thy heavens, the work of thy fingers, the moon and the stars which thou hast ordained."* Instead, the human worships the works of his own hands, those multiple things which his own fingers have formed and which in some way can carry his brand – a brand of pride.

BUT SOMETHING IS HAPPENING – SOMETHING IS IN THE PROCESS OF CHANGING ALL THAT WE SEE AND KNOW. We are creatures of vanity. We tend to produce that which is vain – ultimately useless – the corrosion, ruin, destruction of HOPE. But there is something that is moving in upon the world which is the opposite to that vanity. IT IS THE GLORY OF GOD. We are wise if we refuse and forsake all human arguments about it and just WORSHIP AND ADORE – in the light of His Word. The whole mathematical knowledge of man is going to crumble and fail and fall prone before, and within, that GLORY WHICH IS COMING.

In our scripture passage, Matthew 16:27, we have the facts from the lips of Him who IS TRUTH. *"The Son of Man shall come in the GLORY OF HIS FATHER."* Certainty, security forever, established unshakably in the "POWER OF HIS RESURRECTION" is the world-changing and age-blossoming revealed fact that JESUS IS COMING "IN THE GLORY OF HIS FATHER." Not only is He really actually COMING, but, He is coming IN GLORY. Is that YOUR Jesus who is certainly and irrevocably COMING IN GLORY? God's Word is ROCK – UNSHAKABLE ROCK. Believe it and you will find "joy and peace in believing." Peace, sweet peace, the gift of God's unfading LOVE.

R.B.A.

CHAPTER TWENTY

TO WHAT END IS GOD WORKING?

The late Leonard Ravenhill was fond of saying, "God is not whimsical." That phrase stuck with the author, because it highlights a very important truth about the Lord: <u>His work is not aimless</u>. God has a goal in mind for the human race, and though He seems to work slowly, as humans judge time, <u>He moves steadily onward toward the goal He has declared</u>, and IT WILL BE REACHED.

What possibly could be that goal?

Two distinct approaches will increase our appreciation for what *God is now doing*. The first approach uses an analogy. Just as we want our natural children to become healthy, productive adults, so God desires His children to grow up into spiritual maturity. The second approach explores the powerful phrase from Romans 8:29, "For whom He did foreknow, them He also did predestinate to be conformed to the image of His Son, that He might be the firstborn among many brothers."

An Analogy

I will never forget the first time I saw a *Billy Graham Crusade*. I saw one on television long before I attended a live Crusade. The large combined choir impressed me; George Beverly Shea's solo moved me; Billy Graham's message touched me. What meant the most, however, was the response to the invitation he gave at the close of his message. As the choir sang *Just As I Am*, hundreds of people got up from their seats, filled the aisles, and streamed toward the platform to receive Jesus as their Savior. Rev. Graham led them in the "Sinner's Prayer," and trained counselors came alongside each "inquirer" to read Scriptures and firm up the decision to follow Jesus. In fact, the monthly magazine put out by the Billy Graham Association was entitled "Decision Magazine." I remember fighting back the tears as I watched people surrender their lives to Jesus.

If you have ever "led a soul to Christ," you know what a blessed experience it is. "There's no thrill like leading someone to salvation." "Evangelism is the greatest mission of the Church." "Bringing souls to Christ is the greatest thrill a missionary can ever experience."

I grew up hearing those comments. To a certain extent they are correct.

What I heard Billy Graham say later, however, troubled me. "Based on follow-up surveys our organization has conducted, hardly 25% of the people who come forward in my meetings to receive Christ are still practicing Christians after five or more years."[1]

Another remark from Leonard Ravenhill also bothered me. "Doug, if you calculate all the 'conversions' that evangelists claim to have counted in their meetings or through their televised ministries, the entire population of America has been 'saved' at least twice!"

One of my greatest disappointments in forty years of ministry stems from the *failure* of precious souls I have "led to the Lord" to *continue* walking in the truth. Yes, I should be able to "shrug it off" with some simple explanation, such as, "Well, they really didn't get saved in the first place." Or, "Once saved, always saved; don't worry about them." Or, "Even Jesus had a disciple who betrayed Him." Still, it hurts. "Demas has forsaken me," wrote the Apostle Paul, "having loved this present world" (II Timothy 4:10). That bothers me.

Please understand that I am THANKFUL for the 25% of converts in Billy Graham's ministry who follow Jesus for the rest of their lives. I am very thankful for every Christian who professed faith under my ministry and now practices it. I know that the waves of the Spirit for the past one hundred years and more have birthed millions of new souls into the Kingdom of God, especially in Third World countries.

We all love newborn babies – they seem as if they dropped from heaven to earth – so helpless and yet so lovable. Yet how tragic it is if the child's growth is stunted, or disease robs its health, or an accident maims the child for life. It is unspeakably sad when that baby never matures into the adult man or woman it is programmed to become. We may feel compassion, but what must be the heartache of parents who never see their child develop into normal maturity?

Let us make the analogy with God as our Father and us as His children. It is clear that "there is joy in Heaven over one sinner that repents," as Jesus said twice in Luke 15; every soul who comes to Christ is a source of tremendous joy, the kind of joy we have when we cradle a newborn baby in our arms. How much "joy in Heaven" there must have been when the Gospel was planted in Ephesus, Smyrna, Pergamos, Thyatira, Sardis, Philadelphia, and Laodicea?!

Thirty years later, though, those same churches were in trouble spiritually. When we read the *Messages to the Seven Churches* in the Book of Revelation (2:1-3:22), we see God's concern for the lack of spiritual maturity of those Churches; in fact, five of them are seriously ill. *Is it not remarkable that nothing is said in any of those messages about a failure to "see more souls saved"!* Instead, we encounter repeated calls to "Repent" of crippling behaviors in five of those churches, behaviors that are detrimental to further growth and maturity, and inimical with Christ-likeness.

- The Church at *Ephesus* is warned that their light will be removed if it does not return to its First Love and resume doing the First Works.

- The Church at *Pergamos* is threatened with the Lord coming suddenly to fight against them with His Word.

- The Church at *Thyatira* is likewise facing tribulation, and even the death of some of its members, because of extreme corruption being practiced and taught!

- The Church at *Sardis* is strongly warned, and the possibility is raised, of having its members' names blotted out of the Book of Life.

- The Church at *Laodicea* is in such extreme spiritual need that Jesus is OUTSIDE the door, knocking to regain entrance!

Only the Churches at *Smyrna* and *Philadelphia* are doing well – *Smyrna*, because its members are being purged by the fires of suffering, and *Philadelphia*, because they have "kept My word, and have not denied My Name." Both churches, far from being threatened, are encouraged by promises from the Lord: "I will give you a crown of life... I will keep you from the hour of temptation... I will make you a pillar in the temple of My God."

Please understand that I am NOT saying the Church should not make evangelism a priority! What I AM saying is that *the spiritual growth into maturity which follows the spiritual birth is a priority with God.*

Consider the words of Paul to the Ephesian Church which clearly state God's GOAL:

> ...till we all come to the unity of the faith and of the knowledge of the Son of God, *to a perfect man,* to *the measure of the stature of the fullness of Christ;** that *we should no longer be children,* tossed to and fro and carried about with every wind of doctrine, by the trickery of men, in the cunning craftiness of deceitful plotting, but, speaking the truth in love, *may grow up in all things into Him who is the head – Christ –* from whom the whole body, joined and knit together by what every joint supplies, according to the effective working by which every part does its share, causes *growth of the body for the edifying of itself in love.*† (Ephesians 4:13-16)

This is the quite normal, natural desire of a father for his children – "a perfect man"; "grow(ing) up in all things"; "growth of the body"! And it is quite surely the desire of God for His children.

Consider also the words of Paul to the Galatian believers:

> My *little children,* for whom I labor in birth again *until Christ is formed in you,* I would like to be present with you now and to change my tone; for I have doubts about you. (Galatians 4:19-20)

What divine pathos lies in these words! He had *labored in birth* for their salvation; now he *travails a second time* for the **formation of Christ within them!**

Obviously God has not abandoned the goal He set for the Galatian believers. He has worked ceaselessly to bring forth Christ-fully-formed in His people, waiting patiently for the "time of the harvest," as He pictures it in The Parable of the Wheat and the Tares (Matthew 13:24-30). He waits until both the Tares and the Wheat are fully mature and ready for harvesting, and He will not remove the Tares prematurely, lest the Wheat be uprooted also. There is much wisdom in that parable.

James puts it this way: "Therefore be patient, brethren, until the coming of the Lord. See how the farmer waits for the precious fruit of the earth,

---
* "The measure of the stature of the fullness of Christ" = "incorruptible love possessing your whole being, your body as well as your soul" (from Andrews, *Faith Home History, Part 1,* p. 4).
† Not till we all come to an individual perfection, but that as members of Christ's body we corporately express what He is. At some point, we all need to be taken "over the line," so to speak.

To What End Is God Working?

waiting patiently for it until it receives the early and latter rain. You also be patient. <u>Establish your hearts, for the coming of the Lord is at hand</u>" (James 5:7-8).

The two passages from Ephesians and Galatians are not isolated instances of Paul's God-given passion for spiritual maturity in the lives of his converts to Christianity. This passion fills the verses in I Thessalonians 3, a chapter which has no equal in expressive longing.

The spread of the Gospel to the Gentile world delighted the Apostle Paul, as indicated by his salutations to the Thessalonians or to the Romans.‡ Paul's *concern for the new believers* also surfaces in passages full of Divine passion. Listen to his words to the Thessalonians, for example: "For now we live, if ye stand fast in the Lord" (I Thessalonians 3:8).

That statement is the center of an entire chapter dealing with his deep concern for their spiritual condition, because he knew their faith would be tested by suffering. I will put the passage in here, highlighting with italics the almost <u>*parental concern*</u> he has for their growth.

> Wherefore *when we could no longer forbear*, we thought it good to be left at Athens alone; And sent Timotheus, our brother, and minister of God, and our fellow labourer in the gospel of Christ, to establish you, and to comfort you concerning your faith: That no man should be moved by these afflictions: for yourselves know that we are appointed thereunto. For verily, when we were with you, we told you before that we should suffer tribulation; even as it came to pass, and ye know. For this cause, *when I could no longer forbear*, I sent to know your faith, lest by some means the tempter have tempted you, and our labour be in vain.
>
> But now when Timotheus came from you unto us, and brought us good tidings of your faith and charity, and that ye have good remembrance of us always, desiring greatly to see us, as we also to see you: Therefore, brethren, we were comforted over you in all our affliction and distress by your faith: *For now we live, if ye stand fast in the Lord. For what thanks can we render to God again for you, for all the joy wherewith we joy for your sakes before our God; Night and day praying exceedingly that we might see your face, and might perfect that which is lacking in your faith?*

---

‡ See I Thessalonians 1:6-10 and Romans 1:8.

Now God Himself and our Father, and our Lord Jesus Christ, direct our way unto you. And the Lord make you to increase and abound in love one toward another, and toward all men, even as we do toward you: *To the end He may stablish your hearts unblameable in holiness before God, even our Father, at the coming of our Lord Jesus Christ with all his saints.* (I Thessalonians 3:1-13)

This demonstrates extreme pastoral concern for the development of their faith from initial salvation to spiritual maturity, from their new birth, to the fixed state of "hearts unblameable in holiness," when Jesus returns. Paul is obviously expressing the Passion of Christ for His own ones to have their faith perfected.

Here is another illustration of the point I am making, taken from the opening of Paul's letter to the Philippian believers:

For God is my witness, how greatly I long for you all with the affection of Jesus Christ. And this I pray, that your love may abound still more and more in knowledge and all discernment, that you may approve the things that are excellent, that you may be sincere and without offense till the day of Christ, being filled with the fruits of righteousness which are by Jesus Christ, to the glory and praise of God. (Philippians 1:8-11)

Paul is looking ahead to "the day of Christ" and praying earnestly that the hallmark of Christian faith, abundant love, will result in fully developed Christian character and action.

In the light of the above observations, the Apostle John's remark in Third John intrigues me: "*I have no greater joy than to hear that my children walk in truth*" (v. 4). Think of all the things about his ministry that he could have chosen as "my greatest joy"! Healings, deliverances, and conversions, probably numbering in the thousands! One of only three witnesses to Christ's Transfiguration! An eyewitness to the Resurrected Christ! A key figure in the extension of the Church from Jerusalem to Samaria to the uttermost parts of the earth in his lifetime! **Yet his "greatest joy" is hearing the report that his spiritual children are walking in the truth he had taught them.** This should help us answer the question, "To what end is God working?"

Many more examples in the Epistles attest to God's interest in *children who grow into maturity,* who *become like Jesus* – "*conformed to the image of His Son,*" to use again the phrase from the magnificent Chapter 8 of the Epistle to the Romans.

To What End Is God Working?

Romans 8 sums up God's plan so beautifully and connects to other similar chapters, such as First Corinthians 15, and Revelation 7. We leave it to the reader to develop a love for every phrase in those chapters. To accomplish the purpose in writing this book, this recommendation (to read such chapters) is meant to help us **discern God's hand in moving His people toward His goal in our time**, as expressed succinctly in Romans 8:29 – conformity to Jesus' likeness.

"Conformed to the Image of His Son"

We need, I believe, to develop a deeper understanding of His Divine Purpose: to have a people "conformed to the image of His Son" (Romans 8:29). This is no small matter! A. T. Robertson comments on this verse as follows:

> **Conformed to the image** (summorphous tēs eikonos). Late adjective from *sun* and *morphē* and so an inward and not merely superficial conformity. *Eikōn* is used of Christ as the very image of the Father (II Corinthians 4:4; Colossians 1:15). See note on Philippians 2:6 for *morphē*. Here we have both *morphē* and *eikōn* to express the gradual change in us till we acquire the likeness of Christ the Son of God so that we ourselves shall ultimately have the family likeness of sons of God. Glorious destiny.[2]

Yes, yes, yes! A "Glorious Destiny" indeed! Robertson's choice of the word "gradual," however, reflects the almost universal belief among God's people that the transformation into Christ's likeness takes place slowly and unnoticeably, almost as though it is just beyond the reach of *our present faith*. This often results in an unconscious dampening of our hunger to be like Jesus now, and an unrighteous acceptance of our spiritual *status quo*.

Do you remember the line from Martha Robinson's testimony that took her beyond that dampening of hunger and acceptance of her present spiritual state? Here it is again:

God got the light to me that it would be blessed to be utterly gone. And that was a Real Light.

This entire book is based on that "Real Light."

What does it mean, both in theology and in practice, to "be conformed to the image" of Christ? And how do we look at Church History if this is the purpose for which we have been saved?

If we look at the *Holiness Movement* from this standpoint of spiritual history, we see God's great Mercy to the Church in drawing us into sacred and holy communion with Himself, in which the Power of the Cross reaches deeply into the heart, will, motives, and actions of every Christian, to purify us in these elements of daily living. It can hardly be otherwise, if we are to be like Christ. The *Holiness Movement* gave the Church an increased awareness of this need. So many of the greatest and most beloved hymns from that period reflect the longing to be utterly pure.

Some years ago I did a thorough study of the word "pure" (and related words) in the Scripture, discovering in the process that "purified" represents the state of impure souls made pure by the ongoing, daily, refining fire of the Holy Spirit. Without the longing for it, who would even want to endure this refining fire to become "pure in heart"?

This God-given hunger for heart-purity appeared in John Wesley's writings of the 18th Century, and in his brother Charles' hymns, before it burst into fullness some 100 years later. From that time and to the present, that hunger remains. One sees it in the penetrating messages of the late Leonard Ravenhill, for example, or in the ministry of Paul Washer. The point is simply that God is Himself the originator of this hunger, for it leads naturally to the cry, "*Oh, to be like Thee, precious Redeemer, pure as Thou art!*"[3]

Almost (but not quite) as an aside, I am reminded of an exchange between Rex Andrews and one of the young students in his Bible class on Galatians (not the author). It went something like this:

"Brother Andrews, you say that we should pray to be like Jesus, but I have a friend who contradicted that by saying, 'I already have the mind of Christ. Paul said so.' What can I say to him?"

"Just look him right in the eyes," Andrews replied, and ask him, "*Do you?*"

That jarred me, because there is a vast difference between what one CLAIMS to have or be, and what one actually knows by experience. To say, "I received everything I will ever need as a Christian when I received Christ," may sound theologically correct, and in fact may BE theologically correct, but where are the believers who have pursued that theology to its logical conclusion? And who, in pursuing it, have managed to stay clear of fanaticism? And who are obviously, and evidently, living out the Christ-life as it is pictured in the Gospels? Is there a willingness in you, dear reader, to acknowledge that there is a difference between all that is available to you in Christ and what you have actually experienced?

The *Holiness Movement* fanned the flames of hunger to be like Christ in every area of the believer's life. As far as Martha Robinson is concerned, as well as the other founders of the Zion Faith Homes, they willingly surrendered to that flame of hunger, and it motivated them to "seek the Lord with the whole heart," as Psalm 119:2 puts it (and the echo is found five more times in that Psalm, in vv. 10, 34, 58, 69, and 145).

Turning now to the *Divine Healing Movement*, and endeavoring to look at it from God's vantage point, can we not see the Lord nudging His people to accept His actual touch on their bodies? To testify, as thousands have, "Jesus healed me," is to make the Savior personal, active, and real in a believer's life. Jesus is no longer distant and impersonal.

Testimonies like that abounded in Dr. Dowie's ministry, and although skeptics also abounded, the evidence is overwhelming that Jesus DID directly and personally heal many of incurable diseases. Martha Robinson is one of those, and her complete testimony is available for anyone to read and to judge for themselves its validity.[4] The same is true of Elder Eugene Brooks and his wife Sarah Brooks, as testified to by both in their own words, and by their daughter Ruth, whom I knew personally. Their healings were a major factor in their growth in God and in their understanding of a personal, intimate relationship with Jesus that went beyond the theoretical.[5]

As documented in Gordon Gardiner's remarkable book, *Out of Zion*, God raised up a large number of healing evangelists whose ministry continued long after Dr. Dowie's departure from the scene. I am aware that deconstructionist theology attempts to discredit the entire *Divine Healing Movement*, but the evidence is in and it is indisputable. Ruth Brooks, for example, who as a young person attended divine healing services conducted by F. F. Bosworth, told me she saw an eye created in an empty socket in a man Bosworth had just prayed for. My mother Nancy gave me a copy of *The Real Faith*, by Dr. Charles Price, saying, "I attended his meetings when I was first saved."[6] I found it to be the best book on "faith" outside of the Bible, and, encouraged by its thesis, I myself was healed completely of *ulcerative colitis*, considered an incurable disease. My Sunday School teacher, Rev. John W. Collins, personally witnessed many instances of divine healing as a young man attending an Assembly of God church in Chicago, Illinois. He later became an instrument of healing for several people with life-threatening diseases.

If there is to be a "recovery" of Jesus' life and ministry, it must include divine healing, as well as casting out devils (which I will leave out of this discussion for now). Certainly the early days of the Faith Homes bore witness to His power both to heal and to deliver.

Looking now at the *Pentecostal Movement*, and endeavoring to do so from God's vantage point, it is not difficult to see in it a further step toward God's plan of "full redemption, body, soul, and spirit." Though all of the denominational movements in America initially experienced the fires of revival, by the end of the 19th Century, they had been severely weakened by European Rationalism which had made its way to the United States. The approach to theology in the great seminaries in Europe took the pathway of "Higher Criticism," which undermined the authority and infallibility of the written Word of God. Humanistic thought took aim at the purity of the Gospel.[7]

The outpouring of the Holy Spirit world-wide, as documented by many, swept over the Church and breathed fresh life into it.[8] Literally millions of believers were "baptized in the Holy Spirit," bringing a reviving of the Gifts of the Spirit with it.[9] The awareness of Christ's Presence among and in His people increased tremendously. "Jesus is WITH us! His Spirit is flooding my soul! He is speaking His Word again among His people! He is sending us out with the burning message of the Gospel, and of His soon Return!" Such remarks appear frequently in early Pentecostal literature.

There appeared excesses, of course, but one could not deny that the power of the Holy Spirit had "come upon" God's people physically. People "shook" under that power; they were "slain in the Spirit"; they spoke in unknown tongues. As you recall, just prior to his baptism in the Spirit, Rex Andrews felt warm oil being poured out on his head and running down over his body.

Certain Scriptures came alive with fresh meaning, such as:

And the very God of peace sanctify you wholly; and I pray God your whole spirit and soul *and body* be preserved blameless unto the coming of our Lord Jesus Christ. (I Thessalonians 5:23)

And thou shalt love the Lord thy God with all thy heart, and with all thy soul, and with all thy mind, and *with all thy strength*: this is the first commandment. (Mark 12:30; Luke 10:27)

Meats for the belly, and the belly for meats: but God shall destroy both it and them. Now *the body* is not for fornication, but for the Lord; and *the Lord for the body.* (I Corinthians 6:13)

What? know ye not that *your body is the temple of the Holy Ghost* which is in you, which ye have of God, and ye are not your own? For ye are bought with a price: therefore glorify God *in your body,* and in your spirit, which are God's. (I Corinthians 6:19-20)

The light of the body is the eye: if therefore thine eye be single, *thy whole body* shall be full of light. (Matthew 6:22)

The *light of the body* is the eye: therefore when thine eye is single, thy *whole body also is full of light*; but when thine eye is evil, *thy body also* is full of darkness. If *thy whole body* therefore be full of light, having no part dark, the *whole [body]* shall be full of light, as when the bright shining of a candle doth give thee light. (Luke 11:35-36)

Possessed by God

The Scriptures present a forward movement to God's possession of the body, and it is not fanatical to say so. During a conversation with Rev. Hans Waldvogel about the Baptism of the Holy Spirit, he recollected Martha Robinson saying, "When I and others in this Work arise to preach, we do that with the power of the Holy Ghost upon our bodies. In other words, He moves our bodies. Our bodies are His instruments. *That is what God had in mind when He launched the Pentecostal Movement – to get hold of the bodies of His people.*"[10]

How will we ever be "conformed to the image of His Son," if God does not "get hold of the bodies of His people"?

Consider these Scriptures, which are often quoted at funerals, but without regard to context:

> For our citizenship is in heaven, from which we also eagerly wait for the Savior, the Lord Jesus Christ, *who will transform our lowly body that it may be conformed to His glorious body,* according to the working by which He is able even to subdue all things to Himself. (Philippians 3:20-21)
>
> But if the Spirit of Him who raised Jesus from the dead dwells in you, He who raised Christ from the dead will also *give life to your mortal bodies* through His Spirit who dwells in you. (Romans 8:11)

Without going into further detail, as one who has been in Pentecost his whole life, it is clear to me that God intends a full salvation, for "spirit, soul, *and body.*"

Though it is difficult for us to grasp, because of our limited experience in God, if we have a prayer life of "seeking the Lord with the whole heart," we sense the direction in which God is moving His people.

Look once more at Martha Robinson's testimony, not in the light of your experience, but in the light of her experience, noticing especially her references to the body:

> ... [W]e passed over into a change, which was not like anything we had ever heard of. It included *everything from head to foot.* We found out it was A TASTE OF SOMETHING GOD IS GOING TO DO IN THE LAST DAYS. At that time we did not understand that we had come into it by the crucifixion, or death to self. In a moment we were gone and a Greater One was there. Entire spirit and soul *and body* were in a new and divine control. We walked *out of the natural into the spiritual, in BODY as well as in Soul.* That was the experience God opened This Work with...
>
> And the mystery was so enormous and so wonderful; and I felt my God moved – as it were eliminated me – Christ was living in me; and yet I didn't seem to live at all. My mind didn't work at all – my spirit off in heaven. It seemed that *Christ was just borrowing, as it were, my body.* (Emphases added.)

What encouragement we receive when we recall that *"It was a taste of something that God is going to do in the last days... It is not meant for one, but for many."*

God has a goal in mind for His people. We may not yet understand fully all that John saw in his *Revelation of Jesus Christ*, but we can immerse ourselves in the words of Romans 8, until the goal named by God in verse 29 motivates us to "present *our bodies* a living sacrifice, holy, acceptable to God." We are destined, nay, <u>pre-destined</u>, **"to be conformed to the image of His Son."** HALLELUJAH!

As her experience with God deepened and her understanding of God's goal became ever more clear, Mrs. Robinson wrote:

> It is God's Plan that there should be New Bodies in the world, and BE New Body Work.[11]

I write about such things with some trepidation, for the term "New Body," although it was *God's* term, became a battleground of intense conflict, spiritually. For a time, the Vessels were asked by the Lord not to use the term publicly. Furthermore, there arose in Pentecost a number of heresies about *the body*, some of them rather childish in nature, and others very pernicious, leading to all kinds of wild behavior and immoral actions.

I have to make it clear that I am not a "teacher" on the subject of "the New Body." God called me to His ministry in the Faith Homes and I am simply testifying to the truth, and to the reasonableness of Jesus' works in those Homes. And I am convinced that He wants me to write this record.

There remains one more area of spiritual understanding to explore before touching further on "God's Plan that there should be New Bodies in the world, and BE New Body Work." That area concerns the importance of "The Inside World" (the realm of CAUSE), compared to "The Outside World" (the realm of EFFECTS).

If the servants of God are resting on God's promise that they will be "sealed in their foreheads" (Revelation 7:3), it must happen to them as an *invisible* action, a CAUSE. And that "sealing" will certainly have its EFFECT.

May God grant to us "purity of heart" so that we can "SEE GOD" in that invisible realm, and participate in the amazing transition from "this present evil world" to "the world to come."

CHAPTER TWENTY-ONE

THE INSIDE WORLD VS. THE OUTSIDE WORLD

In order to understand more clearly what is meant by the phrase "till we have sealed the servants of our God in their foreheads" (Revelation 7:3), it is helpful to explore what the Bible teaches about The Inside World vs. The Outside World. This will lead to a separate discussion of The World of Cause and its relation to The World of Effects, especially as the Bible portrays it.

Jesus' words in Luke 11:40 distinguish The Outside World (*that which is without*) from The Inside World (*that which is within*). Jesus said to "a certain Pharisee" with whom He was eating, "Ye fools, did not he that made *that which is without* make *that which is within* also?" (Luke 11:40). In the next verse (v. 41), Jesus preserves the distinction: "But rather give alms of such things as ye have; and, behold, all things are clean unto you." "Such things as ye have" = "those things that are within" (ESV); the Greek reads *ta enonta*, literally, *the things being within.*

Though the atheist denies it, every sincere believer accepts the fact that "in the beginning, God created the heavens and the earth" (Genesis 1:1) in all their fabulous variety and countless systems. It is *The Outside World* of created things, of creatures, of nature. Just as fabulous, however, is *The Inside World* that God created, the world of self-consciousness, the world where decisions are made, the world of the invisible. Paul states, "[Jesus] is the image of the invisible God, the firstborn of every creature: For by Him were all things created, that are in heaven, and that are in earth, visible and invisible, whether they be thrones, or dominions, or principalities, or powers: all things were created by Him, and for Him" (Colossians 1:16). Two worlds, one *visible*, the other *invisible*.

Modern science posits a completely materialistic explanation for all origins. This places it at odds with Bible truth, of course. The human race will have to face the dictum of the Psalmist some day: "The fool has said in his heart, 'No God'" (literal translation of Psalm 14:1).

If the entry into *The Outside World* is labeled WHAT, then the entry into *The Inside World* is labeled WHY. Referring to the word "invisible" in Colossians 1:16, A. T. Robertson comments, "*invisible (means) 'the world of spirits.*'" "Spirit" has to do with the will, motives, "thoughts and intents of the heart" (Hebrews 4:12). "Be renewed," Paul says, "in the spirit of your mind" (Ephesians 4:23). Will is the most sacred, most protected, and most sensitive spot in *The Invisible World*. It is penetrated only by asking questions about motives: "*Why* did you decide to take that course of action?", for example. Jesus asked, "*Why* call ye Me, 'Lord, Lord,' and do not the things which I say?" (Luke 6:46). There are more than 70 places in the Gospels alone where *Why?* highlights motives.

The rashness ascribed by Jesus to that Pharisee with whom He was eating (*you foolish ones, rash ones*) was due to over-emphasis on outward religion, rather than on religion of the heart. Jesus' preface to the designation "you foolish ones" shows how misplaced that emphasis can be: "Now do ye Pharisees make clean the *outside* of the cup and the platter; but your *inward part* is full of ravening and wickedness" (Luke 11:39-40).

The two greatest commandments must be obeyed in The Inside World long before the results are seen in The Outside World. "This people honors Me with their lips," said the Lord Jesus, quoting Isaiah, "but their heart is far from me" (Mark 7:6). Love for God starts in the heart, as does love for one's neighbor. Where does love originate? In The Outside World? Surely not. For that matter, what IS love? Even the *visible* acts of "bestow(ing) all my goods to feed the poor, and giv(ing) my body to be burned" (I Corinthians 13:3), do not guarantee that love is the *invisible inward motive* of my heart!

Love is a dwelling place *in the heart*, a home for someone else, *invisible*, but real.

Even the ungodliest of societal critics, such as Andrew Sullivan, or the late Christopher Hitchens, or Camille Paglia, constantly question the motives of Christians.[1] Hitchens was especially critical of Mother Theresa, for example! Bloggers of every stripe gain traction with their readers by (supposed) insightful, incisive, and even "incite-full" observations about the *motives* of the people they write about, especially Christians. It is their tacit admission of the reality of The Inside World. But what kind of Inside World do these writers live in?!

The point is simply that any serious attempt to understand what it means to be *SEALED IN THE FOREHEAD* must take account of The

The Inside World vs. The Outside World

Inside World of mankind, the world of MIND, and WILL, and HEART, and MEMORY. God created that Inside World just as certainly as He created the Outside World.

Satan appealed to Eve's Inside World in order to overthrow her Love for her Creator. He raised a "Question" about God's character based on a deceitful presentation of God's Inside World. He persuaded her to make a decision that darkened her Inside World. She was deceived; Adam willingly transgressed (see I Timothy 2:14). The CAUSE was the devil's incitement; the EFFECT was Death to the Creature and Curse to the Creation.

Jesus, as the "last Adam," was attacked and tempted by the Same Tempter, but "all the fiery darts" (designed to inflame the imagination to do evil) never found a target in Jesus' Inside World. He said, "Be of good cheer: I have overcome (conquered) the world" (John 16:33)! What *world* did He overcome? *Kosmos*, of whom the devil is described thrice by Jesus as "the Prince of this world (*kosmos*)."

The *sealing of God's people in their foreheads* is the natural and logical extension of Jesus' victory over that Evil Prince. It takes place in The Inside World. The effect of it becomes visible in The Outside World.

Jesus' life is explicable only if one understands His Inside World. *Why* did He do what He did? *Why* did he say what He said? What motivated His actions? What were His internal desires?

Here is an Old Testament look into His Amazing Inside World:

> "Sacrifice and offering Thou didst not desire; Mine ears hast Thou opened: burnt offering and sin offering hast Thou not required. Then said I, Lo, I come: in the volume of the book it is written of Me, I delight to do Thy will, O my God: yea, Thy law is within My heart." (Psalm 40:6-8)

The Hebrew words for "within My heart" graphically picture His Inside World: *baytoqh mai-ayee*, meaning, *in my bowels, in the deepest part of my being, in the midst of my heart.*

God's purpose for His people is nothing less than a Pure Heart, or, to be more precise, a Purified Heart. Jesus pronounced a Superlative Blessedness on those who are *pure in* (clear into) *the heart*. What is that Blessedness? "They shall SEE God." Where? In The Outside World? No, in The Inside World. That is equivalent to saying "the heavens will be opened" to them as sons and daughters of God on the earth. It is also equivalent to saying that their faith in the literal fulfillment of the New Covenant has been rewarded. Seven amazing promises of God have become the conscious life of The Sealed Ones (from Hebrews 8:8-12):

1. I will put my laws into their mind.
2. (I will) write them on their hearts.
3. I will be to them a God.
4. They shall be to Me a people.
5. They shall all KNOW Me.
6. I will be merciful to their unrighteousness.
7. I will remember their sins no more (*ou me*, a double negative in Greek, meaning, *not at all*).

Have you never longed for such inward righteousness as described in these seven statements, beginning with the ultra-amazing first two? "The battle is for the mind," wrote Jessie Penn-Lewis in her classic booklet by that name. Do you not desire that **every thought** would be brought into Christ's captivity? If the heart is "what you are" (the simplest definition I know of), then what will it be like to have God's laws governing every aspect of what you are?

Do not such considerations increase our understanding of Peter's words in his First Epistle:

> ... an inheritance... reserved in Heaven for you, who are kept by the power of God through faith unto salvation, *ready to be revealed in the Last Time.* (I Peter 1:4b-5)

> ... be sober, and hope to the end for the Grace that is to be brought unto you *at the Revelation of Jesus Christ.* (I Peter 1:13)

Or in his Second Epistle:

> We have also a more sure word of prophecy; whereunto ye do well that ye take heed, as unto a light that shineth in a dark place, until *the day dawn, and the day star arise in your hearts...* (II Peter 1:19)

Or in Paul's promise recorded in his epistle to the Thessalonians?

> When he shall come to be *glorified in his saints*, and to be *admired in all them that believe* (because our testimony among you was believed) in that day. (II Thessalonians 1:10)

The Inside World vs. The Outside World

There exists in Christendom as a whole a tragic confusion about Jesus' Coming. The Great Problem arises because Christians think God is going to take over The Outside World, with Jesus ruling and reigning, without God taking over The Inside World of His people!

With due respect for sincere attempts to "explain" the Lord's Coming, and especially what is commonly called "The Rapture," we might do well to consider the words God spoke through one whose Inside World was completely filled with Jesus:

> He wants His people to be prepared for His Coming. He is coming, but in a different manner than most people suppose when they study out this subject. Command this people to know it in a greater way: When is God coming? And unto whom is God coming? It is not yet found out in this world (1934), not yet taught. And the people who are so ready to argue about it are those who are the most ignorant on the subject. Hold your heart open, and when He calls He will not be unknown to you. Jesus knows and will not leave us ignorant.*

> "Jesus is coming TO His people before He comes FOR His people." ~Martha W. Robinson.

As all Christians should, we long for the Lord's enemies to be subdued, to be put under His precious feet. The Psalmist promises it: "He shall subdue the people under us, and the nations under our feet" (Psalm 47:3). At the same time, should we not have a longing for Jesus to subdue *us* to Himself? And is not this glorious conquering within His people related to His Second Coming?

Paul writes in Philippians 3:20-21,

> For our conversation (citizenship) is in Heaven, from whence also we look for the Savior, who shall change our vile (natural) body, that it may be fashioned like unto His glorious body, according to the working whereby he is able to subdue all things unto Himself.

The Opening of the Sixth Seal, and the accompanying *sealing in the forehead*, begin the process by which God's people are subdued in body, soul, and spirit. His Presence in The Inside World then affects the Outside World. There cannot be the latter without the former.

---
* From notes taken down during a talk by Martha Robinson on November 14, 1934.

In such a sealing by God, He subdues all the powers of the mind (*forehead*), including the memory, the understanding, and the will. If the mind is sealed, and the mind and heart obey instinctively and explicitly the will of God in all things, then the body is also conquered. No longer can "the lusts of the flesh, and the lust of the eyes, and the pride of life" (I John 2:16) have dominion over His people. In the testimony of Martha Robinson quoted above, "Entire spirit, soul, and body were in a new and divine control."

The following article expresses these amazing love-intentions of God for His own ones, as this present age reaches its climax. (It is of unknown date, but of known experience.)

"MADE FOR GOD"
TO
BE POSSESSED

We do not know how to ask of God: If we really knew what we lacked we should know what to ask for. Your body, soul and spirit were *NOT made for you*. "It was made for God." How much you give to God is how much you will have. The Lord is trying to make it plain that He will GIVE us ALL things. If He has given us Himself, how much more will He give us of other things? We still don't know how to ask of God and what to ask for. Your body, soul and spirit were *made to be possessed* by the Holy Ghost.

Even before Paul died they were already getting full of confusion and divisions because of trying to figure out in their natural minds. The greatest reason *why* the Holy Spirit was poured out was that you might be possessed. It was the "wisdom of this world" that crucified Jesus, and the wisdom of the world will destroy you if it has a chance. It tried to find a testimony against Jesus to destroy Him. It sought to crucify Him, and it did crucify Him. The wisdom of the world is getting stronger, *but God* is beginning to raise "His Standard" and will raise it; but by "that time" you had better be possessed. That "Beautiful Marred Face" is going to be the "Light" that is going to shine by the Holy Ghost into the heart. It is the lack of One thing that has caused schisms and divisions in the world amongst God's children: it is because they are not possessed by the Holy Spirit.

The Inside World vs. The Outside World

Our natural birth is the opportunity for life, but *not* "Life," for we were born into death, but when we are born again – "THAT IS LIFE."

The "Spirit" and "Wisdom" of this world has such a knowledge of things; the world has increased in wisdom and knowledge until there are hundreds and thousands and millions of offerings for the people to draw them into the world. It is a terrible time, and there are many who will not give up the world and the things of the world.

Jesus is trying to get you to the "Oneness" – in the 17th chapter of John. Jesus prayed that "they might all be one." John is full of two words (in the 17th chapter) – "God," and the "World." This book is the "Gospel" of "Oneness." The complete possession of the Holy Ghost in you makes you "one" with Jesus and the Father. There are so many things in this 17th chapter of John that sort of tie up in a bundle all the mystery of God ("The bringing into Oneness"). There isn't anything in your being that will function according to the Will of the Creator until you are possessed by the Holy Ghost, especially your mind. "Bless the Lord, O my soul, and all that is *within me*" – What a surrender there is in that expression!†

Every cell in your brain was meant to pick up the "Light" and the "Knowledge" of God and to give you "Light" of Him. There are only a few of your brain cells that ever came to the place where God meant them to be, to reflect the "Light" and the "Glory" of God, and *NOT* of self.

How will I come into the place to reflect Him? By knowing Jesus. We have to abandon ourselves – mostly in what we think we know, and what we think we can do ourselves. How do we do this? By knowing Jesus. Most people have not progressed a step beyond what they know when they received Jesus, because they will not "let go" and be possessed. Then they lose what they received. He wants to possess us so completely that these temples will become the temple of God. Does that make us crazy? NO! *That* makes us see and understand.

The teaching to know Jesus was partially defeated in this

---

† Psalm 103:1

Work (Faith Home work). If all that had been swept aside, there wouldn't be any Work here. Why was it defeated? Because the reasoning mind and self did not give to Jesus the possession of self completely; we are at this point in this Work. It does not make any difference to God if some refuse to press forward on this point; it will not stop Him from completing the possession of His people. But in His love for you personally, it does matter to God whether you do, or you don't, come and let God do this in you. God wants to fulfill in everyone who comes here. I am working on a Judgment line and it is cutting right through. We are at a point and are winning it. He is going to bring a people to Himself right here in these Homes. He is carrying it out to establish a people who have "given themselves." How will He do it? By taking possession of them by the Holy Ghost until there is nothing that belongs to you any longer. If you have given up everything to Him, then what He has is yours, His Mercy is yours, His Lowliness and all else of His He gives to you. It is only "Merci-ers" who can bear the image of lowliness. In these last 40 years, the wisdom and the spirit of this world has been struggling and wrestling with the Children of God as to whether God Himself can take control of His own *with* or *in* complete possession. He has been training a people that will bear the image of God. They have to lose their lives. He brings you to "poverty" by giving you a "fortune." You will find you are taking steps and making progress. Is this to happen a few years from now? NO – now a few things have been fought out in the heavens that were not fought out a few years ago. Many have been giving their lives in prayer and sacrifice, the last 40 years, to fight this out and make it possible for you to obtain now. Now you can make the progress if you want to.

You have to *know* what the expression means, "The Power of the Holy Ghost will come upon you" and "ye shall receive power after that the Holy Ghost has come upon you." ‡ What is this power of God? To be seen in the Life of Jesus Himself. We think of this power as a noticeable and an outside power to do something. Jesus said, "I have power to lay my life down."§

---

‡ Luke 24:49 and Acts 1:8
§ John 10:18

This is the power you will have – to be able to lay your life down – to lose your life; you must know what it means; to know what the possession of the Holy Ghost is. You are laying your life down as the Holy Ghost takes possession, you are dying to self.

What a beautiful way to die – not a gloomy death – this is the power of God! In these Homes we bring it to this issue all the time, in the kitchen and in the meetings. Are you willing to give up your life? How are you going to keep the power? By letting your daily life become a testimony to who Jesus is and what He does. Through constant conflict and constant triumph, you will find in your life steadily the power of God. How quickly can you recover when your pride is brought low, when you find you aren't doing as well as you thought for God? Just in the proportion that you are able to lay your life down are you in the proportion of the power of God.[3]

By now it should be clear to anyone reading this that God intends this kind of experience to be the normal life of His redeemed ones, not just of a small number who may have been familiar with the Zion Faith Homes. "It [Jesus' possession of her] is not meant for one, but *for many*," said Martha Robinson.

This act of God, by which He completes what Jesus died to give us, will be the CAUSE that brings about the End of This Age and the emerging of "a New Heavens and a New Earth, wherein dwells righteousness." Only God knows how to do it, but He has given us a Divine Preview in the last book of the Bible, "The Revelation (Unveiling) of Jesus Christ."

Let us examine the CAUSE in more detail, and then look at the EFFECT in the visible world.

If we examine the relationship between *cause* and *effect* at the time of Jesus' First Advent, we will find it easier to see how cause and effect interrelate when Jesus comes The Second Time.

In one of the most succinct statements ever made about History's Hinge Point, the Apostle Paul says, "But when the fulness of the time was come, God sent forth his Son, made of a woman, made under the law, to redeem them that were under the law, that we might receive the adoption of sons." (Galatians 4:4-5)

How did God "send forth His Son"? Did He appear out of nowhere, suddenly a full-grown man with commanding presence and supernatural signs? No, Jesus was "made of a woman." How did that happen? Luke quotes Gabriel as telling Mary, who wondered "How?",

> The Holy Spirit will come upon you and the power of the Highest will overshadow you. (Luke 1:35)

Here the CAUSE is clearly stated. It happened in The Inside World, the very real but unseen world, the world of "spirit" and "will" and "decision." No one saw it in The Outside World, not even Mary. What unfathomable, infinite, holy mystery is in those words: "The Power of the Highest will overshadow you"! Repeating, that was the CAUSE of history's greatest turning point.

What was the EFFECT then, in the visible world, The Outside World? The actual Presence and Fulness of God in human form – The Word made Flesh – who tabernacled with us. Jesus Christ APPEARED in bodily form, the Perfect Image of God, the Last Adam, the Redeemer of Mankind.

From the outset, the "Prince of the Power of the Air," the "Ruler of This (fallen) World," opposed that Last Adam, trying either to kill Him before His time, or to corrupt Him, or to keep Him from The Cross. Satan, who is AN EVIL SPIRIT, was the CAUSE of the opposition against the HOLY SPIRIT Who possessed Jesus utterly.

The Gospels describe the EFFECT of the cause, both in the outworking of Jesus' ministry – healing the sick, casting out devils, raising the dead, teaching and preaching and living the Kingdom of God on earth – and in the opposition aroused to a killing hatred of Him, His words, and His ministry.

If we examine the conversion of Paul with the same thing in mind, *i.e.*, the relationship between *cause* and *effect*, we understand more clearly what actually took place. His Encounter-with-Jesus happened in The Inside World of Paul, visible to him, but not visible to those who were with him. He was blinded by the glory of a Light from Heaven, brighter than the sun at noon, as Jesus was REVEALED in him, but those with him did not see what Paul saw. He describes it in Galatians 1:10,

> But when it pleased God... to reveal His Son **in** me...

Something happened to him in his Inside World, with the result that enormous changes took place in the Outside World, in the world of

EFFECTS. His life and ministry, so dominated by Jesus within him, brought historic change to the world of his time. In addition, his "epistles" (more than a dozen) continue to change the life of mankind worldwide.¶

Paul's opposers fought him everywhere he went, though the worst opposition arose within the Jewish communities where he ministered. What was the CAUSE of the opposition? Not any crimes he had committed, not people he had hurt, not havoc he had wrought; no, it was his testimony of Jesus revealed to him and within him that aroused such hatred. He also preached a Resurrected Christ, seated in the heavenly places at God's right hand, "far above" all other invisible powers in that realm. Those invisible powers were beaten back by one man whose inner life was possessed by that Living Christ. The opposition could only do to him what they did to Jesus: KILL HIM. In the end, of course, it only resulted in an increase in the Arising Word, as the Power of Resurrection made void the power of death.

The history of the Church furnishes many examples of events transpiring in the World of Cause that precipitated large changes in the Outside World, the World of Effects. For the purposes of this book, however, we leave that fascinating history and move ahead to the REASON the Zion Faith Homes came into being.

To summarize what has already been presented in this book, the CAUSE for the emergence of the Faith Homes was *the Revelation of Jesus Christ within Martha Robinson*. She simply followed the powerful leading of the Spirit to "pray through to know Jesus"; she had no grandiose idea of becoming a notable saint, much less the leader of a ministry. We can search her life to find ambition, or fanatical zeal, or the desire to be "The One," as shaping factors, but we will search in vain. She simply prayed for nine months what narrowed down to a single cry: "*Let me die.*" And Jesus, overshadowing her one fateful night in November 1907, answered her cry, and *revealed Himself in her.*

I have described somewhat the EFFECT of that CAUSE, although, as Miss Brooks once said to me, "No one could ever write a complete history of the Faith Homes. There are too many people involved, too many events to describe. Besides those limitations," she continued, "if the full story were to be properly recorded, no one would believe it." Please

---

¶ To this day, the Bible remains the world's best-selling book. The goal of *Wycliffe Translators,* to put a Bible portion in all of the world's languages, is within reach by the year 2025.

remember that she spent 89 of her 93 years within the boundaries of the Faith Home ministry, and she should know!

Now we come to the point of these few paragraphs on the relationship between CAUSE and EFFECT.

It is the year 2013 as I write. We have come, I believe, to another of History's Hinge Points. So many prophecies in both the Old and New Testaments await fulfillment. For the first time in the world's history, three things have come to the full.

1. **Death-dealing power**, in the form of nuclear and biological weapons, threatens the destruction of our entire race. Think of it: from simple weapons like knives and swords, to bows and arrows, to battering rams and cannon balls, to "lead arrows" of long range, to missiles and rockets carrying death, and now finally, to explosive devices that release atmospheric radiation of sufficient strength to annihilate all living things! And not one, but several nations, some ruled by demon-possessed dictators, stock-pile such weapons and can easily unleash their death-dealing power by a single command.**

2. **Evil imaginations** have now come to the full and circulate world-wide by means of fantastic technical advances. Anyone, anywhere, can see every kind of evil that the imagination can produce, pictured endlessly to his vision. All the works of the flesh, yes, all of them, are acted out for anyone to see, whenever one wishes. The very essence of evil – the lusts of the flesh, the lusts of the eyes, and the pride of life – literally fills the air as electronic pulses transmit it world-wide. It is a staggering thought, how the Adversary has managed to corrupt the world and its inhabitants to the extent that God's lament in Noah's day could apply to this present generation: "every imagination of the thoughts of his heart was only evil continually" (Genesis 6:5).

3. **The power to control buying and selling** lies in the hands of the world's business powers. This is a present possibility,

---

** Today, March 6, 2013, the top headline on the *Drudge Report* reads: "North Korea Vows Pre-Emptive Nuke Strike on USA."

not a future dream. Slowly but surely the secrets of electricity have birthed a world-wide computer-based system by which all transactions involving money can be absolutely controlled. What Germany did to the Jewish community in the horrible years of 1938-1945, by shutting them off from all business dealings, can now be duplicated world-wide by the powers-that-be against any group of people they wish to dominate and/or destroy, including Christians.

What is the CAUSE of such present-day realities? <u>It is the power of evil controlling the Inside World of men whose motives are not pure</u>, *i.e.*, who are outside of the understanding of righteousness. Such a description occurs in Psalm 2, for example:

Why do the heathen (nations) rage, and why do the people IMAGINE a vain thing? The kings of the earth set themselves, the rulers take counsel together against the Lord, and against His Anointed, saying, "Let us break their bands asunder, and cast away their cords from us." (Psalm 2:1-3)

The cause is not "poverty," or "social unrest," or "class-warfare," or "wage inequities." The cause is in the IMAGINATION, resulting in their "taking counsel together." The decisions made in their Inside World result in far-reaching effects in the Outside World. One only needs to think of the Inside World of Adolf Hitler, for example, to see what happens when IMAGINATION becomes evil and corrupt.††

However, the Devil is NOT a creator! His specialties are DECEPTION and DESTRUCTION. God has already set in motion in the invisible realm of conflict, the Inside World, the MEANS by which the devil and his works will be utterly overthrown. <u>Jesus' Death and Resurrection guarantee it!</u>

---

†† A recent biography of Mao Ze-Dong clearly shows how his Inside World became the CAUSE of massive destruction in the Outside World, resulting in the death of at least 70 million of his own Chinese people! "The worst thing one can do," he said as a teenager, "is listen to one's conscience"!!! The book is called *Mao: The Untold Story,* by Jung Chang and Jon Halliday, (New York, NY: Random House, 2005).

CHAPTER TWENTY-TWO

THE OPENING OF
THE SIXTH SEAL

Introduction

As we have seen in *Interlude Three*, it is vital not to lose sight of the simple fact that "the Son of Man is Coming in the Glory of His Father." Because His Coming is another "Hinge of History," and because Jesus repeatedly warned to be ready for His Coming, we are *wise* if we look at the Scriptures again and again to see what the Bible teaches about this world-changing event.

I use the word *wise* deliberately. Some years ago the Holy Spirit guided me in a study of the instances in which Jesus used the words *fools*, and *foolish*, in the Gospels. I tracked the usage in Greek, rather than in English. My motive was simply to learn what constituted *foolish behavior*, and thus avoid it. I knew that Jesus would not call someone a *fool* in the way He forbade the use of that word as an accusation of condemnation or despising. His use of the word would point us in the direction of *wisdom* rather than *folly*.

Five passages emerged (and a sixth, but already absorbed within the five). They are:

- The Wise and Foolish Builders (Matthew 7:24-27)

    o The *foolish* behavior to be avoided is, hearing what Jesus says, but not doing it.

- The Wise and Foolish Virgins (Matthew 25:1-13)

    o The *foolish* behavior to be avoided is, *being casual about His coming,* not caring enough to make adequate preparation.

- The Foolishness of Discounting the Inside World (Luke 11:37-41)*

    o The *foolish* behavior to be avoided is, *discounting God's interest in the Inside World* of motives and will, mistaking the Outside World to be His primary focus.

- The Foolishness of Covetousness (Luke 12:16-21)

    o The *foolish* behavior to be avoided is, *stock-piling goods for one's earthly future*, instead of being "rich toward God," *i.e.*, treasure in Heaven.

- The Foolishness of Not Being Sufficiently Immersed in the Scriptures about His First Coming, and not believing what the Prophets predicted about His First Coming (Luke 24:25-27)

    o The *foolish* behavior to be avoided is, *failing to immerse oneself in what the Bible teaches about Jesus' Coming(s), and to believe it.*

It is this last mention of reference, "O fools, and slow of heart to believe all that the prophets have spoken," that motivated me to become thoroughly acquainted with Bible teaching on the Second Coming.

With Jesus on the Road to Emmaus

The account of Jesus walking to Emmaus after the Resurrection (Luke 24) and talking with Cleopas and the other unnamed disciple appeals to me greatly, just the way a "Tell me that one again" story appeals to a child's imagination. The details are a child's delight – Jesus' patience with their re-telling of the weekend's events, when He was Himself the center of it all; the hiding of His identity until the very last moment; His way of getting from them an invitation to stay for supper; and Jesus' "disappearing act" at the end. Ha! Makes me chuckle again just to think of it! Jesus is so amazing, isn't He!

Concealed in the story, however, is a very grown-up matter. It has to do with Jesus saying to them, "O *fools* [*anoetos* = unintelligent, judging by sentiment, not by fact] and slow of heart to believe all that the prophets have spoken..." (Luke 24:25). Why, oh why did Jesus use such strong

---

* Here is where the sixth passage fits in, The Foolishness of Phariseeism (Matthew 23:1-39).

language with them? To say to their faces, "O fools!"? Couldn't He have been "nicer" than that?

The answer lies somewhere in the following truth: *There was no excuse for the disciples on the Emmaus Road not to have been thoroughly familiar, "soakingly" familiar, with all the Scriptures in the Old Testament that spoke of His First Coming.* Jesus' rebuke implies they should have known the meaning of the mysterious events of the past few days, based on their familiarity with the Old Testament. Their failure was due to their ignorance of the facts, leaving them with confused and emotional reactions.

Such observations lead to the following conclusion:

We too are without excuse if we are not thoroughly familiar, "soakingly" familiar, with all the Scriptures in both the Old and New Testaments that speak of Jesus' Second Coming.

If we treat the subject of The Second Coming lightly, we are "foolish" in the sense in which Jesus used that word in Luke 24. When things happen which we cannot understand, we likely will base our opinions on "unintelligent" evaluation, instead of on "fact." Our jumbled emotions may get in the way of seeing events for what they are in God's view. *Many prophetic writers in previous years have succumbed to this temptation, much to their chagrin.*† God HELP us!

The story of the Emmaus Road disciples doesn't end with Jesus' disappearance, thank God. Jesus DID explain to them the meaning of the Scriptures concerning His death and resurrection, even as they talked in the way before they knew who He was. And their burning hearts prompted them to hurry back to Jerusalem where they shared their startling story with the eleven. Suddenly Jesus appeared AGAIN, despite locked doors! (I confess a child's delight in this detail, too!) This time He *"opened their understanding, that they might understand the Scriptures."* Precious, faithful Jesus! Blessed, lowly, incomparable Holy Spirit, Teacher without equal!

Are you comforted to know that God will open to you the understanding of Jesus' Second Coming, if your heart is capable of "burning"? Would it not comfort Him, if we could understand it somewhat BEFORE HE COMES?

---

† During World War II, the outstanding Canadian pastor Oswald J. Smith, for example, published a paper declaring that Benito Mussolini was the Anti-Christ.

It seems to me that passages about Jesus' Second Coming are like gems in a Divine Treasure Box. I feel this way especially about certain passages in the New Testament. They are precious to me. I love to take them out of the box and hold them up to the light, to revel in their priceless beauty and worth. I would never want to "cast them before swine," for the world cares so little about His Coming. Some things need to be pondered in the heart, not shared indiscriminately or apart from the Holy Spirit's leading.

If you have read this far, surely you also love the exquisite jewels in God's Treasure Box. You love to retreat to your trysting place with Jesus and open the lid to look again at the contents of the Box. Their beauty transfixes you; their worth takes your breath away. They are part of your "Hope Chest."

The Transfiguration, a Preview of His Coming

The Gospel accounts of Jesus' Transfiguration are among the gems. Let us take a loving look at the account in Luke 9:28-36, with the six verses that precede it:

> Saying, "The Son of Man must suffer many things, and be rejected of the elders and chief priests and scribes, and be slain, and be raised the third day." And he said to them all, "If any man will come after Me, let him deny himself, and take up his cross daily, and follow Me. For whosoever will save his life shall lose it: but whosoever will lose his life for My sake, the same shall save it. For what is a man advantaged, if he gain the whole world, and lose himself, or be cast away? For whosoever shall be ashamed of Me and of My words, of him shall the Son of Man be ashamed, when He shall come in His own glory, and in his Father's, and of the holy angels. But I tell you of a truth, there be some standing here, which shall not taste of death, till they see the kingdom of God.
>
> And it came to pass about an eight days after these sayings, He took Peter and John and James, and went up into a mountain to pray. And as He prayed, the fashion of His countenance was altered, and His raiment was white and glistering. And, behold, there talked with Him two men, which were Moses and Elias: Who appeared in glory, and spake of His decease which he should accomplish at Jerusalem. But Peter and they that were with Him were heavy with sleep: and when they were awake, they saw His

glory, and the two men that stood with Him. And it came to pass, as they departed from Him, Peter said unto Jesus, "Master, it is good for us to be here: and let us make three tabernacles; one for Thee, and one for Moses, and one for Elias": not knowing what he said. While he thus spake, there came a cloud, and overshadowed them: and they feared as they entered into the cloud. And there came a voice out of the cloud, saying, "This is My beloved Son: hear Him." And when the voice was past, Jesus was found alone. And they kept it close, and told no man in those days any of those things which they had seen.

Notice the context, the "velvet background" that brings out the beauty of this gem. Jesus introduces the subject of His impending death and speaks of the necessity for disciples to follow Him into that death. See how He speaks so clearly of "death-to self" in verses 23 through 26! Hear Him place infinite value on the "soul," and then declare there is only one way it can be "saved"! Does He not link these statements with His Coming by saying that some of the disciples would soon have a preview *of the kingdom of God* (Luke's words) *come with power* (as Mark puts it)? Amazing, isn't it?

What is the supreme brilliance of this Transfiguration "jewel" as it unfolds in the next several verses? Is it not the figure, yes, the *trans-figured figure*, of Jesus Himself?! Look at His face, brighter than the sun! What kind of glory is He in, a glory-light so powerful it shines through His clothing? And what is this Opening of the Heavens which reveals two other persons in conversation with Jesus? What are they talking about? And is this the Father speaking, in an *audible* voice?

Oh God, we tremble before You! *Do we have in this description a foreview of Your Son's Unveiling in this world now?*

Peter believes so. In his Second Epistle he writes with the authority that comes with being an "eyewitness." Here are the words of Second Peter 1:16-19:

> For we have not followed cunningly devised fables, when we made known unto you the power and coming of our Lord Jesus Christ, but were eyewitnesses of His majesty. For He received from God the Father honour and glory, when there came such a voice to Him from the excellent glory, "This is my beloved Son, in whom I am

well pleased." And this voice which came from heaven we heard, when we were with Him in the holy mount.

We have also a more sure word of prophecy [all that the prophets have spoken], whereunto you do well that you take heed, as unto a light that shines in a dark place, <u>until the DAY DAWN, and the DAYSTAR ARISE IN YOUR HEARTS</u>.

Are we not looking at something exceedingly precious, dear reader? Do not you love that phrase, "until...the Daystar arises in your hearts"? This must refer to *"something God is going to do in the last days"*; it must be connected in some way with Jesus' body being *transfigured* before the wondering eyes of Peter, James, and John.

The Sixth Seal

This chapter only introduces the subject of the Opening of the Sixth Seal. If you are interested, you can read what Rex Andrews wrote about it in Chapters 21 and 22 in the *Meditations in the Revelation*. What I share now summarizes those chapters.

Do you remember what the Lord said through Martha Robinson in a public meeting on November 14, 1934, about His Coming? Here is the last paragraph of that message:

Command this people to know it in a greater way: <u>When is God coming? And unto whom</u> is God coming? It is not yet found out in this world, not yet taught. And the people who are so ready to argue about it are those who are the most ignorant on the subject. Hold your heart open, and when He calls He will not be unknown to you. Jesus knows and will not leave us ignorant.

God is looking for a people who, unlike the Pharisees, "hold their hearts open." Did not the Lord have open hearts in Mary and Joseph, who were truly ready for Messiah's birth? Did not He have the hearts of Anna and Simeon, who lived for the moment when the infant Jesus would be brought into the Temple? Were not Peter and James and John and the other disciples prepared to leave all when Jesus said, "Follow Me." Glory to God! And will there not be "five wise virgins" who go out to meet the Bridegroom when He comes — yes, possibly "half" of the total number of virgins expecting His arrival?

Do you insist that you "know it all" when it comes to Jesus' Second Coming, or can you approach the subject with a broken spirit, a humble attitude, and a heart that trembles at God's Word?

Revelation 6 and 7

Question: What is the scroll-book, the opening of which is so supremely important?

Answer: It is simply the pre-determined, humanly unknowable plan and directive of God by which He recreates this world to be "the world to come" (Hebrews 2:5). Its writings unfold "the regeneration," as Jesus termed it in Matthew 19:28. All of the ongoing Revelation (Unveiling) of Jesus Christ which follows Revelation 5 flows out of the scroll-book as Jesus opens it in Chapters 6, 7, and 8. Whatever is written in the scroll-book is carried out in the balance of the vision.‡

Question: What is the significance of the seals, with which the scroll-book is held tightly clasped?

Answer: Simply the hindrances, or blocks, which have to be overcome before the scroll-book can be opened completely and its contents be put into action in the world. Jesus Christ breaks the seals one by one, in sequence. Since He is the "Lamb with horns and eyes," He alone has the power and the wisdom to break them, thus eliminating the hindrances to the re-creation of this poor, sin-cursed world. His action (of breaking the seals) allows certain powers of the Enemy to come forth, but never without Jesus opening the seal first. He is carrying out the destruction of The Destroyer's works in the same way He taught us to do: "Be not overcome of evil, but *overcome evil with good*" (Romans 12:21). The tares (of the Adversary's planting) are allowed to grow along with the wheat (of God's planting), lest the uprooting of the tares uproot the wheat also. All things must wait "until the time of the harvest" (Matthew 13). With long patience the Divine Husbandman "waits for the precious fruit of the earth" (James 5:7).

The opening of these seals corresponds with Jesus' prophetic words in Matthew 24:4 to at least verse 14. The history of the world from His

---

‡ Such statements may seem presumptuous to some – "How can he just say such things without proof?!" – but they are practically self-evident if we are able to read these passages without being blinded by preconceptions and human reasonings.

death until now is accurately, so accurately, described there in Matthew 24 and Revelation 6.§

All this terrific commotion (spiritually speaking, but manifested in the world), has as its goal the UNVEILING of JESUS CHRIST to this world. God has never swerved from His promises! Hallelujah! Psalm 37 (for example) is still true, word for word, line for line! No one but God Himself could possibly know how to tie up the ends of this age, but HE DOES KNOW! Glory to Jesus forever, who was found worthy to OPEN THE BOOK!

This brings us to our last Scripture for this topic.

A Closer Look at Revelation 6:12–7:17

Question: What is this which happens when Jesus opens the Sixth Seal, and why is there such a long description of it?

Answer: It is clear that two things are happening when Jesus Christ opens the Sixth Seal.

First, *something happens in our astronomical heavens which shakes the world as we know it and evokes tremendous fear in the general populace.* Not since the upheaval in Egypt when God was freeing the Israelites nearly 40 centuries ago, followed by the giving of the First (Old) Covenant at Mt. Sinai, does the Bible record such a tremendous shaking in nature as this one in Revelation 6. The prophets predict it, to be sure; and a look at Isaiah 24-27, or Isaiah 2 (for example), should alert us to it. But when the Sixth Seal is opened by Jesus, THE SHAKING HAS COME!!! THE GLORY OF GOD RETURNS!!!

There are many Old Testament prophecies that point to this terrible shaking. Isaiah 2, for example, where twice it is said, "When He arises to shake terribly the earth" (vv. 19, 21). Another descriptive passage is Isaiah 24-27, which ought to be very familiar to all Christians. What about Joel 2:31-32; Jeremiah 25:15-38; Habakkuk 2; Isaiah 34; and the great descriptions of the Fall of Babylon in Jeremiah 50 and 51? Are you "soakingly familiar" with these great prophecies? Not to mention the amazing visions of Daniel 2 and Daniel 7?

---

§ Again, unless our analytical minds insist on tearing things to pieces, such observations as I am making are practically self-evident. May I humbly urge you, dear reader, to search the Scriptures for yourself "to find out whether these things [are] so" (Acts 17:11 NKJV).

The Opening Of The Sixth Seal

The writer of Hebrews says,

> See that ye refuse not him that speaketh. For if they escaped not who refused Him that spake on earth, much more shall not we escape, if we turn away from Him that speaketh from heaven: Whose voice then *shook the earth*: but now He hath promised, saying, Yet *once more I shake not the earth only, but also heaven* [the astronomical heavens]. And this word, Yet once more, signifieth *the removing of those things that are shaken*, as of things that are made, that those things which cannot be shaken may remain. Wherefore we receiving a kingdom which cannot be moved, let us have grace, whereby we may serve God acceptably with reverence and godly fear: For our God is a consuming fire. (Hebrews 12:25-29)

Beloved ones, are you READY FOR THE SHAKING???

Second, *God's own ones, both Jews and Gentiles, are sealed in the forehead.*¶ God is going to keep The Second (New) Covenant with the remnant of Abraham's seed in Israel, and THOUSANDS OF MODERN JEWS will find themselves in the GLORY-LIGHT OF THE OPENED HEAVENS just as Saul of Tarsus did on the Damascus Road! Equally true, God is going to seal an UNTOLD NUMBER OF GENTILES IN THEIR FOREHEADS, as the wording of Revelation 7:14-17 shows:

> And I said unto him, "Sir, thou knowest." And he said to me, "These are they which came out of great tribulation, and have washed their robes, and made them white in the blood of the Lamb. Therefore are they before the throne of God, and serve Him day and night in His temple: and He that sitteth on the throne shall dwell among them. They shall hunger no more, neither thirst any more; neither shall the sun light on them, nor any heat. For the Lamb which is in the midst of the throne shall feed them, and shall lead them unto living fountains of waters: and God shall wipe away all tears from their eyes."

¶ Rotherham's translation brings out very clearly that two groups are being *sealed in their foreheads*, one group numbering 144,000, and a second group that no man can number. I realize this is not the ordinary dispensational way of looking at this passage, but such teaching unrighteously diminishes the enormous significance of the *sealing*.

Someone might say, "Well, it doesn't *say* this group is sealed in their foreheads." And my answer would be, the wording itself describes that sealing! Much the same argument could be made concerning Jesus' baptism in the Holy Spirit. The Scripture does not say directly, "Jesus was baptized in the Holy Spirit at His water baptism." But Luke does record that while Jesus was praying, the heavens were opened to Him, and God spoke audibly over Him, and the Spirit descended in a bodily form like a dove upon His head (Luke 3:22). That is a description of Holy Ghost baptism, is it not?!

Likewise here in Revelation 7, we have statements which describe what it means to be sealed in the forehead. Let us consider the phrases one by one –

they are standing before God's throne, and before Jesus
> like all who "stood before the Lord" in the Old Testament

they are clothed with white robes
> like Paul, they are "found in Him, not having their own righteousness" (Philippians 3:9)

they have palms in their hands
> in a vast fulfillment of "Palm Sunday" – caught up in supreme exaltation of Christ

they have come through great affliction
> the trial of their faith shines like gold as Jesus comes! (I Peter 1:7)

they have washed their robes and made them white in Jesus' blood
> "Redeemed, how I love to proclaim it! Redeemed by the Blood of the Lamb!"[1]

they are before the throne of God
> "And Elijah the Tishbite... said unto Ahab, 'As the LORD God of Israel liveth, before whom I stand...'" (I Kings 17:1)

they serve Him day and night in His temple
> "What? know ye not that your body is the temple of the Holy Ghost which is in you, which ye have of God, and ye are not your own? For ye are bought with a price: therefore glorify God in your body, and in your spirit, which are God's." (I Corinthians 6:19-20)

He that sitteth on the throne shall dwell among them
>They are where He is, and He is where they are!

they do not hunger or thirst any longer
>like Moses on Mt. Sinai, without food or water for 40 days in God's Presence (Deuteronomy 9:9) *Satisfied in the eternal life of God!*

they are not subject to heat and cold
>like the three Hebrew children in the fiery furnace (Daniel 3:25)

the Lamb in the midst of them feeds them
>"The Lord is my Shepherd: I SHALL NOT LACK ANYTHING." (Psalm 23:1 AMP)

Jesus leads them to living fountains of waters
>"Ho, every one that thirsteth, come ye to the waters, and he that hath no money; come ye, buy, and eat; yea, come, buy wine and milk without money and without price." (Isaiah 55:1) *and the bride says come! come to the waters.*

God wipes away all tears from their eyes
>"He will swallow up death in victory; and the Lord GOD will wipe away tears from off all faces; and the rebuke of His people shall He take away from off all the earth: for the LORD hath spoken it." (Isaiah 25:8)

>"For I reckon that the sufferings of this present time are not worthy to be compared with the glory which shall be revealed in us." (Romans 8:18)

Can you find a better description anywhere in the Bible of what it means to be "sealed in the forehead"? And the lengthy description of the sealing magnifies its tremendous importance.

Conclusion

All of these Scriptures are meant to give us some idea of the significance of the Opening of the Sixth Seal by Jesus. The opening of the Sixth Seal is the PRELUDE TO HIS UNVEILING, and as such it is PART OF HIS COMING. IT IS JESUS REVEALED **TO** HIS PEOPLE BEFORE HE COMES **FOR** HIS PEOPLE. It is the fulfillment of numerous prophecies in both the Old and New Testaments. It precedes the Opening of the Seventh Seal, which is "The Blowing of the Seven Trumpets." When the Seventh (Last) Trumpet sounds, **"THE MYSTERY OF GOD WILL BE FINISHED as He hath declared to His servants the prophets"** (Revelation 10:7).

What IS "the mystery of God"? Simply, **"CHRIST IN YOU, THE HOPE OF GLORY"** (Colossians 1:27). It is **"GOD'S GREAT VICTORY OF THE AGES,"** *which begins with the sealing in the forehead, and ends in the complete possession of God's people by Jesus, spirit, soul, and body.*

"Even so, come, Lord Jesus!" (Revelation 22:20)

EPILOGUE

Knowing it is time to conclude, I wish to make a few observations, despite the risk of stating the obvious.

1. The word "simplicity" occurs numerous times in this book. In the King James Version of the Bible, the word occurs three times in the New Testament:

> Or he that exhorteth, on exhortation: he that giveth, let him do it with **simplicity**; he that ruleth, with diligence; he that sheweth mercy, with cheerfulness (Romans 12:8).
>
> For our rejoicing is this, the testimony of our conscience, that in **simplicity** and godly sincerity, not with fleshly wisdom, but by the grace of God, we have had our conversation in the world, and more abundantly to you-ward (2 Corinthians 1:12).
>
> But I fear, lest by any means, as the serpent beguiled Eve through his subtilty, so your minds should be corrupted from the **simplicity** that is in Christ (2 Corinthians 11:3).

Each of these occurrences reflects the Greek word *haplotes*, which A. T. Robertson refers to as "an old and expressive word from *haplous* (simple, without folds)."[1] It is also the root word for the expression, "a single eye." A pure heart harbors no hidden agendas, no double motives. I saw it lived out in the Zion Faith Homes for many, many years. It remains my earnest desire to stay within the boundaries of that simplicity.

The "sealing in the forehead" is also a great simplicity. To the pure in heart it is not complicated, but spiritually logical, understandable, simple, and desirable. Martha Robinson lived in a foretaste of that sealing, as did the others who labored with her. That is why this book is testimony, not merely doctrine.

2. The word "vast" implies something beyond measurement, especially as it refers to the ability of the mind to grasp something larger than itself, something beyond visual or mental comprehension. What has been written in the preceding pages in no way reaches the limits of the vastness of the "simplicity that is in Christ." The words of Isaiah 64:4 apply to this truth: "For since the beginning of the world men have not heard, nor perceived by the ear, neither hath the eye seen, O God, beside thee, what he hath prepared for him that waiteth for him."

3. "Someday you will understand that it must be ALL JESUS. Then you will understand." ~ Martha Wing Robinson

4. The accompanying Appendices can be read as a vital part of the history of the Faith Homes and what it stands for. The final paragraph of Appendix E makes a fitting conclusion to *A Vast Simplicity*:

> "The Time is NOW when He wants to manifest HIS PRESENCE to His own. NOW! The Times have run out, and we are slipping over the line into His Time and into His DAY. The Adversary may do terrible things, and destructions may overtake the evils of the world, BUT JESUS WILL NEVER DESERT HIS SHEEP. He will carry them through to the end MORE THAN CONQUERORS — those who live by His Blood; who love not their own lives unto death; and who have the testimony of the MERCY THAT ENDURES FOREVER."

ALL GLORY TO JESUS

AFTERWORD

For those Faith Home friends still living who might read *A Vast Simplicity*, their response is not hard to imagine: "But you left out so much, especially about those who served the Lord in the Homes for many years. Couldn't you have written a chapter about them?"

The answer is, "I did." In previous drafts, I included sketches of many who blessed the Work of God in the Faith Homes and whose memories I cherish. Some served in leadership positions, such as Mrs. Beulah Andrews (Rex's wife), Rev. Marie Robinson, Rev. and Mrs. Murdoch MacLean, Rev. Ruth Lade (Schleicher), Violet van Hellen, Ruth Jackson, Rev. Eugene Waldvogel, Rev. Dorothy Miller, Rev. George Rundblom, Rev. James Thomas, Rev. and Mrs. Lee Allen, Rev. and Mrs. Ofer Amitai, Rev. Rose Simon, Rev. and Mrs. David Leopold, Rev. and Mrs. Richard Brogden, Sr., Rev. Lucille Simon, and Rev. Rowena Miller.

Subsequently, however, in celebration of the 100th year anniversary of the Zion Faith Homes in 2009, the present leaders prepared a forty-page booklet for the occasion that was distributed to guests and interested friends. It contains many pictures of historical interest, as well as brief summaries of various aspects of Faith Home life and ministry, including a complete list of Faith Home residents for the past 100 years.

Primarily for that reason, another chapter along those lines became unnecessary. I trust that no one who remembers "those days" will feel slighted.

Secondarily, *A Vast Simplicity* is not written to satisfy those who, out of curiosity, might be attracted to read about such an unusual place. The Zion Faith Homes yielded to the "Law of Change"; a visit to the Homes today will confirm that observation. This writer's intention is to make seekers-after-Jesus to know assuredly that God is going ahead with His pre-ordained plan to have a people for Himself. The unchangeable Creator/Redeemer has seen the travail of His Son's soul, and is satisfied. A seed shall serve Him. *What God has started He will complete.* "Looking unto JESUS, the Author – and the Finisher – of our faith" (Hebrews 12:2)!

Father in Heaven, please use this small account of Your Work to fan the flames that You have kindled in many hearts, to the praise of the Glory of Your Grace in Christ Jesus. Amen.

Rev. Douglas D. Detert

March 29, 2013

Appendix A

Studies In Psalm 136, *The Great Halal*

An abbreviated analysis of the Psalm…

(v. 1) We are enjoined to *give thanks unto the LORD*, the Eternal Fountain of Being, **because He is good.**

> His goodness is *the reason* for giving thanks. Since the Garden of Eden, God's Adversary Satan has insinuated that God is NOT good, has ulterior motives, and should NOT be worshiped as God. Giving thanks because God IS good and because His mercy IS forever, unmasks the Deceiver.

(v. 2) We are to *give thanks* (frequently rendered "praise") *to the God of gods*, the One who is Supreme over all Supreme Ones.

> Why? Because there is no other Being, imagined or created, whose eager, ardent desire to supply the needed good of life to all His creatures never ceases; as such, He is SUPREME, and His basic GOOD-NESS far surpasses all other "gods."

(v. 3) We are commanded to render and cast forth praises *to the Ruler and Sovereign over all other rulers and sovereigns.*

> Why? Because His love-in-action, that gives Him complete authority in the Universe, will never cease to be.

(v. 4) We are enjoined to give thanks to, and to worship Him who is the Only One of whom it can be said that *He does great wonders.*

> Why? Because His deeds are now, have been, and always will be GREAT WONDERS, deserving of our utmost admiration, conceived and enacted by unending Love-in-action.

(v. 5) Who *made the heavens by wisdom and understanding;*

> Why should this statement evoke the response, "because His Mercy is forever"?

Because His Wisdom and Understanding, by themselves, uphold the infinite System-of-Systems that we call the Universe, and prevent the Second Law of Thermodynamics from destroying everything.* In addition, the love-behind-all-created-things will never cease to be.

(v. 6) Who *stretched out the earth upon the waters;*

Where is the mercy in such a statement? It lies in the implicit and inalterable division between land and sea. It is God's mercy that restrains the oceans behind boundaries, making land habitable. [As a direct consequence of the fact that violence filled the earth and the thoughts of man's imagination were only evil continually, the Flood in Noah's time breached that restraint, resulting in widespread death (see Genesis 6:5,11-13).] However, His unending mercy will never allow that to happen again! (See Genesis 9:15, with context.)

(v. 7) Who *created great lights;*

It is not hard to see that our planet's two *great lights* not only support life as we know it, but truly *govern* day and night, giving structure and rhythm to man's existence. As such, the sun and moon exquisitely express God's unending mercy!

(v. 8) that is, *the sun*

The *sun* is the source of heat and light for our planet, thus "funding" life; it also *rules the day, i.e.*, it makes normal life possible, even livable; *light* is part of God's mercy to the earth, part of the system by which man-as-we-know-him exists. The *sun* and its placement at the center of our solar system is one of many vital factors supporting life on earth, as described by Astronomer Hugh Ross.[1] And the mercy, which the sun represents, will never cease to be.

(v. 9) also, for example, *the moon and the stars*

While the *sun* governs days as a result of the *earth's rotation*, the *moon* governs months by virtue of *its revolution* around the earth.

---

* "According to the second law, the entropy [amount of energy no longer available] of any isolated system, such as the entire universe, never decreases. If the entropy of the universe has no maximum upper bound then eventually the universe will have no thermodynamic free energy to sustain motion or life, that is, the heat death is reached." Accessed July 23, 2013 at http://en.wikipedia.org/wiki/Second_law_of_thermodynamics.

APPENDIX A

For centuries, the *stars* governed travel at night. Scientists still do not fully understand the effect stars have on earth-life; the ages-old belief in Astrology may turn out to be a perversion of the true understanding of the effects of stars on man's existence. Perhaps in yet unknown ways, (gravity, regularity of orbits, background radiation, *etc.*) the moon and the stars show forth the unfailing-ness of God's Mercy.

We are urged to render thanksgiving to the Eternal Being, to Him:

(v. 10) Who *smote Egypt in their firstborn*;

> How could the death of Egypt's firstborn evoke thanksgiving to God? The answer lies in the relation of God's wrath to God's Mercy. If the definition of God's wrath is correctly given as "His power to save all those that put their trust in Him,"† then the Tenth Plague represents an enormous mercy to those whom Pharaoh had determined to oppress and enslave indefinitely. Does God take pleasure in the death of the wicked? Absolutely not! However, if Egypt's oppression of the Jews had not been stopped, God's plan of Redemption would have been blocked, and God's promise to Abraham would not have been fulfilled. Thank God that His Will-to-deliver-and-set-free is still unchanging!

(v.11) Who *brought out Israel from among them* (the Egyptians);

> All the statements following (vv. 12-15) are part of the life-giving mercy by which Israel was thrust out of Egypt and guided into the Promised Land.

> What happened to the Egyptians (always a type of unbelieving, God-defying people) approximately 3,500 years ago is but a tempest in a teapot compared with the Mercy that God will show to all His people to set them and the whole Creation free from *the bondage of corruption* in days immediately ahead. This is so, precisely because His Mercy is unto always!

---

† For most of us, this quote from the writings of Rex Andrews is not an intuitive definition of God's wrath. But consider this paragraph from his booklet, *The Will of God*: "Does not the Bible speak about 'The wrath of The Lamb'? Yes, it surely does. But the wrath of the Lamb and of God is not like human wrath. That same blazing glory which looks like wrath to people who are in wrath themselves, is the very same fire that is burning in my heart right now. To people who are in evils, the fire and the glory of God seems like wrath - and IS wrath to their evils. But it makes me alive and I want to live in it. 'Life' destroys 'death.' And Love destroys evil. And Mercy – Lovingkindness - destroys evil forces, violence, wrath, and whatever destroys life." (p. 9).

(v. 12) Who *brought out Israel with a strong hand, and with a stretched out arm;*
BECAUSE, if it were not true that God's Will of *Mercy* is age-abiding, there never would have been an "exodus" at all!

(v. 13) Who *divided the Red Sea into parts.*
WHY give thanks to God for *that?* BECAUSE the fact that God *saved* them from otherwise certain slavery and death (by opening a way for them when there was no way), shows the *unfailing, no-exception* quality of God's Blessed Will, which is loving-kindness. What was "life" for the children of Israel became "death" to Pharaoh's army.

(v. 14) and *made Israel to pass through the midst of it;*
BECAUSE, at the hour when they passed through, in a very real sense, they were *utterly* at the Mercy of the Creator, and, Glory to God!, such loving-kindness can be counted on and lived in forever!

(v. 15) but shook off and *overthrew Pharaoh and his host in the Red Sea;*
BECAUSE, the same Mercy that *saves* those who are willing to repent also destroys those who are bent on destruction. Such loving-kindness is our hope in this world forever.

We are urged and enjoined and commanded to continually cast forth praises to the Eternal Creator, our Father, to Him:

(v. 16) Who *led His people through the wilderness.*
WHY give thanks to Him for leading them through the wilderness? BECAUSE that's another way one finds out that God's mercy sustains life under the most inhospitable conditions. We find *manna and water* in the wilderness! And such mercy remains, despite repeated provocations.

(v. 17) Who *smote great kings;*
BECAUSE His Mercy surpasses the power of earth's greatest rulers, bent on destroying God's people. Such mercy will not suddenly abate or disappear in the face of some great force-power of evil. It simply **IS**, forever!

(v. 18) Who *slew famous kings;*
Mercy is not intimidated by the reputation of ANY king, no matter

how glorious a history of domination he may have had. There *is* a King *of* kings who lives and reigns forever, and His Kingdom is Love.

Give thanks to Him:

(v. 19) Who *slew the great and famous king Sihon of the Amorites*,

Because the overthrow of an Amorite king in whose kingdom wickedness had come to the full (Genesis 15:16), demonstrates that God's love-in-action for the best good of all His creatures *is* forever.

The Canaanite culture surpassed any other culture unearthed by archaeologists for immorality and perversion of every sort.‡

(v. 20) *Who slew Og, king of Bashan*;

Because any act of God by which He destroys and puts away something which has reached the height of corruption is an act of love; and Og represented a formidable opponent of everything good, a man so huge he needed an enormous iron bedstead, and who ruled over 60 cities.

For the Israelites, it was another proof that God's sheer mercy upon them would NEVER cease.

(v. 21) Who *gave their land for a heritage*;

Because, the Mercy by which He could actually bring that many people into the Land of Promise after, and in the face of, almost continual rebellion and disobedience, must be *Eternal*, and age-abiding.

(v. 22) *even a heritage unto Israel His servant*;

Because, God saw Israel as His "Prince with God"! He gave them what was not earned or deserved! He kept His Word to Abraham as the fulfillment of the promised Mercies! Surely it is because His Loving-kindness is forever.

We are enjoined to cast forth praise, and to render thanksgiving to Him:

(v. 23) Who *has [earnestly] remembered us in our low estate* and imprinted us [on His heart] (Amp);

Because the sole cause for such inconceivable regard for man by the Almighty Creator is simply that His *Will* (that Spirit which

---

‡ This was stated by Dr. Robert Cooley in a class on Biblical Archaeology taken by the author.

constitutes <u>God's desire</u>, what He <u>thinks</u> and <u>feels</u> toward His creatures) was, and is, and always will be, <u>MERCY!</u>

(v. 24) Who *has redeemed us* [rescued us, snatched us away] *from our enemies* – those who would destroy us (Amp);

> Why? Because the ONLY thing that ever comes between any of God's creatures and the force-power of evil that seeks to *destroy* us by every means, is the everlasting Will-Desire of God <u>to GIVE LIFE TO</u> and <u>PRESERVE</u> and <u>NOURISH</u> and <u>WATCH-GUARD OVER</u> all of His created ones.

(v. 25) Who *gives food to all flesh*;

> Because <u>all flesh is fed by and through the Mercy-Lovingkindness of the Creator</u>; that is, Mercy is God's <u>supply</u> system by which He <u>meets the need</u> of all creatures everywhere, and *that* Lovingkindness IS forever.

(v. 26) *O give thanks unto the Supreme One of Heaven – the King who rules and presides over the Kingdom of Heaven* (Amp);

> FOR His Mercy and Lovingkindness simply IS, and WAS, and ALWAYS WILL BE!!!

Appendix B

The Definition Of Mercy: Is It Biblical?

The following sentences comprise "the Definition of Mercy" as it appears in *What the Bible Teaches about Mercy*.[1] The Scriptures that follow each phrase or sentence substantiate the rightness of the definition.

> MERCY is God's supply system for every need everywhere.
>
> Mercy is that kindness, compassion and tenderness which is a passion to suffer with, or participate in, another's ills or evils in order to relieve, heal and restore.
>
> It accepts another freely and gladly AS he is and supplies the needed good of life to build up and to bring to peace and keep in peace.
>
> It is to take another into one's heart JUST AS HE IS and cherish and nourish him there.
>
> Mercy takes another's sins and evils and faults as its own, and frees the other by bearing them to God.
>
> This is the Glow-of-love. This is the ANOINTING.

MERCY is God's supply system for every need everywhere.

> The eyes of all wait upon Thee; and Thou givest them their meat in due season. Thou openest Thine hand, and satisfiest the desire of every living thing. (Psalm 145:15-16)
>
> My God shall supply all your needs according to His riches in Glory by Christ Jesus. (Philippians 4:19)

Mercy is that kindness, compassion and tenderness which is a passion to suffer with, or participate in, another's ills or evils in order to relieve, heal and restore.

kindness

> But after that the **kindness and love** of God our Saviour toward man appeared, not by works of righteousness which we have done, but **according to His mercy** He saved us, by the washing of regeneration, and renewing of the Holy Ghost... (Titus 3:4-5)

compassion and tenderness

> To give knowledge of salvation unto His people by the remission of their sins, through **the tender mercy** of our God; whereby the dayspring from on high hath visited us... (Luke 1:77-78)

passion

> To whom also He shewed himself alive **after His passion** by many infallible proofs, being seen of them forty days, and speaking of the things pertaining to the kingdom of God. (Acts 1:3)

suffer with, or participate in, another's ills or evils

> For even hereunto were ye called: because **Christ also suffered for us**, leaving us an example, that ye should follow His steps. (I Peter 2:21)

> For He hath **made Him to be sin for us**, who knew no sin; that we might be made the righteousness of God in Him. (II Corinthians 5:21)

> He is despised and rejected of men; a Man of sorrows, and acquainted with grief: and we hid as it were our faces from Him; He was despised, and we esteemed Him not. Surely **He hath borne our griefs**, and **carried our sorrows**: yet we did esteem Him stricken, smitten of God, and afflicted. (Isaiah 53:3-4)

> He shall see of the travail of His soul, and shall be satisfied: by His knowledge shall My righteous servant justify many; for **He shall bear their iniquities.** (Isaiah 53:11)

> **In all their affliction He was afflicted.** (Isaiah 63:9)

It accepts another freely and gladly AS he is and supplies the needed good of life to build up and to bring to peace and keep in peace.

freely and gladly

> Come unto Me, all ye that labour and are heavy laden, and I will **give you rest**. Take My yoke upon you, and learn of

Me; for **I am meek and lowly in heart**: and ye shall find rest unto your souls. For **My yoke is easy, and My burden is light.** (Matthew 11:28-30)

Ho, every one that thirsteth, come ye to the waters, and **he that hath no money**; come ye, buy, and eat; yea, come, buy wine and milk **without money and without price.** (Isaiah 55:1)

AS he is

And he [**the dying thief**] said unto Jesus, "Lord, remember me when Thou comest into Thy kingdom." And Jesus said unto him, "Verily I say unto thee, **today shalt thou be with Me** in paradise." (Luke 23:42-43)

and supplies the needed good of life

And Jesus said unto them, **"I am the bread of life**: he that cometh to Me shall never hunger; and he that believeth on Me shall never thirst." (John 6:35)

to build up, and to bring to peace

But now in Christ Jesus ye who sometimes were far off **are made nigh by the blood of Christ. For He is our peace,** who hath made both one, and hath broken down the middle wall of partition between us. (Ephesians 2:13-14)

and to keep in peace.

To give light to them that sit in darkness and in the shadow of death, **to guide our feet into the way of peace.** (Luke 1:79)

It is to take another into one's heart JUST AS HE IS and cherish and nourish him there.

take another into one's heart

For we have not an high priest which cannot be touched with the feeling of our infirmities; but was in all points tempted like as we are, yet without sin. (Hebrews 4:15)

JUST AS HE IS

And when the Pharisees saw it, they said unto his disciples, "Why eateth your Master with **publicans and sinners?**" But when Jesus heard that, He said unto them, "They that be whole need not a physician, but **they that are sick**. But go ye and learn what that meaneth, 'I will have mercy, and not sacrifice': for **I am not come to call the righteous, but sinners to repentance**." (Matthew 9:11-13)

and cherish and nourish him there

For no man ever yet hated his own flesh; but **nourisheth and cherisheth it, even as the Lord the church**. (Ephesians 5:29)

Mercy takes another's sins and evils and faults as its own, and frees the other by bearing them to God.

faults as its own

For He hath made Him to be sin for us, who knew no sin; that we might be made the righteousness of God in Him. (II Corinthians 5:21)

Who **His own self bare our sins in His own body on the tree**, that we, being dead to sins, should live unto righteousness: by whose stripes ye were healed. (I Peter 2:24)

and frees the other

The Spirit of the Lord GOD is upon Me; because the LORD hath anointed Me to preach good tidings unto the meek; He hath sent Me to bind up the brokenhearted, **to proclaim liberty to the captives, and the opening of the prison to them that are bound.** (Isaiah 61:1)

by bearing them to God

For ye were as sheep going astray; but are **now returned unto the Shepherd and Bishop** of your souls. (I Peter 2:25)

This is the Glow-of-love. This is the ANOINTING.

The Spirit of the Lord is upon Me, because **He hath anointed Me** to preach the gospel to the poor; He hath sent Me to heal the brokenhearted, to preach deliverance to the captives, and recovering of sight to the blind, to set at liberty them that are bruised, to preach the acceptable year of the Lord. (Luke 4:18-19)

Appendix C

Two Possible Great Calls

The following article was copied from a letter written by Brother Rex Andrews on July 3, 1969.

There are two possible Great Calls. One, a great ministry of Evangelism and Healing. This is visible in the very prominent leaders of our time who have risen since 1947. Two: A hidden ministry of Prayer, Suffering, Forerunners blazing a Trail for others. A call to be NOTHING, that God might be ALL. Mrs. Robinson had these two Calls offered to her. One Path, He said, [was that] she could be an Evangelist, go up and down the country, and win many souls. The Other Path was different; she would not be popular; would suffer more than anyone she knew of. She said, "Jesus, you choose for me." This record was by Hilda Nilsson.

God led Mrs. Robinson as He chose. He put her into the Revelation of Jesus. As she expressed it: "That was the experience that God opened This Work with." And *The Faith Home Work* is that Work. It can never be anything else. Everyone wishing to be a part of it must adjust to This Work, and not the reverse in which This Work would have to adjust to some other person's type of work. Mrs. Robinson came into it "by the Crucifixion or death to self." This Work is that kind of Work, and all of the ministers in This Work are that kind of ministers. And The Teaching here, blessed of God through years of simplicity, is that kind of Teaching... Long years ago, when the organ was in the other corner and there were three rows of chairs where the organ is now, I remember so clearly getting down on my knees by the back row, and saying to God in a real Power meeting: "Father, I want Your will absolutely. And if it should ever happen that I don't want Your will, take what I am saying now, and do this, and not what I might want then." Well, He has done it. Taken 50 years more or less. But it is my testimony that He has done it, and is completing the process.

There are two ways possible sometimes. 1.) To be a great evangelist and go about reaching many souls and having honor with men – with sufferings. 2.) A Path of The Lord's own choosing which seems to come to nothing, or at least seems to BE NOTHING. The first seems to BE SOMETHING. In that path one's own will may not be completely broken and "annihilated." The second is the reality of NOTHINGNESS. One has only God, only Jesus. The second was M.W. R.'s lot and her Work. And that has to be The Faith Home Work. But only "Nothings" can keep it so.

Appendix D

John G. Lake's Letter to Elder Brooks and His Reply

Introduction by Rex B. Andrews

Following are two letters written over 60 years ago; one by John G. Lake and the other by Elder Eugene Brooks in reply. We are printing them here because they present, in their substance, a problem of the Christian ministry – as well as of the life of any follower of Jesus. That problem is: The enormous need that is latent in the life and experience of those whom God blesses and uses. So many need to understand how to go on with God, and how to retain their life with Jesus and to grow in it. Especially in these days of what seems an almost over-emphasis – in some quarters – on great works and great gifts. We say over-emphasis because of the under-emphasis, in even some of the greatest of the leaders of our times, upon the growth in God of the daily life of the child of God. It is a startling fact that in many cases Christians and Christian workers do not know what to do, and how to proceed on and into the FULLNESS OF GOD. This is an almost unbelievable common failure. So many talk and teach about "prayer" who do not actually PRACTICE in their lives a vital PREOCCUPATION WITH GOD in their private lives. Or, they gradually lose out in their walk-with-God by becoming too much involved in goings, and doings, and efforts to become "great," or "GREATER." Anyone who does not realize his need to have from two to four hours alone with God daily, will almost surely find himself in a wilderness facing into a spiritual loss and vainness as the spirit-of-this-world opposes advance and seeks to render void the fruitfulness of their life which was begun in the wonder of the power of the HOLY SPIRIT. These letters are offered as studies in spiritual contrasts. They will be greatly rewarding to any who are willing to read, and study, ponder, and digest what is expressed in them.

John Lake and Elder Brooks were both mighty men of God – each in his own way and calling – as their letters clearly show. And those of us who knew them both quite intimately can add our testimony that such an estimate is true.

Rex B. Andrews

Rev. John G. Lake's Letter to Elder and Mrs. Brooks
June 16, 1916

Dear Brother and Sister Brooks:

For some days I have been moved by the Spirit to write to you. At the time of our marriage I felt that God had really laid upon your souls the burden of my need in God. As I moved out in faith at that time, endeavoring to trust God for physical strength and guidance and grace from heaven to accomplish His will, He richly blessed my soul and our work was accompanied by the power of His Spirit.

While at Philadelphia the Spirit of the Lord came mightily upon me for healing, and wonderful healings took place. Later we came to Spokane, Wash. The first door God opened here, strangely, was a door in what is known here as The Church of The Truth, a New Thought body. Their pastor was formerly a Universal preacher. He had seen Christ through Christian Science teaching. He was a hungry soul. He invited me to preach at his church. I said to him, "My message is not yours. I preach the Christ and Him crucified." He replied, "Brother, preach your own message, and as much of it as you want to. You are in the hands of the Spirit of God."

After the first sermon, he invited me to take one of the healing rooms in their church, and pray for the sick throughout the week. God gave wonderful healings. The church was mightily moved. It was a new manifestation of the power of God to them. I was invited to teach their weekday classes on the subject of the baptism of the Spirit. God showed me four persons in the church at that time who would receive the baptism. We ministered there about six months, then started our own work about Feb. 1st, 1915.

The first lady from the Truth church to be baptized in the Spirit was a Mrs. P. She received her baptism at the first service we conducted in our own hall. At the close of the Sunday morning service the Spirit fell on her, and she was baptized in the presence of the congregation.

Mrs. P. told me that five years before, while in a great agony of soul, she fell on her knees and cried out for deliverance and light and help, saying, "Oh God, is there no one anywhere who can bring me the light my soul needs and show me God as my spirit craves?" And the Spirit spoke to her and said, "Yes, in Johannesburg, South Africa." On the day of her baptism as she was under the power of the Spirit, the Lord reminded her that He had fulfilled His promise to her, and that I had come from Johannesburg, S. Africa in response to her soul's call and the soul call of others who needed God.

Another lady from The Church of The Truth was likewise baptized in the Spirit, Mrs. F. The Spirit revealed Christ and the Blood and His cleansing power. They have been beautiful souls, as also the other two.

In connection with our work we maintain healing rooms, open from 10 a.m. to 4 p.m. every day, where the sick and otherwise needy souls come for prayer. We also have a hall connected with the healing rooms, where we have our weekday and weeknight meetings. Our Sunday services are all held in the Masonic Temple. Sunday School in the morning, preaching at 11 a.m. and the large public service at 3 p.m.

Our work here has been characterized with wonderful healings, and many of them. When I wrote the stories of the wonders God was performing in Africa to America, the people largely said, "We do not believe it." Satan tried in many ways to make the world believe it was not a fact. But our work here has been under the eye of such competent witnesses of such high character, and so many of them, that Satan cannot longer deny the stories of what God has done. The news has reached all the Pacific Coast states. People are coming, not the sick only, but teachers, particularly from among the Truth people of the Coast country, to inquire what it is, and what is the difference, and what do we mean when we talk about the baptism of the Holy Ghost, and how do you get it?

During the year 1915, 8,030 persons were healed. Mr. Westwood ministers with me in the work, and has the adjoining healing room. Mr. S. P. Fogwill, formerly a deacon of Zion City, is also with me. He makes the calls from home to home throughout the city all day with the Ford car. Usually we minister to one hundred persons per day, sometimes more sometimes less.

Among the remarkable cases of healing are three of recent occurrence, which I want to give you. They are out of the usual order of healings, and in my judgment belong to the class of miracles of creative order.

One is Mrs. Pn., a trained nurse, a graduate of Trinity Hospital, Milwaukee. She was operated upon and the generative organs were removed, womb and ovaries in July last. In November she was operated upon again for gall stones. After the operation the bile broke loose and flowed from her body in quarts, to such an extent that death became imminent. Indeed, during the time she was being prayed for she passed into a state of coma, apparent death, and for about half an hour there was no evidence of life, and no breath passed her lips. Mr. Westwood was with her. He had been with her all night. It was about 4 a.m. The Spirit of God took gradual possession of her being in such power that she was healed entirely of the gall stone difficulty. Her generative organs regrew, and last month she became a perfectly normal woman. Mrs. Pn. is now the matron of our Divine Healing Home.

The second case is that of Miss K., a victim of glandular tuberculosis. She was operated on 26 times, and was treated by 56 different physicians, and finally left to die. One after another abandoned the case.

In one of her operations an incision was made in the lower abdomen. This was done in an endeavor to remove a great quantity of pus that had formed in the body. On account of the tubercular state of her flesh, the wounds would not heal nor hold stitches. Three times she was opened and sewed up, but without avail. The consequence was that a normal movement of the bowels could not take place. This condition lasted for six and a half years.

While down in the city she fainted on the street. They were about to take her to St. Luke's Hospital for an operation when she became conscious, and refused to go. She came to our home and spent the night with us. We prayed for her.

On the next day, Sunday, as she sat in the tabernacle in the afternoon service, while public prayer was being offered, she said it seemed to her as if a hand was placed inside of her abdomen, and another hand on her head. The voice of the Spirit spoke within her soul and said, "You are healed." She arose from her chair, and became perfectly normal.

Number three. Mrs. L., the wife of a Main St. merchant here, fell downstairs some ten or twelve years ago, which caused a prolapse of the stomach, bowels and female organs. She became an invalid. After several years of operations and suffering she was attacked with rheumatics and became a helpless cripple. When the doctors had failed, she was recommended to take bath treatments at Soap Lake, one of the hot lakes in Washington, where the water is very hot and very much mineralized. The treatments had this strange effect, that the disease left her body and centered entirely in the right leg. A formation of bone, as large as a large orange came on the inside of the right leg and the bone of the leg began to grow until the leg was 3 inches longer than the other one, and the foot became almost an inch longer than the other one.

Her lungs had fallen in through tuberculosis. She was prayed for one day in the healing rooms, and as she went out to get in the car she was amazed to discover that her lungs were raising up, and her chest filling out. She was perfectly and instantly healed of that.

Later while I prayed for her concerning the lump on her leg, the Spirit came upon her powerfully, and she burst into great perspiration, which ran down her person into her shoes. The leg which was 3" longer than the other one at that time, shortened at the rate of an inch a week and in three weeks was perfectly natural and the same length as the other. The foot also shortened in length, and now she wears the same sized shoes on both feet, and her legs are of equal length.

God wants to do something new in connection with my work. It is not clear to my soul yet just what it is. Finances have been tight lately. There has not been the usual flow of financial help. Healings have not been so powerful for some 3 weeks. My spirit is disturbed. I recognize it as one of the stirrings that come to the soul previous to a change in the character of the work and ministry. I feel the need of your prayers. I know that God put me on your hearts. I know I am on your hearts still and will always be, for I believe God has laid the burden of intercession upon you dear ones for my life.

I may not always see the guidance of God as you see it, but I desire to assure you of my deep personal love for you all, and of the bond in the Holy Ghost with you that is intense and powerful. I want your prayers.

Our work has extended into the country round about. We now have a congregation at Bovill, Idaho, another at Moscow, Idaho, the seat of the state University, and another at Pullman, Washington where the Washington Agricultural Schools are located. We have another congregation in the north part of Spokane, aside from the central work.

Beloved, you know that we can trust God to apply to the soul that discipline that is necessary for its subjection to God. As I look back over the way, though it seems hard, I can see that every step of the way has been necessary for my soul's discipline, not only that God's humility might reign in me, but that God's power might be made manifest through me, and my faith strengthened in God.

I feel I have never yet attained that place in God where I can accomplish the real life work that He desires through me. There is a broader ministry that God wants accomplished. I feel He has called me to it, but the way has never been opened so far, nor have I felt that my soul was really ready for it.

I have given you a good deal of detail concerning myself, for John Lake has always been a good deal of burden to himself, and I feel that I want your loving prayer and holy faith in my behalf, that the real will of God may be done in me and through me to the glory of God. God bless you.

Give our love to all the dear ones.

Your brother in Christ,
(John G. Lake)

Reply to John G. Lake's Letter by Elder Brooks
July 1, 1916

My Dear Bro. Lake:

Your long and interesting letter was received and read with much pleasure.

We were exceeding glad to hear from you and to know that God has been so abundantly blessing you. I do praise Him for all He is doing in and through His people.

We have been in a severe strain of work for some weeks – spending as much as 14 hours a day at times.

It did seem as if your request would have to go unheeded, for we knew that a short prayer would not meet the demands in your case. But the Lord said we were to have a 3-hour prayer for you; and in order to get it, we dismissed our usual meeting last night and called all the people in the 3 homes together and prayed for 3 hours, strong and powerful.

I'm sure our God has heard that cry and we believe that God will manifest the answer in the way and at the time of His choosing.

We do not need to tell you that we love you and greatly desire that you should measure up to the Divine requirements, therefore no apology is needed for a little word of admonition. My soul seems to sense a possible error you are making in reference to your self and work. I do not say I am correct at this point, but I have the soul sense that you have your eyes in the wrong direction. You say "God wants to do something <u>new</u> in connection with my work." I do not doubt that. But what is it? Is it enlargement? Development? Aggression? Gifts and dominion?

It may be all these or none of them, but one thing is true - that if your eyes get on these, somewhere you will fail.

While I do not claim wisdom for these words, yet I am quite sure of the correctness of the statement that no man can be used as largely as you have indicated and not be treading on most dangerous ground. And while it is true that greater conquest, enlargement, dominion, etc. may be intended by the Lord, one thing is absolutely necessary, if these victories are to be continued, and that HUMILITY, genuine, deep, lasting – shall be yours.

You know that a man may be called and greatly anointed for a certain work and yet not be as powerful in God as some other not so greatly called. But have you learned that the man thus largely called must find that grace and depth in God or <u>lose</u> his stewardship and disgrace his name and profession? God needs certain works to be done and calls whom He will to do it, <u>but He will sacrifice the work to save the worker</u> – with God the <u>worker</u> is important, with man the work – God has His eye on the <u>man</u> – the man has his eye on the work. Your letter shows that you have the vision though somewhat mixed. You see God and you see your need, but you also see other things and these other things <u>needing</u> you.

The real vision is to see "Jesus only" and to see nothing else. Not Jesus <u>and</u> – just Jesus. The "single eye" sees none but Jesus – the double eye sees Jesus <u>and</u>.

If I could put into words the soul-sight of this you would get the idea and seek to impart it, but it is an experience and not a doctrine. It is the absolute sufficiency of Jesus for <u>every need</u> and the utter uselessness of every human effort.

Just as long as there are <u>things</u> and <u>doings</u> in our vision Jesus cannot be so mighty. When He alone is seen, He <u>takes care</u> of the things and doings. We <u>try</u> and fail until we are willing to give up and admit we cannot – then we may turn to Him.

My Bro. we are absolutely useless without Him. What if we have been used a bit when we were not recognizing Him? That does not prove our sufficiency, but His grace. He knew we were blind and was therefore patient. But our blindness and folly must be exposed and we fail and then awaken to find our springs had all been in Him all the time. It is the folly of the natural man to suppose that <u>he</u> is doing it until his conceit is exposed, and then finds that God made a vessel to honor because He had need, but when the vessel took glory to itself He broke the vessel that He might make it again.

Now, you know as well as I the things I am saying. Then why do I say them? Just to stir up your "pure mind."

But there is one thing which you perhaps do not know as well as I – the unfailing and only way to attain that desired end. You are the one called and equipped (because of the need) without much effort on your part. I not being thus called must needs find at the foot of the cross what was imparted to you at the start, because of the need. Is God unrighteous? No not at all. Then sometime, somewhere you too will have to go down at the foot of the cross to retain that which has been imparted for the time of need, or you will find yourself someday the "broken vessel." No, I by no means indicate you should do as I do, nor by any means go the way I go – but I do say that go what way you may you have got to go on your knees. Nor do I think you would have to spend the time in prayer that we do, for your call being different the requirement would be different. But certain it is that if the prayer closet is neglected because of the stress of work, God will neglect the work sometime.

We can argue ourselves out of the victory with the thought that God will excuse our declension in prayer because we are so engaged in the vineyard. But when we turn to the life of our Lord and find Him leaving the multitude, who had come to be ministered to, and going off to pray, we have to admit there is no excuse left.

But surely I have exceeded the limitations of propriety. I simply intended to say a few loving words by way of remembrance, and lo, I have been preaching to you at a wild rate, and still have not said the thing yet I desired to say, for I did wish to just hold up Jesus and make you look at Him from every angle and see how transportingly beautiful He is – how all sufficient He is – how He fills all – meets every requirement – satisfies every longing – is Himself the equipment for every service. Oh, John Lake, there is no other need of ours in this world or that to come but Jesus. I know I'm not making it clear - I can't, but it is true all the same.

It is <u>so</u> true that it is supreme folly to look for, desire, or be tempted with ought else. If He is "The Way" we can't get lost. If He is "The Life" the devil can't kill us. If He is "The Truth" we can't be deceived by lies. What do we need besides Jesus? If everything proceeds from Him – if all things culminate in Him – if He is the embodiment, the fulfillment and the consummation of all things, why should we seek after or even think of anything else?

No, I haven't told you <u>yet</u> and now I despair of doing so, for Jesus is so infinitely wonderful that all words fade when referring to Him. Oh, my Bro. John, I once looked for <u>power</u> – wanted <u>equipment</u>, sought <u>usefulness</u> – saw gifts in the distance – knew that dominion was somewhere in the future, but glory to God! One by one these faded, and as they faded there was a <u>form</u>, a figure emerged from the shadows which became clearer and more distinct as these other things faded and when they had passed I saw "Jesus only."

The Lord bless thee my Brother and fulfill all His purposes in thee. Our very earnest love to you and your dear wife.

All the saints greet thee in love. Wife and I among them.

In the bonds of Christ,
   (Eugene Brooks)

Appendix E

To One Asking For Forgiveness

Feed My Lambs   Serial No. 28   August 1959
Zion Faith Homes, Zion, IL

The following letter is an answer written in 1946, to one who wrote asking for forgiveness for unkind words. It is now 13 years since sending it.* Except for a few places where the wording has been slightly revised for the sake of clarity, it remains the same. It is a record, report, and testimony of one who went headlong into the depths of hopelessness for seven years. One who after more than two decades in the ministry was trapped in sin, and in the ensuing discouragement went slam-bang to the depths of both hopelessness and of caring-no-longer. Everything seemed futile: "You can't win'" seemed blazoned in strong words on every side. "It is useless to try any longer, you can't win, you will fail" was the title in capital letters over all that could be visualized of the future.

In this letter is described at least part of The Recovery which God gave to me — after seven years. We print it now in the hope that someone reading it may find a new and living hope, and act on it. The phrasing may seem stilted to some. To others the whole setting may seem disgusting. There are those who can never quite get the sense of despising out of their hearts for one so weak and so vile — even when GOD has cleansed and renewed into a triumph, which in despair seemed forever beyond reach. There are others, thank God, who possibly considering themselves, have not only tolerated both the person and testimony, but have urged the expressing of it. They have said, "Tell it. Others are longing to hear it."

The times we are living in are increasingly requiring a knowledge in us all, of HOW-to-triumph in the MIDST of evils which are rising to

---

* Of course it is now more than 65 years since this was written. The 13 years mentioned here refers to the period when the letter was first written in 1946 until it was published as an article in *Feed My Lambs* in August 1959.

a climax of power in human life. After 15 years, I can say, it all remains the same. Yet, those 15 years have been a conflict of wading through such opposing evils as would seem fantastically overdrawn if pictured in words. "Who always causeth us to triumph in Christ," are words which stand today.†

Rex B. Andrews

* * * * * * *

Dear Brother:

You are freely and fully forgiven. It seems very odd for me to have someone ask me to forgive them. I thought that I was the only one who had need of forgiveness. I do not seem to have any memory of anything you said. So I will just say, The Lord bless you and comfort you in every way.

Yes, Jesus let me fall so that I would "know that it is all just Jesus." And in that knowledge, there has come an understanding of God and of His mercy which I never even faintly dreamed of before. My idea of "mercy" was that The Great God was so loving and condescending that no matter how low a person had fallen, if he would come to Him and ask for forgiveness, He would freely forgive him. And that is so. But the reason that Got so forgives is not that He condescends to do so, but simply that He IS mercy. And His willingness to forgive anyone who asks Him for forgiveness is but one phase of His boundless mercies.

When one has been blessed in the instructing of others, especially of persons of what we call the "low" type of sins and vices, there comes into the heart, unconsciously, an assumption that, "I understand all about the mercy of God." But the simple fact is that there is very little understanding in the world of what the mercy of God really is. And the assumption that I knew all about the subject sort of precluded me from making any very thorough search, even in the Scriptures, concerning the mercy which in so many places is translated also by the word, "lovingkindness."

Throughout the whole Universe of Creation, in which are unnumbered worlds, humanly speaking, and countless hosts of beings of all types and intelligences,‡ there is an intricate system of the OUTFLOW of life from the

---

† II Corinthians 2:14

‡ In using the phrase "countless hosts of beings of all types and intelligences," Mr. Andrews seems to be referring to different classes of angels, not to a belief in extra-terrestrial beings living on other planets.

Love of God. That outflow from His Love is MERCY – Lovingkindness. The life of every creature everywhere, in the heavens and on the earth, is sustained by mercies. Mercy, or Lovingkindness, is life-giving radiation of Love.

When God creates, He creates within everyone and everything a Way for the flow into it of its own quality of existence. Then He creates The System by which that flow is maintained. That System is a system of mercies and the life which flows into the creature is in mercies. There is no one in the universe capable of receiving the FULL FLOW OF THE PURE LOVE OF GOD except the only Begotten Son, who is Himself the exact Image, or form, of that Love. IN, and through The Son of God, there is the breaking down into qualities and lesser degrees so that The Love of God will not consume the one into whom it flows. In other words, God levels His Love down TO THE CAPACITY of the individual creature. And that is MERCY.

The Love flows forth from God as the mercy of His Love. In the one who receives it, that mercy IS Love. And in the leveling down to the capacity of the Little One, is Something so indescribably holy and so entrancingly wonderful, that once he gets a real glimpse of it he is changed forever, and becomes, by choice, a lowly slave of The God of Love. Some, of course, shrink from and almost abhor the term "slave." But those who understand it prefer that term, describing God's possession of them, rather than even the somewhat easier sounding word, '"bond-slave." But either word describes it.

That something, so indescribably holy and entrancing, is the UTTER LOWLINESS OF GOD who is both OVER all His works, and is also UNDER all of them. I repeat: when one gets just a little glimpse of the reality of the lowliness of God, he is changed forever, not by some long process then of praying through, but by the inrush into his being, in that moment, of the pure Mercy of God. In that inflow of mercy God is also willing to impart His own utter lowliness to any who want it and seek for it.

That Utter Lowliness is in its very essence something which "I" am NOT, for it is something which HE IS. Unless "I" can receive that Lowliness of God as of pure mercy, and of pure mercy alone, then I can never receive it. For if the true Lowliness of God did not come into me as pure mercy, in which there is no merit of any kind, then I would easily become proud of my lowliness. And the Adversary himself is capable of such a pride.

If we search for lowliness by the accumulation of works we shall never find it. For the reckoning up of our "works" as being of merit, is in itself not lowly. Yet the "REST" we want and seek for is in utter lowliness. Where shall we find it? In Jesus alone. For HE is the pure mercy of God. He said, "Come unto Me... and you shall find rest... For I am meek and lowly in heart."§ He will give, in mercy, the lowliness and the rest as to one with whom He is joined-in-spirit. That joining with Him begins the moment we give our all to Him, and we do that as we "see" how He gave His all for us.

There are, however, many lessons of faith that have to be learned before we come to understand how real it is that we are actually part of Jesus Christ — part of His very life. In the learning of those lessons, we come to find that His "lovingkindness (mercy) is BETTER THAN LIFE."¶ Really so. And as we learn to trust Him and receive all from His pure mercy, we learn the lessons of abiding IN HIM. And there the Adversary cannot reach us any longer, that is, he cannot defeat us there. As we become rescuers of others the Adversary may fight us, and even be allowed to test thoroughly our life in God. But he cannot reach us there to DEFEAT us.

In learning to abide in God, we find ourselves in the necessity of being keepers of His Words. For in all His words are the instructions for mercy-ing others as we have been mercied. I found out that I cannot know what it is to ABIDE in Jesus without a mercy-ing heart. For unless I am willing to do to others THE SAME MERCY which He has done to me, then I am in that respect like the Adversary, because the essence of all evils is in these two things: 1.) A self-will to exalt myself. 2.) A coveting to possess, which refuses to pass on freely to others the mercies by which I live. And out of those two arises the third evil: the WRATH of frustrated pride and self-exalting, and of failure to make gain out of others. (Those things can be stated in other ways. This is not intended to be a final technical treatise on the matter.)

That may sound a little complicated. It would not be so if we were not such incorrigible "thinkers." We think and think, and think, and try to do everything by thinking. We think instead of pray. We think instead of believe — in fact we use the words interchangeably: "I think" for "I

---
§ Matthew 11:28-29
¶ Psalm 63:3

believe." We think instead of yield. And in our thinking there is just one person in the center, and on top, and at the end of everything. That person is "I." That "I" stands in our being squarely IN THE SPOT WHERE JESUS HAS TO APPEAR. Right there. Exactly there. And that brings us back again to the idea of utter lowliness. For when at last I am leveled down to the level of SIMPLE MERCIES, there I find Jesus. And where do I find Him? Rising in my soul in the very place where "I" always occupied the center-of-everything. And it becomes a reality, conscious and substantial: "NOT I, but CHRIST LIVETH."**

Why have I written all of that? Perhaps to take your thought away from self and self-processes. It really doesn't matter whether one can follow to the depth of what has been expressed. There is a living FIRE in it. I cannot myself fathom all the depths of it, yet, this is testimony of actual experience. I know what I am saying. Yet, at the same time, I also know that I do not, of myself, know anything about it. It is all freely given, for to "know the Lord," as He is, is pure mercy.

Just knowing The Glorious One, in even the tiny glimmer that has been given to me, appears in a leveled down condition of self where I can see all the time that I DO NOT KNOW ANYTHING AT ALL. I simply have found mercy, and am willing to testify to what I have found. And the one great cry to God is that never, under any circumstances, will He for any reason at all ever allow me to think of myself, or see myself, in any form of self-exalting. I could not bear to live if I thought that I would ever again exalt myself in any way at all. The mere thought of doing so is pain.

But I know too that mercies are the Living Flame of God, albeit they may be leveled down into such a lowliness as to be but drops of moisture in application to one's need. Yet whether His mercies be of flame or of moisture they are life-giving flames and life-giving moisture. I am not trying to give your brain a workout, though that might seem to be the case. I am trying to put into words a flow of something which burns its sweet way into the very core and fiber of the being itself, and, having burned its way in, comes alive and says, "Peace, beloved, I am from Jesus to give you FREELY everything that you need." And that is just what Jesus did with me.

** Galatians 2:20

It was in the early part of 1944, when for some reason my Bible was by my plate one day at breakfast time. I do not know how it came to be there. I had not used it – nor prayed – for about seven years. Maybe I did pray, but it does not seem to me that I had done so. Anyway, I just "happened" to have the Bible there. And I just "happened" to open it while I was waiting for the breakfast to be put on the table. It opened to Isaiah 53.

That was the beginning of a long list of things which happened so supernaturally and so accurately, for over two and a half years, that I seemed to be living in the kind of things you read about in the Bible. As I read down the chapter that morning, something like an arrow of light flashed straight through my being. I thought, "I will finish this chapter." It seemed to come all alive. More so than it had ever done in my life previously, I was almost startled at the reality of it, and I said to myself, "I will try reading that again." And I did.

As days went on, when coming home from work, I would seem to have a desire to get down on my knees while waiting for supper. And I found stealing over me such a sweetness and such a comfort as a tired and bruised and lonely little child might find in his mother's arms. Such mercies of God are incontestable. When He begins to move in with His mercies, all seems to give way before them. And I started reading my Bible and praying with never a thought that I would ever belong to the Lord again, or anything like that. I had lived for seven years in a complete, utter, and final hopelessness, in which there was not a single ray of light, nor a single apparent care about it. I did not have any idea of actually being back in what I had known of "His Will," even though He took me into some remarkable understandings of Himself. Utter hopelessness is not a thing which can be put into words, I guess.

I cannot remember the exact dates in 1944, nor even the months when these things began, though it was near the beginning of the year. Looking back, I seemed to be coming out of a thick darkness of sleep. Anyway, I did start reading the Bible and praying, and it grew on me to such an extent that I took off days, and finally a week, and then weeks, in order to have time to pray and read MORE.

One day I was reading in John 13, where Jesus laid aside His garments and took a towel and girded Himself and WASHED THE FEET of His disciples. Suddenly it all opened out to me: the Creator, the Almighty One, the All-Highest, quietly arose among them. His own feet UNwashed by anyone, and like a house-slave washed their feet. More than that, lovingly washed them. Lowliness! Mercies! My heart seemed like a kodak film receiving the imprint of the wonder of such a Master. And I wept, and prayed that if He would just let me have the privilege of washing some of His disciples' feet with His world-and-sin cleansing mercies, I would be willing to be just a love-slave for Him forever. And I seemed to know the desire was granted.

One day while I was reading the Bible, somewhere in Isaiah I think, suddenly there seemed to be a way opened up from my heart and inner eyes to some point way, way, way, way up into the Beyond. And there was the clear knowledge-impression of an Angel standing there. Nothing dramatic about it like this might sound in telling it. It just seemed as matter of fact as though I looked out of the window and saw someone in the field across the fence. But I said to myself, "There is an Angel." That was the first time in my life that I had had an experience like that.

As I remember it, from that time on I began to tarry to be revived in my old prayer life: breath of the Spirit in prayer as I had known in the days long since gone. And I began to tarry and pray lying on my face as I had once done. Then I found myself being guided to pray for "poverty of spirit." "Make me POOR IN SPIRIT." And I began to realize that one of the main reasons for all of my defeats and turnings away and failures and sins had been that I had never prayed through to be truly poor in spirit.

I began taking off much time from work so as to be able to pray and wait on the Lord. Then one day while praying, quietly, the knowledge of God opened in me in words something like this: "The One who is truly poor is the Holy Spirit, Himself, for He is willing to be given, sent from the glory of God, and given to you." And in that moment I saw and understood what poverty-of-spirit, and true lowliness, really is. It is an utter selflessness of having nothing of one's own, and a willingness to give all one's life to God for others.

It is difficult to put into words all that I could see, because it was of the very essence of simplicity. So utterly simple was it that it seemed impossible NOT to see through it all. GOD was like that. Jesus was like that. The Holy Spirit was like that. And I could be like that, by being filled with The Holy Spirit who was willing to be given to such a vile and filthy wretch as I. HE would be the lowliness, not I. He would FILL me, and that would be the lowliness of God. Then I would be truly lowly, and truly "Poor." Yet it would not be "I," but it would be HE, The Most High God, who is of such pure mercy in His dealings with His creatures that I would be lowly like Him, because He was dwelling IN me. That is also the essence of purity.

I do not think that I went over all of those ideas at that moment though. I did not need to for it was clear as daylight – C L E A R. The wonder of it grows, and Grows, and GROWS. Because it is real. And that is what Reality is. That is to say, there we find Reality: the utter Lowliness of God, and the mercy which flows out through that Lowliness into the very least of all and unto the uttermost. To see yourself as the least-of-all is true freedom.

I repeat: at that moment I became bound to God as His possession. I mean utterly and finally. And that is all I am, ever can be: or ever want to be: just a love-slave to the God, who in contact with His creatures is utter Lowliness and pure Mercy. All I ask is to be like that. That is Jesus Christ my Lord.

But though all of those things transpired, it did not occur to me that I was really getting back to God, or would ever be back in His service. It just seemed as if I were sort of turning back into some way which was the way things ought to be. Oh, I cannot explain it all nor tell it right. All I can do is to try to make visible the reality of His mercy and the simplicity of His Lowliness.

One day while praying, it was after coming home from work, I was kneeling with my face down in my easy chair where I generally did my reading. Quietly my physical heart seemed to be enclosed as within hands, or within a ball of something light and soft. And I felt the touch of the pure Love of God. In the moment it lasted, I seemed to be able to peer away out into the horizon of the Universe. It seemed as though from the very highest point of bliss that a human being would be capable of knowing, or of the most perfect love that a perfectly mated couple could find – from that point one could catch a glimpse on the horizon of the Universe of the light of the pure Love of God – the primal love from which all true loves descend. It probably did not last around my heart for more than half a minute. But in that time it seemed to me that if it were to remain for one whole minute I would literally explode into a million million fragments. So utterly pure was it.

Since that time it has become plain to me that what is called the "First

Love" of the child of God for Jesus, and for God, is of that same quality. There is nothing else like The First Love. I do not mean "first" simply in reference to time or sequence in one's experience. It can mean that. But mainly the word, "first," means: chief, head, supreme. Oh, the wonder of the First love. It is the losing of THAT which becomes, in the deceivings of the Adversary, the confusion and defeat of our souls. And to that the whole Kingdom of God is always seeking to bring us in again.

This wonderful One has been restoring to me not only everything I ever had, and vastly more with it, but He is restoring me to, or to me, whichever it is, that which is above all other things which He does for us: the utterly simple LOVE for HIM which is just simple reality of God. What can one say? There is a place where speech fails; where one simply becomes wordless; the heart "fixed on Thee"; the mind confounded into silence; the whole being still; in the adoring acknowledgment, "From everlasting to everlasting, THOU ART G0D."†† So is the meaning of the Word once given us in a message of Wisdom: "The First Love is not a great desire to go to work. It is THE AWAKENING OF THE HEART TO THE WONDER OF JUST JESUS CHRIST HIMSELF."[1]

And as you say, "The mercy of God to you gives some encouragement." It should. For there is no way to calculate all the evils from the pit of which Jesus raised me up and set me free. It seems incredible, but He has never offered me a single reproach. To be sure He mightily convicted me of the awful reality and destruction of sin, but He did not reproach me by throwing my sins up to me. Confessed, they were forgiven and blotted out. I had not supposed that I would ever get back to God. When I did once or twice think about it, I seemed to "know" that when kneeling at the altar I would be faced with all the terrible evils I had been guilty of. And how could I stand it? I would be crushed to the earth and simply expire under the awful light of God. So have I heard some teach it. So would I probably have taught it at one time. But God has reversed a great deal of all that I thought I knew. He has shown me "The way He takes." It is a way of repentance by which one TURNS eternally TO God.

That mercy crushed out of me all resistance to Him. I have had a hard way to learn to really KNOW GOD, that is, to be known of Him, in the little way of reality which He has given. But it would be

---

†† Psalm 90:2

worth spending a thousand years in such distresses and conflicts and death to find it. Aside from the distresses and pain caused to others, I would willingly go the route again, if it had to be so, just to find the LOWLINESS AND MERCY OF GOD.

Likely those who enjoy the ideas of a God of force and destruction will think me beside myself and as though I were riding a hobby. But it is being clearly shown to me that God is PURE MERCY in His contact with His creatures and with His creation. The WRATH and DESTRUCTION arise in THE OPPOSITION to His mercies of Love, but all the motions of God Himself are generated in mercy. The man with the legion came TO Jesus, but the spirits said, "Have you come to torment us..."♯ Those evil spirits were the real tormentors. They had been tormenting the life out of the man. Jesus had not come to torment anyone. He had come to DO MERCY. But to those who OPPOSED the mercy, the very mercies seemed to be torments – and were. For nothing is so tormenting to evils as pure mercies.

All the motions of GOD are generated in Mercy, which is Lovingkindness. All that He asks of us is that we GIVE FREELY TO OTHERS WHAT HE GIVES TO US SO FREELY. And on that simple condition, which is the law of Faith and of Life, He is willing to give through Jesus' Blood, absolutely everything – just GIVE it. For it is mercy He wants and will have, "not sacrifice."§§

The Time is NOW when He wants to manifest HIS PRESENCE to His own. NOW! The Times have run out, and we are slipping over the line into His Time and into His DAY. The Adversary may do terrible things, and destructions may overtake the evils of the world, BUT JESUS WILL NEVER DESERT HIS SHEEP. He will carry them through to the end MORE THAN CONQUERORS – those who live by His Blood; who love not their own lives unto death; and who have the testimony of the MERCY THAT ENDURES FOREVER.

In Him, Brother Rex

♯ Mark 5:7
§§ Hosea 6:6; quoted by Jesus in Matthew 9:13 and Matthew 12:7.

Appendix F

Thoughts On Being "Possessed"

There are several Scriptures which emphasize God's expressed intention to DWELL in His people as His own possession. For example:[1]

1. I Corinthians 6:12-20 (I will bold various phrases for emphasis)

> *All things are lawful unto me, but all things are not expedient: all things are lawful for me, but I will not be brought under the power of any ["become the slave of anything" Amp].*
>
> *Meats for the belly, and the belly for meats: but God shall destroy both it and them. Now* **the body is** *not for fornication, but* **for the Lord**; *and the Lord for the body.*
>
> *And God hath both raised the Lord, and will also raise up us by His own power.*
>
> *Know ye not that your bodies are* **the members of Christ**? *Shall I then take* **the members of Christ**, *and make them the members of an harlot? God forbid.*
>
> *What! Know ye not that he which is joined to an harlot is one body? For two, saith He, shall be one flesh.*
>
> *But he that is joined unto the Lord is one spirit...*
>
> *What! Know ye not that your body is the temple of the Holy Ghost which is in you, which ye have of God, and* **ye are not your own**?
>
> *For ye are bought with a price: therefore glorify God in your body, and in your spirit,* **which are God's**.

Notice the clear implication of these phrases. We are God's possession, both as something He purchases, and as something He dwells in.

2. **II Corinthians 6:16-18**

> *And what agreement hath the temple of God with idols? For ye are the temple of the living God; as God hath said, "I will **dwell in them**, and walk in them; and I will be their God, and **they shall be My people**."*
>
> *"Wherefore come out from among them, and be ye separate," saith the Lord, "and touch not the unclean thing; and I will receive you, and will be a Father unto you, and **ye shall be My sons and daughters**," saith the Lord Almighty.*

This is language which recalls the terms by which God spoke of Israel, as "My people," and "Israel My possession." Sometimes He would say, "and they are Mine." Also, because He refers to New Testament saints as "the Temple of God," then we must carry over into our lives the same sense of REVERENCE for God's earthly dwelling place that characterized the true worship of God in the Temple made with hands in the Old Testament. That earthly Temple was God's possession on earth and as such was sacred to the *nth* degree as HIS PLACE ON EARTH.

With that understanding, it is not surprising that God refers to the baptism of the Holy Spirit as a SEAL, God's SEALING of His own, a SEALING which points to full POSSESSION of His people. Thus we have:

3. **Ephesians 1:13-14**

> *In whom ye also trusted, after that ye heard the word of truth, the gospel of your salvation: in whom also, after that ye believed, ye were sealed with that Holy Spirit of promise,*
>
> *which is the earnest of our inheritance until **the redemption of the purchased possession**, unto the praise of His glory.*
>
> *That last verse reads in the NIV as follows: "who [the Spirit] is a deposit guaranteeing our inheritance until the redemption of **those who are God's possession** – to the praise of His glory."*

4. **Romans 8:23** (context, as always, is tremendously important)

> *And not only they, but ourselves also, which have the firstfruits of the Spirit, even we ourselves groan within ourselves, waiting for the adoption, to wit, **the redemption of our body**.*

"Redemption" refers to purchasing back something that rightfully belongs to the original owner. The whole of Romans 8 expresses the REALITY of being POSSESSED by the Holy Spirit, in a measure now, and fully then, *i.e.*, at the time of "the manifestation of the sons of God."

These two chapters, Romans 8 and Ephesians 1, deserve much worshipful study.

5. II Corinthians 1:21-22

> *Now he which stablisheth us with you in Christ, and hath anointed us, is God; who hath also **sealed us**, and given the earnest of the Spirit in our hearts.*

The word "earnest" is the same word as is used in Ephesians 1 (#3 above), meaning, "the deposit, pledge, or guarantee, both a down payment and a taste of what eventually is paid for, and experienced, in full." "Sealed" bespeaks ownership.

Since James speaks of the tongue as the most "unruly" member, it is not surprising that the tongue being controlled by God, (as evidenced by speaking in tongues or prophecy or both), would become the primary means by which God would signal His Presence in the human temple. The subjugation and control of the tongue by God becomes a "deposit" toward the subjugation, control, and possession of the entire body.

By contrast, when an individual becomes "demon possessed," his tongue becomes an instrument of Satan. Such a possession is often indicated by demonic control of that person's body as well (e.g., the demoniac in the tombs).

6. Acts 2:3-4

> *And there appeared unto them cloven tongues like as of fire, and it sat upon each of them.*
>
> *And they were all **filled with the Holy Ghost**, and began to speak with other tongues, as the Spirit gave them utterance.*

First "filled," then "began to speak." Jesus said to the Pharisees, who spoke evil from their hearts, "O generation of vipers, how can ye, being evil, speak good things? Out of the abundance of the heart the mouth speaketh" (Matthew 12:34; also Luke 6:45).

This clearly implies that God's intention, when baptizing an individual in the Holy Ghost, is to take possession of his heart, and thus to get His pure word spoken out of that person's mouth, a word which is untainted by any other spirit.

This description is also reminiscent of the many references to "fire" in the Old Testament, but especially reminiscent of the fire which fell on acceptable sacrifices. Such offerings BELONGED TO GOD, and His acceptance of them was indicated by FIRE.

7. John 6:63

It is the Spirit that quickeneth [gives life]; the flesh profiteth nothing: the words that I speak unto you, they are spirit, and they are life.

If it is true that His words ARE SPIRIT, then to be full of the Holy Spirit, (possessed by the Spirit), means we are FULL of HIS WORDS. That means, of course, not "full" in the sense of having memorized many verses, but "full" in the sense of "fully experiencing" them, having them made REAL to us, so our daily lives are fully shaped by what Jesus said and taught.

This brings us naturally to the first seven "Beatitudes" [pronouncements of BLESSING], where Jesus describes for us what a truly "Spirit-filled life" consists of. These seven "words" correspond to "the Seven Spirits of God," which is a term appearing only in the Book of Revelation. One needs time in those amazing utterances of Matthew 5:3-9 for them to lodge in the heart, thus changing what we "ARE" into a possession of God, a dwelling place for Him. The "sealed ones" in the Book of Revelation become God's "firstfruits," His peculiar possession.

8. Galatians 5:1 - 6:10 (which is too long to quote here)

In this passage God describes the possession of the heart by the Spirit, (and hence, possession of the tongue as well), as "walking in love." There are details given in this passage which tie many things together. For example, notice the contrast between the flesh and the spirit, and the resulting BEHAVIORS of each, depending on who possesses the human being: the Lord or Satan. There is not a word in this passage about speaking in tongues, but surely "walking in love" would correspond nicely to the word "edify" in First Corinthians 12 and 14.

Appendix F

9. **Titus 2:15** [Amp] (with which we conclude this brief study)

   [the Messiah, the Anointed One,] Who gave Himself on our behalf that He might redeem us (purchase our freedom) from all iniquity and purify for Himself a people – to be peculiarly His own – [people who are] eager and enthusiastic about [living a life that is good and filled with] beneficial deeds.

Prayer:

Father, please open our hearts to the divine pleasure of being filled with the Holy Spirit. Give us a distaste for "all filthiness of the flesh and spirit." Make us hungry to be filled with Your beautiful, lifegiving Spirit. Lead us, blessed Father, into the offering of ourselves to you, in the pathway of Your Son, "who through the Eternal Spirit offered Himself without spot to God."

"We are waiting, beloved, for the light, and the sight of The Son of God, into which all self-knowledge disappears."[2]

Notes

PREFACE

1. From the third verse of *This Is My Father's World*, written by Maltbie D. Babcock in 1901.

PROLOGUE

1. *Ellicott's Commentary on the Whole Bible, Vol. VI* (Grand Rapids, MI: Zondervan, 1982) p. 439; the emphasis on the word "actual" is in the original.
2. Gordon P. Gardiner, *Radiant Glory: The Life of Martha Wing Robinson*, (Brooklyn, NY: Bread of Life, 1962). It was slightly revised in 1987. It is now available in its entirety on the internet, the publishers having chosen not to renew the copyright.
3. Rex B. Andrews, *Meditations in the Revelation*, (Zion, IL: Zion Faith Homes, 1991) p. 209.
4. *Ibid.*, p. 225.

CHAPTER 1

1. Gardiner, *Radiant Glory*, a biography of Martha Wing Robinson, the acknowledged founder of the Zion Faith Homes; and Gordon P. Gardiner *The Fighting Elder: Conflicts in the Narrow Way*, (Zion, IL: Zion Faith Homes), a biography of Elder Eugene Brooks, published in booklet form, and now also available on the internet.

CHAPTER 2

1. There are many links to his work and writings. His official website can be accessed at http://www.jedwinorr.com/
2. You can read the full introduction at http://www.revival-library.org/leadership/sp_wallis_revrecovery.php
3. His life and work is summarized in an obituary found at http://ag.org/top/News/index_articledetail.cfm?targetBay=c97d4d5c-a325-4921-9a9e-e9fbddd9cdce&ModID=2&Process=DisplayArticle&RSS_RSSContentID=20102&RSS_OriginatingChannelID=1184&RSS_OriginatingRSSFeedID=3359&RSS_Source=
4. A fair summary of his life is available at http://en.wikipedia.org/wiki/H._Vinson_Synan
5. See Wheaton College's profile of her at http://www.wheaton.edu/Academics/Faculty/B/Edith-Blumhofer
6. "The mid-nineteenth century Evangelical Awakening which became worldwide commenced as a leaderless movement, but it produced effective leaders and it energized or established societies that extended it into *evangelism, missions, and social reform for forty years at least*" (emphasis mine). http://jedwinorr.com/Orr_Revival_and_Revivalism.pdf, p. 25.
7. Its focus is, according to its own statement, "To promote Bible teaching at an annual Convention in Keswick and on other occasions with the aim of encouraging holy and Biblical lifestyles."
8. Keswick's official history, *The Keswick Convention: Its Message, Its Method and Its Men*, edited by Charles F. Harford, M.A., MJX, (Hong Kong: Forgotten Books, August 2010) is available at http://www.archive.org/stream/keswickconvent00unknuoft/keswickconvent00unknuoft_djvu.txt

9. 1) Gordon Lindsay, *John Alexander Dowie: A Life Story of Trials, Tragedies, and Triumph,* (Dallas, TX: Christ for the Nations, Inc., 1980) available online in its entirety at http://hopefaithprayer.com/books/JohnAlexanderDowie-GordonLindsay.pdf.

    2) Arthur Newcomb, *Dowie, Anointed of the Lord,* (New York, NY: The Century Company, 1930). The book can be downloaded at https://sites.google.com/site/leavesofhealing/leavesofhealingpartone:thelifenewcomb1.

    3) Rolvix Harlan, *John Alexander Dowie and the Christian Apostolic Church in Zion,* (Evansville, WI: R.M. Antes, 1906), available for purchase at http://shop.revival-library.org/ProductDetails.asp?ProductCode=407_harlandowie. According to the accompanying description, "This is the major biography of Alexander Dowie who was correctly regarded as the father of the 20th century Healing Movement. He ploughed a furrow of ministry which others in the Pentecostal revival later took up in the early years of the twentieth century. His teaching on healing laid a great foundation for the new Spirit-filled churches to build on."

10. For more information, please visit David Eames's helpful website at https://sites.google.com/site/leavesofhealing/. He writes, "A host of respected Pentecostal pioneers including F.F. Bosworth, Lilian Yeomans, John G. Lake, and Martha Wing Robinson had their roots in Dowie's city of Zion. (The full testimony of Mrs. Robinson's healing was published in Leaves of Healing in November, 1900 and can be [accessed at https://sites.google.com/site/leavesofhealing/leavesofhealingparttwo%3Atheministry4].)"

11. See Philip L. Cook, *Zion City, Illinois: Twentieth-Century Utopia,* (Syracuse, NY: Syracuse University Press, 1996) for more information.

12. http://www.truthinhistory.org/life-ministry-of-john-alexander-dowie.html

13. As cited in Gardiner, *Radiant Glory,* p. 75, referring to: Sarah Frances Smiley, *The Fulness of Blessing; Or, The Gospel of Christ, as illustrated from The Book of Joshua,* (New York, NY: Anson, D. F. Randolph & Co., 1876). Smiley's book is out of print, but available online at http://archive.org/stream/fulnessofblessin00smil#page/n7/mode/2up.

14. See especially, Edith Blumhofer, *Restoring the Faith: The Assemblies of God, Pentecostalism, and American Culture,* (Champaign, IL: University of Illinois Press, 1993).

15. See picture in Gordon P. Gardiner, *Out of Zion Into All the World,* (Companion Press, Shippensburg, PA, 1992) p. 47.

16. Gardiner, *Radiant Glory,* especially Chapter IX - XVII, pp. 52-109.

17. Cook, *Zion City, Illinois.* p. 224.

18. See Gardiner, *Out of Zion,* pp. 331-342, Appendix 2, "When God Breathed on Zion," by Bernice C. Lee, who was present in those meetings.

19. All of this and more is recounted in Gardiner's *Out of Zion.*

20. Gardiner, *Out of Zion,* p. 1.

21. See Gardiner, *Radiant Glory,* p. 118, for the details.

CHAPTER 3

1. Gardiner, *Radiant Glory*, p. 19. This quotation is not in the original transcription.
2. *Leaves of Healing*, Vol. IV, No. 10, p. 195.
3. "Written Testimony of Miss Martha Wing," *Feed My Lambs*, Vol. 1, No. 2, (July-Aug. 1950) p. 2-4, and Vol.1, No.3 (Sept.1950) p. 1-3.
4. Jeanne Guyon, *The Autobiography of Jeanne Guyon*, (Chicago, IL: Christian Witness Company, 1917).
5. *Ibid.*, p. 1-2.
6. *Ibid.*, p. 59.
7. *Ibid.*, p. 61.
8. *Ibid.*, p. 81.
9. See Gardiner, *Radiant Glory*, p. 171, for example, or Andrews, *Meditations in the Revelation*, pp. 97-98.
10. Martha Wing Robinson, as cited in Rex B. Andrews, "Something God Is Going to Do in the Last Days," unpublished article (Sept. 1972) p. 1.
11. Rex B. Andrews, "Faith Home History," Part 1, an unpublished article.

CHAPTER 4

1. Letter from Rex B. Andrews to Ruth Lade (Schleicher), April 1960, unpublished.
2. Andrews, "Faith Home History," Part 1, p. 9.
3. Gardiner, *Radiant Glory*, pp. 193-194.
4. Gordon Gardiner quotes extensively from that diary in *Radiant Glory*.
5. Martha Wing Robinson, as cited in Andrews, *Meditations in the Revelation*, pp. 230-235.
6. Gardiner, *Radiant Glory*, p. 175.
7. Rex B. Andrews, "Record of Truth," unpublished article, (July 1959) p. 3.

CHAPTER 5

1. Robinson, "Something God Is Going to Do in the Last Days," as cited by Andrews in *Meditations in the Revelation*, p. 230.
2. Andrews, "Something God Is Going to Do in the Last Days," p. 1.
3. Andrews, "Record of Truth," pp. 2, 4, 5.
4. For additional material on this matter, Chapters XXVI to XXIX of Gardiner's *Radiant Glory* are helpful, though not comprehensive.
5. The term "just Jesus" does not refer to "One-ness Doctrine," but to the pre-eminence of Jesus in everything. Some people later condensed the teaching of the Faith Homes into those two words, but often without understanding that it meant the elimination of anything else in one's life that took Jesus' rightful place.
6. The man was Alexander Campbell, who later became one of the Vessels. Details of this momentous night are given in full in Gardiner's, *Radiant Glory*, pp. 197-199.
7. Gardiner, *Radiant Glory*, p. 215.
8. *Ibid.*, p. 175.
9. Andrews, "Record of Truth," p. 2.

10. Gardiner, *Out of Zion*, p. 285.
11. Andrews, "Record of Truth," p. 8.
12. Rex B. Andrews, "Clarification of the Term 'New Work'," unpublished letter, (July 1950) p. 3.
13. Madame Guyon, *The Autobiography of Madame Guyon*, (Gutenberg eBook, 2007) p. 5, accessed at http://www.gutenberg.org/files/22269/22269-h/22269-h.htm#I_1.
14. Andrews, "Record of Truth," p. 3.

CHAPTER 6

1. Charles Wesley, *O for a Heart to Praise My God*, accessed July 23, 2013 at http://www.hymnal.net/en/hymn.php/h/410.

CHAPTER 7

1. Andrews, "Clarification of the Term 'New Work'," p. 3.
2. Guyon, *Autobiography*, pp. 302-303.
3. Many such letters are preserved, primarily due to the efforts of her biographer, Gordon Gardiner, and Rev. Hans Waldvogel, who knew they contained "treasures of wisdom." In later years Rev. Gardiner compiled a small booklet with a quotation from Mrs. Robinson for every day of the year. It was called *Treasures of Wisdom*.
4. That record, titled, NOVEMBER 14, 1934 MRS. MARTHA ROBINSONS BIRTHDAY is available to anyone who asks for it; the details are given at the end of this book.
5. Andrews, "Something God Is Going to Do in the Last Days," p. 5.
6. Andrews, "Clarification of the Term 'New Work'," p. 1.

CHAPTER 8

1. Andrews, "Faith Home History," Part 3, p. 1.
2. See Heidi Baker's wonderful book, *Compelled by Love*, (Lake Mary, FL: Charisma House, 2008) Chapter 1, for similar stories.
3. Andrews, "Record of Truth," p. 8.
4. Annie Schisler, *I Saw the Lord: Visions Given to Annie*, Book IV, "I Looked and I Saw Visions of God," R. Edward Miller, ed. (Peachtree City, GA: Shiloh Christian Church, 1974) pp. 29-30.
5. Rex B. Andrews, "What Are You Here For?, Talk #6: Bearing the Cross," (1967). This entire series of talks is reprinted in Chapter 19.
6. Andrews, "Record of Truth," p. 7.

CHAPTER 9

1. Their story, written by Gordon P. Gardiner, under the title *The Fighting Elder: Conflicts in the Narrow Way*, was never published in book form, but is available on the internet.
2. Various authors have traced the fascinating history of Zion. See Notes: Chapter 2, Note 9 for references.
3. *Feed My Lambs*, Serial No. 14 (Oct.-Dec. 1955) p. 6.
4. "Tongues and Interpretation by Elder Brooks April 22, 1945," *Feed My Lambs*, Serial No. 6 (April 1953) pp. 5-6.

5. Andrews, *Meditations in the Revelation*, p. 209.
6. Andrews, "Clarification of the Term 'New Work'," p. 1.

CHAPTER 10

1. See his best-selling testimony, *Tortured for Christ* (Bartlesville, OK: Living Sacrifice Book Company 1967, 1998).
2. The words were written by Joseph Lincoln Hall, (1866-1930).
3. Lelia N. Morris, *Sweet Will of God,* accessed at http://www.hymnal.net/en/hymn.php/h/383 on July 24, 2013 .

INTERLUDE ONE

1. *Feed My Lambs*, Serial No. 12, June 1955.

CHAPTER 11

1. *Faith Home Bulletin*, September 1964. Everyone was encouraged to vote, however.

CHAPTER 12

1. Rex B. Andrews, letter to the Faith Home Council dated January 9, 1961.
2. Rex B. Andrews, "Faith Home History," Part 2, (July 1961).

CHAPTER 13

1. "That I Might Know Him," *Feed My Lambs*, special edition (April 1976).
2. Andrews, "Record of Truth," p. 7.
3. For a brief autobiographical description of this period of his life, see Rex B. Andrews *What the Bible Teaches About Mercy*, (Zion, IL: Zion Faith Homes, 1985) pp. 168-169.

CHAPTER 14

1. Prophecy given by Elder Eugene Brooks, April 23, 1944, as cited in *Feed My Lambs,* Serial No. 14 (Oct-Dec 1955) p. 6-7. As you may remember, this was just prior to Rex Andrews' restoration from his backsliding.
2. I do not have the exact words of this "conversation," but my recounting of it is pretty close to what happened.
3. Notes taken down on September 19, 1971.
4. The late R. Edward Miller, in whose home Annie had resided for some time, compiled a record of those visions, *I Saw the Lord: Visions Given to Annie*, R. Edward Miller, ed. (Peachtree City, GA: Shiloh Christian Church, 1971)

CHAPTER 15

1. As recorded in her own testimony; see *Leaves of Healing* (Nov. 1900) or Rex B. Andrews, "The Right Attitude," *Feed My Lambs*, Serial No. 14 (Oct.-Dec. 1955) p. 1.
2. Andrews, *History of the Faith Homes*, Part Two, p. 1.
3. Please see *Appendix B: The Definition of Mercy.*
4. Rex B. Andrews, "The Mind of Christ vs. The Natural Reasoning Mind," p. 1.
5. *Ibid.*, p. 4.

6. From a talk given by Martha Robinson on her birthday on November 14, 1934. Four stenographers took notes and compared them in order to obtain an accurate record of what was said.
7. *Ibid.*

CHAPTER 16

1. Rex B. Andrews, "The Will of God," transcription of a sermon given in September 1949, (Zion, IL: Zion Faith Homes, March 1960).
2. For more on "The Black Box," see http://prezi.com/b76gjjvvbpsx/black-box/
3. Andrews, *What the Bible Teaches About Mercy*, p. 3.
4. The original poem has 14 verses! See them at: http://www.poemhunter.com/poem/the-will-of-god-2/
5. See one of many explanations of Hebrew couplets, or parallelism, at http://www.crivoice.org/parallel.html
6. Andrews, *What the Bible Teaches About Mercy*, p. 63.
7. See Andrews, *What the Bible Teaches About Mercy*, especially pp. 192-195.
8. Written by William Booth-Clibborn, grandson of the founder of the Salvation Army.
9. This can be looked at in detail by studying Chapter 35 of Andrews, *What the Bible Teaches About Mercy*, p. 225ff.
10. *He Looked Beyond My Faults and Saw My Need*, written by Dottie Rambo in 1967.
11. He passed away in the early 1990s; see this link for a newspaper article about him, written in 1986: http://news.google.com/newspapers?nid=1310&dat=19860912&id=igpWAAAAIBAJ&sjid=uOEDAAAAIBAJ&pg=6868,2671840

CHAPTER 17

1. Quoted from a longer reply to a question I asked him about the similarities between the Synoptic Gospels.
2. My personal thanks to Miss Grace Savage, who took my crude drawing and digitized it so well.
3. Andrews, *What the Bible Teaches About Mercy*, p. 199.
4. Andrews, *Meditations in the Revelation*, p. 30.
5. *Ibid.*, p. 57.
6. *Ibid.*, pp. 54-55.
7. *God in Heaven Hath a Treasure* was written in 1915 by Francis Ridley Havergal.
8. Andrews, *What the Bible Teaches About Mercy*, p. 199.
9. *Ibid.*, p. 200.
10. *Ibid.*, p. 110.
11. The refrain of the hymn, *Satisfied*, written by Miss Clara Tear Williams (1858-1937).
12. I highly recommend Tim Keller's book, *The Prodigal God* (New York, NY: Dutton, 2008) to illuminate what Jesus was teaching in this story.
13. Rex B. Andrews, *The Prophet Abraham*, Part 1, (Zion, IL: Zion Faith Homes, 1952) pp.15-16.

CHAPTER 18

1. As told to the author by Rev. Leonard Ravenhill.
2. Read about the unusual prayer travail that preceded the outpouring of the Spirit in California in 1907, as recorded by Frank Bartleman in his book, *What Really Happened at Azusa Street*, (New Kensington, PA: Whitaker House, 2000).
3. See Mary Meade Clark's book, *A Corner in India*, (Philadelphia, PA: American Baptist Publication Society, 1907).
4. *In Evil Long I Took Delight*, a hymn penned by John Newton in the late 1700s.
5. Rex B. Andrews, "God's Blessing Pact," *Feed My Lambs*, Vol. 20, Serial No. 73 (Sept.-Nov. 1970) p. 9.

CHAPTER 19

1. *Jesus, Lover of My Soul*, a hymn of Charles Wesley penned in 1740.
2. As noted before, these words were written by Joseph Lincoln Hall, (1866-1930).
3. From the hymn, *I Worship Thee, Sweet Will of God*, by Frederick Faber.

CHAPTER 20

1. See Jeremy Myers, "Is Crusade Evangelism Effective?", Till He Comes, accessed July 20, 2013 at http://www.tillhecomes.org/crusade-evangelism-effective/; also Massimo Lorenzini, "The Modern Invitation System Examined," Frontline Ministries, accessed July 20, 2013 at http://www.frontlinemin.org/decisionism.asp.
2. A.T. Robertson, *Word Pictures in the New Testament*, accessed October 25, 2013 at http://www.ccel.org/r/robertson_at/wordpictures/htm/RO8.RWP.html.
3. From the chorus of the hymn, *Oh to Be Like Thee*, written by Thomas O. Chisholm (1866-1960). He also wrote the words to the well-known hymn, *Great Is Thy Faithfulness*.
4. See "Written Testimony of Miss Martha Wing," *Feed My Lambs*, Vol. 1, No. 2 (July-Aug. 1950) p. 2-4, and Vol. 1, No. 3 (Sept. 1950) p. 1-3.
5. See Gardiner's *Conflicts in the Narrow Way*.
6. Dr. Charles S. Price (1867-1947) held meetings throughout the United States during the years 1921-1945. My mother was converted in 1936.
7. See Eric Metaxas' biography of Dietrich Bonhoeffer to see how far into mainstream Protestantism humanism had penetrated. It is called *Bonhoeffer: Pastor, Martyr, Prophet, Spy*, (Nashville, TN: Thomas Nelson Publishers, 2010).
8. See Chapter 2, *Converging Streams*, p. 25.
9. Note that "tongues" and the rest of the gifts had not been totally unknown or lost. See John Sherrill's book, *They Speak with Other Tongues*, (Grand Rapids, MI: Chosen Books, 1964, 2006).
10. From a personal interview Hans R. Waldvogel had with Martha Robinson sometime between 1932 and 1936, as cited in Gardiner, *Radiant Glory*, p. 300.
11. Martha W. Robinson, as cited by Rex B. Andrews in "Something God Is Going to Do in the Last Days," p. 7. In writing his article, Rex Andrews copied Mrs. Robinson's quote as originally written down by Hilda Nilsson (one of the vessels in the Faith Homes), dated April 6, 1921.

CHAPTER 21

1. To learn more about Andrew Sullivan, visit http://www.theatlantic.com/andrew-sullivan/. See Christopher Hitchens' vitriolic article on Mother Theresa, at http://www.slate.com/articles/news_and_politics/fighting_words/2003/10/mommie_dearest.html.
2. See Paul Johnson's book, *Intellectuals*, (London, UK: Harper Collins, 1990), for an examination of seventeen culture-shapers of enormous influence in the past 150 years, whose inside "light" (understanding) wrought havoc in society. Their words portrayed one thing, their lives another.
3. Rex B. Andrews, "'Made for God' To Be Possessed," unpublished article, date unknown.

CHAPTER 22

1. From the hymn, *Redeemed,* written by Fanny Crosby in 1882.

EPILOGUE

1. A. T. Robertson, *Word Pictures in the New Testament*, comment on Colossians 3:22, accessed October 1, 2013 at http://www.thebible.net/reference/ntwordstudy/COL3.RWP.txt.

APPENDIX A

1. See http://www.reasons.org/articles/planet-habitability-requires-a-lifetime-of-fine-tuning (accessed February 2, 2013).

APPENDIX B

1. Andrews, *What the Bible Teaches About Mercy*, p. 2.

APPENDIX E

1. This message of Wisdom was given through Martha Robinson.

APPENDIX F

1. These thoughts were written down by the author in April of 2001, in response to Rex Andrews' article, "'Made for God' To Be Possessed," (see Chapter 21, pp. 376-379).
2. Andrews, *Meditations in the Revelation,* p. 33.

Resources

For further information, or to request materials, please contact Evergreen Center, Inc.

Mailing address: Evergreen Center, Inc.
                                N7101 14th Court
                                Almond, WI 54909

Phone number: 715.366.7003

E-mail address:
      evergreencenter@evergreencenterinc.org